JUSTICE AND AUTHORITY IN IMMIGRATION LAW

This book provides a new and powerful account of the demands of justice on immigration law and policy. Drawing principally on the work of Adam Smith, Immanuel Kant, and John Rawls, it argues that justice requires states to give priority of admission to the most disadvantaged migrants, and to grant some form of citizenship or non-oppressive status to those migrants who become integrated. It also argues that states must avoid policies of admission and exclusion that can only be implemented through unjust means. It therefore refutes the common misconception that justice places no limits on the discretion of states to control immigration.

Justice and Authority in Immigration Law

Colin Grey

·H A R T·
PUBLISHING
OXFORD AND PORTLAND, OREGON
2017

Hart Publishing

An imprint of Bloomsbury Publishing Plc

Hart Publishing Ltd
Kemp House
Chawley Park
Cumnor Hill
Oxford OX2 9PH
UK

Bloomsbury Publishing Plc
50 Bedford Square
London
WC1B 3DP
UK

www.hartpub.co.uk
www.bloomsbury.com

Published in North America (US and Canada) by
Hart Publishing
c/o International Specialized Book Services
920 NE 58th Avenue, Suite 300
Portland, OR 97213-3786
USA

www.isbs.com

**HART PUBLISHING, the Hart/Stag logo, BLOOMSBURY and the
Diana logo are trademarks of Bloomsbury Publishing Plc**

First published in hardback, 2015
Paperback edition, 2017

British Library Cataloguing-in-Publication Data
A catalogue record for this book is available from the British Library.

ISBN: PB: 978-1-50991-544-6
HB: 978-1-84946-599-1

Typeset by Compuscript Ltd, Shannon
Printed and bound in Great Britain by
Lightning Source UK Ltd

To find out more about our authors and books visit www.hartpublishing.co.uk. Here you will
find extracts, author information, details of forthcoming events and the option to sign up for our
newsletters.

To RL

ACKNOWLEDGEMENTS

This essay began as a dissertation for the Doctor of Juridical Science (JSD) programme at the New York University School of Law. In writing it, I greatly benefitted from the guidance of Professors David Golove, Jeremy Waldron, Cristina Rodríguez, and Lewis Kornhauser. My intellectual debts to Professor Waldron will be especially evident, both to his writings and for his suggestion—made 22 January 2008—that I examine Adam Smith's arguments against the Laws of Settlement, a turning point in my thinking. Someone from outside NYU to whom I owe an equal if not greater debt is Joseph Palumbo, unaffiliated but endlessly wise, who read and gave comments on my dissertation and then again on the manuscript prior to publication. Many others offered intellectual and other forms of support along the way. The list includes my colleagues at the NYU JSD programme: Omer Kimhi, Doreen Lustig, Eran Shamir-Borer, Nourit Zimerman, Yun-chien Chang, Galia Rivlin, Juan Gonzalez Bertomeu, and Jean Thomas. It also includes others from my time in New York: Theresa Chan, Aditya Dutt, Aliya Haider, and Boris Ayala-Ayanovich. I am grateful to Maren Behrenson, Matt Lister, and Chantal Thomas for comments on portions of the work. Parts of Chapter Six appeared in an earlier article: 'The Rights of Migration' (2014) 20 *Legal Theory* 25. I thank Cambridge University Press for granting permission to reproduce them here. Finally, while revising the manuscript for publication, I have been a legal adviser for the Immigration and Refugee Board (IRB) of Canada. None of the views or arguments that follow should be attributed to the Government of Canada, including the IRB.

CONTENTS

Acknowledgements vii

Introduction 1
    I.   Four Predicaments 1
    II. Justifying Immigration Policies: Rawls, Kant, and Smith 3
    III. Some Parameters and Stipulations 10

Part I: Preliminaries

1. Justice, Authority, and Immigration 15
    I.   Introduction 15
    II. Justice and Authority 15
          1. Justice 15
          2. Authority 17
    III. The Universality of Justice 20
          1. An Absolutist Objection 20
          2. Smith's Theory of Moral Judgement 23
          3. Judgements about Justice 25
          4. Why Social Justice is not a Special Relationship 28
    IV. Justice and Authority in Immigration Governance 31
          1. The Problem of Justice in Immigration Governance 31
          2. The Problem of Authority in Immigration Governance 34
    V. Moving on 37

2. Inegalitarianism in Immigration Governance 39
    I.   Introduction 39
    II. Some Considered Judgements of Injustice in Immigration 40
    III. Discretionary Doctrines 44
    IV. Inegalitarianism in Immigration Law 48
    V. Inegalitarianism: Four Examples 51
          1. Economic Migration and Guestworker Programmes 51
          2. Family Migration 52
          3. Refugees 54
          4. Illegal Immigration 55
    VI. Moving on 56

Part II: The Authority of Immigration Regimes

3. The Rightful Governance of Immigration 61
   I.   Introduction 61
   II. The Argument for the Postulate of Public Right 63
   III. The Moral Standing of States and Required Forms of Partiality 68
        1. Juridical Integration and the Moral Standing of States 69
        2. Partiality Among Members...73
   IV. The Duty to Govern Immigration Rightfully 77
        1. The Juridical Nature of Migration 79
        2. The Function of Immigration Regimes 81
   V.   Immigration Regimes as Status Regimes 86
        1. Status in the Governance of Immigration 87
        2. Justifying Immigration Status...88
        3. Status and Discretion in Immigration Governance 91
   VI. Moving on 92

4. Two Absolutisms 93
   I.   Introduction 93
   II. An Absolutist Schematic 96
   III. Communitarian Absolutism 99
        1. Complex Equality...99
        2. Complex Equality and Immigration Governance 102
        3. Domination at the Border 104
        4. Thin Morality at the Border 106
   IV. Liberal Pessimism 107
        1. Immigration and Egalitarian Justice 107
        2. Pessimism about Legitimacy...110
        3. Hope..111
   V.   Moving on 113

5. The Authority of Immigration Law..114
   I.   Introduction 114
   II. Consent 117
   III. Fairness 122
   IV. The Natural Duty of Justice as a Principle of
       Political Obligation 126
   V.   How Just Immigration Regimes Can Have Authority.....................133
        1. Reasonable Deviations from Justice 134
        2. Reasonableness and Obligation...137
        3. Reasonableness in the Circumstances of Immigration 141
   VI. Moving on 145

Part III: Justice in Immigration Governance

6. The Indirect Principle of Freedom of Migration............................149
   I.   Introduction 149
   II. Two Frameworks 151
   III. The Value of Freedom of Movement 158
       1. The Capabilities and Our Considered Judgements.............159
       2. 'An Evident Violation of Natural Liberty and Justice'.........164
   IV. The Global Distributive Justice Alternative 168
   V. The Indirect Principle 172
       1. The Indirect Principle...173
       2. The Relevance of the Indirect Principle.................176
       3. The Critical Force of the Indirect Principle.............178
   VI. Moving on 180

7. Priority of Admission for the Worst-off Migrants...........................181
   I.   Introduction 181
   II. Contextualism and Universalism 183
   III. A Contextualist Universalist Method 185
   IV. A Constructivist Approach to Immigration 189
   V. Free and Equal Migrants 191
   VI. A Basic Liberty 194
   VII. A Non-lexical Liberty 199
   VIII. Prioritizing the Worst off 204
   IX. Principles for the Just Governance of Immigration 207

Conclusion 210

Bibliography..215

Index 225

Introduction

I. Four Predicaments

TO BECOME A migrant is to enter a precarious condition. Migrants uproot themselves. They put themselves at the mercy of their states of destination and transit. Their journeys may test the limits of endurance for privation and inhumanity. And, not always but uncomfortably often, the experience ends badly. This may seem a melodramatic way to begin a work of legal and political philosophy, but the special vulnerability that attends migration is too often ignored in the academic philosophical literature on the subject. Because the most striking migration flows today run from poorer to richer parts of the world—because Americans, Australians, and Europeans are not huddling into boats bound for Haiti, Indonesia, and Libya—the debate over justice in immigration governance is sometimes subsumed within larger discussions of international or global distributive justice. Alternatively, when immigration *is* the primary focus, the literature has largely concentrated on whether and how a right of exclusion or to admission can be justified in principle. While an inquiry into justice in immigration governance must be undertaken against background concerns about international or global justice, and while the possibility of rights of admission or exclusion are clearly important to any such inquiry, we should not overlook the many adverse consequences that the exercise of state power to control immigration may have, whether or not a gun is ever brandished at the border.

The vulnerability of migrants is one of four predicaments an inquiry into justice in immigration governance must confront. The second predicament is that of the states, and their members, doing the governing. Anyone who has studied immigration will have been struck by the recurrent patterns of rhetoric and policy response. To see this, it is enough to compare the waves of American nativism in the nineteenth and early twentieth centuries, chronicled in John Higham's classic work *Strangers in the Land*,[1] to contemporary reactions in countries facing large influxes. To be sure, these anti-immigrant refrains betray more than a measure of alarmism. However, they also reflect the defensible anxiety that, through the introduction of new human beings, immigration may significantly change the societies affected by it, and that such changes will disadvantage some and benefit others. At the limit, and ascending to abstraction, immigration can destabilize a

---

[1] J Higham, *Strangers in the Land: Patterns of American Nativism* (New York, Atheneum, 1981).

state's political conception of justice. And the alarmism itself is part of this desta-bilizing dynamic.

Yet despite the potential threat posed by immigration, it is a striking fact that no prosperous liberal constitutional democracy (our concern here) bars immigration outright. There is an important reason for this forbearance. The governance of immigration is an inescapably 'properly public purpose', one that, together with natural reproduction, is one of two ways states have of 'creating, sustaining, and improving' their political conceptions of justice, over time.[2] Like the family, by injecting new cohorts of prospective members, it ensures the 'orderly production and reproduction of society and its culture from one generation to the next'.[3] Immigration, then, is both essential to the ongoing viability of justice within wealthy liberal constitutional democracies and a threat to it. Faced with this ten-sion, such states have concluded that the best policy options are inegalitarian, tending toward admitting the advantaged and imposing greater restrictions on the less advantaged. Such policies run up against prevailing worldwide migra-tion flows. As a result, less advantaged migrants are more likely to suffer adverse consequences—to be arrested and detained; to be exploited, abused, raped, or murdered; to die in deserts of dehydration; to asphyxiate in cargo containers; or to drown or get eaten by sharks at sea. The upshot is a troubling correlation between disadvantage and vulnerability during the migration process.

Political–moral inquiry into immigration governance should focus on whether this form of self-reproduction by states is consistent with social justice. At the very least, we should ask whether social justice has any purchase in this domain. Otherwise, our liberal constitutional democracies may be built on an injustice not of some centuries-old colonial past, but that daily renews itself.

This challenge leads to the last two predicaments, one legal and one method-ological, which can be taken up together. Traditional liberal theories have tended implicitly or explicitly to presume bounded communities, despite the fact that the idea of limiting our moral obligations territorially seems antithetical to the core liberal premise of equal moral personhood. And it is well known that John Rawls in particular develops his theory of justice for the basic structure of a well-ordered but closed society, entered only at birth and exited only at death.[4] This is so well known, and so often mentioned, that I feel apologetic for repeating it. However, it will come up again and again in the pages that follow.

Rawls's limitation to his theory resonates in the realm of immigration gover-nance in part because it tracks the foundational legal doctrine of immigration

---

[2] A Ripstein, *Force and Freedom: Kant's Legal and Political Philosophy* (Cambridge, Harvard Univer-sity Press, 2009) 26–27.

[3] J Rawls, 'The Idea of Public Reason Revisited' in S Freeman (ed), *Collected Papers* (Cambridge, Harvard University Press, 1999) 595. Walzer makes the same connection between immigration and natural reproduction: M Walzer, *Spheres of Justice: A Defense of Pluralism and Equality* (New York, Basic Books, 1983) 34–35.

[4] J Rawls, *A Theory of Justice*, revised edn (Cambridge, MA, Belknap Press, 1999) 7; J Rawls, *Politi-cal Liberalism*, expanded edn (New York, Columbia University Press, 1996) 20; J Rawls, 'The Idea of Public Reason Revisited', above n 3 at 577.

law, under which states enjoy broad discretion over immigration governance. The third, legal predicament that arises in the study of immigration law is how to interpret this discretionary doctrine. At its strongest, it is sometimes interpreted as unfettered, which naturally suggests a corresponding view in political morality according to which justice has no role to play in immigration governance. Henry Sidgwick, in *The Elements of Politics*, calls this kind of political–moral view the 'national ideal' of immigration governance. This ideal holds as follows:

> [T]he right and duty of each government is to promote the interests of a determinate group of human beings, bound together by the tie of a common nationality—with due regard to the rules restraining it from attacking or encroaching on other states—and to consider the expediency of admitting foreigners and their products solely from this point of view.[5]

Views of this kind, which I will throughout call 'absolutist', consider that justice does not constrain immigration governance. Though the ongoing validity of the strong reading of the discretionary legal doctrine is disputed, it is fair to say that states generally continue to govern immigration as though they have an absolute right to exclude any and all migrants based exclusively on some conception of national self-interest. This style of immigration governance, and the corresponding interpretation of the discretionary legal doctrine, would be legitimized if absolutism could be defended.

I will argue that absolutism is implausible. Yet if we are to reject it some method for specifying the principled limits of states' discretion over immigration governance must be arrived at. That is the fourth predicament.

II. Justifying Immigration Policies: Rawls, Kant, and Smith

The vulnerability of migrants, the pressures faced by states governing immigration, and the ambiguous but possibly extraordinarily permissive legal doctrine under which such governance takes place, motivate the two questions asked in this essay: Do obligations of justice toward migrants constrain immigration regimes? If so, what principles of justice apply? With absolutism as foil, I have sought to address these questions by drawing on Rawls's work, together, most importantly, with that of Immanuel Kant and Adam Smith.

The chief advantage of placing Rawls's work at the centre of this inquiry is the rich and systematic way in which, over the course of his writings, he lays out and elaborates his methods of justification. Heavy reliance on Rawls brings the obvious drawback that those inclined against his theory will be inclined against the argument presented here. Perhaps more to the point, objections that tell against

---

[5] H Sidgwick, *The Elements of Politics* (New York, Cosimo Inc, 2005) 295.

Rawls may tell against my argument.[6] These disadvantages are outweighed, in my judgement, by the benefits. In particular, Rawls's systematicity facilitates the adaptation of his justificatory methods to the problem of justice in immigration governance. Thus, at different points, I examine if and how Rawls's methods of wide reflective equilibrium and constructivism, as well as his idea of public reason, which is not properly called a method, can be applied to the problem of immigration governance. Even if one disputes the validity of these approaches to justification, or the conclusions that they give rise to, their adaptation and application advances the debate over justice in immigration governance by making mistakes clearer and disagreements easier to pursue. This has seemed to me a promising way forward.

The dependence on Rawls does not mean I assume his conception of justice as fairness, with its two well-known principles of justice. I do not need to, so I do not. I do, however, take on a number of Rawls's methodological starting points and guiding ideals. Most important is the liberal ideal, incompatible with absolutism, of reciprocity: the idea that immigration governance can be undertaken, and justified, on terms that do not require migrants to view themselves as subservient, dominated, or worse but instead evince respect for them as free and equal persons (though, crucially, not as free and equal *citizens* or *members* engaged in social cooperation). Further, while the bulk of the argument assumes, more or less, our own, non-ideal world, when I turn at last in Chapter Seven to developing principles for policies of indefinite admission, I assume that the problem is one of establishing principles for the governance of immigration into an ideal, well-ordered liberal society within a non-ideal world. By a well-ordered society, I mean what Rawls means, namely, a domestic society in which members accept, as compatible with their sense of justice, and know that all other members accept in the same way, a reasonable political conception of justice that regulates all major social and political institutions.[7] By a non-ideal world, I mean a world that comprises at least one well-ordered society and a disordered remainder. This configuration of ideal and non-ideal theory allows us to provide guidance for the evaluation and reform of the immigration regimes of wealthy liberal constitutional democracies in today's world of vast global inequalities.[8]

This is not the approach that Rawls himself takes to immigration, which explains why the answer he comes up with is in part unsatisfying. In *The Law of Peoples*, he writes that: 'The problem of immigration ... is eliminated as a serious problem in a realistic utopia.'[9] Here Rawls is concerned only with the ideal part

---

[6] Joseph Carens avoids such an approach largely for this reason: J Carens, *The Ethics of Immigration* (New York, Oxford University Press, 2013) 298.

[7] J Rawls, E Kelly (ed), *Justice as Fairness: A Restatement* (Cambridge, MA, Belknap Press, 2001) 8–9; Rawls, *Political Liberalism*, above n 4 at 35; Rawls, *Theory*, above n 4 at 397–405.

[8] On this role for ideal theory see Rawls, *Theory*, above n 4 at 215; AJ Simmons, 'Ideal and Nonideal Theory' (2010) 38 *Philosophy & Public Affairs* 5.

[9] J Rawls, *The Law of Peoples* (Cambridge, Harvard University Press, 1999) 9.

of his theory of international justice. He is relying on the contention that what he takes to be the major causes of immigration—persecution, oppression, famine, and population pressure—would not arise in a reasonably just world. Rawls makes only two other vague remarks about immigration governance. Still operating within the realm of the ideal, he suggests that there is 'at least a qualified right to limit immigration'[10] that flows from the need for a state's government to ensure the capacity of its territory to support its members in perpetuity. Members from one state 'cannot make up for their irresponsibility in caring for their land and its natural resources by conquest in war or by migrating into another people's territory without their consent'.[11] When he further extends his ideal theorizing to relations between liberal and non-liberal but 'decent' hierarchical states, he argues that the latter should 'allow and provide assistance for the right of emigration', although he denies that this implies a corresponding 'right to be accepted as an immigrant'.[12] Here treatment of the issue stops. In Rawls's non-ideal international theory, he considers only how to bring so-called outlaw states and burdened societies within the society of well-ordered peoples,[13] but he never considers how immigration should be governed during this period of transition. Since the transitional period is likely to last a long time, this seems like a regrettable omission.

Many who have sought to go beyond Rawls have worked within a framework of debate between closed and open borders, or, between an absolute right to exclude and an absolute right to migration. This framing of the debate, indeed, follows Sidgwick, who thought that if we reject the 'national ideal', the alternative is to embrace the 'cosmopolitan ideal', under which:

> [A state's] business is to maintain order over the particular territory that historical causes have appropriated to it, but not in any way to determine who is to inhabit this territory, or to restrict the enjoyment of its natural advantages to any particular portion of the human race.[14]

There is no reason, though, to suppose immigration governance has only these two extreme alternatives open to it. Instead, I will argue that Rawls is right to say there is a 'qualified right to limit immigration'. This proposition suggests, though it does not follow as a matter of strict logic, a right of immigration of some sort on the part of some migrants. But how do we get to that conclusion? And how can we come to an understanding of either right so that we can assess, first, the absolutist claim and, second, if absolutism turns out to be unsupportable, the scope of just immigration governance? From the perspective of Rawlsian theory, these are 'problems of extension',[15] which require lifting the closed-society presumption.

---

[10] ibid at 39, fn 48. The 'at least', though, seems to reserve the possibility of a stronger right to limit immigration. Note that Rawls here cites Walzer, who I take to be one of strongest exemplars of philosophical absolutism: Walzer, *Spheres of Justice*, above n 3.

[11] ibid at 39.

[12] ibid at 74 and in fn 14.

[13] ibid at 89–90.

[14] Sidgwick, *Politics*, above n 5 at 295.

[15] Rawls, *Political Liberalism*, above n 4 at 20–21; 244–45.

One important aspect of the closed-society presumption is, of course, that Rawls restricted his initial inquiry to the question of which principles of justice would apply to the major social institutions, or basic structure, of a domestic well-ordered society, proceeding only later to questions of international justice. As important when theorizing justice in immigration, however, the presumption only allows for natural entry and exit, through birth and death. The stipulation that members will live out their entire lives within the well-ordered society plays a crucial part in Rawls's argument for the stability of justice as fairness based on his account of moral psychology within a well-ordered society, as well as his argument for the legitimacy of any reasonable political conception of justice arrived at through public reason.

On Rawls's account, the moral development of members within the society into which they are born explains in part why they develop an allegiance toward the principles of the political conception of justice that regulate the society's basic structure and why they are predisposed to turn to those principles when engaged in debates over political matters. That is, the fact that one has come to maturity within a well-ordered society helps explain how one's developed sense of justice comes to be approximately aligned with the developed sense of justice of other members, with the principles of justice governing the arrangements under which they live, and with the specific institutional rules and policies that implement those principles. Public reason, in turn, supports stability because it represents a commitment on the part of members to debate fundamental matters by recourse to reasonable political conceptions of justice that it is believed other reasonable members could accept and because, when debate is carried out on these terms, political obligations of obedience result. Finally, stability is assured because members know that the legitimate expectations, which they form under the rules of society developed through public reason in accordance with their broadly shared conception of justice, will be honoured. Such knowledge allows them to live purposively, to adopt more or less structured plans of life in keeping with some idea of what would be good for them and those to whom they are attached.

So the stability of the well-ordered society depends, perhaps essentially, on its closed nature. And stability for the right reasons, according to Rawls, is a criterion for assessing any conception of justice. Immigration disrupts this stability because it injects cohorts of would-be members who may unsettle existing members' prior expectations, either because migrants will become rival claimants to certain goods or because the public institutional rules of the basic structure, and perhaps the political conception of justice itself, may change. Moreover, the need to come to a just and authoritative agreement over how to resolve such disruptions is hampered by the fact that immigrants will generally be adults who have progressed through the stages of moral development in other societies. At least upon arrival, they will likely have senses of justice that are not supportive of the stability of the political conception of justice in the receiving state. A mismatch results between the senses of justice of migrants and members, as well as a mismatch between migrants' senses of justice and the political conception of justice of the state to which they have come. This absence of a shared political conception of justice presents an obstacle to public reason, since it will presumably be harder for each group to argue along lines that the other will find reasonable. Thus when we lift the closed-society presumption, new questions present themselves about how to secure the conditions of stability and authority necessary for a state to be well-ordered. These challenges to stability provide the starting point for grasping the nature of the 'qualifications' of the right states might have to exclude and, by implication, the 'qualified' nature of the right migrants might have to enter.

While Rawls's work allows us to pose these questions, it does not allow us to answer them, at least not without adjustments. Thus, to address the problems of justice in immigration raised, I make several moves that take us beyond Rawls, or at least Rawls as he is conventionally understood.

The argument begins in Part One by framing the problem of justice and authority in immigration governance. First, in Chapter One, drawing on Smith's *Theory of Moral Sentiments*, I go back to a classical understanding of the concept of justice, and, more importantly, injustice, as unjustified injury wrought by human agency. This concept lays the foundation for later argument in several ways. First, it allows me to address a fundamental absolutist challenge, namely that an inquiry into social justice in immigration governance is not intelligible because social justice is a special relationship. The answers to this challenge turn out to be, first, to deny any strong distinction between social and personal justice or injustice and, second, to claim that the inquiry into social justice in immigration governance is intelligible so long as such governance leads to injuries. The inquiry is simply into whether such injuries are justifiable. The second way that the Smithian concept of justice lays the foundation for later argument is that it allows us to understand the problem of authority as the problem of reconciling conflicting views about justice. While I avoid systematic exegesis, I believe this understanding of the relationship between the ideals of justice and authority is faithful to both Rawls and Kant. I end Chapter One with an abstract statement of the problem of justice and authority in immigration governance. Briefly, this problem is to ensure that the injuries imposed by state immigration regimes on migrants are justified in a manner consistent with the justification of the ongoing political inequality, and the various other inequalities grafted onto this political inequality, between the members and non-members of constitutional liberal democracies.

Chapter Two continues the table-setting begun in Chapter One by doing four things. It lists a series of what Rawls calls 'considered judgements' about justice in immigration governance to be employed in later argument. It provides an overview of the structure of immigration law and policy, in particular by introducing the discretionary doctrine that lies at the heart of immigration law. Finally, it attempts to make the abstract statement of the problem of justice in immigration governance more concrete. If the problem of justice and authority in immigration governance in the abstract has to do with the justification of political inequality between members and non-members of constitutional liberal democracies, a more urgent though contingent problem is to develop principles that allow us to evaluate the inegalitarianism that in practice characterizes the immigration law and policy of such states. Inegalitarianism here refers to a general tendency among constitutional liberal democracies to favour long-term admission of the moneyed, skilled, or otherwise advantaged and to exclude or impose greater restrictions on the less advantaged. A principal aim of this essay is to evaluate the justice of inegalitarianism in immigration governance.

Having framed the inquiry in Part One, Part Two then seeks to answer the first question: Do obligations of justice toward migrants constrain immigration regimes? I argue that they do because unless immigration regimes strive to be just toward migrants, they will have no authority over them. This argument seeks to refute a second version of absolutism, which makes the contrary claim that immigration regimes can have authority even if they do not strive to be just. I cast the debate between these views partly as an interpretive problem focused on the proper reading of the discretionary doctrine introduced in Chapter Two. The interpretive issue is whether this discretion is to be interpreted as absolute or principled.

In Chapter Three I argue that Kant's political philosophy offers us several important resources for tackling the problem of justice and authority in immigration governance. Chiefly, this is because he begins his account of justice with the idea of individuals in the state of nature and develops from this heuristic the postulate of public right, a principle that requires individuals to place themselves under a 'rightful condition', in the standard case to place themselves under the authority of a state, to escape the insecurity brought about by the indeterminacy of justice. The resulting account, first, gives us a justification of the state as guarantor of a political conception of justice, which, second, provides a plausible justification of the political inequality between members and non-members. Such political inequality is justified first by the achievement of an authoritative political conception of justice, which is a good all persons should recognize. But it is further justified by the joint integration of members' senses of justice with the political conception of justice guaranteed by the state which, among other things, gives rise to legitimate expectations which must be respected. The third conclusion yielded by the Kantian account, I argue, is that the postulate of public right extends to the problem of immigration governance. It instructs states to enter a rightful condition with migrants, hence to govern immigration on socially just terms. This Kantian argument is meant to support the claim that the discretionary legal doctrine in immigration governance must be interpreted by officials of a receiving state as being constrained by this duty. I call this the principled account of immigration governance.

I provide two more arguments in Part Two against the absolutist position that immigration regimes can have authority without seeking to comply with the dictates of justice. First, in Chapter Four, I argue that to support the claims to legitimacy of immigration regimes, and to avoid grotesque moral implications, absolutism must give way to some form of principled account. I make this argument by analyzing the philosophical absolutist views of Michael Walzer and Thomas Nagel.

Then, in Chapter Five, I argue that under absolutism immigration regimes cannot give rise to political obligations among migrants and so cannot have authority. Absolutism therefore has difficulty making sense of the fact that wealthy liberal constitutional democracies govern immigration through law. Chapter Five also provides an affirmative account of how immigration regimes can have authority by seeking to comply with principles of justice in immigration. This account builds on Rawls's discussion of the natural duty of justice from *A Theory of Justice* together with his accounts of public reason and the principle of liberal legitimacy, from *Political Liberalism* and his late paper, 'The Idea of Public Reason Revisited'. The focus of argument is on the problem of sustaining authority in the absence of democratic institutions and in the face of likely disagreement over what justice in immigration governance requires. I argue that to have authority, immigration regimes must strive to be governed according to a reasonable conception of justice in immigration governance that reasonable migrants could accept.

This high level result does not include a statement of what reasonable principles of justice in immigration governance might look like. Accordingly Part Three takes up the second overarching question posed in this essay: What does justice in immigration governance demand? This question might be thought of as an attempt to meet a third and last absolutist claim. Absolutism might concede that social justice is not a special relationship and also concede that immigration regimes must strive to be just to have authority. It might nonetheless rejoin that justice makes no demands in immigration governance. If so then once again justice does not constrain immigration regimes. One answer is that this claim is contradicted by the fact that we do have considered judgements, canvassed in Chapter Two, about justice in this domain. This answer is equivocal because those judgements may be subject to revision. A better answer is to try to develop at least an incomplete account of justice in immigration, as I do in Chapters Six and Seven. The resulting account is incomplete in two ways. First, it does not purport to offer a complete evaluative framework for all aspects of immigration policy. Second, it is developed without any ideal conception of global or international justice in mind; without such a conception, it will be impossible to say definitively if the principles developed might not retard the attainment of some global or international ideal.

Chapter Six suggests two principles. In keeping with the Kantian account, I argue that immigration policies can only be justifiably capped in order to ensure the stability of a state's political conception of justice and to protect the legitimate expectations of its members. Next, I develop what I call the indirect principle of freedom of migration by drawing on an argument found in Smith's *Wealth of Nations*, against restrictions on the movement of labourers imposed under the early modern Laws of Settlement in England. The indirect principle states that immigration laws and policies of admission or exclusion will be unjust if they require unjust implementation or give rise to other forms of collateral injustice; if, say, their implementation would require indefinite detention or excessive force, or would give rise to exploitation or abuse by smugglers or traffickers. While I argue that this principle has non-trivial critical force, it is nonetheless limited in that it does not directly address the justice or injustice of inegalitarian laws and policies of admission or exclusion. The practical implications of the indirect principle depend on the extent to and ways in which inegalitarian policies require unjust enforcement or lead to collateral injustice.

Chapter Seven attempts to develop a principle that can provide the basis for a more robust critique of inegalitarian admissions. To do so, I sketch a modified form of Rawlsian constructivism: that is, a modified version of the hypothetical social contract device that Rawls calls the original position. I argue that parties to an original position adapted for the problem of immigration governance would choose to protect freedom of migration as a basic liberty, albeit not one that, as is the case for basic liberties in Rawls's domestic theory of justice, has absolute priority over socio-economic principles. I further argue, however, that to respect the reasons for deeming freedom of migration a liberty, the admissions policies of liberal constitutional democracies must prioritize the worst off, that is, those whose lack of freedom and capabilities most compromises their ability to exercise and develop their two moral powers, namely the capacities for a sense of justice and a conception of the good. Inegalitarian admissions policies must defend themselves by showing that they are consistent with this form of prioritization. I conclude the argument by asking whether the indirect principle from Chapter Six and the prioritarian admissions principle from Chapter Seven accord with our considered judgements and by assessing their evaluative salience with respect to the problem of inegalitarianism in immigration governance.

III. Some Parameters and Stipulations

In developing these arguments, I will usually use the term 'migrant' rather than 'immigrant' or 'emigrant'. By 'migrant', I refer to individuals who desire, intend, or are forced to travel, work, study, take up residence, or naturalize in a state that is not their own. I prefer 'migrant' to 'immigrant' or 'emigrant' as it is more encompassing, although I occasionally use the narrower terms where appropriate. Refugees, for purposes here, are subsumed in the broader migrant category. Finally, the terms 'migrant', 'immigrant', or 'emigrant' are contrasted with the term 'member' rather than 'citizen', unless context otherwise demands. This approach avoids having the argument constrained by legal categories. We should be open to the possibility that some immigrants to a state may count among its formal citizens and that some members may not.

The argument addresses how the immigration of migrants ought to be governed by the immigration regimes of stable and wealthy liberal constitutional democratic states. Each of these five adjectival stipulations is adopted for a different reason: 'liberal', 'democratic', and 'constitutional' because I am working within the liberal, constitutional, democratic tradition of political philosophy and, more particularly, with the liberalism of Smith, Kant, and Rawls; 'wealthy' because it is the wealth of liberal democracies that largely leads to the problem of inegalitarianism which presents the most pressing issue of justice in immigration governance; and 'stable' because most of the arguments would simply not be relevant if such liberal constitutional democracies faced the prospect of collapse. However, much more is said about the issue of stability as we progress.

This is not a study of the actual immigration laws and policies of particular liberal constitutional democracies. However, to the extent that real world examples are used, I draw upon the United States and Canada. This is simply because I know their laws and policies best, and I do not think that this focus introduces distortions. Bias might arise because of the exceptional nature of these countries' immigration rules (for example, the United States in particular places an emphasis on family migration and also faces a uniquely large illegal immigration problem); their histories as countries of immigration and their resultant internal diversity; and their forms of political organization (such as, for instance, Canadian policies of multiculturalism and the national minority status of the Québecois). As long as none of my conclusions are driven by these exceptional elements, the integrity of the argument should not be compromised. I do not think it is, but, if I am wrong, I accept that fact and leave it to future work to achieve a higher level of generalization.

The argument could have been cast wider in another sense. At its broadest, it might have addressed how the movement of migrants, their emigration and immigration, is and ought to be governed by migration regimes, where these might have included the emigration regimes of states and global or regional arrangements regulating migration. Further, it might have covered some international instruments that govern migration incidentally, as part of efforts to regulate other aspects of international practice, such as trade or human rights. Finally, different national regimes form a world system, through shared governance strategies, such as passports, or simply through the combined impact of their policies. Some of these different levels and structures of migration governance do play a role in the argument from time to time. However, the focus is, as I said, on the immigration regimes of stable and wealthy liberal constitutional democracies. While many of the principles and arguments here could be adapted for other contexts, that task, too, will have to await a further study.

Part I

Preliminaries

1

Justice, Authority, and Immigration

I. Introduction

IN THIS ESSAY I seek to refute the plausibility of absolutism, the view that justice does not constrain immigration governance, and to develop a principled alternative. To get underway, sufficiently clear definitions of justice and authority are needed. These are provided in Section Two. But no starting point is entirely neutral. At the outset, we run up against a first, foundational absolutist claim that the inquiry into justice in immigration governance is unintelligible because social justice is a special, not a universal, relationship. No doubt unsurprisingly, I deny this claim. While what is required by justice may vary with context, its scope is limited only by the human capacity to injure one another. These points emerge in Section Three through an exposition of Adam Smith's account of our judgements of justice. Finally, Section Four broadly frames the inquiry into justice in immigration and explains the distinctive challenges of theorizing justice and authority in immigration governance.

II. Justice and Authority

1. Justice

My focus is on the evaluation of immigration regimes from the standpoint of social justice and, importantly, injustice. Social justice, as I will understand it here, is an ideal that aims at the elimination of oppression, where this term refers to unjustified damage to human purposiveness, responsibility for which is traceable to impersonal human agency. Purposiveness, the capacity to set and act on purposes, is a central aspect of what it means to be human. When purposiveness coalesces, individually or in community with others, into a more or less structured conception of how one's life should be lived, we can call this structured conception a conception of the good.[1] A conception of social justice can be theorized through the specification of principles and rules that achieve an appropriate

---

[1] J Rawls, *Political Liberalism*, expanded edn (New York, Columbia University Press, 1996) 19–20.

distribution of rights, duties, benefits, and burdens by major social institutions or practices; that is, to introduce a Rawlsian term, through the basic structure. A condition of social injustice can always be described, or redescribed, in terms of an inappropriate distribution of these things. Such redescriptions may seem artificial or trivial in some cases, for example, cases of torture.[2] That does not mean they are unavailable.

Much in the above paragraph will be unpacked and developed as we go. Most important, to start, is that this way of thinking about justice combines two strands in the literature. According to the first, justice is primarily occupied with the distribution of rights, liberties, powers, and benefits as well as of duties, burdens, restraints, and pains.[3] A theory of justice provides principles for the apportionment of these goods and ills. According to the second strand, justice aims foremost at the elimination of oppression.[4] This second strand, at least recently, has generally been offered up in explicit or implicit criticism of the first. But, as I will use them here, rather than being in tension, these two strands of thought merely come at the problem of justice in different but related ways. Injustice leads to a distinct form of complaint, to which principles of justice respond. Smith states this relationship succinctly: 'The end of justice is to secure from injury'.[5]

A further point is that the focus of inquiry is on social justice. However, the definition provided does not support a strong distinction between 'social' justice or injustice and 'personal' justice or injustice. I have taken the idea of injustice as unjustified injury through human agency pretty much wholesale from Smith, and I will expand on Smith's account below in Section Three. On this understanding, the distinction between social and personal justice or injustice lies in the human agency that has brought it about, and the kinds of justification appropriate given such agency. Personal injustice results from wrongdoing by identifiable perpetrators. Social injustice, or oppression, is characterized by injuries brought about by impersonal human agency, such as through institutional or social rules, practices, or dynamics. Thus personal and social injustice occupy opposing ends of a spectrum characterizing injuries in accordance with the way we assign responsibility for injury.

---

[2] J Gardner, 'The Virtue of Justice and the Character of Law' (2000) 53 *Current Legal Problems* 1, 27.

[3] H Sidgwick, *The Methods of Ethics* (Indianapolis, Hackett Publishing Co, 1981) 265–66; J Rawls, *A Theory of Justice*, revised edn (Cambridge, MA, Belknap Press, 1999) 4; HLA Hart, *The Concept of Law*, 2nd edn (Oxford, Clarendon Press, 1994) 158–59; J Waldron, 'The Primacy of Justice' (2003) 9 *Legal Theory* 269, 277.

[4] E Anderson, 'What is the Point of Equality?' (1999) 109 *Ethics* 287, 313; IM Young, *Justice and the Politics of Difference* (Princeton, Princeton University Press, 1990) 39ff; I Shapiro, 'On Non-Domination' (2012) 62 *University of Toronto Law Journal* 293.

[5] A Smith, RL Meek, DD Raphael, and PG Stein (eds), *Lectures on Jurisprudence* (Indianapolis, Liberty Fund, 1982) 399. Note that the focus on injury avoids the debate over whether immigration restrictions are coercive: A Abizadeh, 'Democratic Theory and Border Coercion: No Right to Unilaterally Control Your Own Borders' (2008) 36 *Political Theory* 37; D Miller, 'Why Immigration Controls Are Not Coercive: A Reply to Arash Abizadeh' (2010) 38 *Political Theory* 111–20. Coercion would be a special form of injury, perhaps requiring a special kind of justification.

To illustrate, on my usage when someone is the victim of a mugging, she has been subject to personal injustice. When someone lives under conditions rendering it more likely she will be mugged, perhaps because she belongs to a marginalized group or lives in a poor neighbourhood, she may be the victim of social injustice. Oppression can be distinguished in part by the special helplessness we feel when injustice begins to approach a state of being. It is brought about not by an identifiable individual or set of individuals, not by a thug or two, but by an ideology, culture, or set of institutions that empowers or enables thuggery. As this example shows, social and personal injustice may be, and often are, experienced together. The search for the causes of oppression can mark the refusal to accept that the explanation of one's victimization stops with the bad intentions of a few men or women. Where social injustice has occurred, its converse can rarely be restored solely through the punishment of a few wrongdoers. Potentially an entire society may be implicated. Reform, not punishment, may be the appropriate remedy.

2. Authority

There is a tight connection between problems of social justice and problems of political authority. Oppression raises problems of political authority because political power will often lie behind the injury complained of and also, of course, because political power will often be the only realistic means of addressing such complaints. These two facts are related. The very fact that political power might be deployed to eliminate injuries may be grounds for concluding that the political system is complicit by omission.

Political authority, I will say, is a term that aims to capture a relationship of governance in which a person or entity is capable of exercising power over a collection of subjects. A descriptive theory of authority tells us how to identify when a person or entity in fact has authority. A normative theory of authority tells us when it is right and proper that a person or entity has authority. Such a normative theory may have two parts. First is a theory of the legitimacy, meaning the moral justification, of the exercise of power. Second is a theory of political obligation, meaning the vindication or not of the governing entity's claims to be owed political obligations, in particular an obligation of obedience to its commands.[6] If political obligation is owed to a legitimate political authority, I will call it a complete political authority. A complete political authority possesses wide-ranging normative power over its subjects.[7] By this, I mean that a person or entity

---

[6] In this chapter and later, in Chapter Five, I ignore technical distinctions between 'obligation' and 'duty'. An obligation, narrowly construed, is a moral requirement incurred through promise, contract, or some other performative act. A duty is a moral requirement that attaches by virtue of one's status, including potentially one's status as a human being. When I refer to 'political obligations', however, I mean political obligations *or* duties.

[7] J Raz, 'Legitimate Authority' in J Raz, *The Authority of Law: Essays on Law and Morality*, 2nd edn (New York, Oxford University Press, 2009) 16–19.

with authority may command, legislate, grant permissions, give authoritative advice, adjudicate, and so on and that, when it acts in these ways, it may change the normative situation of its subjects.[8]

Legitimacy and obligation need not run together. For instance, it is sometimes said that Lockean consent theory provides independent theories of legitimacy (a legitimate state is one that could have been consented to in an ideal history) and political obligation (political obligation can only come from express or tacit consent).[9] This conceptual separation of legitimacy and obligation is disputed by some, who see the two ideas as mutually entailed.[10] I think the claim of mutual entailment is wrong. It seems possible to have a legitimate political authority that is not owed obedience, such as within a prisoner of war camp or in a justly occupied territory.[11] From the other direction, however, it is hard to conceive of an illegitimate government able to command political obligations. Accordingly, legitimacy may be a necessary condition of obligation, but this does not amount to logical correlation. The perhaps slight conceptual space between legitimacy and obligation means that by arguing for legitimacy, one will not necessarily have established the authority of a regime. On the other hand, an argument that a regime can give rise to political obligations on the part of its subjects will usually also establish its legitimacy, hence its complete political authority. The argument in Chapter Five for the authority of immigration regimes asks how immigration regimes can give rise to political obligations. It is therefore an argument of the second kind, aiming at political obligation but in the process establishing legitimacy.

The demand for the justification of the social and institutional arrangements that govern our lives is central to justice and both aspects of authority, yet each ideal responds to this demand in different ways. A claim of social justice seeks to justify a social arrangement by showing that no one under it is oppressed; that the arrangement results in no unjustified injuries of human provenance. The need for such justification arises when there are disagreements between persons over how to live their lives that cannot be resolved by appeal to some higher-level shared conception of the good. In contrast, a claim that a social arrangement has political authority seeks to justify the arrangement by showing that it ought to be accepted and obeyed. We lean on justifications of authority as the prospect for resolution of disputes over justice recedes.

It might be said that where justice pertains to an area of non-ideal theory relative to conceptions of the good, authority defines an area of non-ideal theory

---

[8] AI Applbaum, 'Legitimacy without the Duty to Obey' (2010) 38 *Philosophy & Public Affairs* 215, 219.

[9] J Rawls, *Lectures on the History of Political Philosophy* (Cambridge, MA, Belknap Press, 2007) 128–31 (on legitimacy) and 131–35 (on political obligation).

[10] AJ Simmons, 'Justification and Legitimacy' in *Justification and Legitimacy: Essays on Rights and Obligations* (New York, Cambridge University Press, 2001) 130.

[11] See T Christiano, 'Authority' in EN Zalta (ed), *The Stanford Encyclopedia of Philosophy* (Spring 2013 edn), available at: plato.stanford.edu/entries/authority.

relative to justice.[12] We fall back on justice when moderate scarcity and conflicts of interests, combined with ordinary human failings, lead to circumstances in which the potential for injury arises but where we cannot rely on a common conception of the good to resolve it. These are the circumstances of justice.[13] We fall back on authority when a shared conception of justice cannot be achieved and disagreements over what is right threaten to take on the same heat as disagreements over what is good. These are what Jeremy Waldron has called the circumstances of politics.[14] Disputes at this level can ultimately become more heated, since the initial sense of aggrievement may be compounded by the sense that a set of higher-order impartial standards has been violated. It may not simply be our way of life that is insulted, but an attempt to accommodate other ways of life, including those of the offending parties, at some cost to ourselves.

Theories of authority are to be worked out against background disagreements about justice. One of the reasons it is appropriate to talk about 'political' authority where above I invoked only 'social' justice is that at this level of compromise, it seems unlikely social arrangements can continue in a stable manner without some centralized, governing power; in the standard contemporary case, a state. After all, what is being asked of subjects is to dampen their resentment or indignation, to revise their feelings of being oppressed, while working within official channels to arrive at mutually acceptable arrangements. Political authority in this sense demands a radical reconstitution of the individual self; radical because it involves a revision of their sense of what their own dignity demands. It is hard to imagine how such demands can be consistently effective without political power, at least initially.

Political authority connects to legal authority in a contingent manner. This point is important because in immigration governance the challenge of theorizing justice and authority is presented, in the first instance, by a legal doctrine authorizing broad discretion in immigration governance. Other than by governing through law, political authority could not achieve the aim of coordinate, conflict-free coexistence. That is why Joseph Raz is correct to argue that all legal systems attached to a centralized political authority assert legitimate power to regulate any type of behaviour within their jurisdiction and also claim to be owed obedience by their subjects, in the sense that their subjects have a moral obligation to obey the law because it is the law.[15] The claims of the law and the necessary reliance on law as a tool for governance go hand in hand. Thus the presupposition of authority is an important feature of the self-representation of legal systems

---

[12] I am indebted for this idea to A Applbaum, 'Democratic Legitimacy and Official Discretion' (1992) 21 *Philosophy & Public Affairs* 240, 252 (1992). See also T Nagel, *Equality and Partiality* (Oxford, Oxford University Press, 1991) 170.

[13] Rawls, *Theory of Justice*, above n 3 at 109–12.

[14] J Waldron, *Law and Disagreement* (Oxford, Oxford University Press, 1999) 102.

[15] J Raz, *Practical Reasons and Norms* (Oxford, Oxford University Press, 1990) 151–53; Raz, 'The Claims of Law' in *The Authority of Law*, above n 7 at 29–33; J Raz, *The Morality of Freedom* (Oxford, Clarendon Press, 1986) 100–101.

because they are part of the project of achieving the political authority needed to resolve disagreements about justice.

A theory of political authority must therefore set out and defend the terms of the relationship between a government and its subjects. The government should be shown to be justified in coercively imposing upon subjects (legal) rules of coexistence that fall short in some or most respects of those subjects' ideas of justice and the good. The subjects in turn should be shown to incur obligations defined by the government's rules. Because theories of authority must be multi-perspectival, the task is forbiddingly complex. The authority of those in power can depend on how they came to power. The authority of their pronounce-ments can depend on an array of procedural or institutional mechanisms, such as the rule of law, democracy, and due process. Such authority can depend on a showing that any pronouncement does not violate certain basic or human rights. It can also depend on officials complying with certain role obligations, such as obligations not to act in bad faith, in a conflict of interest, or with undue bias.[16] Depending on whether such conditions are met, the attitude of the subject might be one of complete submission, selective obedience and disobedience, or outright defiance; of acquiescence, respectful scrutiny, or prosecutorial interrogation. Finally, obligations might be directed at those who are not in authority. Subjects might be morally required to exhibit certain attitudes toward one another that coalesce into obligations to obey a political power. Members may have obliga-tions to other members, migrants to other migrants, or members and migrants to each other. Once the many potential components of an account of authority are understood, one begins to see the difficulty of providing a theory of the authority of immigration regimes.

III. The Universality of Justice

1. An Absolutist Objection

To describe the concepts of justice and authority as I have has many substantive implications for the argument that follows. First, coming at injustice through the idea of oppression emphasizes the resentment one feels upon falling victim to an injustice. Felt judgements of injustice, in turn, provide a way to take a first step toward what Rawls calls reflective equilibrium, the method of justification that, at the highest level, I will apply to the attempt to theorize both justice and authority in immigration governance.

The basics of reflective equilibrium can be stated briefly. One begins with a set of judgements made under favourable conditions. These are 'considered judge-ments', which are used to explicate a set of principles. One moves back and forth

---

[16]   M Hardimon, 'Role Obligations' (1994) 91 *The Journal of Philosophy* 333.

between the principles and judgements, making mutual adjustments to ensure they are consistent with one another, until there is no need to make further revisions. At that point, reflective equilibrium is achieved. While Rawls emphasizes that considered judgements can be judgements at any level of generality, when investigating an area where the place of justice is uncertain, as in immigration governance, our judgements about particular instances of injustice provide a more secure starting point. I present a set of considered judgements in the next chapter. These considered judgements are then applied together with others that are the product of argument to develop the ensuing account.

This proposed method runs into a substantive objection from absolutism. As noted in the Introduction, it is well known that Rawls confines his theory of justice as fairness to the case of a closed domestic society. Rawls's official reason for this limitation is methodological.[17] Some argue, however, that this restriction is also substantively sound. Justice, it is said, is a special relationship of limited scope. If so, that raises the metaethical question of whether judgements of justice or injustice across political boundaries, such as judgements of justice or injustice about immigration governance, are intelligible in the first instance. The putative unintelligibility of the inquiry into justice in immigration governance may explain the other two absolutist positions considered later, namely that immigration regimes can have authority without striving to be just or that justice makes no demands in immigration governance.

To support the claim about the limited scope of justice, some philosophers have relied on the coercive nature of political power within states; some on the bounded nature of the cooperative practices distinctive of states; and some on shared communal identities within states.[18] On this last form of argument, principles of justice derive from communal shared understandings.[19] Alasdair MacIntyre, for instance, argues that our pre-reflective attitudes about justice are rooted in desert and, further, that

> the notion of desert is at home only in the context of a community whose primary bond is a shared understanding both of the good for man and of the good of that community and where individuals identify their primary interests with reference to those goods.[20]

Community is prior to justice because our judgements of desert are developed within an existing tradition. Although Michael Walzer's project is very different from MacIntyre's, Walzer's theory of justice, called complex equality, similarly relies on the idea of a community's shared understandings of the proper distribution of different kinds of goods. It seems to follow from these views that when

[17] See, eg Rawls, *Political Liberalism*, above n 1 at 20.
[18] For this useful breakdown, see D Miller, 'Justice and Boundaries' in *Justice for Earthlings: Essays in Political Philosophy* (New York, Cambridge University Press, 2013) 151–61.
[19] See M Walzer, *Spheres of Justice: A Defense of Pluralism and Equality* (New York, Basic Books, 1983); A MacIntyre, *After Virtue, A Study in Moral Theory*, 2nd edn (Notre Dame, University of Notre Dame Press, 1984).
[20] MacIntyre, *After Virtue*, ibid at 250.

a member of one community injures a member of another, injurer and injured will not have shared understandings with which to settle the question of whether the injury is justified, hence just or unjust. They may, in fact, not have sufficient shared understandings to agree on what counts as an injury. Although the lines of argument differ, similar conclusions follow from the other two kinds of view that claim justice is a special relationship.

To be sure, this picture runs contrary to the reaction most would have that, say, assault by a non-compatriot would be an injustice. If the argument for the limited scope of justice operated at the level of personal injustice, it would seem absurd. Accepting this point, one absolutist reply is to admit that there can certainly be personal injustice against non-compatriots, but not social injustice, judgements of which require a deeper appraisal of social and political context. Judgements of justice or injustice in immigration governance would be judgements of this second kind.

A further reply for absolutism is that while there may be some minimal claims of justice that can be recognized across borders, there is something special about questions of membership that resists such judgements. This may be the position taken by Walzer, when he writes that, 'The distribution of membership is not pervasively subject to the constraints of justice. Across a considerable range of the decisions that are made, states are simply free to take in strangers (or not) [.]'[21] Walzer's point is not obviously confinable to his theory of complex equality. Formulated in Rawlsian terms, it might be said that if judgements of social injustice are judgements regarding the unjustified injuries visited upon us by a basic structure, it is unclear such judgements can intelligibly be brought to bear on the question of which basic structure we ought to belong to, or which ought to belong to us. Rather, the question of belonging to a basic structure seems to be a non-justiciable given, just as shared understandings are.

Here Rawls's well-developed discussions of philosophical justification prove frustrating because they do not appear to offer a way to engage either the general claim that social justice is a special relationship or the specific claim that questions of membership are not constrained by social justice. This is obvious with respect to the constructivist original position, the hypothetical social contract device developed in *A Theory of Justice* and *Political Liberalism* only for closed societies. In *The Law of Peoples*, Rawls expands his constructivism to a global society of peoples (not persons) and states. He does so, however, in a way that largely elides problems of social justice that might arise between individuals and states to which they do not belong. Nor does Rawls's discussion of public reason, which is, roughly, a method for working out fundamental political questions by reference to a family of reasonable political conceptions of justice, allay this concern. If one cannot work out a political conception of justice for the governance of immigration, then perhaps one also cannot engage in public reason about immigration governance. Perhaps that is why political discourse over immigration

---

[21] Walzer, *Spheres of Justice*, above n 19 at 61.

often seems unreasonable. Finally, Rawls sees reflective equilibrium as relating in important ways to constructivism and public reason. Reflective equilibrium is used both to assemble the component parts of the constructivist procedure and to assess its output principles. Public reason itself may be thought of as a form of political discourse that aims at a reflective equilibrium that is 'general and wide, or what we may refer to as full'.[22] Perhaps Rawls limits the scope of these other two methods because of limits in reflective equilibrium as well. Perhaps if there is a substantive basis for limiting the scope of social justice to the basic structure of a domestic society, one should also read down the scope of reflective equilibrium regarding matters of social justice.

2. Smith's Theory of Moral Judgement

Such a reading down would be a mistaken interpretation of Rawls and a mistake on its own terms. In what follows I only explain why it is a mistake on its own terms. The explanation will begin with an exposition of Smith's account of judgements of justice and injustice in *The Theory of Moral Sentiments*. Such exposition is also called for because this conception of injustice lies behind much of the ensuing argument.

Smith's conception of injustice rests upon his broader theory of judgement, the central cog of which is the moral-psychological mechanism of sympathy. Sympathy is a natural faculty through which we judge others' behaviour by imagining ourselves in their situation. Once we have carried out sympathetic identification, if we find our passions are the same as those that motivated their behaviour, we judge that behaviour to be proper and approve of it; if we feel otherwise, we judge it to be improper and disapprove.[23]

So sympathy is the faculty through which we judge others. At the same time the judgements of others, carried out through their own exercises of sympathetic identification, discipline us. We are aware of being the objects of sympathy. What is more, we desire sympathetic approval.[24] This desire for sympathy is so powerful that we prefer to temper our emotions, if possible, to achieve it. We 'flatten' the

---

[22] See J Rawls, E Kelly (ed), *Justice as Fairness: A Restatement* (Cambridge, MA, Belknap Press, 2001) 31. See also Rawls's remarks in *Political Liberalism*, above n 1 at 384–85, fn 16: In a well-ordered society 'not only is there a public point of view from which all citizens can adjudicate their claims of political justice, but also this point of view is mutually recognized as affirmed by them all in full reflective equilibrium. This equilibrium is fully intersubjective: that is, each citizen has taken into account the reasoning and arguments of every other citizen.'

[23] A Smith and K Haakonssen (ed), *The Theory of Moral Sentiments* (Cambridge, Cambridge University Press, 2002) 11–17, 20–23 [I.i.1 and I.i.3]. Square brackets refer to part, section, chapter, and paragraph numbers. Some parts of the book are not broken down into sections, in which case the square brackets refer to part, chapter, and paragraph numbers. I have been greatly helped and influenced in interpreting Smith's theory by K Haakonssen, *The Science of a Legislator: The Natural Jurisprudence of David Hume and Adam Smith* (New York, Cambridge University Press, 1981); S Darwall, 'Sympathetic Liberalism: Recent Work on Adam Smith' (1999) 28 *Philosophy & Public Affairs* 139; S Darwall, 'Equal Dignity in Adam Smith' (2004) 1 *Adam Smith Review* 129.

[24] Smith, *Theory of Moral Sentiments*, above n 23 at 17 [I.i.2.1].

sharpness of the natural tone of our emotions. In this way, the sentiments of the spectator and the original actor 'may … have such a correspondence with one another, as is sufficient for the harmony of society. Though they will never be unisons, they may be concords, and this is all that is wanted or required.'[25] Thus the judgements of any two people achieve a degree of concordance through a process in which each exercises sympathetic judgement with respect to the other's actions, sympathetically imagines the others' judgement of him or her, and exercises self-command to try to bring their passions, behaviour, and judgements into accord. Collective moral judgements and social harmony become possible through the ongoing reiteration of this process throughout a group.

Without more, sympathy may suggest a relativist or subjectivist view of moral judgement. Smith acknowledges that various 'corruptions' impede our judgements. A group's collective store of judgements may simply be the sum of its biases and errors. The first corruption Smith mentions is our disposition to admire the rich and powerful and to despise the poor and marginalized, which is 'the great and most universal cause of the corruption of our moral sentiments'.[26] Throughout *Theory of Moral Sentiments*, he enumerates several more. Among the most relevant to the inquiry into justice in immigration governance are natural partiality, that is, the inclination to see even our slightest misfortunes as far outweighing the graver misfortunes of others[27] and self-deceit, or the tendency to deceive ourselves about the propriety or impropriety of a course of action.[28] The impartial spectator tempers, but does not eliminate, the first; the development of general rules addresses the second.

The impartial spectator, an idealized judge who evaluates our behaviour with full information and weighing appropriately the interests of all involved, is a regulative ideal that installs a demand of equal consideration at the heart of Smith's theory. To adopt the perspective of the impartial spectator, we must seek full information and equidistance between our interests and those of others:

> We must view them, neither from our own place nor yet from his, neither with our own eyes nor yet with his, but from the place and with the eyes of a third person, who has no particular connexion with either, and who judges with impartiality between us.[29]

In any paradigmatic two-person interaction, either party may claim a preferred interpretation of impartiality in a given case. The party that can demonstrate that their perspective is more fully shorn of undue partiality and takes better stock of the relevant facts is more likely to have achieved a properly objective judgement. Because of our desire for sympathetic concordance, moreover, we will tend to

---

[25] ibid at 27 [I.i.4.7].

[26] ibid at 72 [I.iii.3.1], although he later also says that: 'Of all the corruptions of moral sentiments, therefore, factions and fanaticism have always been by far the greatest': TMS III.iii.43. See also III.ii.24 (factionalism and intrigue among poets).

[27] See, eg ibid at 157–58 [III.iii.4].

[28] ibid at 182–88 [III.iv.1–12].

[29] ibid at 157 [III.iii.3].

converge on more rather than less objective judgements, since they will naturally garner the sympathy of more individuals. That in turn brings a tendency to internalize, though imperfectly, the perspective of the impartial spectator.

The impartial spectator is an ideal. We have a limited capacity to enter its perspective. In particular, the corrupting power of self-deception often overwhelms our efforts at impartiality. We are least capable of entering into the perspective of the impartial spectator before we act, when swept up in the 'heat and keenness' of our motivations.[30] After acting, it is 'disagreeable to think ill of ourselves' so 'we often purposely turn away our view from those circumstances which might render that judgment unfavourable'.[31] Rules develop so that we may act morally despite these corrupting tendencies: 'Our continual observations upon the conduct of others, insensibly lead us to form to ourselves certain general rules concerning what is fit and proper either to be done or to be avoided.'[32] Prohibitions develop out of actions that shock us, and which meet a similar reaction in others.[33] Rules that provide affirmative guidance develop in obverse fashion.[34] We follow these rules because, Smith argues, we develop a 'sacred' regard, or sense of duty, toward them out of a compound of factors, which include 'discipline', 'education', 'example',[35] superstition,[36] and philosophical reflection.[37] Particularly important are those rules that render us punishable: those are the rules of justice.

3. Judgements about Justice

On Smith's account injustice consists of two elements: (1) an injury that was (2) motivated by sentiments or reasons that would be rejected by an impartial spectator:

> [T]he violation of justice is injury: it does real and positive hurt to some particular persons, from motives which are naturally disapproved of. It is, therefore, the proper object of resentment, and of punishment, which is the natural consequence of resentment.[38]

Injustice, we might say, is the form of complaint we lodge against injuries that exhibit disregard for the equal respect to which we, as persons, are entitled. This understanding is the source of the concept of justice set out in Section Two, above, as unjustifiable injury wrought by either personal or impersonal human agency.

Unlike other judgements, judgements about justice paradigmatically involve three-way, rather than two-way, sympathetic intercourse. We first consider

---

[30] ibid at 182 [III.iv.3].
[31] ibid at 183 [III.iv.4].
[32] ibid at 184 [III.iv.7].
[33] ibid.
[34] ibid at 184–85 [III.iv.7].
[35] For the last three, see ibid at 189 [III.5.1].
[36] ibid at 190–91 [III.5.4]: '[R]eligion, even in its rudest form, gave a sanction to the rules of morality, long before the age of artificial reasoning and philosophy.'
[37] ibid at 191 [III.5.5].
[38] ibid at 93 [II.ii.1.5]. Note that this idea of injustice as 'positive harm' dates back at least to Cicero: S Fleischacker, *A Short History of Distributive Justice* (Cambridge, MA, Harvard University Press, 2005) 22.

whether an alleged wrongdoer in fact injured the person who levies the charge of injustice. Next, we ask if that injury arose out of improper motives, requiring us to imagine ourselves in the role of the alleged wrongdoer and to judge whether an improper passion moved him or her. Finally, we ask if the wronged party's resentment is proportional to the injury and the motives from which it sprang. If the resentment is excessive, its violence makes us recoil; if too mild, its weak spirit appals us; but if proportional to the wrong, in the eyes of the impartial spectator, we will not only approve of the wronged party's desire to punish the wrongdoer, we will want to participate in the punishment.

Smith sometimes seems to consider that the first element of injustice, the 'real and positive hurt', will be self-evident:

> That a man has received an injury when he is wounded or hurt any way is evident to reason, without any explanation; and the same may be said of the injury done one when his liberty is any way restrain'd; any one will at first perceive that there is an injury done in this case.[39]

However, Smith's belief in self-evidence likely cannot be sustained. For example, and anticipating later argument, Smith claims that the early modern Laws of Settlement, which restricted the movement of English labourers from one parish to another, were 'an evident violation of liberty and justice'. However, Smith also says, that the 'common people of England ... never rightly understanding wherein' their liberty consists, have suffered this 'oppression without a remedy'.[40] Even 'evident' violations of justice and liberty, then, can be missed under social conditions where injuries are obscured or where we are discouraged from making claims by, say, a devalued sense of our own self-worth.[41]

To fill in the gap left once self-evidence is off the table, as I have already indicated, I will mean by injury 'damage to purposiveness'. I flesh this idea out in two ways. I will say that purposiveness is a product of our capacity to form and pursue a conception of one's own good, one of our two moral powers. It may also be, subordinately, the result of our other moral power, namely our capacity to understand and act on, together with others, our sense of justice, insofar as acting

---

[39] Smith, *Lectures on Jurisprudence*, above n 5 at 13.

[40] A Smith, *The Wealth of Nations, Books I–III* (New York, Penguin Classics, 1986) 245 [I.x.2].

[41] The claim of self-evidence is similarly undermined, indirectly, by other lengthy arguments Smith himself provides throughout his work against various injustices, such as the laws of primogeniture and entail, most import and export duties, and certain excessive taxes. Among the kinds of injuries Smith mentions in his *Lectures on Jurisprudence*, above n 5, are injuries suffered as a man, as a member of a family, and as a member of a state. Injuries suffered as a man include commutative wrongs (assault, maiming, and murder) but also libel and infringements of liberty. As the discussion in Chapters Six and Seven will show, little is self-evident about infringements of liberty. Injuries suffered as a member of a family include the ill-treatment of one's wife or improper regard by a son, which also seem nebulous forms of harm. Most nebulous of all, as a member of a state, Smith says a subject may be injured by 'oppression' (ibid at 399). Even if Smith means that we will respond with instinctive outrage when confronted with a son's impudence or government oppression, it will rarely be self-evident *why* we perceive injury in such cases. Interpretation is needed to identify some interest or valued good that has been damaged.

as justice requires is part of our conception of the good. Damage to purposiveness, then, can come about through the hindering of the development or exercise of our two moral powers. This understanding of purposiveness does most work in Chapter Seven. Damage to our moral powers, however, cannot plausibly exhaust the ways in which we can be injured. In Chapter Six, I employ the more concrete idea of purposiveness in terms of capabilities, and injury in terms of diminishment of one's capabilities, relying on the capabilities approach to social justice developed by Martha Nussbaum and Amartya Sen.[42] As will be explained, these approaches are mutually compatible and also consistent with Smith's account of justice. Roughly speaking, the idea of the two moral powers corresponds to Smith's notion of moral maturity and the capabilities correspond to what he calls independence.

The second important element of injustice is that of improper motives. In this aspect of injustice, Smith's commitment to equal respect is foregrounded:

> What chiefly enrages us against the man who injures or insults us, is the little account which he seems to make of us, the unreasonable preference which he gives to himself above us, and that absurd self-love, by which he seems to imagine, that other people may be sacrificed at any time, to his conveniency or his humour. The glaring impropriety of this conduct, the gross insolence and injustice which it seems to involve in it, often shock and exasperate us more than all the mischief which we have suffered. To bring him back to a more just sense of what is due to other people, to make him sensible of what he owes us, and of the wrong that he has done to us, is frequently the principal end proposed in our revenge, which is always imperfect when it cannot accomplish this.[43]

It is this aspect of Smith's account of the concept of justice that allows us to speak of him as a deontological liberal and makes it appropriate to think of different claims that he makes about justice as claims that a person or class of persons has been treated with unequal concern and respect.[44] An *unjust* injury, as distinct from an injury, will be one in which the aggressor was motivated by 'unreasonable preference' and 'absurd self-love', terms that I will take to include reasons for action that are unduly partial, unduly disregarding of the injured party's circumstances, or malevolent. Important to later argument, I will also include irrational motives, since to injure someone for irrational purposes cannot be considered proper. All these motives are united because in one manner or another, they

---

[42] I choose to rely on the capabilities approach rather than Rawls's own index of primary goods because I believe they render the idea of injury as damage to purposiveness more accessible; I do not intend to be staking any claim in the debate over the merits of capabilities over primary goods. For discussion, see Rawls, *Justice as Fairness*, above n 22 at 168–76 and M Nussbaum, *Frontiers of Justice: Disability, Nationality, Species Membership* (Cambridge, MA, Belknap Press, 2006); A Sen, *The Idea of Justice* (Cambridge, MA, Belknap Press, 2009).

[43] Smith, *Theory of Moral Sentiments*, above n 23 at 112–13 [II.iii.1.5]. For discussion of this passage, see Darwall, 'Sympathetic Liberalism', above n 23.

[44] 'To hurt in any degree the interest of any one order of citizens, for no other purpose but to promote that of some other, is evidently contrary to that justice and equality of treatment which the sovereign owes to all the different orders of his subjects.' A Smith, *The Wealth of Nations, Books IV–V* (New York, Penguin Books, 1999) at 238 [IV.viii].

represent a willingness to discount the equal dignity of the injured party. The requirement of improper motives is also what suggests the need for injustice to be confined to injuries behind which lay human agency.[45]

The core of Smith's account of injustice, then, is the moral standing of any person to demand a showing that an injury can be impartially justified to the individual or others on his or her behalf. Impartial justification connotes terms compatible with equal respect. If no such showing is possible, resentment is justified, punishment may be demanded, and others may be enlisted in such punishment. Unless either justification or punishment is forthcoming, social dysfunction or disintegration will follow sooner or later. That is because the sense of justice is an 'unsocial passion' that carries within it a destructive spark. Revenge can spiral out of control and excessive punishment of a wrong is itself an injustice, leading to potential for even more excessive revenge. Finally, the resentment incurred by these wrongs, even once any violence dies down, can linger for generations. It is because of the great destabilizing power of injustice that it is necessary that the rules of justice be precise.

Smith claims that the rules of justice are precise. They 'may be compared to the rules of grammar', whereas the rules associated with other virtues are like the 'rules which critics lay down for the attainment of what is sublime and elegant in composition'.[46] I take this to be the statement of an ideal, one that is not reflected in Smith's own discussion of various actual topics under the general heading of justice. In the face of inevitable disagreement about justice, and in light of the unsocial nature of our sense of justice, it is necessary to strive to settle upon rules of justice that 'determine with the greatest exactness every external action which it requires'.[47] It is necessary, that is, to have political authority.

4. Why Social Justice is not a Special Relationship

I have expended many words on Smith because I believe his account of our judgements of justice and injustice is substantially correct. It also sets out a number of important building blocks for later argument.

To begin with, Smith lays out the sense of justice with remarkable psychological acuity; in terms that I find reflect my own experience and that explain the actions and reactions of others as I observe them. Our 'sense of justice' is a set of governing dispositions[48] that gives rise to the moral feelings of resentment and indignation when we feel we have been the victim of an unjustified injury; to sympathetic resentment on behalf of others when we judge that they have been unjustifiably

---

[45] Note that it is injury that requires justification. When one does not injure others, one acts justly regardless of whether one has good or bad motives. Thus Smith's account of injustice is consistent with Kant's view that our duties of right concern only the external use of choice and not our maxims: I Kant, *The Metaphysics of Morals* (Cambridge, Cambridge University Press, 1996) 24 [6:231].

[46] Smith, *Theory of Moral Sentiments*, above n 23 at 205 [III.vi.11].

[47] ibid at 203 [III.vi.10].

[48] 'Governing dispositions' comes from Rawls, *Theory of Justice*, above n 3 at 420.

injured; to the desire to join in the punishment of those who have injured them; to guilt when we have committed such an injury; and to form and follow rules of justice that come to serve as triggers for all these reactions. This account of the sense of justice is also consistent with Rawls's own usage. Rawls generally lays stress on the sense of justice as a capacity 'to understand, to apply, and to act from' principles of justice,[49] but this different formulation is partly a product of his project of formulating a conception of justice for a well-ordered society. It is clear that the reactive attitudes play an important part in Rawls's understanding of the sense of justice, in particular when he turns to the stability of his conception.[50] The combination of these dispositions from the Smithian and Rawlsian accounts, which I take to be compatible, is what I will mean by the 'sense of justice' in later chapters.

Smith's account also explains why justice, as Rawls says, is the 'first virtue of social institutions'.[51] Part of the explanation for according justice primacy is the imperative to show equal respect for one another. This deontological imperative is given consequentialist social force because injustice leads to warranted resentment, which has great destabilizing potential:

> The moment that injury begins, the moment that mutual resentment and animosity take place, all the bands of [society] are broke asunder, and the different members of which it consisted are, as it were, dissipated and scattered abroad by the violence and opposition of their discordant affections.[52]

The primacy of justice is, then, established by the imperative of equal respect and by the fact that, if injustices occur, the chances of achieving mutual coexistence on terms compatible with equal respect become more remote.

The reasons for the primacy of justice provide a reason that stability for the right reasons, as Rawls held, is an important criterion of evaluation for theories of justice. Stability is crucial to any account of political order. Rawls, however, held that a further success criterion for a conception of justice is that it tends to generate its own support through the medium of members' sense of justice: '[A] conception of justice ... is seriously defective if the principles of moral psychology are such that it fails to engender in human beings the requisite desire to act upon it.'[53] If a conception were unstable, then justice would not be assured. Note also that the reasons supporting the primacy of justice suggest that stability is crucial to the evaluation of theories of authority as well. There is a direct relationship between the amount of force needed to govern according to a conception of justice and the degree to which that conception departs from the senses

---

[49] Rawls, *Political Liberalism*, above n 1 at 19.
[50] See Rawls's discussion of the moral sentiments and moral attitudes, in Rawls, *Theory of Justice*, above n 3 at 420–29. See in particular his discussion of guilt, ibid at 423, and of resentment and indignation, ibid at 427.
[51] ibid at 3.
[52] Smith, *Theory of Moral Sentiments*, above n 23 at 100–101 [II.ii.3.3].
[53] Rawls, *Theory of Justice*, above n 3 at 398.

of justice of those living under it. Indeed the use of excessive force to impose a certain set of institutions is more likely to itself be perceived as unjust and would thereby have a destabilizing effect. It is necessary, then, to strive for a conception of justice that can through acceptable means be brought into rough harmony with the sense of justice of subjects to the extent possible. 'The most stable conception of justice,' Rawls writes, 'is presumably one that is perspicuous to our reason, congruent with our good, and rooted not in abnegation but in affirmation of the self.'[54] If theories of justice and authority demand too much of those living under them, in particular if they demand too much repression or reconstitution of subjects' sense of justice, then they will not be stable.

Return now to the absolutist challenge with which this section began, namely that the inquiry into justice in immigration governance is unintelligible because social justice is a special relationship. The first reply to this argument is that Smith's account demonstrates that, while the distinction between social justice and personal justice might be useful as an expository tool, there is in fact no sharp distinction as such. The destabilizing potential of injustice is most clear with respect to commutative injustice, which Smith seems to take as the whole of justice in *The Theory of Moral Sentiments*. But Smith's account can be extended to the wrongs we feel on account of what we call social injustice as well. First, Smith's limitation of his account to commutative justice is a historical artefact, as the very idea of distributive justice had, in effect, not arisen at the time he was writing.[55] Second, Smith in his *Lectures on Jurisprudence* alludes to the possibility of being injured as 'a member of a state', with such injuries taking place through 'oppression'.[56] Third, the various reforms proposed by Smith in *The Wealth of Nations*, and his linkage between these reforms and the ideas of 'justice' and 'equity', for the benefit of the poor speaks to a nascent idea of social justice.[57]

Finally, it simply is the case that the historical expansion of our notion of what constitutes injustice to the social realm represents a willingness over time to recognize forms of injury that previously went unrecognized and to search for appropriate principles for their elimination. The expansion of justice into the realm of the social or the global is itself insufficiently grounded unless an injury can be specified and the search for its justification, or an argument as to why it is not justified, undertaken. The various 'grounds' of justice[58] proposed as support for the claim that justice is a special relationship just specify different ways in which individuals may be injured and different considerations, such as

---

[54] Rawls, *Theory of Justice*, above n 3 at 436.

[55] Fleischacker, *A Short History*, above n 38 at 4.

[56] Smith, *Lectures on Jurisprudence*, above n 5 at 399.

[57] This is a theme in S Fleischacker, *A Third Concept of Liberty: Judgment and Freedom in Kant and Adam Smith* (Princeton, Princeton University Press, 1999); S Fleischacker, *On Adam Smith's Wealth of Nations: A Philosophical Companion* (Princeton, Princeton University Press, 2004).

[58] The notion that different aspects of justice have different 'grounds' is proposed and explained in M Risse, *On Global Justice* (Princeton, Princeton University Press, 2012).

desert, rights, or need, that might come into play in showing why such injuries are justified or not. What unites all discussions of justice, however, is a uniform idea of the kind of complaint being made.

There are at least apparent injuries that result from immigration governance. To maintain the claim that justice is a special relationship that excludes constraints on immigration governance, it must be shown either that all such injuries are justified; that all such apparent injuries are not in fact injuries; or that all such injuries are not the result of human agency. Once engaged in arguments of this kind, we are already making an inquiry into justice in immigration governance. The absolutist claim that justice has no constraining role in immigration governance would have to be the conclusion of such an inquiry, rather than a reason not to embark on it.

In the final section of this chapter, I will seek to explain how this inquiry relates to larger discussions of global and domestic justice and to lay out the particular challenges of theorizing justice and authority in this domain.

IV. Justice and Authority in Immigration Governance

1. The Problem of Justice in Immigration Governance

States make many goods available to their members that are not available to non-members. Such unequal access is at least partly responsible for chasmic global economic inequality, and inequalities of other kinds, based on the seemingly arbitrary facts of birthplace and parentage; at least, these other inequalities would be reduced if inequality of access to state-associated goods were eliminated. One response to global inequality has been to argue for the redistribution of certain goods in the name of international or global justice. Migrants, however, are persons who exercise their purposiveness to seek such goods by physically moving to another state, rather than to have those goods made available to them in their state of origin. Through such exercises of purposiveness conflicts of interest arise with other migrants and with receiving states' members. Real or perceived injuries may result from these conflicts. Hence the question of just immigration governance arises.

Establishing the justice of immigration governance is part of the larger project of establishing whether inequalities between members and non-members of states can themselves be justified, but the problem of immigration holds a distinctive place in this discussion. To explain: TM Scanlon has recently proposed, in a discussion of equality of opportunity, that there is a 'three-level' approach to justifying any inequality. First, it must be shown that it is justified for some person or group of persons to have a superior position to others. Second, it must be shown that there is no unfairness in the selection process for that position. Third, and last, it must be shown that there is no wrong behind the fact that some individual did not have the qualifications necessary to have been successful in the selection process.[59] The justification of any inequality is incomplete if it only takes place at the first level. No inequality of position can be justified unless opportunities for attaining such position are fairly distributed and eligibility for such opportunities itself comes about on terms that are just.

The overall project of justifying global inequality requires that we demonstrate, if possible, that the various inequalities between members and non-members of states can be defended. This is the first-level justification of global inequality. As I will argue in Chapter Three, the justification for inequalities between members and non-members of states must rest on the joint integration of members' senses of justices with the political conception of justice embodied by the basic structure of the state to which they belong. But, as I will also explain, there is nothing in principle about migrants that render them ineligible to become members of a state. Migrants' senses of justice may also become integrated with the political conception of justice of any receiving state; this is especially true of liberal constitutional democracies, whose conceptions of justice are divorced from all but a thin conception of the good. Therefore, the problem of justice in immigration governance lies at the second level of Scanlon's three-level approach. The question is whether access to the goods associated with a receiving state occurs on fair terms in light of the in principle possibility of juridical integration by all migrants. The inquiry into the justice of immigration governance requires that we search for reasons justifying the rules governing such access that cohere with rather than undermine the first-level justification of the inequality between members and non-members. The third level of Scanlon's scheme then would correspond to larger concerns of international or global justice—distributive principles, humanitarian intervention, global trade, and so on—which may or may not undermine the justification of global inequalities even prior to the possibility of migration. At this level, the question would be why, in reality, the possibility of migration is a live one for some groups but not for others.

Thinking about justice in immigration governance as nested within this larger justificatory enterprise with respect to global inequality allows us to isolate certain distinctive features of the problem. First, migrants begin as distant strangers but become proximate ones in a bid to take on the favourable status of membership. Such proximity brings new injury potential. Inside a state, the presence of migrants seemingly leads to the same kinds of conflicts associated with the

---

[59] TM Scanlon, 'Equality of Opportunity' 3rd lecture in *When Does Equality Matter? Uehiro Lectures in Practical Ethics* (December 2013), available at: www.practicalethics.ox.ac.uk/lectures/2013_resources.

circumstances of justice that would have arisen in any event among members. That is, migrant–member conflicts inside a state appear to be conflicts over the same kinds of goods or injuries as in member–member conflicts. So one distinctive element of the inquiry into justice in immigration governance, as compared to other questions of international or global justice, is that immigration is a process, the endpoint of which are circumstances of justice similar to the standard liberal case. An important difference between questions of justice in immigration and this standard case, though, has to do with the powers that a state claims to have over the claimants. When conflicts arise or threaten to arise between members and migrants, a state may respond by excluding migrants *ex ante* or removing them *ex post*. It may also exercise other powers incidental to such exclusion and removal. In contrast, exile or banishment of members is no longer accepted as legitimate.

Thus one way conflicts of justice in immigration are distinctive is the possibility of certain kinds of state action toward migrants in response to conflicts and the kinds of injuries that may result from such state action. Such actions are generally not countenanced toward members, and they are generally not possible toward non-members who are not migrants.

A second form of distinctiveness is the way that entry of immigrants and the exit of emigrants will affect both sending and receiving states. As Samuel Scheffler has written: '[I]mmigration always involves change: *that's the point of it*. It changes the immigrants and it changes the host country.'[60] The nature of the impacts of migration is the subject of an immense interdisciplinary literature. Focus on sending states often leads to discussions of the remittances sent home by migrants or the potentially adverse impact of the brain drain.[61] Focus on receiving states leads to discussion of the impact of immigrants on national or political culture, including political institutions, the domestic economy, the welfare state, mutual civility, and so on.[62] But, of course, social, cultural, economic, or other changes might happen in a vacu-sealed country. What is important is that, in immigration governance, these effects are brought about by the actual addition or subtraction of persons with bodies and moral powers. Thus, just as migrants have a more salient experience of the coercive power of the receiving state, the decisions made by states about migration have self-constitutive consequences that other decisions regarding international or global justice do not because such consequences result from the incorporation or loss of persons. This, indeed, is why many influential

---

[60] S Scheffler, 'Immigration and the Significance of Culture' (2007) 35 *Philosophy & Public Affairs* 93 at 102; see also M Blake, 'Immigration and Political Inequality' (2008) 45 *San Diego Law Review* 963.
[61] For a good survey of these issues, see S Castles and MJ Miller, *The Age of Migration: International Population Movements in the Modern World*, 4th edn (New York, Guilford Press, 2009). For discussion of the brain drain, see ibid 63–67; of remittances, see ibid 59–61.
[62] ibid, 41–44. See also WA Cornelius and MR Rosenblum, 'Immigration and Politics' (2005) 8 *Annual Review of Political Science* 99, 102–106.

discussions of immigration have, plausibly, approached it through the lens of self-determination.[63]

A last form of distinctiveness to note at the outset is that the moral standing of the claimant is not fixed. Immigration changes the immigrants. Claims for justice in immigration governance are claims made by non-members on a state and its members, among whom debates over justice, including the justice of its immigration policies, are up and running. Prior to seeking entry, a migrant plays no part in shaping the social arrangements of his or her state of destination.[64] Migrants will have differing views, from each other and from the members of the receiving state, about whether they should be allowed to enter. It seems correct to say at least as a starting point that their claims should be considered in a different light than those made by members to the same resources and opportunities. But as a result of immigration, in at least some cases, some migrants may take on a new, equal standing: political reception, perhaps formalized, into the ongoing project of working out disagreements within the destination state over justice and the good.[65] The fluid nature of the standing of migrants, from unequal to potentially equal, and the challenge of regulating this process is something an account of justice in immigration governance must seek to capture.

It is clear that the problem of justice in immigration governance relates in important ways to both domestic and international or global justice. Conceptions of international or global justice (perhaps other than those that do away with states entirely) and conceptions of domestic justice would be incomplete without addressing immigration governance. Similarly, any conception of justice in immigration governance would be incomplete without a worked out conception of domestic and international or global justice. Significant progress can be made, however, even treating global and domestic justice as unknown variables. That is how I will proceed.

2. The Problem of Authority in Immigration Governance

The problem of just immigration governance is one that confronts us with a morally fluid situation, as a result of the fact that immigration involves the

---

[63] See Walzer, above n 19; CH Wellman, 'Freedom of Association and the Right to Exclude' in CH Wellman and P Cole, *Debating the Ethics of Immigration: Is There a Right to Exclude?* (New York, Oxford University Press, 2012); R Pevnick, *Immigration and the Constraints of Justice: Between Open Borders and Absolute Sovereignty* (Cambridge, Cambridge University Press, 2011); D Miller, 'Immigration: The Case for Limits' in AI Cohen and CH Wellman (eds), *Contemporary Debates in Applied Ethics* (Oxford, Blackwell, 2005) 199–201.

[64] If he or she did, that may itself be a problem of justice—as when, say, (executives of) powerful companies exert undue influence on foreign countries.

[65] The idea of 'political reception' comes from Michael Walzer: 'The community itself is a good ... that gets distributed. But it is a good that can only be distributed by taking people in, where all the senses of that latter phrase are relevant: they must be physically admitted and politically received.' See Walzer, *Spheres of Justice*, above n 19 at 29.

physical relocation of actual persons. The resulting conflicting claims of justice or injustice must be resolved somehow by some governing entity through the exercise of political power. For the most part, this power is allotted to the immigration regimes of receiving states, which impose laws and policies that not all members, migrants, and other non-members will see as just. The lack of consensus is shown by the problem of widespread illegal immigration, since it is unlikely that all illegal immigrants view themselves as having violated a moral obligation imposed by virtue of the justice of immigration restrictions. A problem of authority is raised by such disagreements. Several distinctive features of immigration regimes complicate efforts to solve this problem.

Joseph Raz's claim about legal regime's self-representation as having authority, noted in Section Two, is made with respect to state-level legal orders. We can also apply his claim to the subcomponents of each legal order. Traffic law regimes represent themselves as imposing general obligations on all who use roads. If you drive, you are obligated to obey the speed limit because it is the speed limit, or so says the law. Such subcomponent legal orders are unambiguously internal, applying largely to members or non-members inside a state. Immigration regimes can also be seen as subcomponents of larger legal orders. However, they are not internal, but liminal. By this I mean a significant portion of their subjects are non-members not otherwise under the state's jurisdiction.[66] Yet it seems clear that immigration regimes, insofar as they are legal regimes, make the same presuppositions as other parts of a state's legal order. Legal orders purport to have authority to regulate immigration for the same reason they purport to have authority over every other area where conflicts of justice arise, that is, because the settlement of such conflicts seems necessary for ongoing peaceful coexistence. The issue with respect to liminal orders is whether non-member subjects should honour these claims to authority.

Liminality is one of five features that render attempts to theorize the authority of immigration regimes difficult. A second feature is as follows. Most laws in the legal systems of wealthy liberal constitutional democracies apply equally regardless of status distinctions. Immigration regimes, however, assign differentiated status—not just between migrants to and members of a state, but between different types of migrants, who may be permanent residents, guestworkers, illegal immigrants, and so on—and treat people differently according to that status by attaching to them different bundles of rights and obligations. The challenge is to show how immigration regimes can impose differential legal status without having it insidiously reflect the view that migrants have lower moral status. The danger is that: 'The excluded can see that they are being treated as if they have a lesser moral standing.'[67] This danger would seem to undermine any attempt to establish authority on recognizably liberal terms.

---

[66] In this respect they are almost, though not entirely, unique. Customs regimes or taxation regimes sometimes claim the right to coercively regulate non-members.
[67] T Christiano, 'The Authority of Democracy' (2004) 12 *Journal of Political Philosophy* 266, 276.

Third, migrants have few avenues of political participation, and in almost all cases no right to vote in national elections. It is an oversimplification to say that migrants by definition are excluded from political participation. In liberal democracies, migrants may be represented by lobby groups or they may be able to express their opinion in protests, speeches, or print.[68] Indeed, the ability to litigate is a way in which migrants might have some say over the application, interpretation, and possibly (through constitutional challenges) validity of immigration laws. Nonetheless, the opportunities for participation and influence are limited compared to those available to members generally. This particular form of exclusion poses a problem for attempts to establish authority in the face of disagreement. It is not clear why migrants ought to accept laws developed without giving them an equal, or anything more than a limited, say.

These three features refer to the governance structure of states and in particular state immigration regimes. Two others relate to the characteristics of the subjects of such regimes. First, the relationship of migrants to each immigration regime is characterized by transience; in most cases the relationship will not last a lifetime, as does generally the relationship between a state and its members. Second, and finally, in addition to being transient, the migrants to a given state are radically heterogeneous. They are not united by any of the kinds of commonalities we may associate with the members of a state. Viewed as a whole, migrants do not share a nationality, territory, religion, language, culture, or class. One might abstractly speak of a 'migrant community'. This community, however, is contingent and diffuse, referring simply to a group of people who happen to be migrants in relation to a given state's immigration regime at a given time. That means that migrants as a group are even likelier than members of a state to have divergent views about justice and the good.

Liminality, unequal status, limited political participation, transience, and diversity are enough to show that establishing the authority of immigration regimes is a daunting task. To see why, go back to the point that it seems possible to have a legitimate government without political obligation, but on any theory it is hard to conceive of how an illegitimate government might generate an obligation to obey the law.[69] It is also sometimes said that to be legitimate a legal order must justify itself by demonstrating that subjects of the law have authorized it. Authorization can occur several different ways, but many theories require that citizens have political voice, through elections or some other form of society-wide normative discussion. We end up with two related propositions: legitimacy is a necessary though perhaps not sufficient condition for political obligation; and legitimacy requires giving voice to the governed at some point in the political process.

---

[68] In the past, several American states have permitted migrants to vote: see M Tienda, 'Demography and the Social Contract' (2002) 39 *Demography* 587. Today migrants are allowed to vote in municipal and regional elections in some countries. New Zealand allows all permanent residents to vote in all elections but not to stand for office. See Castles and Miller, *The Age of Migration*, above n 61 at 285–87.

[69] See G Klosko, *The Principle of Fairness and Political Obligation*, 2nd edn (Lanham, MD, Rowman & Littlefield, 2004) 68.

Immigration regimes, as we have sketched them, coercively regulate the status of outsiders who are denied certain key forms of political participation. Thus we face a circumstance where a key subcomponent of legal orders demands obedience but where the usual means of political authorization are more or less unavailable. We must either refuse to credit immigration regimes' purported claims to authority or identify some account of authority for a regime that seeks to govern a changing, heterogeneous, politically unequal population absent the usual liberal democratic conditions of voice.

V. Moving on

Following Smith, we say that someone has been subject to injustice if they have been unjustifiably injured by another person or persons. Social injustice, or oppression, is unjustified injury that cannot be traced back to identifiable perpetrators but rather resulted from social or institutional rules, practices, or dynamics. Because the injuries that result from immigration governance will often not be traceable to individuals, and even when they are will have an institutional component, the inquiry into immigration governance will in general focus on social justice and injustice. Disagreements over whether any injuries in fact result from immigration governance or disagreements over whether any such injuries are justified must be settled by some political authority. Thus the inquiry into justice leads directly to an inquiry into the political authority of immigration regimes. To seek to bring justice and authority to bear in the realm of immigration governance is to seek to extend a demand of justification to the political relationship between migrant and member. This demand is one that takes place in a morally fluid situation and is set against the overall project of justifying the various inequalities that arise between members and non-members of a state.

On Smith's account, this nuanced and multifaceted problem is taken up by trying to enter into the spirit of the impartial spectator. But Smith is sceptical of anyone's ability to adopt a suitably impartial perspective when matters taking us beyond our own borders are at stake.[70] In those cases, our individual sympathetic shortcomings, our natural partiality, are further corrupted by national prejudice.[71] We do not have to accept wholesale Smith's scepticism to acknowledge that the prescription to consult the impartial spectator does not provide much if any guidance, by itself, as to when an immigration restriction will or will not be

---

[70] Smith, *Theory of Moral Sentiments*, above n 23 at 157–58 [III.iii.4].

[71] ibid at 179 [III.iii.42]: 'When two nations are at variance, the citizen of each pays little regard to the sentiments which foreign nations may entertain concerning his conduct. His whole ambition is to obtain the approbation of his own fellow-citizens; and as they are all animated by the same hostile passions which animate himself, he can never please them so much as by enraging and offending their enemies. The partial spectator is at hand: the impartial one at a great distance. In war and negotiation, therefore, the laws of justice are very seldom observed.'

justifiable. In another context, dealing with a similarly tricky judgement, all Smith tells us is the following:

> If we place ourselves completely in [the impartial spectator's] situation, if we really view ourselves with his eyes, and as he views us, and listen with diligent and reverential attention to what he suggests to us, his voice will never deceive us.[72]

One challenge in carrying out an inquiry into justice in immigration, then, is that of describing the impartial perspective from which to address it. This is a challenge we will revisit repeatedly in later argument. Before proceeding to that argument, in the next chapter I set out a concrete background problem against which it is developed. That problem is a tendency among the immigration regimes of wealthy liberal constitutional democratic states to favour the admission of advantaged migrants. I call this the inegalitarianism of immigration governance.

---

[72] ibid at 267 [VI.ii.1.22]. Smith is addressing the problem of when 'different beneficient affections happen to draw in different ways'.

2

Inegalitarianism in Immigration Governance

I. Introduction

THE LAST CHAPTER closed by setting out the distinctive nature of the inquiry into justice and authority in immigration governance. In this chapter, I attempt to give this inquiry a sharper edge. I argue that justice in first-order areas of immigration governance cannot be treated in isolation from justice in second-order areas. First-order immigration law and policy concerns admission and exclusion: who gets in. Second-order law and policy concerns the implementation and consequences of first-order decisions. It includes such matters as the treatment of resident immigrants; the enforcement of first-order policies through the exercise of powers of arrest, detention, and expulsion, as well as the enforcement of policies regarding the treatment of resident immigrants; and the regulation of private relations formed in response to, or influenced by, immigration law.[1] I make the empirical claim that first-order immigration laws and policies that diverge significantly from the purposes of would-be migrants are more likely to lead to second-order injury. That is one of the reasons current patterns in immigration governance, favouring advantaged over disadvantaged migrants, ought to concern us. A larger aim of this chapter, then, is to introduce the problem of inegalitarianism, which I take to be the central problem of justice in immigration governance today.

Section Two sets out some considered judgements that will be used as a resource for later theoretical argument. Section Three then introduces and discusses the discretionary doctrine that lies at the heart of immigration law. Section Four describes how this discretion is deployed by states to pursue policies aimed at excluding or controlling disadvantaged migrants. Section Five gives further detail by mapping inegalitarianism in the law and policy governing family, refugee, economic, and illegal migration.

---

[1] The distinction between first-order and second-order immigration policy that I adopt maps imperfectly onto that proposed in AB Cox and EA Posner, 'The Second-Order Structure of Immigration Law' (2007) 59 *Stanford Law Review* 809.

II. Some Considered Judgements of Injustice in Immigration

The argument in this essay, at the highest level, seeks to proceed by way of reflective equilibrium, that is, by working back and forth between considered judgements of justice and injustice in immigration governance and possible principles for such governance. The goal is to demonstrate the implausibility of absolutism, the view that justice does not constrain immigration governance. I have already sought to refute one absolutist claim, namely that an inquiry into our judgements of justice in immigration governance is unintelligible. Nonetheless, it remains true that one considered judgement many share is that states enjoy wide-ranging, possibly unlimited, discretion in setting and enforcing first- and second-order immigration laws and policies. For the argument against absolutism to succeed, it must be shown that this judgement ought to be revised in light of others we might hold.

Despite the highly controversial nature of immigration, a list of other considered judgements to the effect that certain actions by immigration regimes would be presumptively oppressive is fairly easy to generate:

1. The return of refugees to countries where they have a reasonable chance of being tortured[2] or where their life or basic human rights would be threatened on account of race, religion, nationality, or political opinion.[3]
2. The separation or the keeping apart of young children from their parents by immigration regimes.[4]
3. The enforcement of immigration or emigration policy using excessive and arbitrary force.[5]

---

[2] Convention Against Torture and Other Cruel, Inhuman or Degrading Treatment or Punishment (adopted 10 December 1984, entered into force 26 June 1987) 1465 UNTS 85, art 3.1.

[3] Convention Relating to the Status of Refugees (adopted 28 July 1951, entered into force 22 April 1954) 189 UNTS 137, art 33. See also the Protocol Relating to the Status of Refugees (adopted 31 January 1967, entered into force 4 October 1967) 606 UNTS 267. Some states protect migrants if they face a denial of basic human rights but do not fall under the strict scope of article 33. See Jane McAdam, *Complementary Protection in International Refugee Law* (Oxford, Oxford University Press, 2007).

[4] For a comparative law analysis of the manner in which citizen children are 'constructively' deported from their countries of citizenship due to the expulsion or exclusion of their parents, see J Bhabha, 'The "Mere Fortuity of Birth"? Children, Mothers, Borders, and the Meaning of Citizenship' in S Benhabib and J Resnik (eds), *Migrations and Mobilities: Citizenship, Borders, and Gender* (New York, New York University Press, 2009) 187. For philosophical discussions of family migration, see M Lister, 'Immigration, Association, and the Family' (2010) 29 *Law and Philosophy* 717; J Carens, *The Ethics of Immigration* (New York, Oxford University Press, 2013) 186–91.

[5] For example: (1) In 1937, Rafael Trujillo ordered the *corte* or 'mowing down' of Haitian migrants in the Dominican Republic. This was an operation carried out by the Dominican Republic's national constabulary and Trujillo loyalists that resulted in the murder of as many as 25,000 men, women, and children who were Haitian or of Haitian descent and living in the Dominican's frontier region and northern Cibao Valley. Haitians living on sugar estates were spared. 'Regardless of the dictator's

4. Expulsion, especially the mass expulsion, of longer-term residents without sufficient due process.[6]
5. The imposition of criminal penalties without trial for breaches of immigration law.[7]
6. The prolonged detention of migrants posing no security or other risk.[8]
7. The private exploitation and other forms of commutative victimization of migrants by employers, traffickers, and smugglers.[9]
8. Barring return to a person's country of citizenship when one cannot naturalize elsewhere[10] and banishment or exile of a citizen.[11]

intentions, no more chilling way could be imagined of conveying to Haitian immigrants that the sugar *bateyes* would thereafter be their only secure place on Dominican soil': S Martinez, *Peripheral Migrants: Haitians and Dominican Republic Sugar Plantations* (Knoxville, University of Tennessee Press, 1995) 44–45. (2) In 1988, the Thai Ministry of the Interior issued a 'pushback' order, deputizing fishermen in Khong Yai to prevent entry of any boats which might be carrying Vietnamese refugees. 'During the first weeks of Thailand's pushback policy, hundreds of asylum seekers were victimized. Those who managed to evade the naval blockade or rammings by Thai fishing boats were abandoned on barren islands without food, water or medicine': AC Helton, 'Asylum and Refugee Protection in Thailand' (1989) 1 *International Journal of Refugee Law* 20, 28. (3) In 2001, Namibia imposed a dusk-to-dawn curfew, with soldiers ordered to shoot violators, along a 450 kilometre stretch of the Kavango River along the border with Angola. This measure prevented Angolan refugees seeking to escape violence in that country's Cuano Cuban Province from being able to seek asylum, since patrols could only be safely avoided at night: JC Hathaway, *The Rights of Refugees under International Law* (Cambridge, Cambridge University Press, 2005) 280.

[6] GS Goodwin-Gill, *International Law and the Movement of Persons between States* (Oxford, Clarendon Press, 1978) 236–37. I use 'due process' here to leave open the possibility of 'substantive due process'.

[7] *Wong Wing v United States*, 163 US 228 (1896) ('[T]o declare unlawful residence within the country to be an infamous crime, punishable by deprivation of liberty and property, would be to pass out of the sphere of constitutional legislation, unless provision were made that the fact of guilt should first be established by judicial trial.')

[8] *Zadvydas v Davis*, 533 US 678, 696 (2001) ('[A]n alien's liberty interest is, at the least, strong enough to raise a serious question as to whether ... the Constitution permits detention that is indefinite and potentially permanent'); but see *Shaughnessy v United States ex rel Mezei*, 345 US 206 (1953) (Excludable alien's long-term confinement on Ellis Island did not constitute unlawful detention.)

[9] See Protocol to Prevent, Suppress, and Punish Trafficking in Persons, Especially Women and Children, supplementing the United Nations Convention against Transnational Organized Crime (adopted 15 November 2000, entered into force 9 September 2003) 2237 UNTS 319; Protocol Against the Smuggling of Migrants by Land, Sea and Air, supplementing the United Nations Convention Against Transnational Organized Crime (adopted 15 November 2000, entered into force 28 January 2004) 2241 UNTS 507. See, eg 'Forced Labor', *The New York Times* (Opinion), 7 September 2010.

[10] See, eg Universal Declaration of Human Rights (adopted 10 December 1948) UNGA Res 217 A(III), art 13(2); International Covenant on Civil and Political Rights (adopted 16 December 1966, entered into force 22 April 1954) 999 UNTS 171, art 12.2; International Convention on the Protection of the Rights of All Migrant Workers and Members of Their Families (adopted 18 December 1990, entered into force 1 July 2003) 2220 UNTS 3, art 8.2.

[11] Universal Declaration of Human Rights, above n 10 at art 9.

At the same time, one can generate a shorter list of fixed judgements regarding aspects of the governance of migrants that are not oppressive, that is, which most people would believe to be justified all else equal:

1. The exclusion of migrants who are criminals, security threats, or public health risks.[12]
2. The exclusion of migrants, and all non-members, from voting in national elections.[13]

These lists are generated using judgements that I happen to hold and that I believe would be widely shared. They are also supported by general patterns of immigration governance and international norms. They will feature heavily in the arguments in subsequent chapters. While none of these judgements is fixed, the ability to account for them or, alternatively, to explain why they ought to be revised is a mark of soundness for a theory of justice in immigration governance.

I have excluded three judgements that are reflected in international law or common practice but about which my intuitions are less secure. These are that it is per se unjust to exclude migrants on racial grounds,[14] that it is per se wrong to prohibit

---

[12] Such exclusions were among the first to appear in immigration regulation. Canada's Immigration Act of 1872 excluded any 'criminal or other vicious class of immigrants' (cited in D Galloway, *Immigration Law* (Concord, Irwin Law, 1997) 10). Canada's Immigration Act of 1906 (SC 1906, c 19) excluded 'the insane, epileptic, deaf and dumb, blind, infirm, those afflicted with a "loathsome" contagious disease, paupers, destitute persons, and those convicted of crimes of "moral turpitude" such as prostitution, pimping, and the like'. Canada's current Immigration and Refugee Protection Act, SC 2001, c 27 [IRPA], states that one of its objectives is 'to protect the health and safety of Canadians and to maintain the security of Canadian society' (IRPA, s 3). IRPA includes grounds of inadmissibility based on public health and public safety (IRPA, s 38(1)(a) and (b)); various forms of criminality (IRPA, ss 35–37); and national security (IRPA, s 34). Migrants can also be inadmissible because they are determined to be unable or unwilling to support themselves and their dependents without relying on social assistance (IRPA, s 39) and for misrepresentation or non-compliance with IRPA (IRPA, s 40(1) and (2)).
In the United States, the first immigration legislation, the Page Act, excluded convicted felons and prostitutes. The Immigration Act of 1882 added paupers, lunatics, and 'any person unable to take care of himself or herself'. The Immigration Act of 1891 added polygamists, migrants with contagious diseases, and migrants 'likely to become a public charge'. The Immigration Act of 1903 added anarchists. (See L Salyer, *Laws Harsh as Tigers: Chinese Immigrants and the Shaping of Modern Immigration Law* (Chapel Hill, University of North Carolina Press, 1995) 6–7, 24, 131.) Today, inadmissibility grounds are listed in §212(a) of the Immigration and Nationality Act (8 USCA 1182) [INA]. These include inadmissibility on health-related grounds (INA §212(a)(1)); criminal grounds (INA §212(a)(2)); and grounds of national security (INA §212(a)(3)). Other grounds of inadmissibility include the likelihood of becoming a public charge (INA §212(a)(4)), failure to meet labour certification requirements (INA §212(a)(5)), and five other general headings.
[13] In the United States, voting can be a ground for deportation: INA, above n 12 at §237(a)(6). See K Semple, 'For Some Immigrants, Voting Is a Criminal Act', *The New York Times*, 15 October 2010. Although it should be recalled, as noted in n 68 in Chapter One, that in the past several American states permitted migrants to vote and that some countries today permit migrants to vote in municipal, regional, and other elections.
[14] Goodwin-Gill, *Movement of Persons*, above n 6 at 85. ('In racial matters, non-discrimination has a normative character and may be adjudged a part of *jus cogens*.')

emigration,[15] and that it is per se unjust to exclude the spouses of individuals.[16] With respect to race-based restrictions, I am not certain that it would not be justified for a racially homogenous country to exclude dissimilar migrants if racial homogeneity were necessary to maintain justice within the state and if exclusion otherwise could be carried out non-oppressively. Though it may be unlikely that these conditions could ever be met, that still does not mean race-based exclusions are in themselves oppressive. With respect to emigration, many of the reasons we might give for limiting ingress may also apply to egress, although the cases appear different because we are less apt to worry about the empirical effects of emigration other than in countries facing brain-drain concerns. Finally, while states generally allow for the reunification of citizens and spouses, I do not have a considered judgement in this regard. In part this is in reaction to an argument from David Miller, taken up later, that all we can lay claim to is 'a reasonable choice of ... marriage partners'.[17] I find Miller's argument plausible enough to lead me to exclude this judgement from my list as well.

One might add to these three a further list of cases or issues about which disagreement seems especially likely. Can suspected terrorists be detained indefinitely on immigration grounds, even when there is insufficient evidence to indict them on criminal charges? Should immigration be a remedy for historic wrongs? Should immigration be allowed for those affected by climate change? Should states be able to design long-term guestworker programmes that bar access to naturalization? Can a government refuse to admit migrants who are criminals, security threats, or who pose a public health risk but who also face the prospect of torture or persecution at home? Should illegal immigrants be given a chance to regularize their status? Should dual citizenship be allowed? This list of controversial questions could go on much longer, descending into ever more fine-grained policy questions. While I hope the argument developed may provide a useful starting point for addressing some of these questions, the issue with which I will be centrally concerned here is whether it is permissible for states to admit the relatively well off and exclude the poor. Legally the answer is obvious because of the discretion states enjoy in formulating and applying their immigration laws and policies. In the next section, I discuss two competing interpretations of that discretion.

---

[15] Universal Declaration of Human Rights, above n 10 at art 13(2); International Covenant on Civil and Political Rights, above n 10 at art 12(2) and 12(3). For arguments in favour of restricting emigration in some circumstances, see L Ypi, 'Justice in Migration: A Closed Borders Utopia?' (2008) 16 *Journal of Political Philosophy* 391, 401ff; G Brock, *Global Justice: A Cosmopolitan Account* (New York, Oxford University Press, 2009).

[16] Matthew Lister argues that states have a duty to allow citizens to bring in non-citizen spouses: M Lister, 'Immigration, Association, and the Family' (2010) *Law and Philosophy* 717, 721. Lister restricts his argument to the claim that this duty is owed to citizens, not to migrants.

[17] D Miller, 'Immigration: The Case for Limits' in AI Cohen and CH Wellman (eds), *Contemporary Debates in Applied Ethics* (Oxford, Blackwell, 2005) 201–202.

III. Discretionary Doctrines

At the heart of immigration law is a legal doctrine granting countries broad discretion over immigration matters. The doctrine first appeared toward the end of the nineteenth century in a series of cases decided in the United States and Britain. These cases all serve as statements of domestic immigration law and also provide the basis for an international discretionary legal doctrine.[18] I will be concerned with the doctrine in both senses.

First in time among the decisions proclaiming the discretionary doctrine is the United States Supreme Court decision, *Chae Chan Ping v United States*:

> The power of exclusion of foreigners being an incident of sovereignty …, the right to its exercise at any time when, in the judgment of the government, the interests of the country require it, cannot be granted away or restrained on behalf of any one.[19]

Chae Chan Ping was followed soon after by two other decisions, *Nishimura Ekiu v United States*:

> It is an accepted maxim of international law, that every sovereign nation has the power, as inherent in sovereignty, and essential to self-preservation, to forbid the entrance of foreigners within its dominions, or to admit them only in such cases and upon such conditions as it may see fit to prescribe.[20]

and *Fong Yue Ting v United States*:

> The right of a nation to expel or deport foreigners, who have not been naturalized or taken any steps towards becoming citizens of the country, rests upon the same grounds, and is as absolute and unqualified as the right to prohibit and prevent their entrance into the country.[21]

Both *Nishimura* and *Fong Yue Ting* expand and strengthen the discretionary power. *Nishimura* makes clear that such discretion extended to conditions of admission. *Fong Yue Ting* applies it to deportation. More than that, they seem to remove the few constraints on the immigration power mentioned in the earlier decision. In *Chae Chan Ping*, Justice Stephen Field had said that the power to 'admit subjects of other nations to citizenship' was 'restricted in [its] exercise only by the Constitution itself and considerations of public policy and justice which control, more or less, the conduct of all civilized nations'.[22] By the time we reach

---

[18] R Plender, *International Migration Law*, 2nd edn (Leiden, Sijthoff, 1988) 2: 'The view that the reception and treatment of aliens is a matter of extensive discretion appears to have arisen in consequence of a series of judicial decisions reached at the end of the nineteenth century in response to a westward migration of Chinese labourers.'

[19] *Chae Chan Ping v United States (The Chinese Exclusion Case)*, 130 US 581, 609 (1889).

[20] *Nishimura Ekiu v United States*, 142 US 651, 659 (1892).

[21] *Fong Yue Ting v United States*, 149 US 698, 707 (1893).

[22] *Chae Chan Ping*, above n 19 at 604.

Fong Yue Ting the immigration power becomes 'absolute and unqualified'. Such uncompromising language is a recurrent feature of the case law.[23]

The status of the discretionary doctrine today is unclear. On the one hand, it sometimes continues to be presented in absolute terms, constrained only by the voluntary legal commitments undertaken by the receiving state in domestic legislation or internationally. Despite repeated predictions and pronouncements of the decline of the absolutist interpretation, executive powers in the United States and elsewhere have shown a tendency to reassert their discretionary authority in times of crisis[24] or in the face of difficult-to-manage migration flows such as, for example, large influxes of asylum seekers.[25] The courts do not always uphold such assertions of absolutist authority, but judicial pushback is almost always delayed and many migrants find no effective remedy.[26]

A harsh and uncompromising interpretation of the discretionary doctrine is therefore available, depending on which government institutions one takes to be primary and which sources of law one uses as a starting point. A lot will depend, for example, on whether one begins with decisions by the judiciary or the executive. It is still possible to assert, as a matter of law, that states may admit whomever they want on whatever conditions they want, or no one at all; that they may expel or detain, for however long, whomever they want; and that, in implementing such policies, they have freedom to design whatever admissions procedures they see fit.

But such harsh assertions of discretionary power over immigration have never had the field to themselves.[27] I have already noted Justice Field's equivocations in

---

[23] Another strong statement is found in the Privy Council decision *Attorney-General for Canada v Cain* [1906] AC 542, 546 ('One of the rights possessed by the supreme power in every State is the right to refuse to permit an alien to enter that State, to annex what conditions it pleases to the permission to enter it, and to expel or deport from the State, at pleasure, even a friendly alien, especially if it considers his presence in the State opposed to its peace, order, and good government, or to its social or material interests.')

[24] For discussion in the context of national security, see D Cole, *Enemy Aliens: Double Standards and Constitutional Freedoms in the War on Terrorism* (New York, New Press, 2003).

[25] For general discussion, see DA Martin, 'Introduction: The New Asylum Seekers' in DA Martin (ed), *The New Asylum Seekers: Refugee Law in the 1980s* (Dordrecht, Martinus Nijhoff, 1988) 6–7; JC Hathaway and RA Neve, 'Fundamental Justice and the Deflection of Refugees from Canada' (1996) 34 *Osgoode Hall Law Journal* 103.

[26] For instance, some courts resisted attempts by the United States government to deny public access to the deportation hearings of designated 'special interest' cases in the wake of September 11, 2001: see, eg *Detroit Free Press v Ashcroft*, 303 F.3d 681 (6th Cir 2002) (Government unsuccessfully asserting right under plenary power to hold deportation hearings closed to the press and public); but see *North Jersey Media Group v Ashcroft*, 308 F.3d 198 (3rd Cir 2002), cert denied, 538 US 1056 (2003) (Finding no historical right of access to deportation proceedings, but not on the basis of plenary power). For earlier pushback by the courts against the Palmer raids, see Cole, *Enemy Aliens*, above n 24 at 122–28. Cole discusses how Louis Post, Acting Secretary of Labor at the time, suspended the vast majority of the deportation orders issued following the Palmer raids. Cole also notes that the federal judge George Anderson roundly condemned the raids: 'A mob is a mob, whether made up of government officials acting under instructions from the Department of Justice, or of criminals, loafers, and the vicious classes.' See *Culyer v Skeffington*, 265 Fed 17, 43 (D Mass 1920), reversed in part sub nom *Skeffington v Katzeff*, 277 Fed 129 (1st Cir 1922).

[27] Partly because they are so implausible. 'Occasionally, the Supreme Court makes a statement about the Constitution that simply cannot be true. Immigration cases seem to attract more than their

Chae Chan Ping. Dicta in a similar vein are often found in immigration decisions, usually but not always in dissent, and often in cases involving expulsion where the claims of absolutism are most jarring.[28] Moreover, in the last several decades, new substantive and procedural inroads have been made. Since the 1970s in the United States the Supreme Court has adopted 'limited responsibility to assure the rationality of substantive immigration policies'.[29] In *Landon v Plascencia*,[30] the US Supreme Court held that returning permanent residents have the right to some due process; in *Zadvydas v Davis*,[31] the Court interpreted the detention provisions of the *Immigration and Nationality Act* to prohibit the indefinite detention of inadmissible aliens who cannot, because other countries will not take them, be removed, stating that the discretionary power over immigration was 'subject to important constitutional limitations'.[32] The Canadian Supreme Court has, for its part, held in *Singh v Minister of Employment and Immigration*[33] that Canada's *Charter of Rights and Freedoms* requires that refugee claimants receive an oral hearing in the determination of their case whenever serious issues of credibility arise. In *Baker v Canada (Minister of Citizenship and Immigration)*,[34] it held that the best interests of the children of a migrant had to be considered when the latter was facing deportation. Such cases provide evidence for the idea that judicial actors have difficulty squaring their role with assertions of an arbitrary power over immigration. The cases do not spell the end of the discretionary doctrine, but they are hard to reconcile with the stronger pronouncements found in cases like *Nishimura* or *Fong Yue Ting*, and other statements of that kind. I will call this as-yet-undefined alternative to absolutism the principled interpretation of the doctrine.

Evidence of the appeal to principle in the exercise of discretion can also be found in international law sources, such as bilateral treaties relating to immigration[35]

---

share of these utterances.' TA Aleinikoff, 'Aliens, Due Process, and "Community Ties": A Response to Martin' (1983) 44 *University of Pittsburgh Law Review* 237.

[28] See, eg the dissents in *Fong Yue Ting*, above n 21 at 737–38 (per Brewer J, dissenting), 744–61 (per Field J, dissenting), and 762–64 (per Fuller J, dissenting); *Knauff v Shaughnessy*, 338 US 536, 551–52 (1950) (per Black J, dissenting); *Shaughnessy v United States ex rel Mezei*, 345 US 206 (1953) at 216–18 (per Black J, dissenting) and 218–27 (per Jackson J, dissenting); *Galvan v Press*, 347 US 522, 534 (1954) (per Black J, dissenting); *Fiallo v Bell*, 430 US 787, 800–16 (1977) (per Marshall J, dissenting).

[29] G Neuman, 'Discretionary Deportation' (2006) 20 *Georgetown Immigration Law Journal* 611, 619, citing *Fiallo v Bell*, above n 28; *Kleindienst v Mandel* (1972) 408 US 753.

[30] *Landon v Plascencia*, 459 US 21 (1982).

[31] *Zadvydas v Davis*, 522 US 678 (2001).

[32] ibid at 695.

[33] *Singh v Minister of Employment and Immigration* [1985] 1 SCR 177.

[34] *Baker v Canada (Minister of Citizenship and Immigration)* [1999] 2 SCR 817.

[35] The Additional Articles to the Treaty between the United States and China, US–China, art V, 28 July 1868, 16 Stat 739 (known as the Burlingame Treaty) recognized 'the inherent and inalienable right of man to change his home and allegiance, and also the mutual advantage of the free migration and emigration of their citizens and subjects respectively from the one country to the other for purposes of curiosity, of trade, or as permanent residents.' For general discussion, see Goodwin-Gill, *Movement of Persons*, above n 6 at 186–89.

and in a growing body of international norms.[36] States 'cannot arbitrarily deprive individuals of this right' and immigration 'rules and regulations should be reasonable. A State does not have complete discretion in this area, and each decision must be properly justified.'[37] Thus, in 2003 the Inter-American Court of Human Rights, in an advisory opinion on the rights of documented and undocumented migrant workers, declared: 'The goals of migratory policies should take into account respect for human rights. Likewise, migratory policies should be implemented respecting and guaranteeing human rights.... [T]he distinctions that the States establish must be objective, proportionate and reasonable.'[38] So, by focusing on a different set of institutional actors and a different body of legal materials, a different interpretation of the discretionary doctrine emerges.

There are therefore two competing readings of the discretionary doctrine, with very different implications. These two readings also face very different burdens of argument in political morality. The absolutist reading is hard-hearted but clear-eyed. Yet it is more difficult to see how it can serve as the foundation for an immigration law that has authority, since in some respects it seems to deny the need for justification at all. On the other hand the principled reading, as its name implies, sends us on a search for principles. It is not obvious how to develop these principles outside the standard, liberal case of a territorially-enclosed state.

---

[36] International human rights instruments impose both indirect (second-order) and direct (first-order) limitations on the immigration power. Indirectly, these instruments prevent admission conditional on a migrant giving up some internationally-protected right, or prohibit certain means of enforcement. Sometimes the resulting guarantees—such as those resulting from the operation of the International Covenant on Economic, Social and Cultural Rights (adopted 16 December 1966, entered into force 3 January 1976) 993 UNTS 3—would be potentially quite significant if respected. These might be thought of as second-order limits. There are also a small number of direct or first-order limits on admissions or expulsions, including: the rule against sending back refugees to countries where they face persecution or torture (non-refoulement) and the rule against restricting admissions using racial criteria. See above nn 2, 3, and 14. Also limiting national discretion over immigration are trade-related instruments. For discussion, see M Klein-Solomon, 'GATS Mode 4 and the Mobility of Labour' in R Cholewinski, R Perruchoud, and E MacDonald (eds), *International Migration Law: Developing Paradigms and Key Challenges* (The Hague, TMC Asser Press, 2007) 112. Finally, of course, freedom of movement within the European Union and efforts in Europe to harmonize immigration and refugee policy with regard to third-country nationals limits the discretion of EU members. For discussion of the European system, see S Benhabib, *The Rights of Others: Aliens, Residents and Citizens* (Cambridge, Cambridge University Press, 2004); G Menz, *The Political Economy of Managed Migration: Nonstate Actors, Europeanization, and the Politics of Designing Migration Policies* (New York, Oxford University Press, 2009).

[37] LB Sohn and T Buergenthal, *The Movement of Persons Across Borders: Studies in Transnational Legal Policy (No. 23)* (Washington DC, American Society of International Law, 1992) 1–2. See also the discussion in Plender, *International Migration Law*, above n 18 especially at 1–4 and 61–84. Following other publicists, Plender refers to the tension between the principle of state sovereignty and the principle of state interdependence: ibid at 1. Peter Schuck, discussing United States immigration law, speaks of a conflict between 'restrictive nationalism' and 'communitarian' principles: see PH Schuck, 'The Transformation of Immigration Law' in *Citizens, Strangers, and In-Betweens* (Boulder, Westview Press, 1998) 20–21. The labels do not matter. It is far more important to figure out why these contrasting views persist, to discern the justification for each, and the stakes in the contest between them.

[38] *Juridical Condition and Rights of the Undocumented Migrants*, Advisory Opinion OC-18, Inter-American Court of Human Rights Series A No 18 (17 September 2003) para 168.

Resolving the ambiguity between the two interpretations is of moment for many controversies with respect to immigration governance, including those revolving around the inegalitarianism of immigration law.

IV. Inegalitarianism in Immigration Law

First-order immigration law and policy has a positive and negative aspect. Positively, it sets out categories for admission, generally broken down according to one of three broad motivations for migration, namely to earn money (economic or labour migrants); to reunite with family (family migrants); or to escape violence or persecution (asylum seekers and refugees). Negatively, it sets out grounds for exclusion or deportation. These grounds may include having a criminal record, having an anarchist agenda, having the potential to make excessive demands on a system of social entitlements, and so on. Other, second-order aspects of immigration policy, such as who gets detained, what rights migrants have upon admission, and so on, are conditioned by, among other things, the logic of first-order policy decisions regarding who should or should not be inside a state.

To be admitted to a country, a migrant must both satisfy the affirmative criteria for a given category and also must not fall under an exclusion ground. Affirmative criteria for refugees, for example, require that refugee claimants show they have an objectively-grounded fear of persecution based on one of five grounds, namely the claimants' real or supposed religious beliefs, political convictions, race, nationality, or membership in a particular social group. Increasingly, countries also grant admission on general human rights grounds not covered by the refugee definition. Affirmative criteria for economic migration typically require a showing that an economic migrant either has arranged employment—though not at the expense of a citizen or already-established permanent resident—certain job skills, or characteristics thought to improve the chances of economic integration. Affirmative criteria for family migrants typically include a showing of a specified relationship of consanguinity or adoption, as well as sponsorship agreements to ensure that new arrivals will not have to draw on public benefits. Categories are often capped at a certain level, so that governments try to meet their policy goals by adjusting the mix of different kinds of migrants. Migrants who meet the affirmative criteria are allowed in, unless inadmissible on one of several grounds, such as criminal conduct; being a danger to national security, public order, or public health; or a likelihood of having to rely on social assistance or other public benefits. The grounds of inadmissibility generally double as grounds for deportation, although the specifics may vary, with no time limit up until the migrant naturalizes.[39] Acquired citizenship can also be lost.[40]

[39] For discussion of the deportation power in United States law, see Neuman, above n 29; AB Cox and CM Rodríguez, 'The President and Immigration Law' (2010) 119 *Yale Law Journal* 458, 510–19. For discussion of deportation in Canada, see JA Dent, 'No Right of Appeal: Bill C-11, Criminality, and the Human Rights of Permanent Residents Facing Deportation' (2002) 27 *Queen's Law Journal* 749.

[40] For Canada, see *Citizenship Act*, RSC 1985, c C-29, s 10 (Canada); for the United States, see INA, above n 12 at §349.

This overall structure, more or less uniform across liberal constitutional democracies, may lead to injury, hence potential injustice, in one of four ways. (1) Migrants may be injured through basic decisions of admission or exclusion, according to which a country seeks to determine what kind and how many non-members to admit or exclude. I call this first-order injury. There are also roughly three second-order ways in which injury can occur: (2) through laws and policies that limit the rights or impose burdens on admitted immigrants; (3) through the enforcement, such as by arrest, detention, and deportation, of first-order as well as other second-order policies; and (4) through the actions of private parties in a position to abuse or exploit migrants, owing to the operation of immigration laws and policies. Recall here that by injury, I mean 'damage to purposiveness'. Thus, the above list provides the different ways in which immigration law and policy may damage the purposiveness of migrants or would-be migrants.

Upon whom do these injuries fall? Prevailing patterns of first-order immigration law and policy are inegalitarian. By this I mean they are geared toward the long-term acceptance of relatively advantaged migrants, those who already possess money, education, saleable skills, and so on, and toward the exclusion of the less advantaged or the restriction of the less advantaged to temporary status. Policies for the permanent admission of economic migrants are designed openly with the goal of attracting migrants with desired endowments, whereas policies for the admission of refugees and family migrants are often applied restrictively. Legally, less advantaged economic migrants are often admitted on a temporary basis, as so-called guestworkers with a restricted menu of rights. Those who come illegally have even fewer rights. As a result, the weight of enforcement measures ends up falling disproportionately on disadvantaged migrants.[41] In immigration law, there is therefore a potentially objectionable correspondence between disadvantage on the one hand and second-order injury on the other.

This pattern of injury results from the fact that immigration regimes are trying to achieve an outcome opposed to the one we would naturally expect, given the sociological forces at work; that is, a result that I will inelegantly call 'countersocial'. Most theories of migration predict that migration flows will run from the poor to rich areas of the Earth. Whether migration is caused by inequalities in wealth and income, labour market dynamics, transnational social networks, or the

---

[41] For instance, it seems that it is primarily poor migrants who are affected by workplace raids. In the 2008 fiscal year, the United States Immigration and Customs Enforcement (ICE) made 5,173 administrative and 1,103 criminal arrests. Most notorious was a raid on a meatpacking plant in Postville, Iowa, which led to the arrest of 389 employees of a meatpacking plant that subsequently faced criminal charges for immigration, labour, and workplace safety violations: '[T]he raid had an immense, deleterious impact on the local immigrant community. Exacerbating matters, the local US attorney for the Northern District of Iowa used the threat of aggravated identity theft, a crime with a minimum two-year sentence, to pressure more than 300 of the 389 workers arrested to plead guilty to lesser crimes, with most receiving five-month prison sentences. Significant issues have been raised over whether the workers received basic due process protections or even understood the charges against them': D Meissner and D Kerwin, *DHS and Immigration: Taking Stock and Correcting Course* (Washington, Migration Policy Institute, February 2009) 38. See also E Camayd-Freixas, 'Interpreting the Largest ICE Raid in US History: A Personal Account' *The New York Times*, 13 June 2008.

creation of a culture of migration in sending states,[42] there is also reason to think that the number of members of poor countries wanting to migrate will continue to grow and that most such migrants, even if they are not among the poorest in their home countries, will be less well off than even the underclass in receiving states, especially if those receiving states are wealthy liberal constitutional democracies.[43] That means many migrants are going to consider it worthwhile to seek to migrate despite the costs. All things considered, it also seems plausible to suggest that a poorer migrant excluded from a wealthy liberal constitutional democracy will suffer a greater setback to his or her purposiveness than a more advantaged migrant.

A further important feature of migration is that it is hard to control. The elaborate visa and identification systems, as well as the administrative tribunals for adjudicating individual claims, put in place by immigration regimes create 'opportunity structures' that migrants can exploit to gain entry to a new country.[44] Each new rule or right creates new channels of entry. For example, even as exclusion laws barred the entry of Chinese labourers to the United States at the end of the nineteenth century, the courts affirmed the right of native-born ethnic Chinese to United States citizenship.[45] That led to tens of thousands of so-called 'paper sons', Chinese migrants who gained entry by falsely attesting to birthright.[46] Today the combined effect of economic migration and refugee admissions rules encourages poor migrants to claim they face a well-founded fear of persecution. As Saskia Sassen has said: 'If a government closes one kind of entry category, recent history shows that another one will have a rise in numbers.'[47] Immigration regimes respond to these migrant strategies with counterstrategies, such as the collection and sharing of biometric information, flying drones over areas where migrants are expected to travel, or the establishment of agreements with sending countries for processing migrants prior to departure. Some of these strategies may work. Some, inevitably, will be more injurious.

I intend to do no more than set out a problem at this point. The claim is not that either the inequality between members and migrants or the distribution of favourable migrant status according to advantage is wrong as such. Neither is it that egalitarianism in our immigration laws and policies is a value that we have

---

[42] For surveys of theories of the causes of migration, see S Castles and MJ Miller, *The Age of Migration: International Population Movements in the Modern World*, 4th edn (New York, Guilford Press, 2009) chapter two; DS Massey et al, *Worlds in Motion: Understanding International Migration at the End of the Millennium* (New York, Oxford University Press, 1998) chapter one.

[43] See Castles and Miller, *Age of Migration*, above n 42 at 5; P Collier, *Exodus: How Migration Is Changing Our World* (New York, Oxford University Press, 2013) 50.

[44] See S Castles, 'The Factors that Make and Unmake Migration Policies' (2004) 38 *International Migration Review* 852, 860.

[45] *United States v Wong Kim Ark*, 169 US 649 (1898).

[46] M Ngai, *Impossible Subjects: Illegal Aliens and the Making of Modern America* (Princeton, Princeton University Press, 2005) 204–206, 218–24.

[47] S Sassen, *Globalization and Its Discontents: Essays on the New Mobility of People and Money* (New York, New Press, 1998) 13.

reason to aim at. Like the inequality between members of wealthy constitutional liberal democracies and migrants to such states, the inegalitarian patterns of immigration laws and policies are indicative of potential injustice. The aim of the next section is to further detail the ways that the injurious effects of immigration law fall most heavily upon the poor or otherwise disadvantaged.

V. Inegalitarianism: Four Examples

Injury in immigration governance will land upon those who are excluded or strictly controlled by first-order rules and upon whom certain second-order consequences fall. In this section I want to further specify concerns regarding inegalitarian patterns of injury in four regulatory categories: (1) economic migration, (2) family migration, (3) refugees, and (4) illegal migration.

1. Economic Migration and Guestworker Programmes

Employers in developed economies have long supplemented their labour supply with foreign workers. Until immigration began to be regulated in the late nineteenth century, such efforts were not a matter for state intervention.[48] Today however governments try to influence economic and labour market outcomes through immigration policy. The key policy tools here are screening mechanisms that try to select migrants based on more-or-less specific labour market needs or according to supposed predictors of economic success, like educational achievement or language ability. Such screening is a core technique of first-order inegalitarianism. Second-order policy tools specific to economic migration include labour certification; the imposition of conditions on certain categories of economic migrants; and the duties and limitations of rights associated with guestworker programmes.

Labour certification requires employers to demonstrate that a permanent or temporary immigrant is not displacing a qualified citizen or permanent resident from a job. It is a form of protectionism that favours citizens and permanent residents over non-resident migrants. It will be inegalitarian to the extent that citizens and permanent residents are better off than non-resident migrants, as will generally be the case when the state of immigration is a wealthy liberal constitutional democracy. It has the injurious effect of depriving some migrants of jobs for which they otherwise might have been hired, which at first blush seem to limit their purposiveness.

Guestworker programmes have featured prominently in recent reform debates. For instance, in 2005 one of the major recommendations of the United

---

[48] C Hahamovitch, 'Creating Perfect Immigrants: Guestworkers of the World in Historical Perspective' (2003) 44 *Labor History* 69, 73–74. See also S Sassen, *Guests and Aliens* (New York, New Press, 1999) especially chapters two and three.

Nations-sponsored Report of the Global Commission on International Migration was for the creation of coordinated, effective guestworker programmes that also protect workers' rights.[49] The appeal of such programmes is fairly obvious. They can generate significant revenue for sending states in the form of remittances.[50] Individual foreign workers get access to wages far greater than those available at home,[51] while employers almost certainly pay less in wages than they would to citizens or permanent residents. Further, such programmes are designed to avoid the spectre of long-term mass immigration. Finally, they can be tailored to meet the labour needs of the receiving state: agricultural workers in the southern United States, construction workers in the Middle East, or miners in South Africa. On the other hand, the inegalitarian concern is quite clear. It is generally lower-paid, lower-skilled workers who are routed into such programmes and who, accordingly, face a resulting risk of exploitation. Regardless of policymakers' intentions, the threat of deportation and a lack of employment rights can lead to the abuse, isolated or systemic, of workers.[52] Such consequences are nothing new. Indeed, historically, guest worker programmes have mutated into forced labour schemes, as the techniques of control necessary to put them in place have proven adaptable to more odious purposes.[53]

2. Family Migration

Family migration provides a way for certain migrants, otherwise inadmissible, to gain access to a labour market, educational system, or other opportunities.[54] It is often said that family migration stymies overall immigration and other policy

---

[49] Global Commission on International Migration, *Migration in an interconnected world: New directions for action* 17–18 (Switzerland, 2005). See also the research paper prepared for the GCIM: Martin Ruhs, 'The Potential of Temporary Migration Programmes in Future International Migration Policy', *A Paper Presented for the Policy Analysis and Research Programme of the Global Commission on International Migration* (September 2005).

[50] According to the World Bank, US$150 billion was remitted in 2004, a 50 per cent increase over the previous five years. The leading recipients were Mexico (US$16 billion), India (US$9.9 billion), and the Philippines (US$8.5 billion): Global Commission on International Migration, *Migration in an interconnected world*, above n 49 at 26.

[51] Migrants who move from lower to higher income economies often earn 10 or 30 times more than they would at home: ibid at 8. Collier puts the figure at 10 times: Collier, above n 43 at 149.

[52] Opponents of guestworkers programmes also often argue that their intended temporariness is a false promise. History, it is said, suggests that such programmes lead to legal and illegal chain migration from sending states, and migrant populations become more or less permanent fixtures. See, eg PL Martin and MS Teitelbaum, 'The Mirage of Mexican Guest Workers' (2001) 80 *Foreign Affairs* 117.

[53] The legislative acts that shaped the apartheid regime in South Africa, for example, had their origins in pass laws instituted in the 1870s, when miners in British colonial South Africa began importing workers from Portuguese East Africa (now Mozambique) who were kept in compounds, paid every six months to discourage truancy, and deported if they refused to renew their work contract: Hahamovitch, 'Creating Perfect Immigrants', above n 48 at 76–78. In both Germany and Japan, guestworkers became forced labourers during the Second World War: ibid at 81.

[54] This dynamic is used to explain how European guestworker programmes, especially in France and Germany, led to large, foreign-born populations: see, eg C Joppke, 'Why Liberal States Accept Unwanted Immigration' (1998) 50 *World Politics* 266.

aims. One criticism of United States immigration law, for example, is that it admits too many family migrants and, as a result, has unjust distributive results within the state, by increasing pressure to lower wages for the most poorly-paid workers.[55] In Canada, large numbers of migrants officially categorized as economic class migrants are in fact the accompanying family members of a principal applicant.[56]

Since family migration provides a means of entry for poor migrants otherwise inadmissible, it may seem to alleviate rather than aggravate the inegalitarianism of immigration policy. That is probably true overall. Nonetheless, attempts to control family migration so that it does not swamp other policy aims can result in inegalitarian patterns of injury. Here the two aspects of family admissions policies of greatest note are sponsorship requirements and the connection between status and statutory rights of family reunion. Both regulatory tools result in interference with family life that seems obviously injurious.

On the first point, sponsorship policies expose families of recent immigrants to the possibility of injury in two respects. They deprive such families of equal access to public provision, even if needed. Furthermore, they tether family members together even past the point where familial bonds have broken down, creating relations of objectionable dependence within families.[57] Such legally-imposed dependency will have the greatest effect on those migrants who most need to draw on social entitlements.

On the second point, citizens have more robust rights of unification than non-citizen permanent residents;[58] temporary migrants have very few if any rights of

---

[55] S Macedo, 'The Moral Dilemma of US Immigration Policy: Open Borders Versus Social Justice?' in C Swain (ed), *Debating Immigration* (Cambridge, Cambridge University Press, 2007).

[56] For discussion, see A Macklin, 'Freeing Migration from the State: Michael Trebilcock on Migration Policy' (2010) 60 *University of Toronto Law Journal* 315, 345.

[57] The standard-form undertaking for sponsorships in Canada includes the following provision: 'I understand that the undertaking remains in effect no matter what may change in my life. For example, if I am divorced, change jobs, become unemployed, and/or go back to school, I will still be responsible to the sponsored person and his or her family members I am sponsoring or for whom I am co-signing.' See form IMM1344AE at p 4, available at: http://www.cic.gc.ca/english/pdf/kits/forms/IMM1344E.pdf. Among the litigants in the Canadian case *Mavi v Canada (Attorney General)*, 2009 ONCA 794, reversed in part, *Canada (Attorney-General) v Mavi*, 2011 SCC 30, a challenge to the enforcement of undertakings, several faced collection action (through the seizure of tax refunds and credits) despite a series of personal setbacks, such as the loss of employment, physical disability, or family ruptures. For example, the Ontario Court of Appeal summarizes the case of one of the litigants this way: 'Mr Hince married his wife in June 2002 while she was visiting Canada. In October 2002, he applied to sponsor his wife and her daughter from a previous relationship for entry into Canada. They arrived in Canada in January 2006 but left Mr Hince after less than a month. In May 2006, his wife began receiving social assistance. In May or June 2006, Mr Hince was informed that his wife was on social assistance and that he would be required to repay all benefits she received. He advised the government that he had offered to support his wife but that she refused his offer; he also claimed that he did not know where she was living.' (See *Mavi*, ONCA at appendix F.)

[58] In the United States, see INA, above n 12 at §201(b)(2)(A)(i) and §203(a). Canada makes few distinctions between citizens and permanent residents: Immigration and Refugee Protection Regulations, SOR/2002-227, s 117(1) and s 130.

reunification;[59] illegal immigrants will have none at all. Here the inegalitarianism of the laws and policies of family immigration is the result of the overall inegalitarianism of immigration policy. Advantaged migrants, who are more likely to be admitted to permanent residence and then citizenship, will thus have an easier time staying together with their family. The less well off in practice enjoy less robust rights to family life and are more likely to be separated or kept apart.

3. Refugees

There is no affirmative right to asylum in international law and states have no legal duty to admit refugees outside their borders.[60] Instead international refugee law, through the principle of non-refoulement, prohibits expulsion of refugees who enter a state's territory.[61] For the most part, state parties process asylum seekers and, if they are found to be refugees, put them on the path to permanent residence and naturalization.[62] Thus refugee protection as a practical matter begins with a determination of whether a claimant is someone who is outside their country owing to a well-founded fear of being persecuted for reasons of race, religion, nationality, membership of a particular social group, or political opinion.[63] This definition is narrow in that forms of hardship that might make it impossible to live a minimally adequate life within one's home country are excluded and in that one is only protected if one faces persecution on one of the five listed grounds. It is also rife with ambiguities.[64] Although several states now allow the admission for protection of individuals on general human rights grounds, that is, so-called 'complementary protection', the narrowness and ambiguity in general carries over to this complementary regime as well. It is not surprising, then, that refugee admissions have become a site of contestation between poor migrants and immigration regimes. Migrants who view themselves as entitled to, or simply very

[59] Only select categories of temporary migrants have the right to bring their family members into a country. An exception in Canada are migrants coming to work as live-in caregivers, who may bring their family members if they have sufficient funds to support them; if their employer has given permission for the family members to live with them; and if the family members are not otherwise inadmissible: Immigration and Refugee Protection Regulations, above n 58 at s 114.

[60] See Hathaway, *Rights of Refugees*, above n 5 at 300; Goodwin-Gill, *Movement of Persons*, above n 6 at 139.

[61] Convention Relating to the Status of Refugees, above n 3 at art 33.

[62] ibid at art 34. ('Contracting States shall as far as possible facilitate the assimilation and naturalization of refugees. They shall in particular make every effort to expedite naturalization proceedings and to reduce as far as possible the charges and costs of such proceedings.')

[63] ibid at art 1.

[64] On these ambiguities, see J Sztucki, 'Who Is a Refugee? The Convention Definition: Universal or Obsolete?' in F Nicholson and P Twomey (eds), *Refugee Rights and Realities: Evolving International Concepts and Regimes* (New York, Cambridge University Press, 1999) 55, 58–60. On the origins of the refugee definition, see JC Hathaway, 'The Evolution of Refugee Status in International Law: 1920–1950' (1984) 33 *International & Comparative Law Quarterly* 348.

much want, entry either push the boundaries of the refugee definition or mis-represent their case. Immigration regimes tend to cling to narrow readings of the definition and put in place procedural strategies to prevent what are represented as fraudulent claims.

Thus international and domestic refugee regimes are characterized by two forms of contestation, over the scope of substantive refugee protection and the procedural means of accessing such protection. The concern that arises in this context is that certain forms of suffering fail to be addressed by domestic and international refugee regimes. Strategies aimed at deterring asylum claims precede the determination of refugee status and so fall equally on those asylum seekers who fit the international refugee definition and those who do not. Further, even those who on any reading do not fall under the definition may suffer from forms of deprivation or poverty that make their exclusion problematic. Finally, asylum seekers tend to be subject to some of the harshest and most peremptory forms of enforcement, most notably detention while claims are processed.

4. Illegal Immigration

Restrictions and controls on movement of economic migrants, family migrants, and refugees determine in part the size of the illegal population. Moreover, growth in the illegal immigrant population drives further second-order policymaking, as strategies are developed for the identification and deportation of illegal immi-grants. For example, the 1882 Chinese Exclusion Act in the United States led to significant fraudulent immigration. In response, Congress passed the Geary Act, requiring all Chinese labourers to apply within one year for a certificate of residence stating that they were lawfully resident in the country. Those without a certificate could be arrested and brought before a federal judge or commissioner to prove their lawfulness in proceedings at which one 'credible', that is, white, wit-ness had to testify on their behalf.[65] Those found to be unlawfully in the country were to be punished by a year of hard labour prior to deportation. So restriction leads to illegal immigration, which leads to new strategies of control with greater potential for injury.[66]

Here the inegalitarian concern is parasitic on the overall policy bias toward the admission of skilled or otherwise advantaged migrants. Presumably any immigra-tion policy will lead to some illegal migration. It is because the disadvantaged are subject to exclusion or strictly controlled by immigration law that the vast major-ity of illegal immigrants are disadvantaged. Illegal immigrants become the target of enforcement measures that may themselves be injurious. Everyday activities

---

[65] See Salyer, *Laws Harsh as Tigers*, above n 12 at 46.
[66] The Geary Act was litigated in *Fong Yue Ting*, above n 21 and *Wong Wing*, above n 7.

like driving, working, or travelling may become illegal. The pall of enforcement may have other injurious results as they augment illegal immigrants' vulnerability to private exploitation. Within the receiving state, the purposiveness of illegal immigrants is therefore severally compromised: what results is the 'revocability of the promise of the future'.[67]

Finally, illegal status can also impact migrants' place in the social hierarchy in their home country. Joshua Reichert has described how in the town of Guadalupe in west-central Mexico, illegal migrants felt subordinate to those migrants who had legal access to the United States. Illegal migrants complained that they 'competed with legal migrants on unequal terms, often complaining that they felt like second-class citizens in their own community'.[68] The status difference between non-migrants and legal migrants was even starker. Therefore where a culture of migration has taken hold, returning or staying home is no way to avoid the stigmatizing differences created by immigration law.

VI. Moving on

First-order inegalitarianism in immigration law creates an inegalitarian pattern of injury through its second-order effects. We have fixed judgements that some of these are oppressive in themselves, although of course these judgements may give way if we come to see that these effects are, in fact, either not injurious or not unjustified. I am troubled by first-order inegalitarianism, but I have no settled judgement about its overall justice or injustice. It is problematic that it has the tendency to result in the forms of injury mentioned. On the other hand, certain considerations point away from concluding that states must, as a matter of justice, pursue more egalitarian policies, that is, policies that either show less favouritism for the advantaged, policies that show no favouritism at all, or policies that favour the disadvantaged. Most plausible to me are arguments that such policies might make domestic social welfare programmes unsustainable or that it is unfair for migrants to make claims upon public benefit schemes to which they have not contributed.[69]

---

[67] NP De Genova, 'Migrant "Illegality" and Deportability in Everyday Life' (2002) 31 *Annual Review of Anthropology* 419, 427, citing DM Carter, *States of Grace: Senegalese in Italy and the New European Immigration* (Minneapolis, University of Minnesota Press, 1997) 196.

[68] JS Reichert, 'A Town Divided: Economic Stratification and Social Relations in a Mexican Migrant Community' (1982) 29 *Social Problems* 411, 418.

[69] The issue is summarized in J Carens, 'Immigration and the Welfare State' in A Gutmann (ed), *Democracy and the Welfare State* (Princeton, Princeton University Press, 1988) 208–13.

Coming to terms with inegalitarianism in the context of our overall global inequality requires facing up to its objectionable consequences while at the same time acknowledging these and other potential rationales. There are three live possibilities: inegalitarian policies are permitted by an absolutist reading of discretion in immigration law; such policies are permitted under a principled reading of discretion in immigration law underlain by a theory of justice in immigration; or such policies are condemned by a principled theory of justice in immigration, which may support a case for reform of the law and reinterpretation of the discretionary doctrine. Part Two, comprising the next three chapters, is given over to making a case for a principled reading of the discretionary doctrine. Part Three, comprising two chapters, then turns to the task of developing principles of justice in immigration governance.

Part II

The Authority of Immigration Regimes

3

The Rightful Governance
of Immigration

I. Introduction

STATES CAN LEGALLY impose inegalitarian policies because they enjoy broad discretion over immigration governance. This discretion runs all the way up to the international doctrine that recognizes national competence and jurisdiction over immigration.[1] And it runs all the way down to the vague standards and broad enforcement mechanisms that characterize domestic regimes.[2] Discretion is a puzzling phenomenon in legal systems generally. What makes this puzzle distinctive in immigration governance is that it points to a controversy in political morality. If states' authority over immigration is 'absolute and unqualified',[3] then the suggestion seems to be that states enjoy an extraordinary moral discretion: authoritative rule over immigration absent the constraints of justice. Inegalitarianism may be licensed because immigration regimes can have authority without striving to be just. The aim of Part Two, comprising the next three chapters, is to challenge this variant of absolutism.

I argue that there is a duty owed by members of receiving states to establish immigration regimes that are reasonably just and a duty owed by migrants to comply with those reasonably just regimes. Underlying both arguments is the claim that the principal value of any state, and the key to the justification of the inequality between members and non-members, lies in the provision of an authoritative and stable basic structure of major social institutions whose rules articulate a political conception of justice. This is a value that both members of and would-be immigrants to a state can recognize. Moreover, it is a value that, because of the primacy of justice, members can demand that immigrants respect.

---

[1] GS Goodwin-Gill, *International Law and the Movement of Persons between States* (Oxford, Clarendon Press, 1978) 3.

[2] See G Neuman, 'Discretionary Deportation' (2006) 20 *Georgetown Immigration Law Journal* 611; D Kanstroom, 'The Better Part of Valor: The REAL ID Act, Discretion, and the "Rule" of Immigration Law' (2006/7) 51 *New York Law School Law Review* 161; D Kanstroom, 'Surrounding the Hole in the Doughnut: Discretion and Deference in US Immigration Law' (1997) 71 *Tulane Law Review* 703; MG Heyman, 'Judicial Review of Discretionary Decisionmaking' (1994) 31 *San Diego Law Review* 861.

[3] *Fong Yue Ting v United States*, 149 US 698, 707 (1893).

From this demand for respect, however, it does not follow that there is an absolutist right to exclusion. Rather, what seems to follow is that restrictions must be justified by reasons that refer back to the need to maintain the state on an ongoing basis as an institution or set of institutions capable of providing authoritative determinations of what justice requires.

In this chapter I focus on the first argument: that there is a duty to strive to govern immigration reasonably justly, where this means to govern immigration in a manner that seeks to avoid the unjustified injury of any person, members and migrants alike. The argument relies chiefly on the work of Immanuel Kant. Unlike John Rawls, Kant works out a justification for the constitutional state that begins with a hypothetical state of nature.[4] It is important to start with such a justification because the problem of immigration governance itself presumes the existence of states and, in any event, it is the states themselves that are doing the excluding.[5] We want to know why states as states, in particular, are justified in doing so.

Kant's justification of the state provides a model for working through the problem of justice in immigration governance. As in the state of nature, migrants to and members of receiving states initially find themselves in a situation where either group can act on their own unilateral judgement of what justice permits or requires. I argue that what Kant calls the 'postulate of public right' applies to this situation of symmetrical unilateralism. The postulate of public right states that 'when you cannot avoid living side by side with all others, you ought to leave the state of nature and proceed with them into a rightful condition, that is, a condition of distributive justice'.[6] Once migrants have become proximate to members, the receiving state and its members must seek to enter a 'rightful condition' with them by striving to govern immigration reasonably justly.

Section Two lays out Kant's argument for the duty to enter a rightful condition, or a state that unites its subjects under a general will, out of the state of nature. This section, with respect to which I claim no originality, takes the form of an exposition of Kant's argument for the postulate of public right. Section Three then explains how the argument for the postulate yields an account of the moral value of states, which in turn supports an account of the justified political

---

[4] 'Rawlsian justification is principally a justification of coercion offered to those who already accept the necessity of living in some kind of state. The only real justificatory question is: What kind of state?' AJ Simmons, 'Justification and Legitimacy' in *Justification and Legitimacy: Essays on Rights and Obligations* (Cambridge University Press, 2001) 143. Hence Rawls eschews the state of nature as a useful philosophical device: '[T]his historical or hypothetical benchmark is simply irrelevant to the question of justice.' (J Rawls 'Distributive Justice' in S Freeman (ed), *Collected Papers* (Cambridge, MA, Harvard University Press, 1999) 135; see also J Rawls, E Kelly (ed), *Justice as Fairness: A Restatement* (Cambridge, MA, Belknap Press, 2001) 54–55.

[5] For this point, see M Blake, 'Immigration, Jurisdiction, and Exclusion' (2013) 41 *Philosophy & Public Affairs* 103, 110.

[6] I Kant, MJ Gregor (trans and ed), *The Metaphysics of Morals* (Cambridge, Cambridge University Press, 1996) 86 [6:307]. Square brackets contain the volume number and page number for the Germany Academy edition of Kant's works.

inequality between members of a state and non-members. Beginning with Section Four, the general Kantian account is applied to immigration governance. I argue that the same reasoning that led to the postulate of public right leads to the conclusion that states must strive to govern immigration 'rightfully', that is, under immigration regimes that are capable of having authority. I claim that to do this, they must strive to be non-oppressive, although the argument for this condition is not worked out in this chapter but must wait until Chapter Five. Thus the postulate of public right applied in the context of immigration governance leads to the principled alternative to absolutism. Section Five adds further specificity to the principled account by considering immigration regimes as status regimes.

II. The Argument for the Postulate of Public Right

The postulate of public right says that 'when you cannot avoid living side by side with all others, you ought to leave the state of nature and proceed with them into a rightful condition, that is, a condition of distributive justice'.[7] Further, 'each may impel the other by force to leave this state [of nature] and enter a rightful condition'.[8] The postulate articulates an enforceable duty to enter with others into, in the first instance, a state embodying a united general will and thus capable of having authority. Here I explain the argument for the postulate, which doubles as a justification for the state.[9]

Kant holds that every person has an innate right to freedom, namely, 'independence from being constrained by another's choice'.[10] This right can only be guaranteed by living in a system of equal freedom, consistent with what he calls the universal principle of right:

> Any action is *right* if it can coexist with everyone's freedom in accordance with a universal law, or if on its maxim the freedom of choice of each can coexist with everyone's freedom in accordance with a universal law.[11]

Individual rights authorize coercion, in keeping with the universal principle of right, to limit others' freedom for the sake of the overall system of equal freedom.[12] Thus the innate right of freedom and the universal principle of right

---

[7] ibid

[8] ibid at 90 [6:312]; see also ibid at 86 [6:307].

[9] My exposition owes much to A Ripstein, *Force and Freedom: Kant's Legal and Political Philosophy* (Cambridge, MA, Harvard University Press, 2009), as well as various papers by Jeremy Waldron, especially J Waldron, 'Special Ties and Natural Duties' (1993) 22 *Philosophy & Public Affairs* 3; J Waldron, 'Kant's Legal Positivism' (1995) 109 *Harvard Law Review* 1535; J Waldron, 'What is Cosmopolitan?' (2000) 8 *Journal of Political Philosophy* 227.

[10] Kant, *Metaphysics of Morals*, above n 6 at 30 [6:237].

[11] ibid at 24 [6:230].

[12] See Ripstein, *Force and Freedom*, above n 9 at 33: '[A] system of equal freedom is one in which each person is free to use his or her own powers, individually or cooperatively, to set his or her own purposes, and no one is allowed to compel others to use their powers in a way designed to advance or accommodate any other person's purposes.'

together lead to a provisional conception of justice, that is, the ideal of a system of equal freedom. This conception is provisional because there will not be any uniquely suitable system of equal freedom.

Different individuals in the state of nature will have different ideas about how a system of equal freedom might be specified. Until matters are settled each person's rights will be under threat. They will live not in a system of equal freedom, but in a realm of 'lawless freedom'.[13] No one in the state of nature has authority over anyone else, so the only way one's views win out is, ultimately, through force. The situation is one 'devoid of justice'.[14]

The insecurity in the state of nature arises because the principles of justice that follow from innate freedom and the universal principle of right will not be determinate, and so judgement is always required to comply with them. However, your best judgement will often not be the same as mine, for reasons rehearsed in Chapter One. That is, divergences in our judgements arise in part because of what Adam Smith calls the 'corruptions' and in part because of what Rawls calls the 'burdens of judgement'. Because of one another's fallibility, in the state of nature I have no reason to defer or subordinate myself to your judgement, since you have no authority over me. Where I defer despite our disagreement, I subordinate myself, allowing my innate right to freedom to be limited by the will of another person.

Thus no one commits a wrong by acting on his or her best judgement of what is right, notwithstanding the injuries to others that may follow. Though from your perspective, my injurious actions may seem arbitrary, from mine they may seem justified (and vice versa). This situation leads to great insecurity, though, so everyone does 'wrong in the highest degree' if they demur from entering into a rightful condition under a central authority which may issue binding judgements of right and wrong.[15] By refusing to enter a rightful condition, one condemns those nearby to live in a state of mutual insecurity and threat.

To illustrate with Kant's main example, property rights are necessary for people to live any but the most rudimentary life. Yet outside a state, no one would have authority on their own to lay claim to a piece of property, excluding all others from the land or object's use and thus hindering their purposiveness. Further, no one would have authority to punish trespasses of the boundaries they have sought to impose. Lastly, no one would have authority to adjudicate disputes of trespass, nuisance, and so on.[16] To have a system of property that allows people to coexist on just terms, you need a government with legislative, executive, and judicial institutions to establish, enforce, and adjudicate such matters.

---

[13] Kant, *Metaphysics of Morals*, above n 6 at 93 [6:316].
[14] ibid at 90 [6:312].
[15] ibid at 86 [6:307–08].
[16] Ripstein, *Force and Freedom*, above n 9 at chapter six.

The example is generalisable to all questions of right.[17] Any rules or principles of justice will be indeterminate.[18] A central authority is required to specify their content, to punish infringements, and to adjudicate disputes. Unless that authority takes the judgement and interests of all parties into account, they will have no reason to defer to it, because to do so would be contrary to their innate right to freedom. In those circumstances, a sufficiently powerful private party, acting on his or her own unilateral will, can always rightfully reopen any dispute. In such a condition, no one's innate freedom can be secure. From all this it follows that there is an enforceable duty, owed by everyone to every other proximate person, to enter into a rightful condition. Only by so doing can everyone's purposiveness be secured.

Note that this argument works even if one does not share Kant's conception of justice as a system of equal liberty.[19] The indeterminacies of justice that lead to the duty to enter a state possessed of authority can involve any conception of justice. Indeed, the argument is strengthened by the possibility of conflicting conceptions of justice. However, you do need to accept certain premises, namely, that justice is a pre-civil moral value, that is, a value that obtains prior to the creation of state institutions; that judgements and principles of justice are indeterminate; and that such indeterminacies lead to objectionable insecurity in the absence of a central authority to resolve them. Further, you need some minimal conception of the freedom and equality of persons, entailing that no one can rightly be subject, without appropriate justification, to coercion according to another's unilateral will. In accordance with what is said later, I will conceive of this minimal sense of freedom and equality as being that all persons are possessed in roughly equal measure of what Rawls calls the two moral powers, the capacity to have a sense of justice and, second, the capacity to form and pursue a conception of the good.[20] Without some such supposition, the question of authority would not arise at all.

The antagonist usually set against the Kantian justification of the state is John Locke, according to whom none may be forced to leave the state of nature

---

[17] ibid at 148.

[18] Joe Palumbo has suggested to me that there are some areas, such as inside a family or within a union, where injury is possible and the rules of justice indeterminate, yet where we would not want the state to intervene. With respect to such there must be a division of labour between the state and the local institution, and the exact demarcation of that division must itself ultimately be decided by the state. I thank Joe for raising this point.

[19] Nor need one rely upon the innate right to freedom, as Kant formulates it. For example, one may not be committed to the idea of freedom as 'independence from being constrained by another's choice'. And one may not wish to follow Kant in concluding that innate freedom entails a commitment to innate equality, that is, independence from being bound by others to more than one can in turn bind them; to the quality of being one's own master and being beyond reproach; and to the idea that one is 'authorized to do to others anything that does not itself diminish what is theirs, so long as they do not want to accept it'. Kant, *Metaphysics of Morals*, above n 6 at 30–31 [6:237–38].

[20] J Rawls, *Political Liberalism*, expanded edn (New York, Columbia University Press, 1996) 332–33.

and enter a civil society.[21] Locke shares Kant's view that there are pre-civil principles of justice. On a Lockean account, however, these are determinate natural laws 'as intelligible and plain to a rational Creature, and a Studier of that Law, as the positive Laws of the Commonwealths, nay possibly plainer'.[22] Everyone has executive power in the state of nature to punish transgressions of and seek reparations for violations of their natural rights. The authority of the state is merely the authority that men already had, transferred to the commonwealth because of inconveniences caused by corruption and viciousness.[23] If we take out the premise that some men will be corrupt and vicious, there would be no reason for rational individuals to proceed out of the state of nature.[24]

A John Simmons takes up Lockean objections of this sort to the Kantian account. Simmons argues first that you are in fact likely to establish sociable bonds with those close to you, rather than posing a mutual threat, if only because you have to go on living with them. These bonds will lessen the chances of conflict. Second, he says there is something wrong with the idea that the postulate applies only to those who are close to one another. Other states or their members can pose greater threats than nearby residents who have opted out of the rightful condition. I can, to use Simmons's example, be attacked by letter bomb. I address these objections in reverse order, explaining first the role of proximity in Kant's argument and then addressing Simmons's contention that proximate persons are less likely to come into conflict.[25]

Proximity is important not in itself but because it is the principal circumstance under which insecurity is likely to arise. Therefore the establishment of states to govern proximate persons is the first order of business. Nonetheless, insecurity and not proximity is the basic worry. This is demonstrated by other formulations where Kant talks about the postulate of public right being a duty owed by those in a position to 'affect'[26] or to 'influence',[27] or who cannot help 'associating' with, one another.[28] The possibility of mailing letter bombs implies a duty to enter a rightful condition among all those who could harm one another in this way, for

---

[21] See J Locke, P Laslett (ed), *Two Treatises of Government* (Cambridge, Cambridge University Press, 1960) 350–51 [II.95]; see also 315–16 [II.73], on the right of children to join themselves to the commonwealth of their choosing. Square brackets refer to volume and paragraph number.

[22] ibid at 274–75 [II.12].

[23] ibid at 275–76 [II.13].

[24] On the contrast between Locke and Kant, see JG Murphy, *Kant: The Philosophy of Right* (London, Macmillan, 1970) 113–27; K Flikschuh, 'Reason, Right, and Revolution: Kant and Locke' (2008) 36 *Philosophy & Public Affairs* 375. For an account more sympathetic to Locke, see Simmons, 'Justification and Legitimacy', above n 4 and AJ Simmons, 'Natural Duties and the Duty to Obey the Law' in AJ Simmons and CH Wellman, *Is There a Duty to Obey the Law?* (New York, Cambridge University Press, 2005) 121.

[25] Simmons, 'Natural Duties', above n 24 at 174–79.

[26] Kant, *Metaphysics of Morals*, above n 6 at 89 [6:311].

[27] I Kant, 'On the Common Saying: "This May Be True in Theory but It Does Not Apply in Practice"' in H Reiss (ed), *Kant: Political Writings* (Cambridge, Cambridge University Press, 1970) 73.

[28] Kant, *Metaphysics of Morals*, above n 6 at 29 [6:237].

example by negotiating an international treaty on postal security—or an international convention on copyright or on criminalizing the trafficking and smuggling of persons: different rightful conditions for different kinds of threat. Kant thinks the response to the threat posed by other states and their citizens, for example, is international and cosmopolitan right.[29]

Simmons's first argument is that proximate persons are in fact less likely to pose threats to one another than distant persons because of human sociability. Simmons may be right that there is less of a chance of conflict among those living side-by-side. However, all the Kantian argument needs to work is the possibility of conflict, since disputes over justice can so quickly get out of hand and resentments caused by such disputes can linger over generations. To deny this possibility, Simmons would have to argue that there is no such threat either because there is no indeterminacy about justice, only corruption and viciousness, which are less likely to be acted on among those living in proximity; because private individuals can have authority to resolve indeterminacy in the state of nature; or because private individuals can resolve conflicts or potential conflicts arising out of indeterminacy based on compromise, without relying on the authority of one of the disputants or of some third party.

I suspect that, at bottom, what is going on here is simply a disagreement about the nature of justice. If one thinks that the requirements of justice are clear, then one will think disagreements about what is just in particular circumstances are less likely. Kant develops his argument most fully with respect to private rights, that is, rights of property and contract. Here the scope for disagreement is relatively obvious, even on an austere conception of justice, as other defenders of Kant's view have shown.[30] Kant himself uses the example of a stolen horse sold to an unsuspecting buyer. Who gets the horse? Each such case contains the seed of conflict, which must be headed off, no matter how likely it is, as a matter of fact, to lead to actual conflict and violence. Violence will no doubt follow sometimes, which is enough to establish the threat.[31] Importantly, when violence does flare up no individual's claim of right can be authoritatively refuted. No individual's claim of what constitutes rightful punishment or compensation can be authoritatively refuted either. Therefore, feuds have the potential to linger and escalate.[32]

---

[29] I Kant, 'Perpetual Peace: A Philosophical Sketch' in *Political Writings*, above n 27 at 93.

[30] Waldron, 'Kant's Legal Positivism', above n 9 at 1538–40.

[31] Ripstein argues that the provisional nature of rights, leading to the duty to enter a rightful condition, is supported by Kant without recourse to the idea of violent disagreement. Kant's emphasis is on the indeterminacy of rights due to the need to apply judgement when deciding upon any matter of right. That means that to create any determinate system of equal freedom, judgements must be made that are equally binding upon everyone. This is true even if violent disagreement does not occur: Ripstein, *Force and Freedom*, above n 9 at 168–69. This contrasts with Waldron's account, which stresses the possibility of violent disagreement: Waldron, 'Kant's Legal Positivism', above n 9.

[32] Kant, *Metaphysics of Morals*, above n 6 at 86 [6:307]: 'Given the intention to be and to remain in this state of externally lawless freedom, human beings do one another no wrong at all when they feud among themselves [.]'

Once more, these claims are supported by Smith's account of justice. And once more, these examples are generalizable beyond cases involving property. They can include disagreements over criminal wrongs. Jeffrie Murphy, for instance, makes the same point using the example of conscientious white supremacists who want to lynch a black man to punish him for the 'crime' of befriending a white woman.[33] They also no doubt can, in the right circumstances, include claims that certain distributions of benefits and duties are oppressive. The answer to the assertion of the determinacy of justice, then, is simply a denial that such determinacy is plausible.

The other two possible arguments in support of the claim that proximate persons are not likely to pose threats to one another simply neglect a problem of regress. Parties in conflict might reach an agreement to resolve matters, perhaps by appointing an arbiter. Disputes can arise about the scope and validity of such agreements, the terms of such arbitration, or disputes with outside parties about the result. One will then need to find a way out of *those* disputes. The need to find another neutral authority, then another, then another eventually leads to the requirement to establish a central government or state.

III. The Moral Standing of States and Required Forms of Partiality

On Kant's argument, rightful conditions are required and justified because they provide the conditions under which it is possible for people to be just to one another on terms consistent with their moral equality. Outside a rightful condition, there is no possibility of mutual relations on just terms because there is no authority to settle disagreements over justice. A state, Kant says, is one of three forms of rightful condition, the others being international and cosmopolitan right.[34] It establishes a rightful condition by uniting members' unilateral wills into a general one, via the establishment of republican institutions. Therefore the argument for the postulate of public right provides a justification of states. This justification has both an inward and an outward dimension. It justifies to members of a state why they are subject to its coercive powers. It also, in a manner to be explored in this section, justifies the exclusion of non-members from the benefits associated with membership in the state. Thus Kant's justification of the state may form part of an account of international or global justice and, more specifically, of just immigration governance.

In this section I begin to depart from Kant in order to describe the outward-facing justificatory power of his account. In particular, I seek to establish why

---

[33] Murphy, *Kant: The Philosophy of Right*, above n 24 at 119.

[34] See the references to 'the three possible forms of rightful condition', with the other two being the right of nations and cosmopolitan right: Kant, *Metaphysics of Morals*, above n 6 at 89 [6:311].

non-members should treat the state as having moral standing, even if it has no value to them, and to establish the forms of partiality that are associated with state membership. To return to Smith's language from Chapter One, the Kantian justification of the state provides part of an explanation of the difference between 'reasonable' as opposed to 'unreasonable preference' among compatriots. These forms of partiality, which I group under the heading of 'justified political inequality', include the provision of state-level rights of political participation to members; the application of range-limited principles; heightened regard among members for one another's self-respect; and respect among members for one another's legitimate expectations. This account of partiality provides the basic justification of inequality between members and non-members to which an account of justice in immigration governance must connect.

1. Juridical Integration and the Moral Standing of States

A state is a rightful condition which, through a constitution and the rule of law, specifies rules of justice that would otherwise be indeterminate. This set of specifications is a political conception of justice. By 'political conception of justice', I do not intend a conception reducible to some grand formula, like the universal principle of right or the two principles of Rawls's justice as fairness. All I intend is that it be a set of rules articulated by a constitutional regime that unites the judgement of individual citizens into a united general will, not that some ideal of justice has been reached. In other words, the Kantian justification of the state operates at the level of non-ideal theory: it justifies our states, to us.[35] To be sure, Kant says that a rightful condition should strive to approximate the ideal of the original contract, which is an 'idea of reason' that 'can oblige every legislator to frame his laws in such a way that they could have been produced by the united will of a whole nation, and to regard each subject, insofar as he can claim citizenship, as if he had consented within the general will'.[36] A state, though, must at most strive, and certainly need not achieve, this ideal to be rightful.[37]

As we have seen, the postulate of public right demands that we establish such a state because without it everyone would live in insecurity. I now wish to explain how this account produces a particular conception of the moral standing of states to make claims against other states and non-members, including migrants.

A state represents an achievement, an articulated though imperfect political conception of justice embodied in its statutes, regulations, judicial decisions, and other government action under the law. To this conception and the basic structure

---

[35] It is for this reason that I use 'political conception of justice' rather than 'public conception of justice', Rawls's preferred label. The term 'public conception of justice' implies compliance with the condition of publicity, part of the ideal conception of justice as fairness. I use 'political conception' to emphasize that the state may be justified without living up to this or some other ideal. Later, in Chapter Seven, when argument proceeds in ideal theory, I use the label 'public conception of justice'.

[36] Kant, 'Theory and Practice', above n 27 at 79.

[37] Kant, *Metaphysics of Morals*, above n 6 at 90–91 [6:313].

embodying it, subjects develop over time what might be thought of as a natural allegiance. It is 'natural' in that their senses of justice over time become jointly integrated with this political conception of justice by living under it together. This is what I think Kant has in mind when he says that 'in an intellectual sense and from the perspective of rights', the members of a state are 'born of the same mother (the republic)' and 'constitute one family'.[38] He is making a point, consistent with Rawls and Smith, about the formative role that a state's conception of justice can have in developing its members' sense of justice,[39] among other ways that a basic structure can influence 'the kinds of persons they want to be as well as the kinds of persons they are'.[40]

The sense of justice is something almost all men and women have. It is what causes us to feel resentment or indignation when we are wronged, and guilt when we do wrong.[41] It is also 'the capacity to understand, to apply, and to act from' the political conception of justice which characterizes the terms of social cooperation in a given state.[42] Both Rawls and Smith provide accounts of how the sense of justice develops. On Smith's version, it is the result of our ongoing sympathetic discourse with others: as we judge one another on matters of justice, we eventually come to share and act on the same store of judgements and rules. Rawls's story is more schematic, but is ultimately compatible with Smith's. According to Rawls, as we come to have faith in the love of our parents, the companionship of our associates, and the justice of our social arrangements, we internalize the principles of our society's political conception of justice. Those principles thereby become a source of motivation for us. In its mature form, our sense of justice is sensitive to this conception and to the way it has been articulated in the rules of the institutions governing our lives. The alignment between members' sense of justice and the political conception of justice articulated by the state's basic structure is what, to return to a Smithian phrase, allows sympathetic concordance, though not identity, of judgement in the important moral domain of justice.

It is through the sense of justice that the political conception of justice embodied by a state's legal system plays a role in shaping members' identities and also forges distinctive ties between them; ties which we might say are deep but not intimate. Members who have incorporated the political conception of justice into their own sense of justice will feel resentment when their understanding of the rules of the political conception or its basic structure is breached. At least some other members will sympathize with that resentment and will mobilize with them to enforce the rules. They will also feel motivated to engage in the political debates

---

[38] ibid at 114 [6:343]; see also Kant, 'Theory and Practice', above n 27 at 74.

[39] See J Rawls, 'The Sense of Justice' in *Collected Papers*, above n 4 at 96; J Rawls, *A Theory of Justice*, revised edn (Cambridge, MA, Belknap Press, 1999) §86; Rawls, *Political Liberalism*, above n 20 at 19.

[40] Rawls, *Political Liberalism*, above n 20 at 269–70.

[41] It is what causes us to become 'enraged' at injustice: A Smith, K Haakonssen (ed), *The Theory of Moral Sentiments* (Cambridge, Cambridge University Press, 2002) 112–13 [II.iii.1.5].

[42] Rawls, *Political Liberalism*, above n 20 at 19.

and procedures through which the political conception of justice continues to be both refined and redefined. They will give one another reasons, that is, based on their shared conception. Thus one's sense of justice is determined not only by its substantive content, not simply by the rules or principles that one takes to comprise the requirements of justice, but also by what I will call its orientation. 'Orientation' to a state, as I will use it, is a commitment to working out the specifics of its conception of justice through further political engagement with other members. It also involves at least a limited commitment to going along with the results even if one considers them wrongheaded. Such a commitment is required at least to the extent necessary to ensure the ongoing viability of the state. Thus even if two states have identical or near-identical political conceptions of justice, their members' sense of justice will be non-trivially different because of their different orientations.

This may seem too demanding. Many, perhaps most, members will not actively engage in politics at any level. But the idea of orientation does not depend on an 'athletic'[43] civic ideal. One shapes a country's political conception of justice even if one is ready to respond to a felt injustice and considers it appropriate to make demands of its public institutions for rectification. This simple posture—the presumption, perhaps quite unthinking,[44] that one is entitled to make claims of a certain kind against a state's institutions and to have them resolved in accordance with the political conception of justice, which one further presumes to correspond, roughly, to that of one's fellow members just as it does with one's own—is enough to say one is oriented to that state. Such latent readiness will have a disciplining effect on the development of a political conception of justice and the rules that embody it.

When a person's sense of justice generally accords substantively with a state's political conception of justice and is oriented toward that conception, I will refer to that person as 'juridically integrated' with the political conception and the corresponding basic structure. Juridical integration is the subjective reconfiguration of a person's sense of justice that corresponds with his or her entry into or belonging to a rightful condition capable of having authority. If this idea of juridical integration is accepted, it follows from the postulate of public right that it is a necessary condition of membership in a state that is effectively regulated by a political conception of justice, where membership connotes being subject to the authority of the state.[45] Juridical integration is not a sufficient condition for

---

[43] I take the word from P Pettit, 'Capability and Freedom: A Defence of Sen' (2001) 17 *Economics & Philosophy* 1, who cites GA Cohen, 'Equality of What? On Welfare, Goods, and Capabilities' in MC Nussbaum and A Sen (eds), *The Quality of Life* (Oxford, Clarendon Press, 1993) 24–25.

[44] 'We often acquiesce without thinking in the moral and political conception implicit in the status quo': J Rawls, *Theory of Justice*, above n 39 at 229. Unthinking acquiescence in the implicit moral and political conception of our state is sufficient to be oriented towards it in the sense that I am using.

[45] Kant, *Metaphysics of Morals*, above n 6 at 91–92 [6:314]: 'The only qualification for being a citizen is being fit to vote. But being fit to vote presupposes the independence of someone who, as one of the people, wants to be not just a part of the commonwealth but *also a member of it, that is, a part of the commonwealth, acting from his own choice in community with others*.' (Emphasis added.)

membership because proximity, that is, the capacity to injure, is also necessary, although it would likely be highly unusual for someone who is outside the range of habitual injury to become or remain juridically integrated with a distant group of individuals. Sympathy depends on our ability to imaginatively identify with others, and imaginative identification is more readily accomplished the more familiar we are with their lives and circumstances.[46] Putting that complication aside, if a group of persons are proximate to one another and jointly juridically integrated with the same political conception of justice then they are co-members. It would be, Kant says, 'wrong in the highest degree' to disavow any proximate member, thus returning them to a situation 'devoid of justice' with respect to other members.

The moral standing of states to make claims of justice on other states and non-members comes from the achievement of a stable political conception of justice and basic structure into which members are juridically integrated. It seems to follow from the duty to enter a rightful condition under such a state that main-taining the conditions for the state's ongoing stability is also a duty. This remark introduces the idea of stability into the argument. Anticipating later discussion, one justification, perhaps the strongest justification, for the exclusion of migrants would seem to be the duty to maintain such stability. Some clarifying remarks about what I mean by stability are therefore needed. These will unfortunately only be stipulative and vague, since it would take me too far afield to provide a thorough discussion of the problem.[47]

At the outset of this subsection, I remarked that by 'political conception of justice', I am referring only to a non-ideal set of principles and rules embodied by a state and its basic structure. What kind of stability does such a state, and its members, have an interest in maintaining? Stability generally refers to the problem of maintaining order. Such order can be achieved, at the non-ideal end of the spectrum, through coercion or deception. At the ideal end, it can result from creating conditions under which the members of a state freely affirm and support its institutions because it corresponds to their sense of justice. In reality, for most states, stability will be maintained through some mixture of coercion and deception on the one hand and of freely-affirmed allegiance on the other. It seems safe to assume, further, that the closer a state gets to maintaining stability solely through coercion and deception, the less likely it is to endure in perpetuity. Members' senses of justice, we would expect, would revolt internally against such a state. In time, we would expect members to revolt externally as well.

Therefore, when I refer to a concern with maintaining the stability of a politi-cal conception, what I mean is the imperative of maintaining conditions in which

---

[46] Smith, *Theory of Moral Sentiments*, above n 41 at 267–71 and 272–73 [VI.ii.2.1-6 and 11–12].

[47] Apart from Rawls's discussion of stability, I have found most helpful B Barry, 'John Rawls and the Search for Stability' (1995) 105 *Ethics* 874; P Weithman, *Why Political Liberalism? On John Rawls's Political Turn* (New York, Oxford University Press, 2010).

a state and its major institutions can foster a reasonable amount of allegiance through juridical integration, as opposed to degenerating into conditions in which it must maintain itself through coercion and deception only. Stability so conceived is the tendency of the major social institutions of a state to remain within or progress toward a range of reasonable political conceptions of justice. As a state comes to approximate the ideal, it will be characterized by what Rawls calls stability for the right reasons, in which members affirm and support the principles of its conception of justice and support its basic structure because those principles and rules correspond to their own sense of justice. The need for some use of coercive power at least can never be eliminated, but it is hoped that it can be reduced to some reasonable minimum.

2. Partiality Among Members

How might the duty to maintain the stability of the political conception of justice give rise to a justification to exclude? The answer to this question is complicated and leads to the further question of whether there can be any permissible or required forms of partiality among compatriots. Many kinds of partiality, say towards families, friends, or co-nationals, seem to play a role in commonsense morality.[48] Because it is also possible that reasonable forms of partiality can or ought to be exhibited toward compatriots, and that such partiality may play a role in justifying immigration laws and policies, any argument regarding the role of justice in the governance of immigration must either delineate required or permissible forms of partiality or explain why no forms of partiality are reasonable.

Two things carry over from Kantian justification of the state in this regard. First, the moral standing of the state depends on its provision of a political conception of justice and basic structure into which its members are jointly integrated. Although the state provides a locus for a plurality of other goods that are the fruits of social cooperation among members, these other goods—which may include a productive economy, the protection of the environment, the production and preservation of great works of art, the development of cultural or ethnic affinities, among many other possibilities—do not directly feature in the state's justification. In fact, such goods themselves give rise to claims of justice, which must be settled authoritatively in accordance with the state's political conception of justice and the rules of its basic structure. Second, to see if any required or permissible form of partiality follows from this justification of the state, the question to ask is: What kinds of partiality must you be permitted or required to express or enact in order to enjoy the appropriate kind of relationship?[49] In the case of the state,

---

[48] This is a theme in several of the essays in S Scheffler, *Boundaries and Allegiances: Problems of Justice and Responsibility in Liberal Thought* (New York, Oxford University Press, 2001).

[49] H Brighouse and A Swift, 'Legitimate Parental Partiality' (2009) 37 *Philosophy & Public Affairs* 43, 45–46. Brighouse and Swift only refer to 'permitted' forms of partiality.

the operative relationship is of joint juridical integration among cooperating members with a political conception of justice. Other forms of partiality involve other goods, which are not part of the justification of the state.

Now it follows from the fact that there is a duty to enter a rightful condition that, if a certain form of partiality is necessary to the achievement and ongoing stability of the state, then it is a required and not merely a permitted form of partiality. The first and most obvious form of required partiality is the provision to members, and the exclusion of non-members, from certain forms of participation in the state-level political process, such as the right to vote in national elections or to run for national office, at least when issues that are not potentially injurious to outsiders are at stake. This form of required partiality is justified by the fact that non-members, by virtue of not having a shared juridical orientation with members, are not committed to working out the principles and application of the state's political conception of justice or to the results of public engagement with such questions. Given this lack of commitment, one would expect their participation in political decision making to tend toward instability. They will not be as invested in the results and so would be expected to make less reasonable contributions. Members will know as much and, as a result, the outcome of any decision-making process may be treated with suspicion. This form of partiality seems to confirm our considered judgement that it is permissible to exclude non-members from the vote in national elections. Note, however, that we do not consistently hold the same judgement with respect to other forms of participation that might shape the political conception of justice, such as local elections or participation in administrative legal and judicial proceedings. This may be because state-level questions of justice are not at stake in such fora. It may also reflect the fact that local juridical integration occurs more readily than national integration.

Next, it will be the case that members who are jointly juridically integrated with a political conception of justice will be mutually vulnerable to a form of injury to their self-respect to which non-members will not be exposed. Self-respect, following Rawls, is the sense of our own value.[50] It 'is not so much a part of any rational plan of life as the sense that one's plan is worth carrying out'.[51] A person's sense of justice is, viewed from this angle, the set of dispositions governed by their belief in their own worth. Through juridical integration, the political conception of justice becomes constitutive of the sense of self-worth of each member. Therefore, at least in a liberal state that recognizes that each person is worthy of equal respect, having a political conception of justice that supports the equal self-respect of each member seems non-negotiable. It is the connection between members' self-worth and the political conception of justice that may create a baseline demand of equality among members; that is, a presumption in favour of equal benefit arises if the unequal provision of that benefit would be damaging to members' self-respect.

---

[50] Rawls, *Political Liberalism*, above n 20 at 318.
[51] Rawls, *Theory of Justice*, above n 39 at 155.

Non-members, whose self-respect in ordinary cases will be tied to some other state's political conception of justice, will not be vulnerable in the same way. Therefore there does not seem to be the same baseline demand for equal respect of non-members; or at least, their self-respect must be honoured in a different way that has not yet been worked out.

Members under the authority of a state recognize that determinations of the requirements of its political conception of justice should, in the ordinary course, be followed. Non-members are not bound by the same determinations. Hence, the determinate principles and rules of justice established within a state are range-limited in that they are in general capable only of binding members, since the rules are the expression of members' united general will. This, then, is a third form of partiality: partiality in the form of principles limited in range to those proximate individuals under the duty to unite under a general will, a will that may authoritatively resolve the indeterminacies and disagreements of justice. Recognize that principles necessary to ensure the equal social bases of self-respect of members are one form of range-limited principles. Note also that while these two forms of partiality are required in that it is necessary to have range-limited principles and, among them, principles attentive to members' self-respect, no specific principles are argued for here.

With respect to immigration restrictions, the justificatory force of these first three forms of partiality is equivocal. If members are required to evince these forms of partiality towards one another to maintain a stable conception of justice, such partiality may provide a counterweight to claims of international or global justice. But it does not seem that they can provide reasons, at least straightforwardly, to exclude migrants or otherwise to justify second-order exercises of power over immigration. A migrant is simply an additional person to whom such principles might apply and the principles themselves say nothing about who should or should not be included. Given that most plausible principles of social justice are sensitive to relative, rather than absolute, levels of goods such as liberties, income, or capabilities, it is in fact difficult to see how the addition of a modest number of migrants could disrupt justice within the state, as measured by consistency with the principles of its political conception of justice.

There are at least two exceptions to this general statement. One is that if a political conception of justice includes a principle guaranteeing provision of the goods necessary to maintain a minimally decent life, then such a principle may justify the exclusion of migrants whose admission would render it impossible to provide the minimum. The second exception arises because of legitimate expectations. As a state establishes and institutionalizes range-limited principles, including principles to ensure the social bases of self-respect, it will create legitimate expectations among members. Members justifiably expect a state to honour the entitlements that they accrue by virtue of having abided by and shaped their lives in accordance with the institutional rules promulgated under a state's political conception of justice. Such expectations are, as Rawls says, the other side of our political obligations.[52] To this I would add, they are also justified by members' juridical integration, since meeting legitimate expectations seems to be required by the due regard that must be had for the manner in which members' self-respect connects with the political conception of justice to which their sense of justice is oriented.

The frustration of legitimate expectations is generally recognized as an injustice.[53] Therefore the possibility of such frustration would also seem to provide reasons that may justify exclusion. The reason in this case appears to be quite strong, because the knowledge that one's legitimate expectations may be denied because of immigration might lead members to defect from their political obligations and to weaken their commitment to the state. For instance, if acknowledging the claims of a non-member would disrupt a member's legitimate expectations to receive certain forms of social entitlements under publicly recognized rules, then that is a consideration that must be taken into account and, all else equal, may justify exclusion.

Note that one of the most important claims that can be made based on legitimate expectations is that the state and its basic structure will continue to treat you as a member with standing to make claims that will be decided in accordance with the political conception of justice; that one need not fear being displaced from the state in favour of a newcomer. It may seem absurd to make this point, but this form of legitimate expectation must be a tacit premise in all discussions of partiality in justice in immigration governance. Otherwise, required or permissible partiality toward members would not establish that current members could not be replaced by new members, who would in turn enjoy the benefits (and share the burdens) of such partiality. From this basic expectation of continued membership, the exclusionary force of all other forms of putative partiality follow. Related to this point is that one has a legitimate expectation in the ongoing stability of the political conception of justice to which one is juridically integrated. This may be the most important form of legitimate expectation. Undermining this stability would be wrong because such political conceptions are great goods. However, such disruptions are also a potential injustice to each individual member.

A question might be asked at this point about the place of other forms of partiality that commonsense morality suggests we have. Do these have any exclusionary force? The answer is yes, they do, but only insofar as they are protected by the political conception of justice and, for this reason, give rise to legitimate expectations. Special responsibilities associated with families or various other forms of 'social unions'[54] create goods that may be a benefit to some and a burden to others. Accordingly, they lead to ways in which individuals may be injured and in that regard they are a proper subject for the state's political conception of justice. With respect to non-members of the state, claims based on such sub-state

[52] ibid at 275.
[53] ibid at 273; see also JS Mill, *Utilitarianism* (New York, Oxford University Press, 1998) 90; H Sidgwick, *The Methods of Ethics*, 7th edn (Indianapolis, Hackett, 1981) 271–73.
[54] Rawls, *Theory of Justice*, above n 39 at 460.

special relations justify only the forms of partiality discussed above. In particular, the question is whether there is a legitimate expectation that this or that special relationship, and the goods associated with it, would be protected within that conception. These remarks point to the many, many interests that legitimate expectations may protect and their considerable importance to questions of justice in immigration governance. Indeed, it points to the fact that it may be wrong to limit the range of possible claims made under the heading of legitimate expectations to those formally recognized under the rules of a political conception of justice and its basic structure. It may be that members also develop legitimate expectations in goods that flourish unmolested within a relatively just state. It at least does not seem absurd to suggest that this might be the case.

It can be seen that legitimate expectations might play a complex role in the examination of whether immigration restrictions are justified. Such expectations may operate at many levels. If the possible frustration of legitimate expectations looks like it may undermine the stability of the state's political conception of justice, then it seems that they would provide a strong reason to exclude. Short of this scenario, however, the reasons given are more equivocal. Exactly what counts as a legitimate expectation that would justify exclusion in the face of countervailing claims by migrants to be admitted needs to be worked out. There may need to be some sort of accommodation between the legitimate expectations of members and the claims of migrants in order to achieve just immigration governance. In seeking such an accommodation, another question of partiality arises, namely how to weigh members' legitimate expectations against the claims of migrants. Unfortunately, I make no further attempt to answer this difficult question. For the remainder of the essay, I will refer rather broadly to the need to respect members' legitimate expectations, without working out exactly what such respect might require.

IV. The Duty to Govern Immigration Rightfully

Recall from Chapter One Michael Walzer's idea that the question of who gets to be a member of a state appears to be a non-justiciable given: 'Across a considerable range of the decisions that are made, states are simply free to take in strangers (or not) [.]'[55] While the discussion in the last section identified some reasons that can be brought to bear in the justification of injuries arising from immigration governance, there has so far been no argument establishing that such reasons need to be given. In this section, returning again to the postulate of public right, I present the beginning of such an argument. Immigration regimes, like the states to which they are appended, must be rightful, that is, capable of having authority.

---

[55] M Walzer, *Spheres of Justice: A Defense of Pluralism and Equality* (New York, Basic Books, 1983) 61.

To be so capable, they must strive to be just, which implies that they must strive to ensure that their rules demonstrate reasonable as opposed to unreasonable preference.

Kant stresses often in his political writings that the circumstances of justice, circumstances where there is a potential for injury that cannot be resolved by resort to a common conception of the good, arise in part because of the inevitable fact of movement over and around a spherical world.[56] As a result, people 'stand in a community of possible physical interaction'.[57] When humans encounter one another on this sphere, they are duty-bound to enter a rightful condition. If no pre-existing rightful condition is in place, a state must be founded. The situation will be different, and more complicated, where a state already exists. Extant states have a moral standing, which must be respected, by virtue of having united the wills of their members into a general will. The demands of the postulate of public right must take this moral standing into account.

Cosmopolitan right is Kant's interpretation of what the postulate of public right demands when individual non-members encounter an already-established state. Kant holds that in such cases, the non-member enjoys a '*right of resort*' but not '*the right of a guest*', and that the

> natural right of hospitality, i.e. the right of strangers, does not extend beyond those conditions which make it possible for them to *attempt* to enter into relations with the native inhabitants. In this way, continents distant from each other can enter into peaceful mutual relations which may eventually be regulated by public laws, thus bringing the human race nearer and nearer to a cosmopolitan constitution.[58]

Under Kant's cosmopolitan right, there is no right to be made a guest, only a right of resort. Here resort means the chance to present oneself in the hope of establishing more robust relations of right. But such overtures can be rejected if strangers can be turned away without causing death; strangers also may not be plundered, enslaved, or otherwise treated with hostility.[59]

Arthur Ripstein has interpreted this account as grounded in Kant's own conception of the limits on our innate right to freedom. This right entitles us to use our bodies and our acquired rights to set and act on our own purposes. It does not, however, protect us from interferences that leave our purposiveness intact—that merely 'change the world' in which we act.[60] On Ripstein's reading, the division of the world into separate states simply changes the world in which people act. Therefore, while migrants are free to propose terms of interaction with states

---

[56] Kant, 'Perpetual Peace', above n 29 at 106; Kant, *Metaphysics of Morals*, above n 6 at 121–22 [6:352–53]. Waldron develops this aspect of Kant's theory in Waldron, 'What is Cosmopolitan?', above n 9.

[57] Kant, *Metaphysics of Morals*, above n 6 at [6:352].

[58] Kant, 'Perpetual Peace', above n 29 at 106.

[59] ibid at 105–106. For discussion of Kant's theory of cosmopolitan right, see Ripstein, *Force and Freedom*, above n 9 at 296–99; S Benhabib, *The Rights of Others: Aliens, Residents and Citizens* (Cambridge, Cambridge University Press, 2004) chapter one.

[60] Ripstein, *Force and Freedom*, above n 9 at 41.

that are not their own, residents of those states are 'free to accept or reject such invitations as they see fit'.[61]

I think that Kant's delineation of the requirements of cosmopolitan right is too modest and that Ripstein's interpretation of Kant is problematic. These disagreements, however, are worked out in Part Three, where I turn to the question of what justice in immigration governance requires. In this section I want simply to explain how one would derive such an account, which I call 'principled', from the postulate of public right. To provide this explanation, we need an account of the juridical nature of the individual act of immigration and of the function of immigration regimes.

1. The Juridical Nature of Migration

I begin by assuming a world that is divided into so many rightful conditions, non-ideal states each with its collection of members whose wills are juridically integrated into the imperfect political conception of justice of their own state. At the same time, each member of a given state is a non-member of every other state. Therefore, between each non-member and the states to which he or she does not belong there is a condition 'devoid of justice' where there is no authority to resolve disagreements about justice.

This is not a problem so long as each person exercises purposiveness inside his or her own state. They participate in the constitutional procedures through which the united general will is formed. They are motivated by a sense of justice that corresponds to the political conception of justice specified by that will. Disputes can be resolved by an authority representing a general will that includes every member's individual will. In the normal course, let us assume, they do not find themselves in relations of possible mutual injury, at least without going out of their way, with the members of other states.

But when a person redirects his or her purposive activity toward another state, lack of shared membership creates a predicament. That is because claims of justice made in such circumstances are not amenable to authoritative settlement. Importantly, oppression can occur even if the members or officials of either state act wholly in good faith, motivated by their sense of justice. Their senses of justice will have been developed within their home state and so may be incompatible. To avoid oppression, a form of negotiation must occur, a working out of what justice requires. The results of any such negotiation, however, will be tentative and insecure, barring some embracing general will.

Immigration represents a distinctive way of redirecting purposiveness toward another state and, hence, a distinctive predicament. The predicament arises because immigration is an attempt to exercise purposiveness by moving *physically* to another state. Through this physical relocation, the migrant comes to interact

---

[61] ibid at 296.

with a new set of proximate others in distinct ways, leading to new kinds of potential conflict, hence new potential insecurity.

The migrant is in a predicament because he or she has entered a condition in which his or her purposiveness is compromised, at least for a time. It is compromised immediately because the migrant's purpose, that is, immigration to a new state, is either directly interfered with or subject to the control of others with whom they are not juridically integrated. It is compromised in a less immediate way because other aspects of his or her purposiveness, the ability to acquire rights or to have rights protected, are less secure in the new society. Both kinds of compromise lead to the need for authoritative settlement.

Thus migrants' purposiveness can be threatened by the failure to resolve questions about immigration in one of two ways. Returning to the language of Chapter Two, there might be first-order indeterminacy about whether they ought to be admitted or allowed to remain, leading to threats to their ability to pursue life projects in a destination state. There will also be second-order indeterminacy relating to his or her other rights, in particular but not exclusively acquired rights of contract and property, within the destination state, as well as indeterminacy relating to his or her rights against enforcement actions by the receiving state or commutative wrongs by the members of that state. The migrant's insecurity is a function of these two orders of indeterminacy. The less settled his or her legal rights to be admitted or to remain are, the less settled his or her other legal rights will be.

The chief aim of migration is to pursue opportunities and other goods that cannot be accessed as easily or efficiently, or perhaps not at all, from abroad. That is, migrants seek to expand their range of purposiveness within the receiving state. Such expansion can take place by pursuing affective relationships, studying, earning wages, acquiring property, and so on: through the various activities through which you live your life. The illegal immigrant pursues these different aspects of human life under a shadow; the legal immigrant less so. Yet both legally admitted and illegal immigrants may face deportation. In both Canada and the United States new deportation grounds or procedures can be adopted with retroactive effect.[62] In the United States especially the grounds of deportation have swollen to a point that large numbers of immigrants are subject to deportation that may or may not be enforced; in practice that means that deportation may be carried out on a discretionary basis by immigration officials, with such discretionary deportation largely immune from constitutional review.[63] Within the receiving state, then,

---

[62] For the United States, see Neuman, 'Discretionary Deportation', above n 2 at 616; *Galvan v Press*, 347 US 522, 531 (1954) ('[W]hatever might have been said at an earlier date for applying the *ex post facto* Clause, it has been the unbroken rule of this Court that it has no application to deportation.') For Canada, see *Medovarski v Canada (Minister of Citizenship and Immigration); Esteban v Canada (Minister of Citizenship and Immigration)* [2005] 2 SCR 539 at para 47 ('There can be no expectation that the law will not change from time to time, nor did the Minister mislead Medovarski into thinking that her right of appeal would survive any change in the law.')

[63] See Neuman, 'Discretionary Deportation', above n 2.

migrants' purposiveness is made insecure by the discretionary deportation power that can be based on retroactive laws. Such insecurity can engender other kinds of insecurity, in particular vulnerability to exploitation.

The members of the receiving state are also in a predicament, although one mitigated by the stark power disparity between the migrant and the receiving state's legal system. Each individual migrant represents a small compromise of the established rightful condition.[64] This is so because they are not incorporated into the society's united general will and so may represent, unless some other ground of obligation might be found, a new form of insecurity for the rights of members, one which did not exist before the introduction of the alien element. Members cannot be sure that migrants have internalized the set of principles or judgements of justice associated with the state's political conception of justice. That makes interactions with them riskier. The potential threat is compounded by the fact that such migrants do not have as strong a reason as members to accept the authority of government in the case of an alleged infringement. The more immigrants there are, the greater the potential predicament. Such worries are no doubt often greatly exaggerated and provide the basis for much anti-immigrant xenophobia. Nonetheless, at the heart of such xenophobia there is a legitimate concern for security that can be explained in Kantian terms.[65]

2. The Function of Immigration Regimes

These twin predicaments can be resolved through juridical integration into the receiving state; that is, when the migrant becomes part of the united general will, motivated by a sense of justice the relevant particulars of which correspond to the senses of justice of other members and to the state's political conception of justice and basic structure. Alternatively, it may be resolved by having the migrant leave the receiving state, to return to the state of origin where he or she, hopefully, is still juridically integrated. The predicament is a moral one: how to restore and maintain a rightful condition. If either the members of the receiving state or the migrant declines to resolve it, they are guilty of 'wrong in the highest degree'.[66] There is a duty on the part of everyone involved, migrants and members, to resolve this mutual predicament, and a right to constrain others toward resolution.

In practice the enforcement of this right falls to the immigration regimes of receiving states. One practical reason for assigning this responsibility to states is that the members and officials of a receiving state will be best placed, including

---

[64] See the remarks by Gerald Gaus on temporary residents in G Gaus, *The Order of Public Reason* (New York, Cambridge University Press, 2011) 463–64. Gaus claims that with respect to temporary residents, the most we can hope for is legitimate coercion, not complete authority.

[65] This sort of predicament is well captured by Robert Nozick's discussion of the threat that independents pose to clients of a dominant protection agency in his argument for the justification of the state: Robert Nozick, *Anarchy, State, and Utopia* (New York, Basic Books, 1974) 54ff.

[66] Kant, *Metaphysics of Morals*, above n 6 at 86 [6:307–308].

by having more of the relevant information available, and motivated to put in place immigration laws and policies that will effectively support the stability of the receiving state's political conception of justice and that will respect existing members' legitimate expectations.

There are also two moral reasons. The first, connected with the practical reason just given, is provided by the simple fact that, perhaps other than for movement within the European Union by European nationals, state immigration regimes are the only likely source of authoritative governance of immigration.[67] The second reason is that each member is juridically integrated into the state confronted with the predicament of immigration. Accordingly, there is a strong reason to think members are entitled to participate in democratic political decision making regarding that political conception of justice.

These moral reasons do not seem decisive. Obviously, the first would no longer hold if states were to establish a rightful international regime for the regulation of immigration. The second moral reason given, like many discussions of the political morality of immigration governance, points us in the direction of something like a right to self-determination. But that members are entitled to a say in the laws and policies governing immigration into their state does not entail that others, and in particular migrants, ought not to have a say. It is therefore not clear that the right on the part of members is an exclusive right. Consider again the idea of the justified exclusion from political participation within a state of non-members to that state. I argued in the previous section that it was justified, in fact required, to exclude non-members from political participation in decision making concerning matters of the political conception of justice or the basic structure that are not potentially injurious to non-members. This argument relied on the claim that political participation by non-members would undermine the stability of the state's political conception of justice in such cases. However, when decisions made by members may injure non-members, a countervailing reason in favour of political inclusion arises. When the potential injury is sufficiently grave—perhaps, as Arash Abizadeh suggests, when it amounts to coercion[68]—then providing some form of political participation to non-members may be necessary. There may be an unavoidable tension between the moral requirement to give affected non-members a say and the moral requirement to ensure the stability of the state's political conception of justice.

That claims to self-determination do not establish that migrants should be excluded from political participation in the decisions made by immigration regimes can also be seen by noting that such decisions concern the make-up of the self-determining group. There are reasons for thinking that we do not view self-determination in the same light when such questions arise. I had no say about where I was born. Neither did other Canadians, apart from my parents. And I as

---

[67] J Finnis, *Natural Law and Natural Rights* (Oxford, Clarendon Press, 1980) 246.
[68] A Abizadeh, 'Democratic Theory and Border Coercion: No Right to Unilaterally Control Your Own Borders' (2008) 36 *Political Theory* 37.

a Canadian do not have any say about the reproductive decisions of my fellow members—about who else is born and their entitlement to membership. It might be objected that states do have discretion to establish policies about who ought to become citizens by birth, but most accept that such policies are constrained by considerations of justice. Further, the two kinds of policies generally accepted as just, *ius soli* and *ius sanguinis*, do not grant the kind of discretion that is claimed by absolutism in immigration governance. It might also be objected that this lack of say over other members' reproductive decisions is because reproductive freedom is basic and deserving of strong protection within a liberal constitutional democracy like Canada. That, however, does not explain why the children of such citizens themselves are entitled to become citizens. Also, at this point the debate has shifted to whether or not there is reproductive freedom, just as in immigration it shifts to the question of whether or not there should be freedom to migrate.[69] All this is simply meant to show that the way we regard self-determination seems different when it comes to the constitution of the population that is self-determining; that is, when it comes to determining the relevant set of selves. This difference, in turn, suggests the mere invocation of the right to self-determination does not establish an exclusive right on the parts of the members of receiving states to make decisions about immigration governance, the way there may be an exclusive right to participation with respect to wholly internal matters.[70]

More to the point, even if the balance of reasons favours exclusive control of immigration by the receiving state, as I will assume going forward (with the balance contingently tipped by feasibility considerations), a decision by an immigration regime that only takes into account the views and interests of its state's members may not be rightful unless the immigration laws and policies of that regime can be said to incorporate somehow the will of the migrants it purports to govern. The failure of immigration regimes to be capable of authority with respect to migrants would be a significant problem on the Kantian account, where the absence of authority perpetuates a condition devoid of justice. A necessary condition to avoid this result is that immigration regimes must strive to carry out their policies justly or non-oppressively by taking into account the interests

---

[69] The point that reproductive rights are the rights of members, and not of non-members, appears to be of only weak relevance here, as reproductive rights are often claimed to be an international human right: see UNHCR, 'UNHCR Note on Refugee Claims Based on Coercive Family Planning Laws or Policies' (Geneva, 2005). If reproductive rights are an international human right then, for example, on Christopher Heath Wellman's account, they may be among the rights that a legitimate state must respect in order to be entitled to self-determination: CH Wellman, 'Freedom of Association and the Right to Exclude' in CH Wellman and P Cole, *Debating the Ethics of Immigration: Is There a Right to Exclude?* (New York, Oxford University Press, 2012) 15–16. By parity of reasoning, it seems to follow that self-determination on Wellman's account cannot establish that immigration is not such a right.

[70] Besides Wellman, other authors have invoked self-determination as a basis for the right to exclude immigrants: Walzer, *Spheres of Justice*, above n 55; D Miller, 'Immigration: The Case for Limits' in AI Cohen and CH Wellman (eds), *Contemporary Debates in Applied Ethics* (Oxford, Blackwell, 2005); R Pevnick, *Immigration and the Constraints of Justice: Between Open Borders and Absolute Sovereignty* (Cambridge, Cambridge University Press, 2011).

and viewpoint of migrants, as it were, in trust. I set out part of the argument for this necessary condition here and complete it in Chapter Five. Before beginning, however, I note that we should not be surprised by the result: The principles of justice in immigration governance will have a significant impact on the lives of migrants, at least potentially a far greater impact than they would have on the lives of the members of a receiving state. It seems reasonable to suppose that the decision about what is required by justice in immigration should at a minimum take the interests of migrants into account. Having made that remark, I turn to the argument.

Recall that the postulate of public right is a response to the provisional nature of justice in the state of nature. The rights and duties of justice are provisional because of their indeterminacy, which leaves them open to individual judgement. Such judgements will inevitably differ, and no one in a condition devoid of justice has authority to impose his or her judgement on others. Insecurity results. In response to this difficulty, there is a duty with a correlative right of enforcement, to enter a rightful condition.

But, and here is the difficulty, this duty and correlative right of enforcement are themselves indeterminate. The indeterminacy comes into play in the means that can be used to bring about a rightful condition. It might be claimed that the duty is to submit to any efforts to establish a rightful condition or, conversely, to do whatever needs to be done. This claim cannot be correct. There can be no duty to acquiesce to evil or extreme violence, say ethnic cleansing or genocide, even if it might succeed in establishing a rightful condition.[71] This seems self-evidently true for the victims of such violence, but this judgement likely extends to those who are not the victims as well. Conversely there can be no duty to submit to violence that has no prospect of successfully establishing a rightful condition. In such cases, the postulate of public right is not engaged.

There are criteria, then, for the nature and degree of force that can be used to establish a rightful condition. The force must be enough to succeed, but not barbaric, brutal, inhumane, or otherwise extreme. This open-ended list of undefined negative qualifiers indicates the indeterminacy of such limits. In the standard case of the postulate, that is, the justification of states, this will present a quandary because there will be no authority to resolve the indeterminacy. While someone using violence to create a rightful condition may not be guilty of wrongdoing, neither would someone who resisted him or her if they believed the violence surpassed some threshold of barbarity or if they believed there was no actual prospect of success. Kant's claim that one commits wrong in the highest degree by

---

[71] Some Kant scholars argue that Kant would not require duty of obedience toward a murderous regime. Ripstein, for instance, distinguishes between despotism and barbarism, with obedience owed to despotic but not barbaric regimes. So the question is: What if barbarism is used along the way to a rightful condition? Ripstein, *Force and Freedom*, above n 9 at 336–43; W Kersting, 'Politics, Freedom, and Order: Kant's Political Philosophy' in P Guyer (ed), *The Cambridge Companion to Kant* (New York, Cambridge University Press, 1992) 342, 361.

refusing to enter into a rightful condition seems to lead to a paradox. It may not be wrong to commit this highest wrong.

The fact that there can be no authority during the founding moment of a rightful condition suggests it will be a moment of heightened insecurity and uncertainty. Therefore there must also be a duty to minimize and abbreviate this initial exercise of arbitrary violence. It must be minimized because force beyond what is necessary would be unjustified, and excessive violence is itself an injustice. It must also be minimized so as not to give rise to historical grievances that undermine joint commitment among members. To be sure, it is well known that Kant says that inquiry into the historical wrongs committed during the founding of a state is off limits:

> It is *futile* to inquire into the *historical warrant* of the mechanism of government, that is, one cannot reach back to the time at which civil society began ... But it is *punishable* to undertake this inquiry with a view to possibly changing by force the constitution that now exists.[72]

We do not need to say Kant is wrong to make the point that a historical grievance, dating back to the moment of founding, will be destabilizing going forward. Resentments may endure for decades or centuries. Surely it is better to reduce such destabilizing forces at the time of founding a state than to suppress it after the fact. Further, the moment of violence is abbreviated so that the period of uncertainty does not last longer than it must. The duties to minimize and abbreviate have the same source as the postulate of public right, namely the duty to create and ensure conditions under which stable relations of justice with others are possible through time. After a contained moment of violence, there must be a period of rightful ascension to a full state, continuous with later ongoing efforts to live up to the ideal of the original contract.[73]

In the non-standard case of immigration, that means facing up to the fact that the initial moment of encounter between the migrant and the immigration regime of the receiving state is one of violence. But this moment of violence must be minimized and abbreviated: no more force than necessary, for no longer than necessary. The remainder of the immigration process must be made part of a rightful condition in which the immigration regime seeks to act as an authority, relying on a general will that hypothetically includes the migrant. This requires that members, judges, officials, and legislators of the receiving state promulgate and enforce immigration laws and policies that they consider justifiable to reasonable migrants as well as to reasonable members. To do so, they must adopt a suitably impartial perspective, viewing matters of immigration governance 'neither from our own place nor yet from his ... but from the place and with the eyes

---

[72] Kant, *Metaphysics of Morals*, above n 6 at 111–12 [6:339–40].

[73] Compare what Rawls says about non-ideal theory in J Rawls, *The Law of Peoples* (Cambridge, MA, Harvard University Press, 1999) 89: Non-ideal theory 'looks for policies and courses of action that are morally permissible and politically possible and likely to be effective'. The creation of a rightful condition seems to be a special instance of non-ideal theory.

of a third person, who has no particular connexion with either, and who judges with impartiality between us'.[74] If this is not done, migrants will have no reason to accept the authority of those laws.

The postulate of public right, therefore, imposes what we might call a condition of rightful non-oppression on immigration regimes. They must govern rightfully. To do that, they must strive to govern justly. Meeting this demand in the case of immigration regimes presents unique challenges. The first is the sheer complexity of the judgement or judgements required, in weighing the potential impact of immigration on the stability of a state's political conception of justice and the legitimate expectations of its members, not to mention any other considerations that might legitimately come into play. The second is the obstacles to providing such judgement in a manner that could be considered authoritative. Immigration regimes are liminal, that is, their subjects are non-members whose senses of justice do not share an orientation with the members of the states to which they wish to immigrate; they are governed through status; and they are without institutional means for political participation by migrants. Further, placing the heterogeneous, transient population of migrants under a united general will seems especially difficult. In the next section, I say more about the problem of governing through status. I take up the other features of immigration governance and how they can be overcome in meeting the condition of non-oppression in Chapter Five, where I describe how immigration regimes can be made capable of having authority.

V. Immigration Regimes as Status Regimes

Most laws in liberal democratic legal systems apply equally regardless of status: everyone enjoys, or is said to enjoy, the status of a free and equal member. For his part, Kant says citizens[75] regard themselves as being 'of equally high birth' and also as superior to those who choose to continue in a state of lawless freedom.[76] A full citizen will be someone who 'wants to be not just a part of the commonwealth but also a member of it, that is, a part of the commonwealth acting from his own choice in community with others'.[77] That is, a citizen is someone whose sense of justice is integrated with a state's political conception of justice.

Kant excludes large groups of 'dependent persons' from the privileged category of full citizen because, it seems, he thinks they will be unable to so engage. Such 'passive citizens' have no 'right to manage the state itself as *active* members

---

[74] Smith, *Theory of Moral Sentiments*, above n 41 at 157 [III.iii.3].
[75] Note that in this section I use 'citizen' rather than 'member' to accord with Kant's usage.
[76] Kant, *Metaphysics of Morals*, above n 6 at 114 [6:343].
[77] ibid at 91–92 [6:314]; see also Kant, 'Theory and Practice', above n 27 at 74. For discussion, see Jacob Weinrib, 'Kant on Citizenship and Universal Independence' (2008) 33 *Australian Journal of Legal Philosophy* 1.

of it, the right to organize it or to cooperate for introducing certain laws'.[78] He infamously sweeps women into this category, along with apprentices, servants, woodcutters, and blacksmiths in India. To these he adds only two groups we might take seriously today, children and criminals.[79] Such persons are defined by their 'lack' of 'civil personality'.[80]

All this is relevant because the assignment of differential legal status is a core strategy in immigration governance. In this section I explore the implications of this strategy, drawing on Kant's discussion of status. Once again, Kant is useful because of an omission by Rawls. Rawls dismisses the idea of unequal status as 'close to being wrong and unjust in itself in that in a status system, not everyone can have the highest rank'.[81] He generally assumes that all members are 'normal cooperating members'[82] and so never directly confronts the problem of how to govern a status society in just terms, apart from his discussion of children.[83] There are no 'passive citizens' in Rawls's theory. But of course that theory nonetheless does imply a status, between membership and non-membership in a closed society, entered only at birth and exited only at death. Part of the task we are left with, once the presumption of a closed society is lifted in order to conduct the inquiry into justice in immigration governance, is how to make sense of this differential status between member and non-member.

I explain first the way status is assigned in immigration law. I then provide what I take to be the most defensible explanation for assigning status. Finally, I describe the implications of this view for the principled interpretation of discretion in immigration law.

1. Status in the Governance of Immigration

'Migrant' is a lesser political status than 'citizen', characterized by lack of access to the national vote, denial of or restrictions on mobility into a country, and other limitations on rights and benefits compared to members. Migrants, that is, are passive citizens relative to a destination state.

Immigration regimes make further status distinctions between permanent and temporary migrants. These are broken down into even more specialized statuses. Permanent migrants subdivide into economic migrants, family migrants, and

---

[78] Kant, *Metaphysics of Morals*, above n 6 at 92 [6:315].

[79] On children: '[T]hese are mere underlings of the commonwealth because they have to be under the direction or protection of other individuals, and so do not possess civil independence.' See ibid at 92 [6:315]. On criminals, see ibid at 92 [6:314]. For Kant's discussion of criminals, see also ibid at 66 [6:283] (those who commit crimes may become slaves) and ibid at 104 [6:329–30] ('Certainly no human being in a state can be without any dignity, since he at least has the dignity of a citizen. The exception is someone who has lost it by his own *crime*, because of which, though he is kept alive, he is made a mere tool of another's choice (either of the state or of another citizen).')

[80] ibid at 92 [6:314].

[81] Rawls, *Justice as Fairness*, above n 4 at 131.

[82] ibid at 18.

[83] ibid at 165; Rawls, 'The Idea of Public Reason Revisited' in *Collected Papers*, above n 4 at 598–99.

refugees. Temporary migrants are typically categorized as guestworkers, students, visitors, tourists, and so on. 'Statuses package certain arrays of rights, duties, etc. under the auspices of a certain entrenched and ongoing concern in the law.'[84] These rights etc allow the receiving state's immigration regime to ensure the migrant carries out the activities that provide the policy rationale for admission. This can be illustrated by several examples. Students' rights of admission are tied to the length of their academic programme and they are generally not allowed to work off campus. When a migrant is admitted because he or she is married to a citizen, most countries impose a requirement that the couple remain married for a certain length of time. The rights attached to economic migrants will vary in accordance with the economic purposes underlying their admission.

The predicament faced by states when governing immigration is the challenge of maintaining the stability of their political conception of justice when confronted with an influx of outsiders who do not share members' sense of justice. Immigration regimes address this predicament by excluding some migrants and transforming those who are admitted into a population of unequal insiders. This governing strategy transforms the predicament into a new one. It now becomes the problem of how to maintain a rightful regime with such a population; how to avoid becoming a caste society without authority over the lower castes.

2. Justifying Immigration Status

The governance of migrants through status has been remarked upon and criticized, most famously by Michael Walzer: 'No community can be half-metic, half-citizen and claim that its admissions policies are acts of self-determination or that its politics is democratic.'[85] This proposition is the conclusion of his criticism of guestworker programmes that grant access to jobs but deny full rights of membership.[86] As I noted in Chapter Two, however, guestworker programmes remain a favoured policy option. Some philosophers have attempted to define terms for them that avoid Walzer's criticisms. For example, Ryan Pevnick has argued that having a humane guestworker programme that protects basic rights is the best moral option for the United States in light of the inevitably large number of Mexican workers seeking to immigrate for jobs and the history of injustice through which the US–Mexico border was drawn. In any event, he notes:

> [I]t is unlikely that foreign workers would prefer a system that promised full legal rights, but accepted very few (thus ushering many into illegal immigration) to a relatively humane guest-worker program that allowed entry for enough to satiate labor demand.[87]

Walzer's point is that differences in status can give rise to exploitation and domination. Pevnick seeks to provide the parameters for a guestworker programme

---

[84] J Waldron, *Dignity, Rank, and Rights* (New York, Oxford University Press, 2012) 73, n 34.
[85] Walzer, *Spheres of Justice*, above n 55 at 62.
[86] ibid at 56–62.
[87] Pevnick, *Immigration*, above n 70 at 179.

that avoids this problem. Thus the academic philosophical literature on immigration governance is already wrestling with the problem of when imposition of unequal status leads to oppression.

Kant provides only Delphic guidance. He says passive citizens have the right to be treated 'in accordance with the laws of natural freedom and equality as *passive* parts of the state'.[88] This right seems to have two components. The first is that the state must still treat them in accordance with their 'freedom and equality as *human beings*'.[89] I take this condition to correspond to what I mean when I say a regime must strive to be non-oppressive—it must seek not to injure passive citizens unjustifiably—in accordance with their status as free and equal persons, as opposed to being free and equal members. But, in keeping with the postulate of public right, decisions about immigration governance must also be made rightfully. That in turn requires imposing laws that migrants, albeit as passive citizens, could recognize as having authority, as though they were part of the general will. Political decisions must be made in trust, that is, on terms a migrant or migrants could have reasonably consented to.[90]

Kant's second condition is that each passive citizen must be given the opportunity to 'work his [or her] way up from this passive condition into an active one'.[91] This condition if defensible has obvious implications for immigration governance. It cannot, though, be a requirement in all cases of status because it is sometimes either justifiably disregarded or incapable of being met. There are some crimes whose commission may allow for punishments, such as execution[92] or life imprisonment without parole, that preclude the possibility of return to full citizenship status. Other status distinctions simply cannot be shed, as when an adult is declared mentally incompetent. In the case of immigration governance, it must be established whether transition to full citizenship is required and upon what conditions.

Giving content to Kant's opaque suggestions requires first a few remarks about status generally. The most important demand advanced by liberal theory, committed as it is to an ideal of reciprocal justification to individuals of social arrangements, is that status be if not justified then at least justifiable to each status holder, at least in principle (a qualifier necessary because of the case of children and the mentally incompetent). The rights and duties that attach to unequal statuses must be explained by a reason or set of reasons relating to the condition of status holders.[93] That is, they must rest on some justifiable distinction such as

---

[88] Kant, *Metaphysics of Morals*, above n 6 at 92 [6:315].

[89] ibid.

[90] For the idea of trust in relations of status, see Ripstein, *Force and Freedom,* above n 9 at 70–81.

[91] Kant, *Metaphysics of Morals*, above n 6 at 92 [6:315].

[92] I stress the 'may'. Kant himself believed that murderers must be executed and that it would be permissible to reduce convicted thieves to the 'status of slave ... permanently if the state sees fit': ibid at 106–107 [6:333–34]. This suggests that the condition that passive citizens be able to work their way up to active citizenship was not universal.

[93] Such a reason or reasons ought to explain 'how the various rights, duties, etc. hang together'. Waldron, *Dignity, Rank, and Rights*, above n 84 at 73, fn 34.

immaturity, past criminal behaviour, or the demonstrated inability to look after one's finances.[94]

Status explanations must be contextually confined. Employers and employees have unequal status in the workplace, but that ought to have no impact on their status with respect to a political authority or their family. Bankrupts have an unequal status within the market but, again, that does not affect their status as voters or as fathers and mothers. It seems that changes in status in one domain of activity ought not in general to imply changes in status in another without some explanation as to why. One form of status that does seem to impart inequality across a range of domains is the status of children. However, even in the case of children the incidents of status will differ in each domain because the facts justifying differential status may have different implications for different sorts of human activity. Within a family, children's immaturity demands that parents 'preserve and care' for them and also that parents have the right to 'manage and develop' them.[95] Those in a position of political as opposed to parental authority have a different set of rights and duties relative to children. Such duties may include the provision of public education, child welfare laws, and special criminal justice regimes for the young. The point is to look for context-specific reasons that justify the unequal status of children within the family, the market, the political domain, or any other identifiable domain of activity.

The best justification for the unequal status of migrants, under the Kantian argument provided in this chapter, is that it is a reasonable assumption that migrants will not ordinarily be, prior to admission, juridically integrated into the receiving state's political conception of justice and that such juridical integration can only take place over time as the migrant becomes immersed in sympathetic interactions with the members of the receiving state. Until integration has occurred, migrants, like all non-members, are justifiably excluded from the united general will because their senses of justice may not be in sufficient substantive accord with that of citizens and/or they are unlikely to be sufficiently committed to the state's political conception of justice to be given a say along with citizens in determining how it and the rules of the basic structure are to evolve.

To move up to the status of free and equal citizen, migrants must come to identify with the receiving state's political conception of justice, as instantiated through the institutional rules of its basic structure. Once this condition is met and they are juridically integrated, they will be qualified to actively engage in the general will and, so long as they are proximate, the necessary and sufficient conditions of membership are met. Exclusion from membership past this point constitutes an injury and, all else equal, would seem to be unjustifiable because

---

[94] There are difficult questions here about whether the justification ought to be addressed to status holders as they are or to 'reasonable' status holders. These issues are most difficult for status holders who have some sort of mental impairment. Since mental impairment does not characterize migrants as a class, I avoid this issue.

[95] Kant, *Metaphysics of Morals*, above n 6 at 64–65 [6:280–6:281]. See T Schapiro, 'What is a Child?' (1999) 109 *Ethics* 715.

of the damage such exclusion would cause to the former migrant's self-respect. Access to the political process and other forms of required partiality may be required, most likely through naturalization, unless some non-oppressive partici-patory scheme that does not require naturalization is developed or unless there is some overriding justification that makes exclusion of the juridically integrated migrant defensible.

3. Status and Discretion in Immigration Governance

Return now to the question of discretion. The principled account of the natural duty of justice instructs that discretion in immigration is to be interpreted as the discretion to govern immigration rightfully and non-oppressively, where the decision as to what counts as oppressive is made on behalf of both members and migrants, with the latter represented in trust. Therefore the discretion over immi-gration governance, to be rightful, must be interpreted as the discretion to exercise judgement about what kinds of governance will be oppressive and to avoid these. This condition of non-oppression applies as a general matter and, more specifi-cally, in the way that different statuses are defined through the assigning of rights and duties.

Thus on the principled account, immigration regimes have power, within limits set by the condition of non-oppression, to establish different forms of status as a means of governing migrants. That implies a power to take into account the pur-poses of the migrant in assigning rights and duties to him or her. It also implies a discretion to decide whether or not, through the assignation of such rights and duties, the aim of physical admission is the juridical integration of the migrant and to decide, also within the limits set by the condition of non-oppression, what rules of status to impose so that integration does or does not occur. There is nothing in the Kantian argument developed thus far that specifies who must be admitted indefinitely or the conditions of temporary or indefinite admission.

The grant of permanent status suggests a migrant has been deemed a candi-date for juridical integration. Such a decision might be made on several different grounds. The migrant might be thought likely to integrate successfully because of his or her economic prospects or his or her family ties. Such non-juridical factors can play a role in predicting whether a migrant can come to identify with a receiv-ing state's political conception of justice. However different statuses are ultimately designed, the incidents of status must suitably reflect the grounds for granting a person admission and some reasonable assessment of how long juridical integra-tion will take. Temporary statuses, on the other hand, reflect a judgement that a migrant should not, or maybe not yet, be a candidate for juridical integration. The conditions imposed on them ought to reflect this aim, but once again the condition of non-oppression must be met. Finally, if a temporary migrant does become juridically integrated then equal political participation and other forms of partiality must be extended, likely through naturalization. Anything else would unjustifiably injure migrants' self-respect. This implies that there is a degree to which states do not have control over who among admitted migrants become members. It should be emphasized, however, that such juridical control is not entirely in the migrant's control either.

VI. Moving on

I have argued that Kant's postulate of public right establishes a duty to govern immigration rightfully and, hence, to strive to govern it non-oppressively. In making judgements about what would or would not count as oppression in immigration law, immigration regimes must consider on the one hand migrants' viewpoint and interests and on the other the impact such immigration would have on the stability of the political conception of justice within the receiving state and the legitimate expectations of members formed under that conception; note that I have not yet considered whether these are the only considerations that must be taken into account. In carrying out this difficult judgement (or these difficult judgements), the members, legislators, judges, and officials in the receiving state are required to show reasonable partiality toward their fellow members, institutionalized by governing immigration through a regime of differential status. I call this related set of propositions the principled account of discretion over immigration governance.

Two things should be noted in closing this long chapter. The first is that the principled account, abstract as it is, does not address many of the issues that divide different accounts of justice in immigration governance currently in circulation. It also does not establish that inegalitarian immigration law and policies are unprincipled. Until we flesh out what principle requires in immigration governance, the only thing that seems incompatible with the principled account is the specific absolutist claim that immigration regimes can have authority without striving to be just. But, and this is the second closing point, no argument against this variant of absolutism has been given. While it seems to follow from the postulate of public right that to be rightful immigration regimes must strive to be just, it has not been shown that they cannot have authority without so striving. I provide such negative arguments over the remainder of Part Two. In Chapter Four, I show that two apparently strong philosophical versions of absolutism ultimately give way to principled accounts. In Chapter Five, I argue that an absolutist immigration regime would be incapable of having authority over migrants.

4

Two Absolutism

I. Introduction

CONTRARY TO THE principled account developed in the last chapter, absolutism in immigration governance claims that immigration regimes can have authority even if they do not strive to be just. Up to now, however, I have provided an affirmative case for the principled account but not a negative argument against absolutism. In this chapter I examine two potential philosophical defences of absolutism that sound in legitimacy, not political obligation, and argue that they cannot be sustained.

Absolutism must be taken seriously in part because it accords with a body of law and practice offering the basis for an interpretation of discretion in immigration law that competes with the principled account. It is at least plausible to claim that the overall immigration policy profile of most wealthy liberal constitutional democracies conforms to what Martin Ruhs and Ha-Joon Chang call 'consequentialist nationalism', in which immigration policy is determined solely 'by an assessment of their impact on (suitably weighted) economic efficiency, distribution, and national identity in the receiving country'.[1] We might say that states often govern immigration *as if* absolutism were a defensible political–moral stance. It is important to see whether that is indeed the case.

The interpretive case in favour of absolutism would include the strongest statements of the discretionary power over immigration, such as the majority decisions in *Nishimura*[2] and *Fong Yue Ting*.[3] Such early pronouncements of absolutism were often made to uphold the racist exclusion of Chinese and other Asian immigrants. Even though such policies are today discredited, the strong statements from the early case law continue to ground an absolutist claim to authority. They provide a defence not just of policies of admission and exclusion, but also of expulsion, detention, procedure, and indeed all aspects of first-order and second-order immigration governance necessary to put today's inegalitarian admissions

---

[1] M Ruhs and H-J Chang, 'The Ethics of Labor Immigration Policy' (2004) 58 *International Organization* 69, 85–86 and 92.
[2] *Nishimura Ekiu v United States*, 142 US 651 (1892).
[3] *Fong Yue Ting v United States*, 149 US 698 (1893).

policies into effect. Here the absolutist can argue that our fixed judgements regarding oppression in immigration, listed in Chapter Two, are recognized only in the breach. It is the persistent pattern of violations that provides the crucial moral data, not our qualms about such breaches. Immigration regimes routinely carry out policies and decisions that result in oppression. This suggests a further fixed judgement that such action is legitimate.

Absolutism as a policy ethos may reach its apogee in efforts to manage inflows of asylum seekers using strategies to discourage migrants from claiming asylum. It is a matter of broad consensus that refugees having a well-founded fear of persecution ought not to be sent back to countries from which they flee and thus should be admitted, if only temporarily. Yet constitutional liberal democracies and other states pursue a wide variety of tactics to discourage asylum claims or to make it harder to successfully pursue them. Such tactics often take the form of procedural manipulation, for example, by abbreviating filing deadlines, expediting hearings, eliminating appeal rights, designating safe countries of origin or safe third countries, interdicting potential claimants prior to their arrival, or creating 'excision' zones deemed beyond the sovereign territory of a receiving state. Once procedures are weakened past a certain point there will be no assurance that the exercise of power will comply with whatever substantive standards of justifiability are in place, in this case the standards set out in the 1951 *Convention Relating to the Status of Refugees*, together with its 1967 *Protocol*.[4] For example, at least some of the 119,520 asylum seekers who have been interdicted on the high seas by the US Coast Guard since 1981 are likely to have been refugees toward whom international obligations apply.[5] Yet, even with on-board screening, interdiction policies return all or most such asylum seekers to their home countries. As procedures become weaker, refugee law approaches an absolutist policy that requires no justifications to be made.[6]

The most uncompromising philosophical defence of absolutism in immigration that I have found can be extracted from the work of Carl Schmitt, the National Socialist jurisprude. For Schmitt, the purpose of immigration governance is to prevent heterogeneity, an aim to be accomplished by the designation of certain migrants (or members) as strangers or enemies and excluding or expelling them. Schmitt sees such designation as necessarily political and incapable of normative regulation. Indeed, designation of an enemy entails the

---

[4] *Convention Relating to the Status of Refugees* (adopted 28 July 1951, entered into force 22 April 1954) 189 UNTS 137, art 33. See also the *Protocol Relating to the Status of Refugees* (adopted 31 January 1967, entered into force 4 October 1967) 606 UNTS 267.

[5] See US Coast Guard, 'Alien Migrant Interdiction: Calendar Year 1982 to Present', available at: www.uscg.mil/hq/cg5/cg531/AMIO/FlowStats/FY.asp. Data is given per year, and I have summed the total myself.

[6] See TM Scanlon, 'Due Process' in *The Difficulty of Tolerance: Essays in Political Philosophy* (Cambridge, Cambridge University Press, 2003) 44. ('Thus, beyond the requirement of institutions that the power they confer be morally justifiable, there is the further moral requirement that there be some effective guarantee that these powers will be exercised only within the limits and subject to the conditions implied by their justification.')

possibility of killing them.[7] On this view immigration governance takes place in a norm-free zone, allowing (to use Schmitt's two examples) for the mass expulsion from Turkey of ethnic Greek citizens and the racist exclusion carried out in the early twentieth century under the White Australia policy. Both of these would today be considered contrary to international law, yet Schmitt clearly sees them as legitimate.[8] Now I do not want to dismiss Schmitt out of hand. The justice or injustice of the policies he mentions has not been explored. Further, Schmitt's idea of immigration occurring in a norm-free zone seems consonant, in a limited way, with the recognition in the last chapter that the initial encounter between a migrant and his or her destination state is one of violence. However, Schmitt's anti-liberalism is in an important way contrary to this decidedly liberal inquiry and his vision of politics is exactly contrary to the ideal of reciprocity that is being used as a guide. To respond to his views would therefore take us too far afield. For that reason, I will not further explore his version of absolutism.[9]

Instead I explicate and offer considerations against what appear to be the more moderate, broadly liberal[10] absolutist accounts provided by Michael Walzer and

---

[7] Schmitt's brief discussion of immigration and emigration policy comes in his preface to the second edition of Schmitt, E Kennedy trans, *The Crisis of Parliamentary Democracy* (Cambridge, MA, MIT Press, 1985) 9: 'Every actual democracy rests on the principle that not only are equals equal but unequals will not be treated equally. Democracy requires, therefore, first homogeneity and second—if the need arises—elimination or eradication of heterogeneity. To illustrate this principle it is sufficient to name two different examples of modern democracy: contemporary Turkey, with its radical expulsion of the Greeks and its reckless Turkish nationalization of the country, and the Australian commonwealth, which restricts unwanted entrants through its immigration laws, and like other dominions only takes emigrants who conform to the notion of a 'right type of settler.' A democracy demonstrates its political power by knowing how to refuse or keep at bay something foreign and unequal that threatens its homogeneity.' That Schmitt cited these examples not just as evidence for a descriptive argument but as support for a normative claim is to be inferred from his larger work. For Schmitt, decisions on immigration would have been one manifestation of the kinds of political decisions needed to maintain the vitality of the state. Political decisions are characterized by the designation of individuals as 'friends' or 'enemies' where the enemy is 'simply the Other, the Alien': C Schmitt, 'Der Begriff des Politischen' (1927) 58 *Archiv für Sozialwissenschaft* 4 cited in E Scheuerman, *Carl Schmitt: The End of Law* 44 (Lanham, MD, Rowman & Littlefield, 1999). Schmitt later developed this idea in Schmitt, G Schwab trans, *The Concept of the Political* (Chicago, University of Chicago Press, 1976). There he made clear that to designate someone as an enemy entails the possibility of killing them in a norm-free zone, the state of exception. See Schmitt, G Schwab trans, *Political Theology: Four Chapters on the Concept of Sovereignty* (Cambridge, MA, MIT Press, 1985).

[8] On mass expulsion, see R Higgins, 'The Right in International Law of an Individual to Enter, Stay in and Leave a Country' (1973) 49 *International Affairs* 341, 351: 'What is not permissible is for a government to order the mass expulsion of a group of persons for discriminatory reasons. One can sympathise with the desire for Africanisation in newly independent African nations. But let it be said that Amin's expulsion of 40,000 Asians, simply on account of their Indian origin and because they held an important position in the commercial life of Uganda, was illegal.' On racial discrimination, see G Goodwin-Gill, *International Law and the Movement of Persons between States* (Oxford, Clarendon Press, 1978) 85: 'In racial matters, non-discrimination has a normative character and may be adjudged a part of *jus cogens*.'

[9] For discussion of Schmitt in the context of a philosophical exploration of immigration law, see B Schotel, *On the Right of Exclusion: Law, Ethics and Immigration Policy* (Abingdon, Routledge, 2012) 75ff.

[10] While it is no doubt true that 'Walzer's liberalism is indeed of a very different character from much that has passed under that name in recent political theory' (D Miller, 'Introduction' in M Walzer, *Thinking Politically: Essays in Political Theory* (New Haven, Yale University Press, 2007) xi), it is also clear that Walzer would be considered a liberal from the Schmittian perspective.

Thomas Nagel. I use the 'what appear to be' qualifier because I argue that their seemingly strong statements in favour of absolutism are unsustainable and in both cases shade into a principled account. The reason for this is that absolutist claims must recognize certain minimal moral conditions to be legitimate; in terms of the list presented in Chapter Two, we would say they need to reflect at least some of our judgements about oppression in immigration law. Once this minimal moral move is made, it is difficult to resist a shift to principled immigration governance. After setting out the absolutist position in schematic form in Section Two, I turn in Section Three to Walzer's arguments and in Section Four to Nagel's.

II. An Absolutist Schematic

Absolutism in immigration, as a philosophical position, subscribes to the following claim:

> (1) Obligations of social justice toward migrants do not constrain the governance of immigration.

The core difference between the absolutist and principled accounts is that absolutism denies immigration governance must be guided by a scheme of principle that aims to eliminate social injustice or oppression. Thus absolutism is distinct from principled arguments for strict limits on immigration. David Miller, for example, who defends the right of states to impose restrictive immigration policies, nonetheless says: 'Potential immigrants have a *claim* to be let in—if nothing else they usually have a strong *desire* to enter—and so any state that wants to control immigration must have good reasons for doing so.'[11] Miller's argument, in my vocabulary, is that significant restrictions on immigration are justified, even if they cause injury, and therefore are not oppressive. In a similar vein, Christopher Heath Wellman has argued that there is a right, derivative from a state's members' right to freedom of association, to exclude all migrants. This right is only presumptive and can be outweighed by other concerns, although Wellman expresses strong scepticism that there will be any interests sufficient to outweigh the right to freedom of association.[12] Both these positions are quite different from absolutism, which claims a lack of principle at the core of the political morality of immigration governance.

---

[11] D Miller, 'Immigration: The Case for Limits' in AI Cohen and CH Wellman (eds), *Contemporary Debates in Applied Ethics* (Oxford, Blackwell, 2005) 199; see also D Miller, 'Immigration, Nations, and Citizenship' (2008) 16 *Journal of Political Philosophy* 371, as well as Miller's discussion of immigration in D Miller, *On Nationality* (Oxford, Clarendon Press, 1995) 128–30.

[12] CH Wellman, 'Freedom of Association and the Right to Exclude' in CH Wellman and P Cole, *Debating the Ethics of Immigration: Is There a Right to Exclude?* (New York, Oxford University Press, 2012) 54–55.

If absolutism is taken to mean there is nothing that we are not prohibited from doing to migrants, it is not plausible. It runs into an argument of the following sort, which Justice Stephen Field made in a dissenting opinion in *Fong Yue Ting*. Against the majority's holding that Congress could direct any Chinese labourer removed from the country without judicial trial or examination, Justice Field objected:

> According to this theory, Congress might have ordered executive officers to take the Chinese laborers to the ocean and put them into a boat and set them adrift; or to take them to the borders of Mexico and turn them loose there; and in both cases without any means of support; indeed, it might have sanctioned towards these laborers the most shocking brutality conceivable. I utterly repudiate all such notions, and reply that brutality, inhumanity, and cruelty cannot be made elements in any procedure for the enforcement of the laws of the United States.[13]

Once social injustice is allowed, 'brutality, inhumanity, and cruelty' follow. Because brutality is an unacceptable feature of the law, the absolutist position cannot be correct. That is Justice Field's argument.

A Schmittian absolutism might accept the possibility of brutality in immigration governance. A more plausible absolutism might alternatively try to contain such morally unacceptable implications by showing that social injustice does not lead to brutality. This can be done by showing that proposition (1) is consistent with something like the following proposition:

> (2) Moral obligations other than obligations of social justice toward migrants may constrain immigration governance. Such obligations may include: (a) obligations of justice toward members; (b) obligations of humanity or other forms of minimal morality toward members or non-members, including migrants; (c) obligations of personal (that is, not social) justice toward migrants; or (d) obligations of virtue of individual legislators, officials, judges or members, for instance, to show compassion.

This approach has some explanatory power. For example (2a) may explain family admissions and the judgement some hold that racial discrimination in immigration admissions are wrong; (2b) may explain refugee admissions; (2c) may explain international and domestic efforts to combat the trafficking of migrants, although it seems to depend on a strong distinction between personal and social injustice that I have denied; and (2d) may explain why sometimes states seem to go beyond these minimal obligations, for example, Canada's codification of a means to apply for permanent residence on 'humanitarian and compassionate' grounds.[14]

---

[13] *Fong Yue Ting*, above n 3 at 756 (1893) (Field J, dissenting). See also *Shaughnessy v United States ex rel Mezei*, 345 US 206, 226–27 (1953) (per Jackson J, dissenting) for a similar kind of argument: 'Because the respondent has no right of entry, does it follow that he has no rights at all? Does the power to exclude mean that exclusion may be continued or effectuated by any means which happen to seem appropriate to the authorities? It would effectuate his exclusion to eject him bodily into the sea or to set him adrift in a rowboat.'

[14] *Immigration and Refugee Protection Act*, SC 2001, c 27, s 25.

A further possible proposition is that:

> (3) There are obligations of justice toward migrants, but not with respect to immigration matters. Such obligations may relate to (a) non-migration aspects of international or global justice or (b) aspects of domestic justice that do not relate to immigration.

As to (3a), perhaps absolutism might deny the possibility of justice in war and other aspects of international or global justice, but it would seem more plausible if it admitted some such principles of justice beyond the state. For its part, (3b) would explain why there may be obligations to provide migrants the same sort of rights as members within the criminal justice system, why migrants may own property, and may sue or be sued in private law. It may also explain why some public entitlements are made available to them, if they are.

Finally, there is a fourth possible proposition that might be held by an absolutist:

> (4) There is an obligation to govern immigration through law.

As Bas Schotel has noted, it is not self-evident that immigration should be governed through law: '[A]uthorities … might have opted for just putting up fences and giving orders to their officials to keep out aliens by all means not prohibited by law.'[15] The decision to govern immigration through law may have normative significance. Whether it does depends on one's theory of law, and in particular, on how closely linked one considers the law and justice to be. It will make a difference whether one believes that legal forms only require formal justice, treating like cases alike, or something more substantial. In the next chapter, I argue that it is significant that immigration regimes hold themselves out to be legal regimes. To be consistent with this self-representation, they must strive to be just. However, I do not further explore the requirements of legality in immigration governance.

Any absolutist theory that embraces some propositions falling under (2), (3), or (4) would have to defend their consistency with (1). The possibility of a theory that succeeded in doing so offers a further reason to take absolutism seriously. It may be possible to argue that some forms of oppression in immigration governance are permissible, even inevitable, without opening the door to brutality, without acquiescing to international or global injustice or the unjust treatment of resident aliens, and without forsaking legal governance. I will argue, however, that neither Walzer nor Nagel, who both moderate their absolutism with principles that fall under (2) or (3) but bypass the question of legality that would fall under (4), succeed in presenting an internally consistent and sustainable absolutism. Their moderating claims lead them away from absolutism, so that they must disavow either these claims (that is, (2) or (3)) or their absolutism (that is, (1)).

---

[15] Schotel, above n 9 at 119.

III. Communitarian Absolutism

1. Complex Equality

The same year that the Haitian interdiction programme began, in 1981, Michael Walzer published a classic essay on immigration, 'The Distribution of Membership', in which he made the following absolutist claim:

> The distribution of membership is not pervasively subject to the constraints of justice. Across a considerable range of the decisions that are made, states are simply free to take in strangers (or not) [.][16]

This is usefully read in conjunction with the following:

> [T]he distribution of membership in American society, and in any ongoing society, is a matter of political decision ... What kind of community do the citizens want to create? With what other men and women do they want to share and exchange goods?[17]

Walzer later characterizes 'political limitations' as potentially 'arbitrary, fixed by some temporary coalition of interests or majority of voters'.[18] Political decisions, that is, are made by horse trading inside the demos but without input from migrants.

Taken together, these passages appear to represent a fairly strong endorsement of absolutism. How strong is unclear. Walzer offers, for instance, a lengthy argument against guestworker programmes; he says that states are required to admit the family of their members; and he opposes the mass expulsion of non-national 'alien elements'.[19] But he also expressly countenances discriminatory immigration policies[20] and, seemingly, would allow the exclusion of some, perhaps large numbers of, refugees, about whom he says: 'One wishes them success; but in particular cases, with reference to a particular state, they may well have no right to be successful.'[21]

Walzer is the only political theorist I know of who has dealt at length with the problem of immigration alongside a complete theory of domestic justice.

---

[16] Walzer first published his chapter in PG Brown and H Shue (eds), *Boundaries: National Autonomy and Its Limits* (Totowa, Rowman & Littlefield, 1981). It was republished as 'Membership' in M Walzer, *Spheres of Justice: A Defense of Pluralism and Equality* (New York, Basic Books, 1983), in which the passage quoted is found at 61.

[17] Walzer, *Spheres of Justice*, above n 16 at 40. Walzer also makes the following claims: (1) Admissions decisions 'are not constrained by any widely accepted standard' (ibid at 34). (2) 'If we cannot guarantee the full extent of the territorial or material base on which a group of people build a common life, we can still say that the common life, at least, is their own and that their comrades and associates are theirs to recognize or choose' (ibid at 48).

[18] ibid at 67. Walzer later concludes that 'there is no alternative to democracy in the political sphere' except when a community enjoys 'an undifferentiated conception of social goods': ibid at 303.

[19] See ibid at 58–62 (guestworkers); ibid at 41 (family); and ibid at 42–43 (mass expulsions).

[20] See his discussion of White Australia: ibid at 47.

[21] ibid at 51.

To further understand his conclusions on immigration, one must examine that theory, which he calls complex equality.

The goal of complex equality is 'a society free from domination'.[22] Each political community is said to have a number of autonomous shared understandings of the value of different goods. These are the 'spheres of justice'. Domination is minimized or eliminated when distribution of each good is determined by the shared understanding appropriate to its sphere. Presumably this is because those who share in a given understanding can be taken to be committed to the corresponding distribution. A form of communal endorsement is at work.

One is dominated, in contrast, when the distribution of valued goods follows an understanding one does not share. Domination occurs whenever one must appeal to an understanding different from one's own, since such an appeal is arbitrary from one's point of view. This conception of domination necessarily includes appeals to the wholly arbitrary will of another, where no shared understanding is possible.

Complex equality is intended to be radically particularist. It appeals to local understandings and does not aspire to set universal standards for the distribution of any good.[23] Thus when Walzer argues that health care should be distributed universally according to need, his argument is meant to rest upon an interpretation of contemporary Western (or the United States') understandings. Different societies, with different shared understandings, may have different principles for the distribution of health care.[24]

The most obvious criticism that can be levelled against this theory is that forms of domination might be internal to some shared understandings. As Brian Barry puts it: '[T]here seems something paradoxical about a theory that implies that a society with slavery, suttee, untouchability, or human sacrifice is a just society so long as the victims share the understandings that legitimize those institutions.'[25] Actually, it may be worse than paradoxical, since Walzer may be committed to the view that the widow who refuses suttee is somehow being untrue to herself. Being burned alive is bad; being the kind of person who is supposed to burn herself alive is worse.[26]

Walzer offers either two or one—they are the same, as I will explain—resources to resist the charge that his theory allows for domination within spheres. First is a set of what I will call structural requirements that he builds into complex equality. Second is an idea that all, or almost all, particularist moralities converge on a set of intuitions that constitute a near-universal 'thin' or 'minimal' morality.

---

[22] ibid at xiii.

[23] For Walzer's criticisms of universal claims in philosophy, see, eg M Walzer, 'Philosophy and Democracy' (1981) 9 *Political Theory* 379.

[24] Walzer, *Spheres of Justice*, above n 16 at 86ff; M Walzer, *Thick and Thin: Moral Argument at Home and Abroad* (Notre Dame, University of Notre Dame Press, 1994) 28ff.

[25] B Barry, 'Intimations of Justice' (1984) 84 *Columbia Law Review* 806, 814.

[26] This formulation was suggested to me by T Nagel, 'Personal Rights and Private Space' in *Concealment and Exposure & Other Essays* (New York, Oxford University Press, 2002) 31, 40 ('To be tortured would be terrible; but to be tortured and also to be someone it was not wrong to torture would be even worse.').

The structural requirements of complex equality include a rule against 'conversion'. Conversion occurs when an individual or group leverages a favourable position with respect to one sphere of goods into a favourable position with respect to another. The wealthy ought not to be able to buy political influence; when they do so, political power ends up being structured by the shared understandings of market exchange rather than, say, democratic participation.[27] Thus, Walzer says, his basic principle of justice is that '[n]o social good x should be distributed to men and women who possess some other good y merely because they possess y and without regard to the meaning of x.'[28] Through application of this principle, complex equality avoids objectionable domination through diversification. No one is supposed to end up in an unfavourable position across several spheres.[29]

A second structural requirement is that shared understandings must be non-coercively inclusive. A majority cannot oppress a minority by operating on a shared understanding that members of the minority do not believe; nor can it wrest avowals of this shared understanding from the minority by force.[30] If full, non-coercive inclusion is not possible within a state that is a sign that it ought to separate.[31] The requirement of non-coercive inclusion seems to me more basic or encompassing than the rule against conversion. Whenever a conversion takes place, the distribution of a good will follow a non-inclusive understanding. At the same time, non-inclusiveness does not always imply conversion.

The idea is that the rule against conversion and the requirement of non-coercive inclusivity will avoid the most dubious implications of a thoroughly relativistic account of social justice. They are shored up by a further claim, developed in later work, that all particularist moralities produce a corresponding set of specific basic requirements like human rights[32] and more abstract ideals like 'justice' itself. Whether this is the case, he says, 'is an empirical matter. It cannot be determined by philosophical argument among ourselves—or even by philosophical argument among some ideal version of ourselves.'[33]

This thin, minimalist morality arises independently within each community's thick, maximalist morality. It must therefore be expressed and interpreted in terms of local moral idioms. The best reading of Walzer is that his two structural requirements, non-coercive inclusiveness and the rule against conversion, are themselves part of thin morality. They are, the claim must be, principles that all political communities will eventually arrive at through their efforts to do away with domination.

Note the following issue. If a given policy accords with thin morality but follows a maximalist interpretation that one does not share, is one dominated?

---

[27] Walzer, *Spheres of Justice*, above n 16 at 11.

[28] ibid at 20; see also Walzer, *Thick and Thin*, above n 24 at 32–33.

[29] On diversification as a strategy for addressing injustice in Walzer's theory, see Scanlon, 'The Diversity of Objections to Inequality' in *The Difficulty of Tolerance*, above n 6 at 217.

[30] For application of this idea to immigration, see Walzer, *Spheres of Justice*, above n 16 at 40.

[31] Walzer, *Thick and Thin*, above n 24 at 65.

[32] ibid at 49.

[33] Walzer, *Spheres of Justice*, above n 16 at 314 fn*.

Walzer must say yes, since any other answer would undermine complex equality's particularism. If one were not dominated so long as the demands of thin morality were met, the particularist shared understandings that are the core of Walzer's theory would cease to be of moral–philosophical interest. Questions of domination could be settled without recourse to them. Thus for Walzer thin morality does not provide the foundation for developing shared understandings nor, through something like John Rawls's overlapping consensus, a theory of justice.[34] This point is important to the argument below. In proceeding with that argument, I will treat the foregoing aspects of Walzer's theory as fixed and correct. That allows me to focus on his discussion of immigration.

2. Complex Equality and Immigration Governance

Walzer treats immigration as an aspect of distributive justice in which the good distributed is either the community itself[35] or membership in the community.[36] These are to be distributed by the community according to its shared understanding of the value of membership or community. Walzer works with state-level political communities. Decisions on immigration are therefore constrained by three things: the structural requirements of complex equality, that is, the rule against conversion and the rule demanding inclusiveness, thin morality, and the shared understanding appropriate to the sphere of community membership. These limits leaven the potential harshness of Walzer's absolutism in immigration, providing the source for obligations that fall under propositions of type (2) or (3), according to the schema set out above in Section Two.

For example, certain specific requirements flow from thin morality. The duty to allow family migration and such succour as we owe refugees are said to be grounded respectively in the 'kinship principle'[37] and in the principle of mutual aid,[38] although these must be interpreted by each community according to its own shared understandings.[39] Walzer's conclusions that the mass expulsion of

---

[34] On overlapping consensus, see J Rawls, *Political Liberalism*, expanded edn (New York, Columbia University Press, 1996) 133ff.

[35] '[T]he community itself is a good—conceivably the most important good—that gets distributed.': Walzer, *Spheres of Justice*, above n 16 at 28.

[36] 'Membership as a social good is constituted by our understanding; its value is fixed by our work and conversation; and then we are in charge (who else could be in charge?) of its distribution.': ibid at 32.

[37] ibid at 41: 'It is a way of acknowledging that labor mobility has a social price: since laborers are men and women with families, one cannot admit them for the sake of their labor without accepting some commitment to their aged parents, say, or to their sickly brothers and sisters.'

[38] ibid at 33, 45–46, and 62.

[39] That might mean that family migration could be regulated according to the receiving community's shared understanding of what a family is and not the migrant's: so American law can restrict Hmong migrants to bringing in one wife, even though a Hmong immigration policy (if one existed) might allow for several. And it might allow for a defence of the supposedly ideological bent of United States refugee policy up to the 1980s, when the preponderance of refugees admitted came from Communist countries.

non-nationals and guestworker programmes are unjust also seem to draw on thin morality. In these cases, Walzer might have said that such policies could not accord with any set of shared understandings that non-coercively incorporated the views of guestworkers or non-nationals. Instead, he relies on two claims of justice that, again, seem to be grounded in thin morality. Non-nationals resident in a state for some time have a 'right ... enforceable against the state ... [to] the place where they and their families have lived and made a life'.[40] For their part, guestworkers resident for a period of time must be allowed to naturalize because as a matter of 'political justice ... the processes of self-determination through which a democratic state shapes its internal life, must be open, and equally open, to all those men and women who live within its territory and work in the local economy, and are subject to local law'.[41] And though Walzer does not say so in this latter case, it is surely the case that the rule against conversion also must play a role: it would be wrong for, as an example, the principles of the market to unimpededly dictate who should be admitted if that ran counter to a community's self-understanding.

Finally, limits may flow from that self-understanding itself. Walzer invokes this kind of constraint only once, in his complicated defence of the White Australia policy, through which that country sought to restrict admissions along racial lines. It is permissible, he says, for a state to limit immigration for the sake of homogeneity, if that corresponds to a community's self-understanding, so long as in doing so it does not seek to reserve for itself unused land that might go to the necessitous.[42] The result would be different if a community's understanding were plural, as with 'Americanness', which, he says in later work, is characterized by cultural 'manyness' and political 'oneness'.[43] He would have to say that such a multicultural, immigrant country could not permissibly restrict immigration along racial, national, or ethnic lines because homogeneity could not be part of a non-coercively inclusive self-understanding of its character.

The idea seems to be that an immigration policy will be unjust if it excludes or admits people based on principles that are contrary to the understanding a community has of its own character. I find this idea, so stated, obscure as well as explanatorily deficient. Nothing here or in Walzer's other constraints can account for restrictions on the immigration of criminals and migrants who pose a danger to a society's security, public health, and public morals.[44] These are some of the oldest types of immigration restrictions, seemingly rooted in existential concerns and not in communal self-understanding. Putting aside the restriction on migrants who pose a threat to public morals, which raises many issues, it seems that it would be at least unjust for a state not to prevent the entry of migrants who

---

[40] Walzer, *Spheres of Justice*, above n 16 at 43.

[41] ibid at 60.

[42] ibid at 46–47. This complex conclusion is another example of the operation of the principle of mutual aid, interpreted in light of the self-understanding of turn-of-the-last-century Australia.

[43] M Walzer, 'What Does It Mean to Be an "American"?' (2004) 71 *Social Research* 633, 638.

[44] Security, for instance, is a good that is distributed among members; it is not part of the shared understanding of membership: Walzer, *Spheres of Justice*, above n 16 at 64.

threaten its existence or the lives of its members. It might be said that part of the shared understanding of membership is the ongoing existence of its members, over the course of their natural lives, and the political community beyond that.

I therefore conclude that Walzer's conception of justice requires that states limit immigration in a manner designed to maintain the conditions that make its own internal, particular, maximalist, complex conception of justice possible. Immigration law must seek to maintain (1) each individual, autonomous sphere of justice, and (2) the overall conditions needed to maintain the kind of integrated set of spheres that allows for complex equality. A constraint of the first kind would mean that a capitalist state may exclude Communists.[45] We might call this a constraint tied to culture, or political culture.[46] A constraint of the second kind means that immigration policy must ensure that public threats are not admitted and must guard against other dangers, such as overpopulation. If either of these requirements is not met, the larger political community is likely to fragment, with members retreating into 'a thousand petty fortresses'.[47]

To the extent that these constraints—those flowing from the structural requirements of complex equality, from thin morality, from existential imperatives, and from the self-understanding of the political community—operate, immigration laws and policies are constrained by justice. That Walzer claims that justice is not pervasive suggests that he thinks there is nonetheless considerable latitude in the setting of such laws and policies. There are many ways to populate a political community to ensure the continuity of its internal character. It would be possible for a country to select migrants who are like-minded and advantaged, rather than those who are like-minded but disadvantaged.

3. Domination at the Border

Walzer faces a difficulty because many or all decisions regarding the governance of immigration will, on his account, be dominating. Domination occurs whenever a good is distributed according to understandings that an individual does not share or, alternatively, according to a thin morality that the individual does share, but which is applied using an unshared maximalist interpretation.

On this view, domination will always be the case within a wide range of politically permissible immigration policies. It will also be the case with regard to those policies mandated by the constraints of complex equality. Non-coercive inclusiveness and the rule against conversion do not extend to migrants. The limits imposed by thin morality are to be interpreted using understandings exclusive of the migrants' perspective. So, in this sense, Walzer's view does indeed seem to be a strong form of absolutism, since it allows for domination at the border.

---

[45] *Immigration and Nationality Act*, §212(a)(3)(D).

[46] Walzer, *Spheres of Justice*, above n 16 at 319: 'A community's culture is the story its members tell so as to make sense of all the different pieces of their social life—and justice is the doctrine that distinguishes the pieces.'

[47] ibid at 39.

Return then to Justice Field's argument, that allowing injustice opens the door to 'brutality, inhumanity, and cruelty'. Can Walzer resist this claim? Yes, if he can show that the thin morality of all receiving states' political communities excludes this possibility. There are two qualifications to this conclusion. The first is that Walzer's own arguments about the range of permissible policy cast some doubt on it. The second is that even non-brutal immigration governance would be dominating.

The first qualification is that the injustice that Walzer allows for includes most notably the exclusion of refugees who might face persecution in their home country. Undoubtedly refugee claims lie along a spectrum of potential suffering and persecution. The exclusion of some refugees may constitute brutality. The exclusion of others may be merely unjust. Walzer's absolutism needs to furnish some argument that identifies a threshold of brutality and explains how that threshold can be made the basis for a viable policy. There seems no reason to think that this could not be done, or rather why it would present any more difficulties than the administration of current refugee law. Substantively, however, some may wish to claim that the exclusion of anyone qualifying as a refugee would be brutal. For those who think so, Walzer's absolutism may have already fallen prey to Field's argument.

Injustice itself need not be illegitimate, if the departure from justice is justified somehow. A necessary condition for justifying injustice would seem to include a showing that it is not brutal, for brutality constitutes a range of behaviour that can almost never be justified. Here too, as the discussion of refugees just showed, there may be disagreement over what constitutes brutality. The second qualification, then, is that Walzer's absolutism has no resources to deal with such disagreement. That is because all justification in complex equality is immanent and exclusively internal. It is never directed at the migrants who object to their exclusion, deportation, detention, and so on. The question asked is not: What can or ought they accept? It is: What can or ought we accept of ourselves in our treatment of them? A community's conclusions about whether or not a given policy is oppresive are presented as established fact.

This is why a world of a 'thousand petty fortresses' would be disastrous. It is also why Walzer uses political communities as his basic moral unit. Each border is a site of domination. Given the aim of minimizing domination, we must minimize the number of borders and maximize the size of '*communities of character*', the 'historically stable, ongoing associations of men and women with some special commitment to one another and some special sense of their common life'[48] that he hopes will constitute states.[49]

No immigration policy will be based on shared understandings that are inclusive of migrants. Similarly, any policy according with thin morality will be interpreted according to the receiving country's thick morality. In either case, the

---

[48] Walzer, *Spheres of Justice*, above n 16 at 62.
[49] See especially ibid at 28–29.

result will be a dominating immigration policy, and possibly a brutal one from the migrant's perspective. On Walzer's account (using Walzer's language) all immigration governance is tyrannical. Therefore injustice in immigration will always be illegitimate. In cases where migrants disagree with a policy, what it means is that immigration policy or decisions will be imposed by naked force alone.

4. Thin Morality at the Border

The only way to avoid this result that I can see is to use thin morality as the basis for justifying immigration policy to migrants. Such an exercise would be contrary to Walzer's view of how thin morality works. Thin morality is meant to be the product of, not the grounds for, the ongoing practices of social criticism and justification through which our shared understandings are scrutinized and developed.[50] Walzer says that: 'Morality is thick from the beginning, culturally integrated, fully resonant, and it reveals itself thinly only on special occasions, when moral language is turned to specific purposes.'[51] Thin morality must be distilled from the thick. Yet I see no alternative but to try to build up from this shared thinness to avoid domination at the border. Besides, the resulting account is plausible.

Across borders, there is no single, presupposed thick morality to serve as the font of thin morality. This possibility seems to be ruled out especially by the transience and heterogeneity of migrants. What must be done is to appeal to each migrant's minimal moral commitments, developed independently within their own home countries, and show how this can be given a reasonable interpretation in terms of the receiving country's maximal morality and its goal of maintaining the necessary conditions for its own conception of justice.

The product of such an exercise may resemble Walzer's description of the inevitable parochialism of attempts at universal philosophy: '[M]inimalism when it is expressed as Minimal Morality will be forced into the idiom and orientation of one of the maximal moralities.'[52] The goal must be to justify immigration policies in terms of thin morality but in the idiom of the receiving country's maximalism. Further, migrants must be invited to engage in the interpretive (critical) discussion. Perhaps, at first they may only be able to grasp intellectually the shared understandings of the receiving country and the conditions necessary for their sustenance. But if the encounter between migrant and receiving state becomes a protracted one, the migrant may begin to identify with those understandings. They may give up their old maximalist commitments and become reoriented toward a new maximalist morality. By engaging with the receiving country's shared understandings, they may begin to share, or even reinvigorate, those understandings. Therefore, to avoid domination at the border, immigration governance must seek to be principled.

---

[50] See M Walzer, *Interpretation and Social Criticism* (Cambridge, MA, Harvard University Press, 1987) chapter two.

[51] Walzer, *Thick and Thin*, above n 24 at 4.

[52] ibid at 9.

IV. Liberal Pessimism

1. Immigration and Egalitarian Justice

An alternative absolutist position can be developed using as a starting point the liberal theory of justice of John Rawls. This fact may strike a discordant note. Nevertheless, as I have already had occasion to note many times, it is notorious, especially for those concerned with global justice, that Rawls's theory of justice presupposes a closed society entered only by birth and exited only by death.[53] Moreover, he ties principles of social justice to the basic structure of individual political societies in a way that later provides the grounds for a statist conception of global justice. This statism can, in turn, be used to develop an absolutist position in immigration.[54]

In this section, I will explore Thomas Nagel's version of this liberal absolutist argument, developed in 'The Problem of Global Justice'. In that essay, Nagel relies in part upon Rawls to argue that the demands of egalitarian justice are confined largely within states. Incidental to this account, he makes a claim for absolutism in immigration. Since the account provided in this essay also relies heavily on Rawls, it is particularly important to address Nagel's absolutism.

By egalitarian justice, Nagel has in mind principles of democracy, equal citizenship, non-discrimination, equality of opportunity, and distributive amelioration. Principles of egalitarian justice have no bearing globally, Nagel argues, since it is state political institutions that give 'the value of justice its application'.[55] This relates to 'the dual role each member plays both as one of the society's subjects and as one of those in whose name its authority is exercised'.[56] Nagel's point here is very close to the link that I have sought to draw between juridical integration and self-respect. Another way of grasping it is by analogy to self-incrimination in the criminal law. A state's members, like criminals, are potentially enlisted in their own injury. Just as there would be something appalling about being forcibly made an agent of one's own punishment, there is something appalling at being made forcibly an agent of one's own oppression. Since all members are implicated in the coercive demands of their state's laws, avoiding self-oppression requires that they be entitled to demand a particularly rigorous form of justification. This form of justification leads to egalitarian justice.

Nagel seemingly has in mind justification carried out through a series of pairwise comparisons 'whereby the situation of each and the potential gains of each are

---

[53] See, eg J Rawls, *A Theory of Justice*, revised edn (Cambridge, MA, Belknap Press, 1999) 7.

[54] As was noted in the introduction, Rawls himself says there might be 'at least a qualified right to limit immigration', citing Walzer in support: J Rawls, *The Law of Peoples* (Cambridge, MA, Harvard University Press, 1999) 39, fn 48.

[55] T Nagel, 'The Problem of Global Justice' (2005) 33 Philosophy & Public Affairs 113, 120.

[56] ibid at 128.

compared separately with those of every other'.[57] Nagel believes that a conception of egalitarian justice arrived at this way will endorse principles and policies that grant strong priority to the interests of the worse off.[58] This priority will result from imaginatively identifying with the points of view of those in that situation.

The stronger demands of pairwise justification do not take hold at the global level because there is no global institution that implicates the will in the same way as state institutions.[59] All that obtains is a less demanding morality consisting of three elements: a minimal humanitarianism owed 'to fellow human beings threatened with starvation or severe malnutrition and early death from easily preventable diseases';[60] a 'duty of rescue from immediate danger';[61] and a set of prepolitical human rights protecting against (in one list) violence, enslavement, and coercion[62] or (in another) bodily inviolability, freedom of expression, and freedom of religion.[63] Minimal global morality results from what Nagel says is a less stringent form of justification, a test of universalisability such as Immanuel Kant's categorical imperative or TM Scanlon's contractualism. In other work, Nagel has said that this test of universalisability provides a criterion of legitimacy, a point to which I return below.[64]

Nagel's conception, then, divides political morality into at least two layers.[65] One layer consists of the robust demands of egalitarian justice within states. The other consists of minimal global moral requirements. It is in illustration of the implications of this statist conception of global justice that Nagel makes the following remark about immigration:

> Immigration policies are simply enforced against the nationals of other states; the laws are not imposed in their name, nor are they asked to accept and uphold those laws. Since no acceptance is demanded of them, no justification is required that explains why they should accept such discriminatory policies, or why their interests have been given equal consideration. It is sufficient justification to claim that the policies do not violate their prepolitical human rights.[66]

---

[57] Thomas Nagel, *Equality and Partiality* (New York, Oxford University Press, 1991) 68. For this interpretation of Nagel's argument, see AJ Julius, 'Nagel's Atlas' (2006) 34 *Philosophy & Public Affairs* 176, 181–82.

[58] Nagel, *Equality and Partiality*, above n 57. See also T Nagel, 'Equality' in *Mortal Questions* (Cambridge, Cambridge University Press, 1979) 106.

[59] Nagel, 'The Problem of Global Justice', above n 55 at 136–40. Nor can the gradual thickening of global institutions lead to weaker demands of egalitarian justice, since such a 'sliding scale' approach to socioeconomic justice would be arbitrary: ibid at 140–43. Nagel is responding to L Murphy, 'Institutions and the Demands of Justice' (1998) 27 *Philosophy & Public Affairs* 251. An argument for a sliding-scale conception of justice is developed in AJ Julius, 'Basic Structure and the Value of Equality' (2003) 31 *Philosophy & Public Affairs* 321.

[60] Nagel, 'The Problem of Global Justice', above n 55 at 118, 130, 131, and 132.

[61] ibid at 131.

[62] ibid at 127, 131.

[63] ibid at 127. Note that in Nagel, *Equality and Partiality*, above n 57 at 159, Nagel also says that liberal toleration is the product of a Kantian test of universalisability.

[64] Nagel, *Equality and Partiality*, above n 57 at chapter four. Chapter fifteen of *Equality and Partiality* contains an earlier statement on global ethics. There Nagel seems to apply the Kantian criterion of universalisability globally in order to express doubts about the possibility of a legitimate world order.

[65] Nagel says morality is 'multilayered': Nagel, 'The Problem of Global Justice', above n 55 at 132, 133, and 141.

[66] ibid at 129–30.

In light of Nagel's larger argument, I read this passage as follows: migrants are not, and cannot be, the agents of their own oppression through immigration law because they are not responsible for that law's genesis. Therefore, there is no possibility of self-oppression and so a more robust form of pairwise justification of immigration law is not called for. Rather, migrants must accept such laws without justification so long as the laws meet a criterion of universalisability, that is, so long as they do not violate prepolitical human rights or the duties of humanitarianism. The only immigrants not yet admitted who might have grounds for complaint, then, would be political refugees and the very poorest. On this picture, egalitarian justice would only be required between members, permanent residents, and perhaps also those resident migrants such as long-time illegal migrants or guestworkers who may have some basis for claiming that the laws of the receiving state are somehow made in their name.[67]

Beyond these limits, Nagel seems to believe his view allows for a great amount of policy freedom, almost certainly including the freedom to enforce inegalitarian immigration policies whose thrust is the exclusion of the poor (though perhaps not those that exclude the very poorest).[68] Such a reading is consistent with other accounts that, relying on statist conceptions of liberal justice, defend broad discretion over immigration law.[69] This view appears to allow for the possibility of illegitimate oppression in immigration governance and hence is absolutist in the following way. For those immigration laws that do not violate prepolitical human rights, Nagel says, demands for justification of claimed injury need not be answered.

Thus Nagel's claim with respect to immigration governance must be understood in light of his broader argument about global justice. Indeed, it can be cast even more broadly. Nagel's rejection of a cosmopolitan conception of global justice and of justice in immigration seems motivated by pessimism about the realisability of worldwide liberal egalitarianism. This pessimism flows from the belief that a political–moral theory must strike a balance between impersonal and personal motives.[70] A liberal egalitarianism that asks too much of us may become pejoratively utopian, by demanding social arrangements that would distort the conditions of living beyond what humans can naturally accommodate. Nagel seems to think cosmopolitan conceptions of justice might be utopian in this sense.

---

[67] The possibility in the last two cases is complicated, however, by Nagel's claim that the obligations of egalitarian justice cannot be forced upon us: '[T]here is no obligation to enter into that relation with those to whom we do not yet have it, thereby acquiring those obligations toward them.' ibid at 121.

[68] They probably also allow for race-based policies unless these cannot be justified to members. For an argument of this sort, see M Blake, 'Discretionary Immigration' (2002) 30 *Philosophical Topics* 273.

[69] See S Macedo, 'The Moral Dilemma of US Immigration Policy: Open Borders Versus Social Justice?' in C Swain (ed), *Debating Immigration* (Cambridge, Cambridge University Press, 2007). Some authors broadly support Nagel's view of global justice but come to a different conclusion about immigration: see A Sangiovanni, 'Global Justice, Reciprocity, and the State' (2007) 35 *Philosophy & Public Affairs* 3, 37–38.

[70] The split between the personal and impersonal standpoint is an old theme in Nagel's philosophy: see Nagel, *Equality and Partiality*, above n 57; T Nagel, *The View from Nowhere* (New York, Oxford University Press, 1986).

Thus Nagel takes Rawls's closed-society presumption to be more than methodological; it represents instead an appropriate boundary defined by the limits of human nature. The 'impartial egalitarian motive'[71] necessary for justice is not feasible beyond the boundaries of a state.

2. Pessimism about Legitimacy

There are many ways to scrutinize Nagel's argument. One might ask whether it is true that migrants' wills are not sufficiently engaged by immigration law to lead to standing to demand egalitarian justification. One might also ask whether Nagel's views provide a plausible account of the grounds of egalitarian justice. The most relevant issue for the argument here, however, is the implications of the test of universalisability.

In his earlier book, *Equality and Partiality*, Nagel proposes using a test of universalisability as a criterion of legitimacy, relying in particular on Scanlon's contractualist formula:

> An act is wrong if its performance under the circumstances would be disallowed by any system of rules for the regulation of behavior which no one could reasonably reject as a basis for informed, unforced general agreement.[72]

Seen in this light, one way of understanding Nagel's argument is as the claim that immigration regimes need not be just but only legitimate.

I find it hard to make sense of this restatement. In part this is because the plain language of Nagel's claim seems most naturally interpreted as the suggestion that even legitimacy is not a concern beneath the threshold of prepolitical human right violations. In part it is because Scanlon's contractualism cannot provide a theory of legitimacy. Contractualism may be thought to provide a substantive theory of legitimacy, in the sense of setting a moral threshold that any legitimate regime must meet. However, no theory of legitimacy can be wholly substantive. People will disagree over what is universally non-rejectable. Some further theory is needed to explain why in some cases one should accept a policy one thinks can be reasonably rejected. A better understanding is that contractualism, or some other test of universalisability, provides the basis for a theory of justice, as I have defined that ideal, in immigration. It needs to be supplemented with a theory of legitimacy, the way Rawls eventually supplemented his account of the reasoning for justice as fairness with a theory of legitimacy using the idea of public reason.

Nonetheless the language of legitimacy is important to understanding what Nagel is trying to accomplish. In the unlikely event that there were universal agreement that an immigration regime was failing to uphold some minimal morality, it is hard to see how it could be legitimate. In *Equality and Partiality*, Nagel applies the language of legitimacy globally, coming to the even starker conclusion that a

---

[71] Nagel, *Equality and Partiality*, above n 57 at 70–71, fn 19.
[72] Scanlon, 'Contractualism and Utilitarianism' in *The Difficulty of Tolerance*, above n 6 at 132.

legitimate world order (including immigration policies) was not possible.[73] Both the rich and the poor could recognize the other's reasonable rejection of their own preferred solutions to global inequality. The ramifications of this situation are potentially bleak: 'If there is no solution that no one could reasonably reject, neither party to the conflict can be reproached for trying to impose a solution acceptable to him but unacceptable to his opponent.'[74] Thus liberal democracies cannot be faulted for imposing inegalitarian immigration policies and migrants cannot be faulted for evading them or any other form of resistance.

If we carry this conclusion forward to his later account of global justice, what Nagel seems to be suggesting is that, so long as the gap between the world's rich and poor remains as wide as it is, there is no possibility of agreement on what the minimal global morality requires, including no agreement on what prepolitical rights ought to be respected by immigration regimes. In the background of Nagel's absolutism in immigration is an even more profound pessimism about the possibility not only of just immigration governance but of legitimate immigration governance.

3. Hope

As I said, Scanlon's contractualist formula cannot provide an adequate theory of legitimacy. A theory of legitimacy would have to explain why one version of what minimal morality requires in immigration can be justifiably enforced against those who disagree with it. Such an account might include certain substantive minima, but it must also surely include institutional considerations of how democracy, constitutionalism, the rule of law, and due process might or might not validate an official determination of such thresholds. In Chapter One, I have explained why that is a forbidding task in the immigration context; I take it up again at length in the next chapter.

The puzzle in Nagel's argument for the political conception of global justice, though, lies in the fact that Scanlonian contractualism, while it cannot offer a theory of legitimacy, can provide a theory of justice.[75] Moreover, it can produce principles of justice that furnish some grounds for resisting the worst effects of inegalitarianism, so long as it can be argued that any relations of domination, demeaning status distinctions, suffering and so on that may result from inegalitarian immigration policies can be reasonably rejected.[76]

---

[73] Nagel, *Equality and Partiality*, above n 57 at 170–71.

[74] ibid at 173. Nagel contemplates the extension of this view to immigration at 179.

[75] Thus Scanlon compares his contractualism with Rawls's original position, suggesting that he views it as arriving at substantive moral positions: Scanlon, 'Contractualism and Utilitarianism', above n 72 at 145–50.

[76] For discussions that emphasize the different reasons to object to inequality, see Scanlon, 'The Diversity of Objections to Inequality', above n 29; Nagel, *Equality*, above n 58; J Rawls, E Kelly (ed), *Justice as Fairness: A Restatement* (Cambridge, MA, Belknap Press, 2001) 130–31; M O'Neill, 'What Should Egalitarians Believe?' (2008) 36 *Philosophy & Public Affairs* 119.

Nagel believes contractualism does not support a strong enough form of egalitarianism, at least within states.[77] Yet in some contexts it may generate more than the limited set of human rights that he lists. The appropriate point of debate with Nagel therefore seems to be not whether obligations of justice constrain immigration governance. Rather, it must focus on what sorts of immigration laws can or cannot be reasonably rejected.

I think Nagel construes the contractualist requirement too narrowly, at least in the domain of immigration governance. The non-rejectability standard seems adequate to explain most of the fixed judgements of oppression in immigration listed in Chapter Two, some of which go beyond his list of prepolitical human rights. It also would allow us to say that migrants, numbering in the thousands, who mounted organized challenges to the Asian exclusion policies of the late nineteenth- and early twentieth-century had acted reasonably.[78] (In terms to be introduced in the next chapter, we could say that they were in compliance with the duty of civility.) Opposition was reasonable because Asian exclusion was irrational, that is, it served no reasonable policy purpose. It was also reasonable because at the same time European migrants faced more favourable admissions policies and so Asian migrants, who could reasonably compare their treatment to another migrant group that was symmetrically situated relative to the receiving state's political conception of justice, were subject to a stigmatizing form of discrimination. Therefore, while Nagel might be correct that Scanlon's formula does not provide for a strongly egalitarian conception of global justice, he is wrong to claim that it produces only a minimal set of human rights and humanitarian duties.

Even if he were correct in this last claim, it does more work than he seems to think. As was discussed in Chapter Two, inegalitarian immigration policies are characterized not only by their first-order policies of exclusion and deportation, but also by second-order policies regarding resident immigrants, matters of enforcement, and private relations that themselves can result in or address instances of oppression. Migrants who disagree with the first-order policies or simply see the potential gains from migration as outweighing the potential costs may come anyway. They insist upon their freedom, as it were, and this may force governments to use oppressive second-order means to achieve their first-order policy aims. There would be no moral permission, however, to carry out such oppressive enforcement of immigration policy under Nagel's argument. That, in turn, might have significant implications for the range of permissible first-order policies. This is a preliminary statement of the indirect principle of freedom of migration, which I explore in greater detail in Chapter Six.

Therefore Nagel's account, which is stated in absolutist terms, turns out to be principled, though not as demanding as his conception of egalitarian justice. To

[77] Nagel, *Equality and Partiality*, above n 57 at 70–71, fn 19.

[78] RP Cole and GJ Chin, 'Emerging from the Margins of Historical Consciousness: Chinese Immigrants and the History of American Law' (1999) 17 *Law and History Review* 325; L Salyer, *Laws Harsh as Tigers: Chinese Immigrants and the Shaping of Modern Immigration Law* (Chapel Hill, University of North Carolina Press, 1995).

return a last time to Justice Field's argument, we may say that Nagel resists the possible tendency of absolutism to slide toward brutality. He does so by producing the germ of a principled account in the form of a test of universalisability that might be used to decide whether first-order and second-order immigration measures are oppressive, and to condemn them if they are.

V. Moving on

I have argued that the discretionary doctrine lying at the heart of immigration law can be interpreted two ways. Under what I have called the principled account, immigration regimes must strive to govern non-oppressively. In contrast, the second, absolutist account says that immigration regimes are not constrained by justice. As a matter of legal interpretation, different aspects of immigration law and practice support each account. I have further argued, however, that two philosophical defences of absolutism in immigration, presented by Michael Walzer and Thomas Nagel, give way on their own terms to a principled reading. This result suggests, though not definitively, that absolutism may not be defensible. The next chapter considers a further argument that under absolutism immigration regimes cannot lead to political obligations among migrants.

5

The Authority of Immigration Law

I. Introduction

THE PHILOSOPHICAL VERSIONS of absolutism discussed in the last chapter address themselves to legitimacy, not political obligation. Yet in actual political discourse absolutism seems to presuppose that migrants who break immigration law are guilty of a moral wrong. How else to explain the outrage targeted specifically at illegal immigrants? I argue in this chapter that this presupposition cannot be made good unless immigration regimes strive to be just under suitably defined institutional conditions. Under absolutism, therefore, immigration regimes are not capable of having authority and so cannot be legal regimes. Since immigration is everywhere purported to be governed by law, this argument suggests absolutism in philosophical and political discourse is explanatorily deficient; that in legal discourse it is incoherent; and that in either of these discursive contexts it is open to the charge of hypocrisy.

Recall that the absolutist position being considered in Part Two holds that immigration regimes that do not strive for justice can have authority. Therefore by showing that absolutist immigration regimes cannot create political obligations among migrants, I establish that they are incapable of having authority and so cannot be legal regimes. The binary is between *striving* and *not striving* to be just, not between being just and being unjust. A regime that suitably strives to be just but fails might still have authority. Further, a regime that meets institutional conditions that enable suitable striving may also be capable of having authority, hence legal, even if it does not always live up to this ideal because officials do not act as they should.

The argument relies on the idea, associated with Joseph Raz but widely accepted, that legal regimes presuppose their own authority, and the further more contentious claim that they must be capable of having authority in order to be legal regimes.[1] It also relies on the stipulated definition from Chapter One that

---

[1] J Raz, *Practical Reasons and Norms* (Oxford, Oxford University Press, 1990) 150–51; J Raz, *The Authority of Law: Essays on Law and Morality*, 2nd edn (New York, Oxford University Press, 2009) 29–30; J Raz, 'Authority, Law, and Morality' in *Ethics in the Public Domain: Essays in the Morality of Law and Politics* (New York, Oxford University Press, 1994) 199–204. Note that I do not rely on Raz's service conception of authority for reasons that would unduly interrupt the argument. Raz discusses

to have authority a regime must both be legitimate, in the sense of being morally justified in exercising power, and command political obligation, in the sense of being able to generate political obligations. As I use the term, 'political obligation' covers both obligations and duties.[2] These may refer to a wide array of require-ments, including political obligations not required by law, such as an obligation to volunteer for military service, to vote, to engage in the political process, and so on. Discussion here will focus on the power to create legal obligations in the stringent sense also specified by Raz. To have an obligation to obey the law in this sense means that you are obligated to do as the law commands because the law so commands.[3] I will take Raz's definition, which has been criticized,[4] to be correct. Indeed, it seems particularly salient in immigration law. For example, refugee claimants might frequently see themselves as having urgent reasons to override legal rules, but if they act on those reasons they are subject to the imputation of having done something morally regrettable. Indeed, refugee law even seeks to regulate the terms of their illegality, absolving them of their putative wrong only under certain conditions.[5]

This argument proceeds by first eliminating the possibility that legal obliga-tions to immigration regimes that do not strive to be just can be grounded under principles of acquired obligation, namely the principles of consent and fairness. The arguments against these principles are elaborations of the argument made in Chapter Three in favour of duty to govern immigration justly. That is, as prin-ciples of acquired obligation, consent and fairness themselves are indeterminate;

---

the relationship between the service conception and the natural duty of justice in J Raz, *The Morality of Freedom* (Oxford, Clarendon Press, 1986) 66–67. See in particular his statement that the natural duty of justice, as a principle of political obligation, is 'dependant on a prior understanding of which institu-tions are just.' Here Raz seems to be relying on the idea that we can come to determinate conclusions about what justice requires outside of a rightful condition, a view I believe rests on a mistake about the nature of justice. I also agree with Stephen Darwall's criticism of Raz's service conception for its reliance on third-personal rather than second-personal reasons, in S Darwall, 'Authority and Second-Personal Reasons for Acting' in *Morality, Authority, & Law: Essays in Second-Personal Ethics I* (Oxford, Oxford University Press, 2013) 135. Darwall's criticism of Raz's service conception of authority on the ground that it relies on non-second-personal reasons connects to the mistake about justice that I attribute to Raz.

[2] Obligations refer to moral requirements incurred through performative acts, such as promises or contracts. Duties refer to moral requirements imposed on us regardless of such acts by virtue of our status.

[3] Raz, *Morality*, above n 1 at 100; Raz, *Authority*, above n 1 at 233–37. For different senses of being under a legal obligation, see J Finnis, *Natural Law and Natural Rights* (Oxford, Clarendon Press, 1980) 354.

[4] See P Soper, *The Ethics of Deference: Learning from the Law's Morals* (Cambridge, Cambridge University Press, 2002) xiv.

[5] *Convention Relating to the Status of Refugees* (adopted 28 July 1951, entered into force 22 April 1954) 189 UNTS 137, art 31: 'The Contracting States shall not impose penalties, on account of their illegal entry or presence, on refugees who, coming directly from a territory where their life or freedom was threatened in the sense of Article 1, enter or are present in their territory without authorization, provided they present themselves without delay to the authorities and show good cause for their illegal entry or presence.'

such indeterminacies must be resolved by some authority; and the only way for the receiving state to act as that authority with respect to migrants is to strive to govern immigration justly. I then introduce John Rawls's formulation of the natural duty of justice as a principle of political obligation and defend it against three objections. These arguments are in Sections Two, Three, and Four.

My claim is that if immigration regimes strive to be just they will be capable of having authority, that is, capable of creating legal and other obligations. Working out the affirmative argument for the natural duty of justice as a principle of political obligation requires developing Rawls's claim that there is a natural duty of justice to support and comply with institutions that are 'as just as it is reasonable to expect in the circumstances'.[6] Specifically, what is required is to establish what would be a reasonable departure from justice in the circumstances. Drawing on Rawls's later account of public reason and the liberal principle of legitimacy, I argue in Section Five that migrants will owe obligations to immigration regimes when three institutional conditions are met by immigration regimes: (1) if they can be represented as being part of an overall design that aims at achieving justice, through a form of what I call institutional reflective equilibrium; (2) if immigration law is developed by members, legislators, judges, and officials seeking to comply with what Rawls calls the duty of civility; that is, seeking to abide by principles of justice in immigration governance that reasonable migrants could accept; and (3) if compliance with the first two conditions is publicly verifiable. This would lead to a requirement of accountability to verify, for example, that immigration laws are constitutional or that officials have acted in good faith and without bias. It would also lead to an interpretive presumption, which migrants can rely on before courts and administrative tribunals, that immigration regimes and those responsible for them have indeed sought to be just. The third condition is crucial. To be capable of having authority, hence legal, immigration law must make itself accountable to a showing that the first two conditions have been met, within reason. These conditions further elaborate the principled account of discretion in immigration governance introduced in Chapter Three. They specify what is meant by the duty to strive to be just.[7]

The role of a theory of authority is to show how governance can be right and proper when consensus over matters of justice is impossible. The question is how any regime, including an immigration regime, can purport to have authority when some, perhaps most, of its subjects will disagree over the justice of its laws. This issue is complicated in the realm of immigration governance for reasons set out in Chapter One. The heterogeneity and transience of migrants as a subject

---

[6] J Rawls, *A Theory of Justice*, revised edn (Cambridge, MA, Belknap Press, 1999) 99.

[7] Note that Bas Schotel has developed a similar argument regarding the authority of immigration law: B Schotel, *On the Right of Exclusion: Law, Ethics and Immigration Policy* (Abingdon, Routledge, 2012) chapter five. However, Schotel relies on Raz's service conception of authority and bases his argument on a different account of what it means to be 'capable' of having authority.

group suggests that problems of disagreement about justice will turn out to be specially intractable. The fact that immigration regimes are status regimes presents a further difficulty. Most modern liberal theories of obligation build on a presumption of moral equality, and so it must be shown that differential status does not render authority impossible. Relatedly, the fact that migrants mostly do not have access to direct forms of political participation, most notably the vote, has the consequence that democratic theories of authority cannot be relied upon in any obvious way.[8] Finally, the fact that most subjects of immigration regimes are not members, what I have called the liminality of immigration regimes, suggests that in most cases there will be no prior ethical relationship between migrants and receiving states. Any account of obligation that relies on such prior relationships cannot ground the obligation to obey immigration law. These would include forms of communitarianism[9] as well as associative[10] or gratitude-based theories.[11] The only eligible theories seem to be those based on acquired or natural obligation. It is to these that I now turn.

II. Consent

The variant of absolutism now under consideration claims that migrants can be obligated to obey immigration law even if the immigration regimes that promulgate and administer that law do not strive to be just. On this view, a migrant would be obligated to obey the summary rejection of a genuine refugee claim; to obey the terms of exploitative guestworker programmes; to obey rulings that would separate them from their young children; and so on. Consent and fairness, addressed in this section and the next, offer accounts of acquired political obligation that might say how this could be so.

We are all accustomed to taking on interpersonal obligations through promising and other performative conventions. As a result, basing political obligation on consent appears unstrained. Additionally, consent, by its very nature, cannot

---

[8] T Christiano, 'The Authority of Democracy' (2004) 12 *Journal of Political Philosophy* 266; J Waldron, *Law and Disagreement* (Oxford, Oxford University Press, 1999).

[9] John Dunn observes that for communitarians 'political obligation ... loses both its starkness and its relative urgency. It becomes hard to distinguish human individuals from their social or cultural obligations; and political obligation is either a logical extension of, or an impertinent competitor with, these other more central and deeply insinuating bonds.': J Dunn, 'Political Obligation' in *The History of Political Theory and Other Essays* (Cambridge, Cambridge University Press, 1996) 71.

[10] R Dworkin, *Law's Empire* (Cambridge, MA, Belknap Press, 1986) 195ff.

[11] Plato, 'Crito' in B Jowett trans, *Five Great Dialogues* (New York, Walter J Black, 1942) 74–75. For discussion see R Kraut, *Socrates and the State* (Princeton, Princeton University Press, 1984) 143ff. For discussion of gratitude theories generally, see AJ Simmons, *Moral Principles and Political Obligations* (Princeton, Princeton University Press, 1979) chapter seven; J Horton, *Political Obligation* (Houndmills, Basingstoke, Macmillan, 1992) 100–102.

be given unknowingly or unwillingly.[12] That appears to allow for an argument that coercive governance, if consented to, does not impinge on the natural freedom of human persons. Consent seems like a plausible way to defend absolutism because it can serve to validate actions that otherwise would be wrong, sometimes very wrong. It would be wrong for you to take one of my French fries, perform surgery on me, or sleep in my basement if I had not consented to it. But if I did consent, the wrong dissipates. Perhaps, then, migrants' consent can validate unjust immigration governance even if unreasonably unjust. I take it that such a suggestion provides the implicit normative heft of, for example, Ryan Pevnick's observation that 'it is unlikely that foreign workers would prefer a system that promised full legal rights, but accepted very few … to a relatively humane guestworker program that allowed entry for enough to satiate labor demand'.[13] The implication may be that migrants would consent to such a rights trade-off, so it would have authority.

The most significant difficulty faced by consent theories in the standard, domestic case is that few natural-born members could be said to have carried out performative acts that might constitute consent to obey their home state's government. Locke, Rousseau, and others attempt to address this difficulty by locating tacit consent in such acts as political participation or continued residence. However, as A John Simmons argues, it is only by abandoning the most appealing aspects of consent—the knowing, uncoerced agreement to be governed—that this principle can be stretched so far. Therefore, in the standard case consent theories either fail to establish legal obligation of sufficient generality, because not enough people will have consented in the proper sense, or they lose what made them attractive in the first place.[14]

---

[12] Most definitions of consent try to capture these qualities. Richard Flatham says that to consent, when appropriate background conditions of choice obtain, a person must (1) know what he or she consents to; (2) intend to consent to it; (3) communicate his or her knowledge of what he or she is consenting to and his or her intention to consent to the person or persons to whom consent is given. R Flatham, *Political Obligation* (New York, Atheneum, 1972) 220, cited in Horton, *Political Obligation*, above n 11 at 28. Raz gives a less stringent definition: 'Consent is given by any behaviour (action or omission) undertaken in the belief that: 1. it will change the normative situation of another; 2. it will do so because it is undertaken with such a belief; 3. it will be understood by its observers to be of this character': Raz, *Morality of Law*, above n 1 at 81.

[13] R Pevnick, *Immigration and the Constraints of Justice: Between Open Borders and Absolute Sovereignty* (Cambridge, Cambridge University Press, 2011) 179. Pevnick is citing D Bell, *Beyond Liberal Democracy: Political Thinking for an East Asian Context* (Princeton, Princeton University Press, 2009). Michael Blake refers to a similar suggestion made by Christopher Heath Wellman in conversation: M Blake, 'Immigration, Jurisdiction, and Exclusion' (2013) 41 *Philosophy & Public Affairs* 103, 120 fn 27.

[14] See the criticism by Simmons, *Moral Principles*, above n 11 in chapter four. The most famous criticism of tacit consent arguments is David Hume's: 'Can we seriously say, that a poor peasant or artisan has a free choice to leave his country, when he knows no foreign language or manners, and lives, from day to day, by the small wages which he acquires? We may as well assert that a man, by remaining in a vessel, freely consents to the domination of the master; though he was carried on board while asleep, and must leap into the ocean and perish, the moment he leaves her.' D Hume, 'Of the Original Contract' in SD Warner and DW Livingston (eds), *Political Writings* (Indianapolis, Hackett Publishing Co, 1994) 172.

On the other hand, it seems more plausible to take the decision to immigrate through official channels as tacit consent to comply with both immigration law and more generally the laws of a receiving state. Indeed, immigration might be a uniquely plausible form of tacit consent. A caveat is that the voluntariness of consent may depend on migrants' initial situation and upon available legal avenues for entry. For example, the express or implied consent of refugee claimants to a system that demands truthful answers may not be considered voluntary for those who have no other means of migrating. As much migration is driven by relative economic inequalities between sending and receiving countries, difficult questions will inevitably arise about when a migrant's need vitiates express or tacit consent. Those questions may undermine the normative force of Pevnick's observation. A poor labourer from Central America who agrees to trade off rights for admission may not be bound to abide by the conditions of entry under a guest-worker programme if he or she came from a sufficiently disadvantaged position.[15]

There are reasons, however, to think that even the kind of involuntariness associated with the plight of refugees and seriously disadvantaged migrants does not invalidate consent to comply with immigration law or the law of the receiving state. Many theorists distinguish between situations where duress was aimed at extorting consent and situations where consent was given under general duress caused by a third party or external situation. You would be bound to abide by the rules of the only hospital that could save your life but not by the promise to give money to a highwayman.[16] Raz's gloss on this issue is that: 'The undesirable aspect of duress is not in the absence of choice but in the fact that it is engineered in order to extract consent.'[17] One reason to think this view is correct is that if duress or involuntariness invalidated consent, then we forfeit another of consent's appealing qualities as a principle of obligation, that is, its seeming clarity. Assuming minimal rationality, we typically consent only to situations that are better for us than the status quo. If so, it would be difficult to articulate when the difference in our circumstances before and after consent would amount to general duress invalidating consent. The difference between voluntary and involuntary consent is therefore one of degree, so consent would always come with a caveat. Restricting invalidating duress to that which is directed at forcing consent avoids this problem.

Even if one accepts this move, other indeterminacies arise with respect to form and content in the immigration context. By form, I mean the sorts of act that

---

[15] See M Blake, 'Discretionary Immigration' (2002) 30 *Philosophical Topics* 273, 278–80. ('What we are doing … is making some individuals offers where the alternative is to remain in a morally prohibited situation.')

[16] For the hospital example, see Horton, *Political Obligation*, above n 11 at 30–31. For highwaymen and gunmen, see Horton, ibid; A Smith, K Haakonssen (ed), *The Theory of Moral Sentiments* (Cambridge, Cambridge University Press, 2002) 390–91 [VII.iv.9–11]; HLA Hart, *The Concept of Law*, 2nd edn (Oxford, Clarendon Press, 1994) 6–7.

[17] Raz, *Morality of Law*, above n 1 at 89.

constitute consent. Here the pressing question is raised by illegal immigration, since it does not seem plausible to suggest that illegal immigrants expressly consent to obey immigration laws.

There are two ways immigration may become illegal. A migrant may enter through official channels but then violate a rule, for example, by overstaying a visa. Such a migrant perhaps may be said to have violated his or her express obligation to comply with immigration law. Alternatively, a migrant may enter a country covertly and never provide any sort of express consent. Any attempt to ground an obligation to obey immigration law for clandestine entrants will fail unless some prior, authoritative obligation to take legal channels is found. One unpromising suggestion might be that individuals have somehow, through their transnational relationships or transactions, consented to border control by individual states. Locke offers roughly this kind of argument when he suggests that the introduction of money represented a tacit agreement to the 'disproportionate and unequal Possession of the Earth'.[18] Today, we might look to globalized commerce. This argument seems to be a highly implausible tacit consent argument.[19]

A second sort of argument for tacit consent by illegal immigrants has more traction. It might be said that although a clandestine entrant does not initially consent to obey immigration law, his or her entry into a reasonably just state constitutes tacit consent to obey all its other laws. For the illegal immigrant this tacit consent might lead to an obligation to regularize status, perhaps by returning home if no other means are available. The argument may catch the clandestine entrant in a catch-22. Whether it does so depends not on the form but the content of the migrant's tacit consent. What did he or she tacitly consent to? Here two issues arise. One has to do with discerning what sort of ethical relationship exists between an illegal immigrant and the receiving state. The other concerns the moral limits of what can be consented to.

It is plain that a migrant's ethical relationship to the state will differ from that of members. For example, Michael Walzer discusses the views of William Edward Hall, who in 1890 asserted that a non-naturalized migrant 'is merely a person who is required to conform himself to the social order of the community in which he finds himself, but who is politically a stranger to it, obliged only to the negative duty of abstaining from acts injurious to its political interests or contrary to its laws'.[20] The purely negative character of the migrant's obligations may not

---

[18] J Locke, P Laslett (ed), *Two Treatises of Government* (Cambridge, Cambridge University Press, 1960) 302 (II.50], but see the entire discussion beginning at 292ff [II.36]. This has been called 'one of the worst arguments' in the Second Treatise: J Waldron, 'Property, Justification and Need' (1993) 6 *Canadian Journal of Law & Jurisprudence* 185, 198.

[19] See the necessary conditions for consent provided by Flatham and Raz, above n 12.

[20] See M Walzer, 'Political Alienation' in *Obligations: Essays on Obedience, War, and Citizenship* (Cambridge, MA, Harvard University Press, 1970) 103.

extend to the obedience of laws of expulsion. It may be plausible to say that by merely entering a country an illegal migrant tacitly consents to obey its laws. It would by no means be clear such an act constitutes consent to the set of laws an illegal migrant has just violated. Even if illegal entry did constitute tacit consent to immigration law, hence an obligation to leave, could the obligation to obey the receiving state's immigration laws persist once the migrant has left the country in conformity with that new obligation? Or does departure constitute tacit renunciation of any acquired political obligations? If so, the departed migrant can once again freely choose to re-enter in contravention of the law, only to once again be under an obligation as soon as he or she came within the country's jurisdiction. A less absurd view may be that the illegal immigrant has tacitly consented to obey all laws except immigration law.

The second issue is that not every possible wrong can be made right by consent. Even Thomas Hobbes says you can not be bound to surrender to execution or to comply with commands to hurt yourself.[21] That seems quite minimal, but how far can we go? Can one consent to any treatment that is unjust? Can a migrant consent to the forms of second-order oppression covered by the considered judgements from Chapter Two? For example, Pevnick does not suggest that migrants' willingness to accept limitations on their rights would justify any such limits. This willingness seems only to allow for 'humane' programmes, where guestworkers may move among employers and have their basic rights respected. So, if tacit consent is playing an implied role in Pevnick's argument, the obligating power of such consent only holds within certain limits.

The various indeterminacies regarding background conditions, form, and content under the consent account all return us to the problem of authority with which Kant begins his argument for the justification of the state. The principle of consent, like any other principle of justice, is indeterminate. An authority is required to establish the conditions under which it can be binding, as well as the necessary form and content of consent.[22] The issue becomes one of uncovering the source of the receiving state's authority to set conditions for the valid form and content of the migrant's consent. Unless the migrant can be assured that the receiving state seeks to establish such conditions reasonably justly, the migrant will have no reason to submit to them. Therefore, even if we cannot say to what extent one can consent to do an unjust act or to submit to injustice, what we must say is that the determination of this question by a duly constituted authority must itself seek to establish those limits reasonably justly.

---

[21] T Hobbes, R Tuck (ed), *Leviathan* (Cambridge, Cambridge University Press, 1996) 151 [111–12].
[22] Horton, *Political Obligation*, above n 11 at 43; A Ripstein, *Force and Freedom: Kant's Legal and Political Philosophy* (Cambridge, MA, Harvard University Press, 2009) 184. Rawls writes: '[T]he content of obligations is always defined by an institution or practice the rules of which specify what it is that one is required to do.' See Rawls, *Theory of Justice*, above n 6 at 97.

III. Fairness

The principle of fairness is perhaps best understood in the domestic case as an attempted corrective to the defects of the argument from consent, in particular the inability to identify consent acts across a large enough group of members. HLA Hart in 1955 proposed that 'mutual restrictions' in any joint enterprise might be the only possible ground for political obligations.[23] Rawls later adopted and elaborated this principle, calling it first the principle of fair play and later, in *A Theory of Justice*, the principle of fairness:

> This principle holds that a person is required to do his part as defined by the rules of an institution when two conditions are met: first, the institution is just (or fair), that is, it satisfies the two principles of justice; and second, one has voluntarily accepted the benefits of the arrangement or taken advantage of the opportunities it offers to further one's interests.[24]

The intuition underlying the principle of fairness is that: 'We are not to gain from the cooperative labors of others without doing our fair share.'[25]

As a standard account of legal obligation, the principle of fairness has faced two sorts of powerful objections and has not necessarily withstood them: the objection, first offered by Robert Nozick,[26] that you should not have benefits thrust upon you against your will; and the contrary objection that, to the extent we say that benefits must be 'accepted' the principle of fairness collapses into a principle of consent and, like consent accounts, displays insufficient generality. The combined effect of these two objections seems to leave the principle of fairness with little scope for application.

George Klosko has sought to rehabilitate the principle of fairness, arguing that it can generate powerful obligations so long as three conditions are met. The goods supplied must be (1) worth the recipients' effort; (2) presumptively beneficial; and (3) have benefits and burdens that are fairly distributed. The presumptive benefit of certain public goods, like physical security, is crucial to Klosko's account. Presumptive benefits address Nozick's objection because they are 'public goods it is supposed that all members of the community want, whatever else they want, regardless of their rational plans in detail'.[27] Therefore, imposition of burdens as part of a scheme to supply presumptive goods cannot be said to impinge on a person's natural freedom. Building on this foundation, Klosko argues that a whole range of discretionary goods that are part of an 'indivisible benefit package' with

---

[23] HLA Hart, 'Are There Any Natural Rights?' (1955) 64 *Philosophical Review* 175, 185.

[24] Rawls, *Theory of Justice*, above n 6 at 96; see also J Rawls, 'Legal Obligation and the Duty of Fair Play' in S Freeman (ed), *Collected Papers* (Cambridge, MA, Harvard University Press, 1999) 117.

[25] Rawls, *Theory of Justice*, above n 6 at 96.

[26] R Nozick, *Anarchy, State, and Utopia* (New York, Basic Books, 1974) 90–95.

[27] G Klosko, *The Principle of Fairness and Political Obligation*, 2nd edn (Lanham, MD, Rowman & Littlefield, 2004) 39.

presumptive public goods might also lead to obligations. Physical security cannot be provided if not bundled together with proper communication and transportation facilities, health care, sewers, market controls needed to maintain a strong economy, and more besides.[28]

The principle of fairness seems unlikely to have much purchase for official immigration. Immigration regimes are simply not cooperative enterprises in the sense required. Neither can the global economic system be viewed this way. In the global economy, gains generally do not accrue to non-participants: there are few opportunities for free riding.[29] So migrants, at least prior to entry, and members do not engage the kind of cooperative system that can ground an obligation under the principle of fairness. Indeed, it might be said that migrants are those non-members who wish to be admitted to such a system. Yet fairness might provide a basis for grounding an obligation to obey among clandestine entrants. Assuming the principle of fairness can ground an obligation generally among members to obey the law, all else equal we would expect illegal immigrants who receive the same benefits to develop the same obligation to obey the law, including perhaps immigration law. This proposal resembles the argument that illegal immigrants tacitly consent to political obligation, discussed in the previous section, and encounters similar problems.

Klosko's account provides the resources to explore this possibility. Say that 'control of membership' is a discretionary public good that is part of an indivisible package with the presumptively beneficial public good of physical security. Here I treat physical security as being different from the kind of insecurity that concerns Kant: the insecurity of being proximate to another person who has authority to act on his or her own unilateral judgements regarding justice. Here, the concern is actual insecurity within a rightful condition. If immigration control is indivisibly part of providing security against such risk, clandestine entrants might be caught in a bind. If they have received the benefits of public security, they might be obligated to comply with the scheme for controlling membership by not working, regularizing their status if possible, or going home.

This story once again has an air of reality. But the connection between control of membership as a good and public security is underdetermined. Most migrants do not pose threats either as individuals or, except in extraordinary situations, because of sheer numbers. Klosko relies heavily on presumptively beneficial public goods because few people could reasonably reject them or dispute that national governments were the only way to provide such goods. The potential for disagreement seeps into his picture when he extends the principle of fairness from presumptively beneficial to discretionary public goods. There will always be room for dispute, as there is in immigration, over which discretionary policies are

---

[28] ibid at 87ff.

[29] AJ Simmons, 'The Principle of Fair Play' in *Justification and Legitimacy: Essays on Rights and Obligations* (New York, Cambridge University Press, 2001) 4.

needed to support the provision of presumptive public benefits. And so Klosko rivets political checks onto his account. Issues of distribution and the provision of discretionary goods must be settled through 'tolerably fair procedures' (that is, a class of democratic procedures 'generally recognized as suitably fair'), which provide outcomes that are 'defensible with reasonable arguments'.[30]

An obvious problem arises. Migrants have limited avenues for political participation. That suggests more pressure must be placed upon the 'defensible … reasonable arguments' as compared to the 'tolerably fair procedures.' But what would those arguments be? They could only be arguments that seek to show that the distribution of membership is not unreasonable, taking into account the perspective of migrants. That is, they could only be arguments of justice. I might seem to have reached this conclusion too quickly. But the appearance of haste is due to the fact that I have not emphasized Klosko's third condition that must be met for the principle of fairness to give rise to obligations, namely that goods be distributed fairly. This is a requirement of justice embedded in Klosko's account of the principle of fairness. It shows that the principle of fairness cannot be made plausible without being subsumed beneath the natural duty of justice.

A requirement of justice in the principle of fairness was first proposed by Rawls in his amendments to Hart's account. Rawls states that 'unjust social arrangements are themselves a kind of extortion, even violence, and consent to them does not bind'.[31] As Simmons notes, Rawls offers no defence of this claim other than asserting that the moral dynamic is 'similar' to the proposition that 'extorted promises are void *ab initio*'.[32]

There seem to be two possible interpretations of Rawls's justice requirement: first, that unjust social arrangements cannot give rise to obligations on the part of an individual when injustice is visited upon insiders to those arrangements; second, that unjust social arrangements do not bind an individual when injustice is visited upon outsiders. Simmons finds the first interpretation of Rawls's claim more appealing, but he argues that it does not accurately represent most people's intuitions. The ability of obligations to attach themselves does not depend on the justice or injustice of a scheme. A better view would be that most of us feel that we should all contribute in proportion to the benefits we receive as insiders. I do not think Simmons is right about this. To insist that a well-off individual owes an obligation in such a case is to insist that they adopt responsibility for the unjust treatment of others. It seems wrong to say that one could be obligated to take on such responsibility. The poorly off in an unjust scheme, for their part, would seem justified in not contributing to a system that presumably treats them unjustly. Simmons's way out for such individuals is to say that they have the option of

---

[30] ibid at 66.
[31] Rawls, *Theory of Justice*, above n 6 at 302.
[32] Simmons, 'The Principle of Fair Play', above n 29 at 1.

refusing to accept benefits. That does not seem a tenable proposition in the case of the very badly off.

Simmons argues that the second interpretation of Rawls's justice condition, regarding the unjust treatment of outsiders, runs wholly counter to our moral intuitions. We tend to feel obligated to do our fair share even with respect to criminal conspiracies. Again, I think Simmons is wrong. Certainly the immorality of particular demands would be grounds for refusing to cooperate. Long-time gang members can suffer sudden attacks of conscience and refuse orders to rob or murder without having done something morally regrettable; so too soldiers ordered to commit war crimes.[33] In such cases, it may be hard to say whether an obligation initially obtained but was overridden, or that no obligation obtained in the first place. Still, many would be uncomfortable with the conclusion that one is even under an initial moral obligation to carry through the immoral imperative. The same argument applies to immoral ends undertaken at the group level. If you have a change of heart and suddenly do not wish to share in the collective responsibility for an organization's immoral ends, it again seems odd to say that we are under an initial obligation that is then overridden.

Therefore Simmons's attack on the justice condition fails. Even so, it remains to be seen if an affirmative case can be made. Again, the argument is the Kantian one. Whether or not participation in a cooperative enterprise can lead to political obligations must itself be determined under conditions of justice. Thus Rawls's claim that 'unjust social arrangements are themselves a kind of extortion, even violence, and consent to them does not bind' misstates things.[34] Under unjust social arrangements, no one can authoritatively say whether extortion does or does not vitiate obligations of fairness (or consent).

Thus justice is a necessary condition for the principle of fairness to ground an obligation to obey immigration law among clandestine entrants. Without a just regime governing the control of membership, clandestine entrants can be under no obligation to regularize their status or otherwise correct their non-compliance because they benefit from the presumptive good of physical security, or any other presumptive good that control of membership indivisibly supports. It is important to note, however, that I have not argued that the principle of fairness can ground political obligation in the case of immigration regimes assumed to be just. First, the structure through time of such an obligation remains peculiar. On the argument sketched so far, the principle of fairness would allow an initial illegal entry and then take hold once the migrant is inside. This peculiarity counts against the conclusion that the principle of fairness can ground political obligations among migrants. Second, the marginalization of illegal immigrants may render it impossible, on any analysis, to view them as

---

[33] Rawls, *Theory of Justice*, above n 6 at 333; Nozick, *Anarchy, State, and Utopia*, above n 26 at 100.
[34] Rawls, *Theory of Justice*, above n 6 at 302.

co-participants in a scheme that justly distributed the presumptively beneficial good of public security or any other public good. That is not to say they would not be under an obligation to obey many laws, but such obligations would arise largely for other reasons. That is, they would not be an obligation to obey the law in itself. Finally, the principle of fairness does not address itself at all to migrants outside the country.

IV. The Natural Duty of Justice as a Principle of Political Obligation

Neither consent nor the principle of fairness by themselves can ground an obligation by immigrants to obey immigration law. If these are the only plausible ways that an absolutist immigration regime can have authority, and if being capable of having authority is a prerequisite of being a legal regime, then under absolutism immigration regimes cannot be legal regimes.

How can we redeem the self-representation of immigration regimes as legal? One way is to turn to the possibility that their authority rests upon the natural duty of justice as a principle of political obligation.

Judgements about which laws and policies to impose in the governance of immigration will usually be made by the members, legislators, judges, and officials of receiving states, and there are non-decisive practical and moral reasons for accepting this fact, as I discussed in Chapter Three. Further, in order for such judgements to have authority, the immigration regimes of receiving states must strive to be socially just, hence non-oppressive. This conclusion, I also argued, follows from Kant's postulate of public right.

However, the argument for the application of the postulate of public right does not specify exactly how immigration regimes are to create the conditions under which it can be said they have authority over migrants, only that it is necessary that such conditions be in place. Kant is less helpful on the question of actual normative authority. He claims that it is only in terms of the idea of the original contract that 'we can think of the legitimacy of the state',[35] but he also makes several claims about state authority that, on their face, seem implausible. Most notoriously, he says that the members of a state have 'a duty to put up with even what is held to be an unbearable abuse of supreme authority' because 'resistance to the highest legislation can never be regarded as other than contrary to law, and indeed as abolishing the entire constitution'.[36] Thus there is a duty to obey even

---

[35] I Kant, MJ Gregor (trans and ed), *The Metaphysics of Morals* (Cambridge, Cambridge University Press, 1996) 93 [6:315].
[36] ibid at 96–97 [6:320].

the unbearably unjust laws of a despotic state, so long as such a state has put in place institutions allowing it to rule by law, thereby uniting its members' wills.[37] Kant also claims that there is a duty not to inquire into historical grievances regarding the founding of the state with a practical aim, hence it is 'a principle that the presently existing legislative authority ought to be obeyed, whatever its origin'.[38] The only permissible form of protest is *'freedom of the pen'*, since it conduces toward the formation of a united general will.[39]

Kant's argument may be that the justification of the state also establishes its near complete authority over its members. If so, that seems to be a non sequitur.[40] While a rightful condition to be rightful, has to be capable of authoritatively settling disagreements about justice, that mere statement does not show how it is so capable. We need a more fully worked out account both of Kant's view and of how states, and particular components of a state's legal order, such as immigration regimes, can claim to have authority. Although I am not in the first instance interested in Kantian exegesis, but in pursuing an account of the just governance of immigration, I think the solution is that Kant believes that there is a duty of obedience so long as the three branches of government—the legislature, the executive, and the judiciary—can be seen publicly to be aspiring to the ideal of the original contract, that is, by asking of each law (or action or decision) whether it is so unjust that the whole people could not possibly agree to it.[41] If so, what is needed is an explanation of what is meant by possible agreement. If we can flesh this out, perhaps we will know on what terms the immigration regimes of receiving states would be capable of having authority over migrants.

We need to identify the conditions of rightful striving for justice that will lead to political obligation being owed by migrants to immigration regimes. In this section and the next, I aim to describe those conditions by explicating the natural duty of justice as a principle of political obligation. I will proceed in this section by considering the natural duty of justice in general as the basis for an account of political obligation, in the course of which I will consider three common objections. I then turn in the next section to the question of how a regime, and specifically an immigration regime, can have authority even if it is not considered to be just in the eyes of some or all its subjects. The account seeks to connect Rawls's discussion of the natural duty of justice from *A Theory of Justice* to his later account of public reason and the liberal principle of legitimacy in *Political Liberalism* and

---

[37] Ripstein, *Force and Freedom*, above n 22 at 339.

[38] Kant, *Metaphysics of Morals*, above n 35 at 95 [6:319].

[39] I Kant, 'On the Common Saying: "This May Be True in Theory but It Does not Apply in Practice"' in H Reiss (ed), *Kant: Political Writings* (Cambridge University Press, 1970) 85; Kant, *Metaphysics of Morals*, above n 35 at 95 [6:319].

[40] It also suggests, as Simmons says, that Kant conflates the questions of the justification of a state with the question of its legitimacy, once established: AJ Simmons, 'Justification and Legitimacy' in *Justification and Legitimacy*, above n 29 at 141.

[41] Kant, 'Theory and Practice', above n 39 at 79.

'The Idea of Public Reason Revisited'. My claim is that with public reason, Rawls is seeking to determine the conditions where there can be a duty to obey the law, as well as other political obligations, even when a basic structure or elements of a basic structure are not perfectly just from any one person's perspective.[42] What I seek to do is work out this relationship within Rawls's thinking and then to modify it for application to the problem of justice in immigration governance.

Having embraced the principle of fairness in an earlier essay, in *A Theory of Justice* Rawls accepts that it is illegitimate to impose political obligations on a person based on receipt of unwanted benefits. Accordingly, he allows that receipt of benefits must 'in some sense' be voluntary for the principle of fairness to give rise to obligations. But there is no plausible account that would locate voluntary acceptance in enough individuals to provide for political obligations to hold generally among the members of a state, although fairness would still hold for those who seek out privileged positions such as government office.[43] Rawls concludes that: 'There is, I believe, no political obligation, strictly speaking, for members generally.'[44] Rawls seems to mean that the general authority of a just state cannot rest on obligations acquired through performative acts, like accepting benefits or expressing consent, as opposed to duties that are binding irrespective of such acts. Rawls, that is, employs the distinction between 'obligations' and 'duties' that I have not adhered to.[45] He proposes instead that the natural duty of justice provides a ground of multiple political obligations—to comply, to do one's share, to support, and to not undermine.[46] All of these various duties are needed to provide the assurance that a sufficient number of other members will do their part in supporting the basic structure to ensure its ongoing stability,[47] since even in a well-ordered society there may be 'many who do not find a sense of justice for their good'.[48] The need for such obligations will be even more pronounced for the non-ideal society.

Rawls's formulation of the natural duty of justice is as follows:

> This duty has two parts: first, we are to comply with and to do our share in just institutions when they exist and apply to us; and second, we are to assist in the establishment of just arrangements when they do not exist, at least when this can be done with little cost to ourselves. It follows that if the basic structure of society is just, or as just as it

---

[42] He is also, he claims, providing an account that resembles Kant's account of the idea of the original contract: J Rawls, 'The Idea of Public Reason Revisited' in *Collected Papers*, above n 24 at 577, fn 16. However, I am not primarily interested in how far Rawls adheres to or departs from Kant.

[43] He calls this a form of *noblesse oblige*: Rawls, *Theory of Justice*, above n 6 at 100.

[44] ibid at 98.

[45] See above n 2.

[46] Among the various duties Rawls seems to derive from the natural duty of justice are a duty not to seek to undermine just institutions that do not apply to us (Rawls, *Theory of Justice*, above n 6 at 302); a duty 'as circumstances permit, ... to remove any injustices, beginning with the most grievous' (ibid at 216); a duty among legislators to try to follow the principles of justice underlying the constitution (ibid at 314); a duty to engage in properly circumscribed civil disobedience (ibid at 319–46); and a duty among soldiers 'not to be made the agent of grave injustice and evil' (ibid at 333).

[47] ibid at 295–96.

[48] ibid at 505.

is reasonable to expect in the circumstances, everyone has a natural duty to do what is required of him. Each is bound irrespective of his voluntary acts, performative or otherwise.[49]

Rawls later makes clear that this duty is, more specifically, a duty to support and further arrangements that satisfy the principles of justice that define a state's political conception of justice.[50] To defend this account of political obligation, we must show how it derives from a basic statement of the natural duty of justice as a duty to seek to have just relationships with other humans regardless of our voluntary acts, prior institutional commitments, or associative ties. That is, it must be shown how our basic duty to act justly toward others with a sense of justice manifests itself as a political obligation toward a reasonably just basic structure.

We can begin with the observation that Rawls focuses on what, in Chapter One, I called social injustice or oppression, not on personal injustice or wrongs. For Rawls 'the primary subject is the basic structure of society'.[51] He claims that the basic structure is to be judged by the two principles of his conception of justice as fairness: (1) the principle of equal liberty; and (2)(a) the principle of fair equality of opportunity together with (2)(b) the difference principle, that is, the principle that social and economic inequalities must redound to the greatest benefit of the least advantaged members of society. Justice as fairness is the theory that these are the principles that must be adhered to avoid oppression. Under Rawls's theory, if our society's institutions tolerably comply with justice as fairness, that disencumbers us so that we may govern ourselves as individuals or groups only according to an interpersonal morality or, at least, a morality that does not need to have in view the justice of an entire society at all times. When we act on the natural duty of justice, by complying with or doing our share in the institutions that make up a society's basic structure, we indirectly fulfil our duty not to oppress one another and help to ensure that others do the same. The natural duty, therefore, helps guarantee the background justice that gives us the moral elbow room we need to live purposively. Thus the duty both addresses an assurance problem and does so in a way congenial to members' purposiveness.

There have been three sorts of objections to the natural duty of justice as a principle of political obligation.[52] First, it is said it has no obvious limitations of range, so we may be required to comply with, do our share in, and assist in the establishment of just arrangements wherever they are or might be needed. Thus it does not capture the fact, assumed by many theorists, that our political obligations are special obligations of the same genus as our obligations to family or friends, and discontinuous with universal duties like the duty not to kill. Ronald Dworkin, for instance, writes of the natural duty of justice that 'it does not tie

---

[49] ibid at 293–94; see also ibid at 99.
[50] ibid at 295.
[51] ibid at 7.
[52] For a discussion of these, see J Waldron, 'Special Ties and Natural Duties' (1993) 22 *Philosophy & Public Affairs* 3, 4–8.

political obligation sufficiently tightly to the particular community to which those who have the obligation belong'.[53] For Dworkin and others, the duty fails because it lacks boundedness. I call this the objection from particularity. Note that this objection is different from the absolutist objection, discussed in Chapter One, that justice itself is a special relationship. If justice were a special relationship, then the objection from particularity would have no bite.

Related to this objection is a second one about whether the natural duty of justice can provide sufficient guidance. If the natural duty of justice has no limits of range, then far from providing moral elbow room, it demands that I support all just institutions anywhere. If, to avoid this problem, I am only required to support some subset of just institutions, such as those associated with my own state, how is that subset to be selected? Were I to choose to support a foreign government rather than my own, it is not clear on what moral ground my government could object. Finally, there is a concern that a universal natural duty of justice may undermine the stability of existing states. Under a universal natural duty, allegiances will divide and governments will no longer be able to depend on the support of a fixed group of members. This family of objections all point to the difficulty of translating the natural duty of justice into an action-guiding principle. Together, I will call them the objections from practice.

A third objection relates to Rawls's stipulation that the natural duty of justice only takes hold with regard to institutions that 'apply' to us. This requirement seems directed at the first two objections. It may go some distance toward restoring the particularity of political obligations. It may also limit the set of institutions we must support, addressing concerns about practicability. Here, however, it is said there is a danger of unilateral application, that is, of institutions that proclaim themselves just and purport to 'apply' to you.[54] This charge resembles Nozick's objection to the principle of fairness, and the argument follows a familiar path. To meet it, some form of prior acceptance on the part of the subjects would be needed. Yet it is difficult to come up with a satisfying account of prior acceptance that does not devolve into something like a requirement of consent, which likely would not capture a broad enough portion of the population to establish a

---

[53] Dworkin, *Law's Empire*, above n 10 at 193.

[54] The most thorough articulation of the unilateral imposition objection was provided by Simmons. Simmons imagines that a new institution with noble ends—an 'Institute for the Advancement of Philosophers'—comes into being and demands that he pay dues: 'I am not morally required to go along with just any institution which "applies to" people of descriptions which I happen to meet, even if these institutions are *just*. People cannot simply force institutions on me, no matter how just, and force on me a moral bond to do my part in and comply with those institutions.' He further denies that an institution can be said to 'apply' to you just because you were born into it: 'my birth is not an act I perform, or something for which I am responsible': Simmons, *Moral Principles*, above n 11 at 148–50. As I say above of Raz in n 1, it seems to me that this example is premised on a mistaken idea of justice: the Institute Simmons describes has noble ends, but it does not aim to resolve conflict between two parties, of which you are one. See also the discussion in Chapter Three, Section Two. Waldron discusses Simmons's example in Waldron, 'Special Ties', above n 52 at 29–30.

duty to obey the law or other political obligations. I call this the objection to the application requirement.

I start with a methodological point. Some academic philosophers of political obligation, following Simmons, have viewed the ability to explain obligation in particularist terms as a desideratum. A viable theory must show that an individual has obligations towards a particular state (his or her own) or fellow members (of the same state), not an obligation toward all states and non-members. Simmons puts the requirement this way: '[W]e need a principle of political obligation which binds the citizen to one particular state above all others, namely that state in which he is a citizen.'[55] This restriction is in tension, however, with the project of investigating obligation in immigration governance or in any other international or transnational context. There are orders purporting to be legal which may not be states or even subcomponents of states and which make seemingly intelligible demands of obedience from non-members, from groups of individuals who do not share membership with one another, or from states. That suggests that particularity is not so intimately tied up with the idea of authority that it should be used as a criterion of theoretical success in all cases. It seems preferable therefore to give up on particularity as a methodological desideratum unless it can be defended on substantive grounds.[56]

Can it? I take the principal worry to be that by proposing a universalized principle of obligation, we are committing a phenomenological mistake. Special obligations can be voluntary, as when I make a promise, or involuntary, as when I owe certain commitments to those with whom I stand in a meaningful relationship, such as a parent or child. And we can view this latter category of special obligation as either derivative of wider, universal obligations or irreducibly particular. The intuition is that the natural duty of justice errs by ignoring the irreducibly particular nature of our special obligations to those with whom we share state membership.

Now we might accept that some special relationships may in fact be irreducibly particular—relationships of family, friendship, even membership in certain groups or associations—and yet deny that the relationship to our co-members, including through political obligations, falls under this category. Note also that irreducible particularity, even if accepted, does not imply exclusivity. There is no obvious reason why the natural duty of justice cannot sit comfortably alongside special obligations. To be sure, this picture may require that we develop a means of weighing competing moral demands, but that is a problem no more difficult than most moral judgements.

Having made these points, though, in fact the natural duty of justice both meets the particularity requirement as Simmons states it and can be applied to contexts

---

[55] See Simmons, *Moral Principles*, above n 11 at 31–32.
[56] For criticism of the particularity requirement, see K Walton, 'The Particularities of Legitimacy: John Simmons on Political Obligation' (2013) 26 *Ratio Juris* 1, 9–13.

outside the state. In showing how this can be so, we also respond to the objections from practice and the application objection.

Here we may begin with a proposal made by Jeremy Waldron in his article 'Special Ties and Natural Duties'. Waldron accepts that there can be insiders and outsiders with respect to any given institutional regime. That leads him to propose a taxonomy of three kinds of principles. The first kind of principle is represented by P1, a range-limited principle of justice administered by an institution, L. Next comes P2, a range-limited principle requiring insiders to accept L's supervision of P1.[57] A third, consequentialist principle of unlimited range, P3, demands 'that both insiders and outsiders refrain from attacking or sabotaging L in its attempts to put P1 into operation'.[58] In this way, Waldron seeks to 'give a reasonably clear sense to the Rawlsian formulation that a person owes support to just institutions that "apply to him."'[59]

On its own, Waldron's scheme is just that, a scheme. However, taken together with a Kantian justification of the state, it becomes richly suggestive. Within a state, those range-limited principles (P1s) are simply those principles settled authoritatively by the united general will. P2 is the natural duty of justice as a principle of political obligation. And P3 is the duty imposed on outsiders not to undermine the political conception of justice made up of P1s because of the great value of a rightful condition. Moreover, we may add still greater specificity by adding that range-limited principles will include some principles ensuring free and equal political participation by members; some principles that are necessary to eliminate the possibility of injustice due to the unequal provision of the social bases of self-respect; and some principles necessary to ensure that the legitimate expectations of members are respected—that is, principles corresponding to the required forms of partiality among members set out in Chapter Three.

What we say, then, is that the rules of a basic structure apply to us, in the sense relevant to political obligation, if we are among those whose will is united under a rightful condition. There is no concern about application being involuntary, since there is a duty to enter a rightful condition. Union under the general will also explains the sense that we owe a particular obligation to the institutional rules of the basic structure within our own state, so long as these are reasonably just. Such union, as I argued, involves the strongly self-constitutive bond of juridical integration, creating a tie that is deep but not intimate. The Kantian account also explains how the natural duty of justice can be suitably action-guiding. First, typically, only the range-limited principles established by our own state will be

[57] Waldron, 'Special Ties', above n 52 at 16. Waldron's paper is not concerned with how outsiders become insiders. He does remark that people 'mark themselves as insiders in relation to L by accepting P2. In general, a person is an insider in relation to an institution if and only if it is part of the point of that institution to do justice to some claim of his among all the claims with which it deals.'
[58] ibid at 17.
[59] ibid at 18.

salient. For the most part, even today, we will not be in a position to injure members of other states. Therefore we will not be overwhelmed by the demands of the natural duty. Second, where we are in a position to injure others, the natural duty of justice does provide guidance: To enter a rightful condition or 'to assist in the establishment of just arrangements where they do not exist'.[60] All of this suggests that Simmons' insistence that the natural duty of justice fails to meet the criterion of particularity flows from his rejection of the Kantian justification of the state. If that justification is accepted, the natural duty of justice does offer particularized, action-guiding obligations without concerns about the involuntariness of the application of this duty.

V. How Just Immigration Regimes Can Have Authority

The three objections to the natural duty of justice as a principle of political obligation are not fatal if one accepts that justice is a pre-civil and indeterminate virtue, as well as the Kantian justification of the state based on those premises. Since I believe the supporting premises and arguments in favour of the Kantian justification are sound, I take it that the objections just canvassed do not show that the natural duty of justice cannot in principle provide a ground for political obligation. It remains to work out an affirmative account of how the natural duty of justice might lead to political obligations owed by migrants to immigration regimes. In particular, what must be spelled out are the conditions under which immigration regimes would have authority, hence able to give rise to political and in particular legal obligations, and also the conditions that would render them capable of having authority, hence able to claim to be legal regimes. There would still be reason to reject the natural duty of justice, as a principle of political obligation, if we could not furnish a plausible account of how it gives rise to such obligations as opposed to merely remaining a personal demand made on each individual with respect to other individuals.

In examining this possibility, the more important claim made in Rawls's formulation is not that there is a duty to comply with, support, do our share in, and not undermine just institutions, but that there is a duty to do so even when such institutions are only 'as just as it is reasonable to expect under the circumstances'. This is a claim that when there is a modicum of justice there will be a duty to obey institutional rules that will strike some or perhaps many as unjust.[61] That is,

---

[60] Rawls, *Theory of Justice*, above n 6 at 293–94; see also ibid at 99.

[61] What about a duty to obey laws that are not required by justice—laws that are non-just rather than unjust? Because of the coercive power that backs such laws, those who object to them will also consider them unjust.

under the natural duty of justice there is a political obligation to do less than what you judge justice requires and to accept certain injustices that you perceive to have been committed against you and others, provided that in either case the deviation from the strict requirements of justice is reasonable under the circumstances. This on its face is a far more plausible claim than Kant's claim that there is a duty to obey tyrannies. However, it still requires defence.

What is a reasonable deviation from justice? In *Theory*, Rawls offers two suggestions. A reasonable deviation from justice includes cases where the burdens of injustice are more or less evenly distributed over different groups. 'Therefore,' he says, 'the duty to comply is problematic for permanent minorities that have suffered injustice for many years.'[62] Further, a reasonable deviation would not include cases where people are 'required to acquiesce in the denial of our own and others' liberties'.[63] But how does he arrive at these conclusions? And how can we know that injustices short of these two examples are reasonable? Indeed, how could these vague suggestions be further specified? It seems once again that the very limits of the natural duty of justice as a principle of political obligation reproduce the basic, persistent problem of indeterminacy and potential disagreement.

Given that, and the powerful moral attitudes associated with our sense of justice, this part of the natural duty asks of us a great deal. In the remainder of this section I set out first a general understanding of the reasonableness condition, drawing on Rawls's later account of public reason and the liberal principle of legitimacy. I then describe specific institutional requirements under which the reasonableness condition is fully met and how that leads to an understanding of when it is capable of being met. Finally, I adapt the resulting account to immigration regimes. The basic thought is that the natural duty of justice gives rise to political obligations for two reasons. The first reason is the Kantian imperative to enter a rightful condition: There must be some authority so that we respond to a basic assurance problem caused by justice's indeterminacy. The second is the Rawlsian answer that, by following public reason, an authority—in the standard case, the state; in our non-standard case, a state's immigration regime—cannot be asked to do more, given the inevitable indeterminacy of justice. There is, quite simply, no reasonable alternative available.[64]

1. Reasonable Deviations from Justice

The idea of 'the reasonable', typically used to describe either principles or persons, has a prominent place in Rawls's writings.[65] As a descriptor of principles,

---

[62] Rawls, *Theory of Justice*, above n 6 at 312.

[63] ibid.

[64] See '*Commonweal* Interview with John Rawls' in *Collected Papers*, above n 24 at 620.

[65] For discussion, see S Freeman, 'Public Reason and Political Justification' in *Justice and the Social Contract: Essays on Rawlsian Political Philosophy* (New York, Oxford University Press, 2007) 227–28 and 237–38.

the 'reasonable' seems to connote acceptability to reasonable persons. For example, in Rawls's first published paper, 'Outline of a Decision Procedure for Ethics', he says:

> The reasonableness of a principle is tested by seeing whether it can function in existing instances of conflicting opinion, and in new cases causing difficulty, to yield a result which, after criticism and discussion, seems to be acceptable to all, or nearly all, competent judges, and to conform to their intuitive notion of a reasonable decision.[66]

And in *Theory*, expanding on the natural duty of justice, he writes: 'As a rough rule a conception of justice is reasonable in proportion to the strength of the arguments that can be given for adopting it in the original position'.[67]

As a descriptor of persons, reasonableness connotes openness to the arguments and points of view of others, as well as a willingness to accommodate others' ends. Thus, in 'Outline', he writes that the 'competent judges' whose judgements become the basis for explicated principles, are 'reasonable' men. Such men show 'a willingness, if not a desire, to use the criteria of inductive logic in order to determine what is proper for [them] to believe'. They show 'a disposition to find reasons for and against ... possible lines of conduct'. They have a 'desire to consider questions with an open mind' and they know, or try to know, their own 'emotional, intellectual, and moral predilections' and seek to take account of these when reaching judgements.[68] In *Political Liberalism*, where the idea of the reasonable takes on a more prominent role, the description of reasonable persons becomes linked to the explicitly political problem of finding fair terms of cooperation in a liberal society characterized by reasonable pluralism. Reasonable persons, in particular, are moved by the ideal of reciprocity to propose and abide by fair terms of cooperation:

> Persons are reasonable in one basic aspect when, among equals say, they are ready to propose principles and standards as fair terms of cooperation and to abide by them willingly, given the assurance that others will likewise do so. Those norms they view as reasonable for everyone to accept and therefore as justifiable to them; and they are ready to discuss the fair terms that others propose.... Reasonable persons, we say, are not moved by the general good as such but desire for its own sake a social world in which they, as free and equal, can cooperate with others on terms all can accept. They insist that reciprocity should hold within that world so that each benefits along with others.[69]

Finally, in 'The Idea of Public Reason Revisited', his last published essay, Rawls tells us that:

> Citizens are reasonable when, viewing one another as free and equal in a system of social cooperation over generations, they are prepared to offer one another fair terms of cooperation according to what they consider the most reasonable conception of political

---

[66] J Rawls, 'Outline of a Decision Procedure for Ethics' in *Collected Papers*, above n 24 at 11.
[67] Rawls, *Theory of Justice*, above n 6 at 310.
[68] Rawls, 'Outline', above n 66 at 3.
[69] J Rawls, *Political Liberalism*, expanded edn (New York, Columbia University Press, 1996) at 49–50.

justice; and when they agree to act on those terms, even at the cost of their own interests in particular situations, provided that other citizens also accept those terms. The criterion of reciprocity requires that when those terms are proposed as the most reasonable terms of fair cooperation, those proposing them must also think it at least reasonable for others to accept them, as free and equal citizens, and not as dominated or manipulated, or under the pressure of an inferior political or social position. Citizens will of course differ as to which conceptions of political justice they think the most reasonable, but they will agree that all are reasonable, even if barely so.[70]

For Rawls, then, reasonableness is that part of the moral sensibility connected with the sense of justice[71] and is a key moral–psychological component of the process of achieving 'full' reflective equilibrium,[72] a reflective equilibrium that is both wide and shared among the relevant group; it is contrasted with the rational, which is associated with our ability to form, revise, and pursue a conception of the good. We might say, stepping over to Smith, that to be reasonable is to make good faith efforts to take on the perspective of the impartial spectator, so that our judgements regarding justice are made taking into account, to the extent we are able, the perspective of others. In this way, they provide a suitable basis for seeking social harmony.

To solve the problem of authority within society, therefore, Rawls endeavours to describe the ideal of the most reasonable impartial perspective available to the members of liberal constitutional democracies when addressing other members. This is the perspective of ideal public reason and it provides a deliberative benchmark for measuring when a departure from strict justice, as assessed from the partial perspective of any single member, is reasonable. The ideal of public reason is realized

> whenever judges, legislators, chief executives, and other governmental officials, as well as candidates for public office, act from and follow the idea of public reason and explain to other citizens their reasons for supporting fundamental political positions in terms of the political conception they regard as the most reasonable. In this way, they fulfill what I shall call their duty of civility to one another and to other citizens.... [C]itizens fulfill their duty of civility and support the idea of public reason by doing what they can to hold government officials to it.[73]

Decisions regarding fundamental political questions made on the basis of public reason are legitimate and create political obligations. Rawls makes this claim in his discussion of the 'liberal principle of legitimacy' and the 'duty of civility':

> Thus when, on a constitutional essential or matter of basic justice, all appropriate government officials act from and follow public reason, and when all reasonable citizens think of themselves ideally as if they were legislators following public reason, the legal enactment expressing the opinion of the majority is legitimate law. *It may not be thought*

---

[70] J Rawls, 'Idea of Public Reason Revisited', above n 42 at 578.
[71] Rawls, *Political Liberalism*, above n 69 at 52.
[72] J Rawls, E Kelly (ed), *Justice as Fairness: A Restatement* (Cambridge, MA, Belknap Press, 2001) 31.
[73] J Rawls, 'Idea of Public Reason Revisited', above n 42 at 576–77.

the most reasonable, or the most appropriate, by each, but it is politically (morally) binding on him or her as a citizen and is to be accepted as such. Each thinks that all have spoken and voted at least reasonably, and therefore all have followed public reason and honored their duty of civility.[74]

Thus if the members of a state comply with public reason in their debates over constitutional essentials and matters of basic justice, then political obligations arise, including a duty to obey legal enactments expressing the opinion of the majority.[75] This passage suggests that, through his development of the idea of public reason, Rawls also works out the problem of how to discern reasonable from unreasonable deviations from justice. The resulting account is largely procedural or institutional in nature. A reasonable deviation from justice is simply one that is the result of decisions by members striving to comply with the ideal of public reason: the result of a debate among members proposing what they believe to be reasonably just terms of cooperation to one another in accordance with reciprocity.

2. Reasonableness and Obligation

Rawls does not actually say why political obligation follows when deviations from strict justice, as understood from the partial perspective of any one member, have been reached through the deliberative process that seeks to comply with the ideal of public reason. I now want to flesh out this claim. That will then allow us to determine how it might be applied in immigration governance, so that we can discern the conditions under which immigration regimes are capable of having authority, as well as the conditions where they might actually have it.

I will assume that the relevant 'circumstances' in which the reasonableness of a deviation from justice must be assessed will always be four-fold. They are, first, whatever circumstances of justice led to the kinds of claims at issue, that is, whatever conflict of interest may lead some persons to believe they may have been unjustifiably injured. Second, the circumstances include the fact that there will always be disagreement about justice because of indeterminacy. Third, they include the fact that each one of us faces other obstacles—corruptions and the burdens of judgement (which, strictly speaking, include indeterminacy)—in coming to matching judgements about justice in the face of indeterminacy. Finally, the fourth circumstance is the limits of institutional design in addressing the first three. That is, although institutions and their rules can make up for human limitations to an extent, they quite obviously cannot eliminate all indeterminacy and disagreement. In particular, they cannot eliminate the ultimate reliance of any institution on the human actors within it, who may not always do what they should. A reasonable deviation from strict justice must be understood

---

[74] ibid at 578 (emphasis added).
[75] ibid at 579.

in terms of what is possible in light of these circumstances. It is unreasonable, that is, to ask for greater assurances of justice than can be provided.

My claim for the standard, domestic case is that, in these circumstances, a deviation from the strict requirements of justice is reasonable, first, if it can be represented as having been generated by a suitable constitutional, legislative, administrative, and judicial process; and second, if members, legislators, judges, and officials who are responsible for the law act from what Rawls calls the duty of civility, that is, the duty to strive to act from just principles that other members can accept as reasonable. Both conditions are subject to a third, namely that the compliance with the first two conditions must be publicly open to scrutiny. A reasonable deviation from justice is one that occurs, therefore, when certain institutional conditions are met and when the relevant legal and political actors publicly fulfil certain role obligations.[76] Fourth and finally, in a domestic setting some form of democratic decision making will be required to resolve lingering disagreement.

To begin, Rawls recognizes that principles of justice require institutional specification through what he calls the four-stage sequence.[77] The first stage is whatever procedure is used to arrive at principles of justice. For Rawls this is the constructivist social contract device known as the original position. The second stage is a constitutional convention in which the aim of the framers is to design a set of rules for the constitutional powers of government and the basic rights of members. The asymptotic goal of such a constitution is to produce exclusively just outcomes, that is, a basic structure that will produce only just laws when the constitutional procedures are followed. The more modest goal is 'to select from among the procedural arrangements that are both just and feasible those which are most likely to lead to a just and effective legal order'.[78] The third stage is legislative, in which laws and policies are proposed and judged according to their consistency with the constitution as well as the principles of justice. Finally, there is the fourth stage, in which the laws are applied to particular cases by judges, executive officials, and conscientious members.

Throughout the four-stage sequence a sort of wide reflective equilibrium is at work. As has been discussed in Chapter One, wide reflective equilibrium is a method through which we work back and forth between considered judgements to arrive at coherent moral principles. Similarly in the four-stage sequence, the best constitution is found 'by moving back and forth between the constitutional convention and the legislature'.[79] The best legislation is found by seeing how well it makes sense of the constitution and how well, when applied, it matches our considered judgements. Even cases of rule application at the fourth stage must be seen

---

[76] MO Hardimon, 'Role Obligations' (1994) 91 *The Journal of Philosophy* 333.
[77] Rawls, *Theory of Justice*, above n 6 at §31.
[78] ibid at 173.
[79] ibid at 174.

as having the potential to force us to revise the principles developed at the first stage.[80] The ability to represent our political institutions as engaged in a process of wide reflective equilibrium is the first condition for political obligation under the natural duty of justice. Through reflective equilibrium carried out across the four stages, the principles of justice provide a substantive check on possible injustice. Scrupulous framers will be mindful of possible justice and injustice in the legislative and judicial edicts of their regimes. When they perceive what they believe to be an injustice, they will seek to correct it at the appropriate stage. If institutional means, including but certainly not limited to judicial review and the possibility of constitutional amendment, are put in place to ensure that this is done so far as possible, then there will be reason to think political institutions will overall tend toward, though without ever achieving, elimination of injustice.

For this to work, all engaged in the various forms of decision making integrated into the institutional process of wide reflective equilibrium must comply with the duty of civility, which might be thought of as a duty to seek reasonable terms of coexistence. For those exercising or seeking to influence the exercise of political power, it is a duty 'to be able to explain to one another on those fundamental questions how the principles and policies they advocate and vote for can be supported by the political values of public reason';[81] that is, a duty to engage in debate in which argument is based on reasons that can be referred back to a sincere belief that the positions or decisions we embrace are consistent with a political conception of justice that all can reasonably be asked to endorse. The duty of civility also finds expression at moments where compliance is demanded of us, as a duty 'not to invoke the faults of social arrangements as a too ready excuse for not complying with them, nor to exploit inevitable loopholes in the rules to advance our interests'.[82] The duty of civility derives from the natural duty of justice in the following way. Peaceful coexistence is itself a great good so justice demands that we not ask too much of one another by insisting too rigidly on our own conceptions of justice. Exactly how this duty is to be fulfilled will no doubt vary in accordance with the individual's position within the basic structure.

Though appealing, these two conditions do not address the problem of disagreement, in particular, disagreement over whether someone has strayed beyond the reasonable. This is a product in part of the way the duty of civility, the liberal principle of legitimacy, and public reason are defined. If we are attentive to Rawls's

---

[80] See the remarks in J Rawls, 'Reply to Habermas' in *Political Liberalism*, above n 69 at 399.

[81] Rawls, *Political Liberalism*, above n 69 at 217; see also Rawls, 'Idea of Public Reason Revisited', above n 42 at 576–77, 594–94. Freeman notes that this statement of the duty may seem too burdensome to be plausible. 'Perhaps the best way to understand the duty of civility is that citizens must sincerely believe that their political decisions are justifiable in terms of public reason, and that, if they are not able to explain this justification, then there should be *someone* whose judgement citizens trust who is in a position to explain their political decisions in terms of public reasons.' See Freeman, 'Public Reason and Political Justification', above n 65 at 374.

[82] Rawls, *Theory of Justice*, above n 6 at 312.

formulations, what they require is the fulfilment of the duty to offer reasons that we sincerely believe that other reasonable persons can accept. It is not a requirement that it actually be the case that others will accept them or even that they reasonably can. From one perspective, this is no doubt realistic: all we can ask of decision makers is that they seek to act on reasons they think others will accept. From the perspective of the members of a state subject to those decisions, however, it may be unclear whether this requirement has been fulfilled. Therefore there needs to be some form of accountability, which leads to the requirement of publicity.[83] Publicity in Rawls has a deep relationship to the demand that a conception of justice provide terms of social cooperation that all can accept. The most important argument for publicity is the idea that public justification is necessary for our acceptance of state institutions: 'For if the basic structure relies on coercive sanctions, however rarely and scrupulously applied, the grounds of its institutions should stand up to public scrutiny.'[84] The requirement of publicity connects with certain checks associated with the rule of law, such as the power to challenge the constitutionality of legislation or government actions, to raise in court the claim that an official acted in bad faith or was biased, or an interpretive presumption that laws, in cases of ambiguity, were in fact promulgated in keeping with the duty of civility. This last possibility would amount to canons of statutory interpretation presuming both constitutional adherence, coherence, and general reasonableness on the part of a legislature. It is through legal challenges of these kinds, in part, that the compliance of the basic structure with the underlying conception of justice can be publicly verified.

Finally, it will be unclear at what point it can be said that an authoritative equilibrium has been reached and, perhaps more important, who gets the final word. The obvious and perhaps only way out in the domestic context is by envisioning the stages in democratic terms, so that the final word rests with the members of a state. Rawls in fact explicitly incorporates an idea of deliberative democracy into his account of public reason.[85] Thus he may be taken as endorsing the claim that to be authoritative, political decisions must comply with public reason and must, in the end, be submitted to the democratic process. It is as part of that process, acting in accordance with the duty of civility, that the members of a state can decide if the decisions by officials have truly been reached in accordance with public reason.

In summary, the authority of the legal enactments of a state with respect to its members is established by having the relevant legislators, officials, and judges strive for justice by complying with the duty of civility within an appropriate institutional apparatus. It is further established by allowing members to hold

[83] Rawls, *Political Liberalism*, above n 69 at 66–71. See also J Rawls, 'Kantian Constructivism in Moral Theory' in *Collected Papers*, above n 24 at 324–26.
[84] ibid at 68.
[85] Rawls, 'Idea of Public Reason Revisited', above n 42 at 579–81.

those officials accountable for doing so through a requirement of publicity, which includes the rule of law, and democracy. The result of this discussion is that we may say that the natural duty of justice may give rise to political obligations if a state's institutions engage with its members in what we might call democratic reflective equilibrium. In effect, at this point, what may be claimed is that any deviations from justice are the responsibility of the members of the state.[86]

3. Reasonableness in the Circumstances of Immigration

Once again, Rawls develops his account of public reason for closed, well-ordered societies, ignoring the possibility that members' political decisions might injure non-members.[87] But the arguments in Chapter Three based on the postulate of public right together with those in this chapter tell us there is a duty to strive to govern immigration non-oppressively in order that the governance of immigration should be rightful. How immigration regimes can establish their authority by striving not to oppress migrants must be set out, especially in light of the fact that immigration is necessarily and, within constraints, justifiably governed through status and the fact that democratic affirmation of the reasonableness of deviations from justice is likely unavailable in this context.

Recall, from the passages quoted above, that the criterion of reciprocity requires that when terms of governance are proposed 'those proposing them must also think it at least reasonable for others to accept them, as free and equal citizens, and not as dominated or manipulated, or under the pressure of an inferior political or social position'.[88] Reciprocity is an ideal of political relations opposed to the Schmittian idea of the political as the sorting of friends from enemies. What must be done is to avoid having the non-member status of migrants lead to forms of immigration governance that are based on domination, manipulation, or worse.[89] To do this, we need to begin by extending Rawls's idea of reasonableness to the immigration context by explaining how the ideal of reciprocity can be applied, such that migrants and members can be seen as jointly engaged in a project of just immigration governance.

Such an explanation begins by divorcing the idea of reciprocity from the idea with which Rawls often twins it, fair social cooperation. Reciprocity can serve as a guiding political ideal whenever two persons can call upon shared values to resolve political questions that arise between them. Within states, cooperation gives rise to a shared good that can serve as the basis for agreement, but the benefits of social cooperation are not the only possible basis of reciprocity. Remember

[86] Democracy 'embodies a principle of respect for each person in the processes by which we settle on a view to be adopted as *ours* even in the face of disagreement': Waldron, *Law and Disagreement*, above n 8 at 109. See also Christiano, 'Authority', above n 8 at 273.
[87] Rawls, 'Idea of Public Reason Revisited', above n 42 at 577.
[88] ibid at 578.
[89] ibid at 574.

that states, and the political inequality between members and non-members, are justified by the successful integration of members under a general will, reflected in a political conception of justice. Because the justification of immigration governance, as I noted in Chapter One, is part of the project of justifying the various other inequalities that rest upon the political inequality between members and non-members, limitations to immigration must be justified based on the ongoing need to ensure the stability of the receiving state's political conception of justice and the need to respect members' legitimate expectations. Immigration is one of only two ways, the other being childbirth, that societies may reproduce themselves. Each state's immigration regime is 'part of the basic structure, since one of its main roles is to be the basis of the orderly production and reproduction of society and its culture from one generation to the next'.[90] It is important to stress that this role of immigration policy is unavoidable. Any state that, improbably, sought to bar all immigration would be making a policy choice to seek the ongoing maintenance of its political conception of justice solely through natural reproduction. Therefore, the primary justification of immigration policies, for members and non-members (including migrants) alike, must be the maintenance of a state's political conception of justice through the regulation of the admission of new permanent or temporary members.

Reasonable members will therefore see immigration regimes, and the proposed immigration of individual migrants, as part of the project of maintaining the political conception of justice of their state. This ongoing project cannot be undertaken without enlisting migrants in its execution. It is easiest to see migrants admitted indefinitely in this light since, as I argued in Chapter Three, the aim is eventually to juridically integrate them into the state. But temporary resident migrants may also contribute to and have claims on the state's social product. Further temporary migrants may themselves become juridically integrated, even in the face of policies designed to prevent them from doing so, in which case all else equal there will be a duty to grant them political equality, likely through naturalization. Finally, even excluded migrants are jointly engaged in the requisite sense. If a migrant's exclusion on fair terms is required to maintain the receiving state's political conception of justice, a reasonable migrant will accept that. One of the characteristics of a reasonable migrant is surely that he or she recognizes the great value of the provision of a political conception of justice that is stable for the right reasons. Reasonable migrants are not rapacious.

It might be objected that this conception of joint engagement between members and migrants forces upon members a relationship of reciprocal justification against their will. Thomas Nagel, for example, writes that 'though the obligations of justice arise as a result of a special relation, there is no obligation to enter into that relation with those to whom we do not yet have it, thereby acquiring those

---

[90] ibid at 595. I have substituted 'immigration regime' for 'family'.

obligations toward them'.[91] The reply to this objection is, first, that it misrepresents facts to suggest that receiving states are merely the passive recipients of immigrant pressure. All liberal constitutional democracies actively use immigration policy as part of efforts to shape their economic and other prospects. In light of contemporary demographic pressures and shortages in Western labour markets, it is highly unlikely that they will stop doing so. This reply may not be fully satisfying, since it is based on what might seem to be a contingent fact. A second reply is simply to deny the objection. There is no limit to the liberal demand that social arrangements, including immigration regimes, be justified to those subject to and potentially injured by them. And it will sometimes be unjustifiable to deny certain moral requirements notwithstanding that we have not sought them out or the circumstances that brought them to bear.[92] Immigration is such a case. Members may not have a duty to help migrants to come and they may not have a duty to admit them (though they may, on both counts). They do have a duty to recognize that immigration laws and policies may be injurious. Migrants' demands for justification of such injuries must be answered on terms that reasonable migrants can accept.

The specification of the reasonableness requirement in the natural duty of justice, applied in context of immigration governance, appeals to this idea of joint engagement between migrant and member in the maintenance of the receiving state's political conception of justice, replacing the idea of fair terms of cooperation in Rawls's domestic theory. This form of joint engagement provides the basis for the application of the ideal of reciprocity as a form of political relationship.

With this basis for reciprocity specified, we can develop the rest of the account of the natural duty as a principle of political obligation for immigration regimes. Here we run up against a further problem. Within a state, when laws are the product of democratic procedures, such that all relevant actors fulfil the duty of civility and the publicity condition is satisfied, the laws despite inevitable imperfections will not fall outside the range of reasonable justice. Though unjust in the eyes of

---

[91] T Nagel, 'The Problem of Global Justice' (2005) 33 *Philosophy & Public Affairs* 113, 121. Christopher Heath Wellman also pursues an argument based on the right of a state's members to freedom of association, which he plausibly claims includes the right not to associate. However, he argues only that such a right is presumptive, which suggests the need to give reasons for not associating: CH Wellman, 'Freedom of Association and the Right to Exclude' in CH Wellman and P Cole, *Debating the Ethics of Immigration: Is There a Right to Exclude?* (New York, Oxford University Press, 2012) 54–55. Finally, Michael Blake suggests a still more moderate view that there is 'a presumptive right to be free from others imposing obligations on us without our consent': Blake, 'Immigration, Jurisdiction, and Exclusion', above n 13 at 115.

[92] See Waldron, 'Special Ties', above n 52 at 27 for a similar claim: 'Despite the conditions we have imposed, someone might still balk at the general idea behind this position. Can an organization simply impose itself on us, morally, in this way? There comes a point when the theorist of natural duty must stop treating this question as an objection and simply insist that the answer is yes. His affirmative answer is, after all, what distinguishes a theory of natural duty from theories of acquired political obligation.'

some members, all laws are proposed as part of a conception of justice that other members can reasonably be asked to accept. There is simply no other way to provide assurance of justice in the face of the indeterminacy of justice.

Democratic decision making is crucial here, as it provides the final guarantee of reasonableness in the face of disagreement. This conclusion seems to suggest that immigration regimes must themselves be subject to a form of democratic decision making that includes migrants. That may well be the case, although under realistic assumptions, I have difficulty imagining a form of democratic decision making that would be both accepted by members and provide for meaningful participation by migrants. Arash Abizadeh has suggested that democratic governance of immigration might involve 'truly global institutions (eg federal or confederal), multilateral state institutions, or transnational domestic institutions'.[93] The development of such institutions would face obstacles that appear to me intractable even in an ideal world, including justified political inequality between members and non-members as well as the transience and heterogeneity of the population of non-member participants.

Failing the development of immigration regimes that could provide for actual, democratic participation inclusive of migrants, the more realistic alternative is for immigration laws to be arrived at through an 'ideally democratic decision'.[94] What I mean by this is that the responsible political actors, who will be members of the receiving state, must turn their minds to migrants in the same spirit as they do in standard democratic debate among members. Members and legislators must conceive of migrants as free and equal persons with their own views and interests. They must ask themselves what decisions reasonable migrants might make, given the shared goal of maintaining the receiving state's shared political conception of justice, if they were juridically integrated—if they, as outsiders, were fully committed to the receiving state's political conception of justice—and had to make a decision regarding immigration law and policy, or its implementation. The members, that is, must make political decisions in trust on behalf of migrants.[95]

The difference between immigration governance and the domestic context is that democratic reflective equilibrium is not, I am assuming, feasible. The question becomes what institutional guarantees, short of democracy, can define the terms of a reasonable deviation from justice. Thus, immigration regimes must

---

[93] A Abizadeh, 'Democratic Theory and Border Coercion: No Right to Unilaterally Control Your Own Borders' (2008) 36 *Political Theory* 37, 55. See also D Miller, 'Democracy's Domain' (2009) 37 *Philosophy & Public Affairs* 201.

[94] See Rawls, *Theory of Justice*, above n 6 at 256: 'All generations are virtually represented in the original position, since the same principle would always be chosen. An ideally democratic decision will result, one that is fairly adjusted to the claims of each generation and therefore satisfying the precept that what touches all concerns all.' Rawls alters his account of justice between generations in Rawls, *Political Liberalism*, above n 69, but the essential idea of assuring the ideal representation of future generations remains intact.

[95] Ripstein, *Force and Freedom* at n 22 at 70–81.

admit of representation as engaged in a process of reflective equilibrium: justice in immigration governance must be seen as their asymptotic goal. The second condition is that those responsible for immigration regimes must act from a duty of civility toward migrants and in accordance with ideal democratic decisions. Finally, there is a requirement of publicity, which leads to rights to challenge laws and acts on the basis that they are unconstitutional, on grounds aimed at ensuring that relevant officials have acted in good faith and without bias, and benefiting from an interpretive presumption, when an immigration decision is challenged, that a law or policy was drafted in keeping with the duty of civility and institutional reflective equilibrium.[96] When no such interpretation is available, the natural duty of justice does not give rise to political obligations and the migrant may be faced with the complicated question, unaddressed here, of how to respond to an unreasonably unjust law.

VI. Moving on

An immigration regime will have authority over migrants if it strives to be just by fulfilling the conditions outlined: if its decisions can be represented as part of a process of institutional reflective equilibrium; if the relevant legislators, officials, judges have acted in accordance with the duty of civility; if members and legislators have made 'ideal democratic decisions' on behalf of migrants; and if migrants

---

[96] To some extent such an interpretive presumption already features in the case law, when courts interpret immigration statutes to avoid constitutional doubt: see, eg *Jean v Nelson*, 472 US 846, 854 (1985) ('Prior to reaching any constitutional questions, federal courts must consider nonconstitutional grounds for decision'); *Zadvydas v Davis*, 533 US 678, 689 (2001) ('We have read significant limitations into other immigrations statutes in order to avoid their constitutional invalidation. For similar reasons, we read an implicit limitation into the statute before us.') Alternatively, it is found when courts have held that they should read ambiguous deportation statutes in the light most favourable to a migrant, due to the harsh consequences of deportation: see *Bridges v Wixon*, 326 US 135, 147–48 (1945) ('We cannot assume that Congress meant to employ the term 'affiliation' in a broad, fluid sense which would visit such hardship on an alien for slight or insubstantial reasons'); *Fong Haw Tan v Phelan*, 333 US 6, 10 (1948) ('since the stakes are considerable for the individual, we will not assume that Congress meant to trench on his freedom beyond that which is required by the narrowest of several possible meanings of the words used'); *INS v Cardoza-Fonseca*, 480 US 421, 449 (1987) (relying on the 'longstanding principle of construing any lingering ambiguities in deportation statutes in favor of the alien'). For discussion of the role of 'subconstitutional norms' in reshaping the United States plenary power doctrine (the US label for the discretionary doctrine as a matter of domestic constitutional law), see H Motomura, 'Immigration Law after a Century of Plenary Power: Phantom Constitutional Norms and Statutory Interpretation' (1990) 100 *Yale Law Journal* 545. Motomura argues that '[i]n immigration law, the "constitutional" norms that actually inform statutory interpretation—which are norms borrowed from public law generally—conflict with the expressly articulated constitutional norm—unreviewable plenary power': ibid at 564. In the terms I have used in developing my argument, what is going on is that the courts are acting to constrain the exercise of absolutist discretion in order to ensure the authority of immigration law. Motomura's 'phantom' constitutional norms are norms that reflect an effort to act from the duty of civility. They are seeking to interpret immigration law based on a political conception of justice that reasonable migrants might accept.

have rights to challenge immigration laws, policies, and decisions to ensure that these requirements have been met. We say further that an immigration regime is capable of having authority if the institutional prerequisites are in place; that is, if the failure to live up to this ideal is the result not of institutional barriers, but of the failures of individuals acting within the relevant institutions.[97] If so, it can represent itself in good faith as a legal regime.

The last three chapters have sought to establish that immigration regimes have a duty to strive to be just, providing a foundation for the principled account of discretion in immigration governance. The main argument for that account, taking off from Kant's postulate of public right, was set out in Chapter Three. In Chapter Four, I tried to show that the philosophical absolutisms of Michael Walzer and Thomas Nagel ultimately give way to a principled account, by way of a concern with legitimacy. In this chapter I have tried to argue that unless immigration regimes strive to govern justly they cannot have authority and therefore cannot be legal regimes. I have also tried, relying heavily on Rawls, to describe sufficiency conditions under which immigration regimes can be said to have authority. In all this, nothing has been said except at very high levels of abstraction about what it would mean for immigration regimes to be just. That task is taken up in Part Three.

---

[97] For a different account of being 'capable' of having authority, see Schotel, above n 7 at 123–29.

Part III

Justice in Immigration Governance

6

The Indirect Principle of Freedom of Migration

I. Introduction

THE CONCLUSION OF the argument in Part Two imposes the daunting theoretical task of developing reasonable principles of just immigration governance that we, members of wealthy liberal constitutional democracies, sincerely believe reasonable migrants would accept. Such principles are needed to establish the authority of immigration regimes, as mandated by the postulate of public right. Members of wealthy liberal constitutional democracies also have an independent reason to seek an understanding of justice in immigration governance, namely so that we can assess the acceptability of inegalitarian policies.

In responding to these imperatives, we have available our earlier discussion and arguments. We know that a reasonable conception of justice in immigration governance ought to mediate between international or global justice and the political conception of justice embodied by a state. To do so, it must be attentive to the justification of the political inequality between members and non-members. This justification rests upon the joint juridical integration of a state's members into a shared rightful condition and the fact that non-members are not so integrated. The fact of joint juridical integration suggests two further corollaries. Members must exhibit certain forms of partiality toward one another, and non-members who become juridically integrated must be given membership, likely through naturalisation. In addition to these propositions, we have from Chapter Two a set of considered judgements. Reasonable principles of just immigration governance must incorporate these into an account that shows the ongoing political inequality, and the other forms of inequality layered on top of this political inequality, between members and non-members occur on fair terms. If a principle does not incorporate one of the considered judgements, it must give us a good reason to revise it.

What would such principles look like? As has been noted in the Introduction, Henry Sidgwick proposed two ideals of immigration governance, the national and the cosmopolitan. The national ideal corresponds roughly to absolutism, of which we may now introduce a third variant. An absolutist may concede that social justice is not a special relationship and that an immigration regime must strive to be just in order to have authority, yet he or she may also claim that the requirements of social justice impose no constraints on immigration governance. Under this view, immigration governance can be both absolutist *and* principled, in the sense developed in Part Two, because justice imposes no demands in this domain. Such an account might result because it can be said either that immigration governance results in no injuries; that any such injuries are not the product of human agency; or that any such injuries are justified. We should continue to take these possibilities seriously. They would provide an explanation for the considered judgement most people have that states have broad and possibly unlimited discretion to control immigration. They may also explain a good deal about the way immigration happens to be governed. In contrast to this absolutist possibility, Sidgwick's cosmopolitan ideal corresponds to what today is often called an open borders view, namely, a view that there is a strong right to migrate freely. This alternative would have to be defended, in near symmetry to the principled absolutist position, by claiming either that immigration would not have any adverse effects on a state or its members, or that any such effects are justified in light of the reasons favouring the right to migrate. For reasons I will explain, I do not consider either of these opposing ideals plausible. The alternative that I propose over the next two chapters searches for a middle ground account that recognizes both a limited right to free migration and a limited right to exclude.

I begin by taking up the hint of an argument found in Kant's account of cosmopolitan right. According to Kant cosmopolitan right holds that states may exclude a migrant if it can be done without killing, once they have provided the migrant with the opportunity to try to enter into rightful relations.[1] This suggests that whatever right to exclude a state may have, that right includes at least one second-order constraint: no killing. From some of Kant's other remarks, it may also include constraints against enslavement and plundering.[2] In this chapter, I argue that second-order constraints of these kinds may impose a non-trivial regime of principle on the discretionary control of immigration by states. Thus I claim that immigration regimes are bound by what I call the indirect principle of freedom of migration. Under this principle, a state may only impose those first-order immigration laws and policies that do not result in second-order oppression. The argument for this principle proceeds in non-ideal theory: that is, my claim is that it applies to wealthy liberal constitutional democracies here and now.

Section Two of this chapter situates the arguments in this chapter and the next within a framework of debate over justice in immigration governance. Section Three argues that migration has presumptive but variable value, which means that all migrants have a prima facie claim to enter a state; this argument helps us to further conceptualize injuries that result from immigration governance.

---

[1] I Kant, 'Perpetual Peace: A Philosophical Sketch' in H Reiss (ed), *Kant: Political Writings* (Cambridge, Cambridge University Press, 1970) 105.
[2] ibid.

Section Four contrasts this account of the value of migration with the value attributed to migration by theories that treat justice in immigration as subsumed within the larger problem of global distributive justice. Section Five provides the argument for the indirect principle.

The indirect principle is non-trivial. To avoid all forms of second-order oppression, immigration policies would have to track the purposes of migrants far more closely than they currently do. As a result, compliance with the principle would tend to push immigration regimes toward the admission of far more of the disadvantaged than is currently the case. The argument is limited, however, since it tackles only second-order immigration governance. It tells us nothing about first-order inegalitarian policies that may be implemented without second-order oppression. That is why I explore a second, ideal argument for a principle of prioritarianism in indefinite admissions in Chapter Seven.

II. Two Frameworks

In the past decade or so there has been an explosion of interest in the political morality of immigration governance, a topic previously only of occasional interest to academic philosophers.[3] Yet the problem of justice in immigration governance has many parts, and these philosophical discussions often do not

---

[3] I make no attempt at completion, which would lead to an even more preposterous footnote. Discussions in books, book-length discussions, and edited volumes include: BA Ackerman, *Social Justice and the Liberal State* (New Haven, Yale University Press, 1980); M Walzer, *Spheres of Justice: A Defense of Pluralism and Equality* (New York, Basic Books, 1983); B Barry and RE Goodin (eds), *Free Movement: Ethical Issues in the Transnational Migration of People and of Money* (University Park, Pennsylvania State University Press, 1992); WF Schwartz (ed), *Justice in Immigration* (New York, Cambridge University Press, 1995); V Bader (ed), *Citizenship and Exclusion* (New York, St Martin's Press, 1997); P Cole, *Philosophies of Exclusion: Liberal Political Theory and Immigration* (Edinburgh, Edinburgh University Press, 2000); M Dummett, *On Immigration and Refugees* (New York, Routledge, 2001); P Meilaender, *Toward A Theory of Immigration* (New York, Palgrave, 2001); S Benhabib, *The Rights of Others: Aliens, Residents, and Citizens* (Cambridge, Cambridge University Press, 2004); M Gibney, *The Ethics and Politics of Asylum: Liberal Democracy and the Politics of Asylum* (New York, Cambridge University Press, 2004); R Pevnick, *Immigration and the Constraints of Justice: Between Open Borders and Absolute Sovereignty* (Cambridge, Cambridge University Press, 2011); B Schotel, *On the Right of Exclusion: Law, Ethics and Immigration Policy* (Abingdon, Routledge, 2012); CH Wellman and P Cole, *Debating the Ethics of Immigration: Is There a Right to Exclude?* (New York, Oxford University Press, 2012); J Carens, *The Ethics of Immigration* (New York, Oxford University Press, 2013). Notable articles include: A Abizadeh, 'Democratic Theory and Border Coercion: No Right to Unilaterally Control Your Own Borders' (2008) 36 *Political Theory* 37; M Blake, 'Discretionary Immigration' (2002) 30 *Philosophical Topics* 273; M Blake, 'Immigration' in CH Wellman and RG Frey (eds), *The Blackwell Companion to Applied Ethics* (Oxford, Blackwell, 2003); M Blake, 'Immigration and Political Equality' (2008) 45 *San Diego Law Review* 963; M Blake, 'Immigration, Association, and Antidiscrimination' (2012) 122 *Ethics* 748; M Blake, 'Immigration, Jurisdiction, and Exclusion' (2013) 41 *Philosophy & Public Affairs* 103; J Carens, 'Aliens and Citizens: The Case for Open Borders' (1987) 49 *The Review of Politics* 251; J Carens, 'Realistic and Idealistic Approaches to the Ethics of Migration' (1996) 30 *International Migration Review* 156; J Carens, 'Who Should Get In? The Ethics of Immigration Admissions' (2003) 17 *Ethics & International Affairs* 95; E Cavallero, 'An Immigration-Pressure Model of Global Distributive Justice' (2006) 5 *Politics, Philosophy & Economics* 97; S Fine, 'Freedom of Association is

engage the same issues. My goal in this section is not to review this literature, as able reviews already exist.[4] Rather, it is to set out two frameworks that can be used to dissect different accounts of justice in immigration governance. The first is a policy framework that, taking into account the function of immigration regimes, breaks down the kinds of questions a theory of justice in immigration governance must answer if it is to offer full practical guidance. The second is a normative framework that suggests the different conceptual resources that must be brought to bear in developing such a theory. These frameworks allow me to situate the arguments for freedom of migration found in this chapter and the next.

One aim of political philosophy is to provide tools to evaluate important social institutions and practices in order to settle controversial questions and furnish, if appropriate, reformist prescriptions. Such evaluations must start with claims about what a given institution's aims are. This is so even if the critique is abolitionist, in which case the claim might be that the aims identified are irredeemably illegitimate. The policy framework that I provide begins with the premise that the aim of migration governance is to regulate the movement of individuals across international borders; the aim of immigration governance, to regulate movement into a state. These functions can be broken down many ways. Most useful in assessing various philosophical discussions of immigration policy is the following five-fold division of policy tasks: (1) cap setting; (2) selection; (3) incorporation; (4) enforcement; and (5) the regulation of private relations.

These five functions are interrelated and need be taken up in no particular order. Cap-setting refers to the question of whether or not it is ever permissible or required to cap immigration and if so how such a cap ought to be set. The second

---

Not the Answer' (2010) 120 *Ethics* 338; A Hosein, 'Immigration and Freedom of Movement' (2013) 6 *Ethics & Global Politics* 25; C Kukathas, 'Immigration' in Hugh LaFollette (ed), *The Oxford Handbook of Practical Ethics* (New York, Oxford University Press, 2003) 567; C Kukathas, 'The Case for Open Immigration' in AI Cohen and CH Wellman (eds), *Contemporary Debates in Applied Ethics* (Oxford, Blackwell, 2005) 207; W Kymlicka, 'Territorial Boundaries: A Liberal Egalitarian Perspective' in D Miller and SH Hashmi (eds), *Boundaries and Justice* (Princeton, Princeton University Press, 2001) 259; M Lister, 'Immigration, Association, and the Family' (2010) 29 *Law and Philosophy* 717; M Lister, 'Who Are Refugees?' (2013) 62 *Law and Philosophy* 345; LE Lomasky, 'Liberalism Beyond Borders' (2007) 24 *Social Philosophy and Policy* 206; S Macedo, 'The Moral Dilemma of US Immigration Policy: Open Borders versus Social Justice?' in C Swain (ed), *Debating Immigration* (Cambridge, Cambridge University Press, 2007); D Miller, 'Immigration: The Case for Limits' in Cohen and Wellman, *Contemporary Debates in Applied Ethics* 193; D Miller, 'Immigrants, Nations, and Citizenship' (2008) 16 *The Journal of Political Philosophy* 371; R Pevnick, 'Social Trust and the Ethics of Immigration Policy' (2009) 17 *The Journal of Political Philosophy* 146; M Risse, 'On the Morality of Immigration' (2008) 22 *Ethics & International Affairs* 25; L Ypi, 'Justice in Migration: A Closed Borders Utopia?' (2008) 16 *Journal of Political Philosophy* 391.

[4] See V Bader, 'Fairly Open Borders' in Bader (ed), *Citizenship and Exclusion*, above n 3, V Bader, 'The Ethics of Immigration' (2005) 12 *Constellations* 331; J Seglow, 'The Ethics of Immigration' (2005) 3 *Political Studies* 317; CH Wellman, 'Immigration' in EN Zalta (ed), *The Stanford Encyclopedia of Philosophy*, Spring 2014 edn, available at: plato.stanford.edu/archives/spr2014/entries/immigration; and S Fine, 'The Ethics of Immigration: Self-Determination and the Right to Exclude' (2013) 8 *Philosophy Compass* 254.

question is how to select migrants for admission. On a view that repudiates a cap, the issue will be which migrants if any should be selected for exclusion. Views that allow for a cap, in addition to categories of exclusion, must also address the issue of how to distribute admission beneath the cap, that is, what admissions categories to create and what mix of migrants to allow in. Third is the question of a state's policies toward migrants who have entered the state. Such policies address, among other things, how long a migrant may stay; the menu of rights and duties granted to and imposed on them; the programmes made available to speed or prevent their integration; and how quickly, if ever, they may qualify for citizenship. I call this task incorporation, but this term should be taken to include non-incorporation as well. Sometimes, as with most guestworker programmes, the policy goal will be to prevent having the migrant come to feel a sense of belonging within a receiving state. Fourth are questions relating to implementation and, more narrowly, enforcement. Every governance strategy for putting into effect other immigration policy choices falls under this category. It is also a self-generating category, since some enforcement or implementation measures may require others. For example, the power of detention requires a power of arrest. Finally, most immigration policies include measures aimed at regulating private relationships that develop as a result of or are otherwise conditioned by immigration law and policy. Such measures might include strategies for preventing trafficking and smuggling, the exploitation of migrant workers, and spousal abuse of migrant women.

To map this framework onto the first- and second-order distinction introduced in Chapter Two, it will be seen that cap-setting and selection are first-order functions. Policies of capping and selecting migrants attempt to establish who will be allowed in. Policies of incorporation, implementation and enforcement, and the regulation of private relations are second-order. The interdependence of these components is important to recognize. The number of migrants that ought to or can be allowed into a country will depend on which migrants are selected and what rights they are granted. It may be, for example, that a country can justifiably exclude some migrants if it cannot provide them with the resources necessary to prevent the formation of an underclass. Or it may be that efforts to exclude certain groups of migrants may generate enforcement needs or forms of objectionable private victimization that require new forms of policing. As I hope to make clear, the extent to which the indirect principle places limits on exclusion policies and thus supports some range of first-order freedom of migration turns on this kind of interdependence. More specifically, it depends on what, also in Chapter Two, I called the countersocial premise: the premise that some first-order policies, that is, those that diverge significantly from the purposes of migrants, are more likely to require oppressive enforcement and incorporation policies or to lead to oppression through the medium of private actors.

A full theory of justice in immigration governance would provide principles for evaluating the justness of policies of cap-setting, selection, incorporation, enforcement, and the regulation of private relations. Every discussion of justice in immigration governance of which I am aware takes up either first-order issues of cap-setting and selection or second-order issues of incorporation, although within legal scholarship there is extensive discussion of issues of enforcement, especially detention and interdiction, and different efforts at addressing private exploitation or abuse.[5]

To fill in the full policy framework, a theory of justice in immigration governance would require the following elements, which I call the normative framework: (1) an account of the value of migration; (2) an account of the value of states; (3) an account of the effects of migration on states; and (4) a framework for judgement. I do not mean each element of the framework is normative, only that they are all necessary to provide a normative theory of immigration governance. Thus, keeping in mind the domain of human activity regulated, there must be some theory of the intrinsic or instrumental value of migration for the migrants themselves. Next, taking note of the fact that we are concerned with migration to and from states, a theory of justice in immigration governance must assign some intrinsic or instrumental value to these political entities or to the various goods that are safeguarded or simply able to flourish within them. Note that it is possible to propose that either the act of migration or states have no instrumental or intrinsic value. Doing so has the natural attraction of solving the problem of the morality of immigration governance through obviation, although it will almost always be an implausible move. The third part of the normative framework is called for by the fact that immigration may lead to beneficial or harmful effects for migrants, receiving states' members, and other aspects of the states themselves, such as its political institutions. Any account of justice in immigration must therefore reckon with the range of defensible empirical claims about these and other possible effects on that which we value in states. Finally, a normative theory must provide some framework for considering whether migration ought to be permitted in light of the reasons underlying the value of migration to the migrants and the likely effects of migration on the value of states. Whatever evaluative framework is proposed must confront the possibility of partiality, that is, the possibility that the reasons underlying the value of states may be treated differently than the reasons underlying the value of migration. Possibilities include either full equality across all possible evaluative dimensions, or the explication of one or more forms

---

[5] See, eg D Cole, 'In Aid of Removal: Due Process Limits on Immigration Detention' (2002) 51 *Emory Law Journal* 1003; G Heeren, 'Pulling Teeth: The State of Mandatory Immigration Detention' (2010) 45 *Harvard Civil Rights-Civil Liberties Law Review* 601; Daniel Kanstroom, 'Deportation, Social Control, and Punishment: Some Thoughts on Why Hard Laws Make Bad Cases' (2000) 113 *Harvard Law Review* 1890; JC Hathaway and RA Neve, 'Fundamental Justice and the Deflection of Refugees from Canada' (1996) 34 *Osgoode Hall Law Journal* 103; CM Rodríguez, 'Guest Workers and Integration: Toward A Theory of What Immigrants and Americans Owe One Another' (2007) *University of Chicago Legal Forum* 219; C Sheppard, 'Women as Wives: Immigration Law and Domestic Violence' (2000) 26 *Queen's Law Journal* 1; MJ Anderson, 'A License to Abuse: The Impact of Conditional Status on Female Immigrants' (1993) 102 *Yale Law Journal* 1401.

of partiality. If the latter, the challenge is, of course, to define and defend that partiality, so that it can be shown to be either permissible or required.[6]

These two frameworks provide a way of interrogating discussions of justice in immigration so that they can be placed in dialogue with one another. Partial theories will address themselves to different aspects of immigration policy. By examining their normative underpinnings, we can come to a rough understanding of their commitments regarding those aspects of policy they have not addressed but that other philosophers may have taken up. Of course, the degree to which a conception can be filled out will depend on the resources developed by the author.

As it happens, in addition to focusing on first-order issues, the bulk of discussions of first-order questions in political philosophy chiefly address the value of states and the reasons states may have (or not have) for excluding migrants. States might be said to be valuable as sites of distributive justice or economic activity; as repositories of national, ethnic, or other forms of culture; as political co-ventures; as security pacts; and so on. The pattern of argument in many articles is to identify some valuable function served by states that can plausibly be called on to justify restriction, to propose some empirical premises about the likely impact of immigration on the ability of states to serve that function, and then to draw conclusions about the permissibility or non-permissibility of different kinds of immigration restrictions.[7] It is less common to find sustained discussion of the value of migration. Most often, the aim of migration is assumed to be the accumulation of wealth and income, valuable only in those terms, and so the problem of justice in immigration is assimilated into questions of global and domestic distributive justice, with exceptions made for refugees.[8] Family migration is rarely even acknowledged.[9]

The arguments in this chapter and the next focus on the relatively neglected issue of the value of migration. Building on two related ways of conceiving that value, they provide a part of a conception of justice in immigration governance. In terms of the policy framework, the concern is largely first-order issues of cap-setting and selection, although the indirect principle is attentive to the interplay between these policy tasks and the tasks of incorporation, enforcement, and the regulation of private relations. In terms of the normative framework, I provisionally assume going forward that we now have a considered judgement that states are valuable as the authoritative guarantors of a political conception of justice. On

---

[6] D Miller, 'The Ethical Significance of Nationality' (1988) 98 *Ethics* 647; S Scheffler, 'The Conflict Between Justice and Responsibility' in *Boundaries and Allegiances: Problems of Justice and Responsibility in Liberal Thought* (New York, Oxford University Press, 2001); A Abizadeh and P Gilabert, 'Is There a Genuine Tension between Cosmopolitan Egalitarianism and Special Responsibilities' (2008) 138 *Philosophical Studies* 348.

[7] A Abizadeh, 'Liberal and Egalitarian Arguments for Closed Borders: Some Preliminary Critical Reflections' (2006) 4 *Ethique/cs & Economique/cs* 1.

[8] See, eg Ypi, 'Justice in Migration', above n 3.

[9] But see Lister, 'Immigration, Association, and the Family', above n 3.

this view, the project of providing a framework for settling questions of justice among members of a state is immensely valuable and if a state were to become what Rawls calls a well-ordered society, it may well be the highest form of good. I also now want to advance the claim that justification of any cap on immigration must be based on the impact immigration would have on the stability of the state's political conception of justice or on the effect of immigration on the legitimate expectations that members might have formed under that conception and its basic structure.

To lend support to what may seem to be a strong claim, imagine as a possible counterexample a state that harbours a valuable good that does not seem to be associated with its political conception of justice. An example might be the Amazon rainforest in Brazil. If Brazil experienced significant immigration that threatened the sustainability of the rainforest, that might seem to provide a reason independent of the political conception of justice for restricting immigration. Moreover, it might seem to be a reason that all reasonable migrants would accept given the importance of the rainforest for the world's ecosystem. Ultimately, though, even in this case exclusion must be justified by recourse to reasons relating to stability and legitimate expectations. To see why, note that within Brazil the need to protect the rainforest will have led to principles and rules that, say, limit the rights of members to benefit commercially from logging or to farm, develop, and live on deforested land. Such rules and principles will be range-limited, established by the Brazilian government to settle potential conflicts among Brazilians. But range-limited principles, as was noted in Chapter Three, do not have any exclusionary force on their own. Their ability to justify exclusion rests on the legitimate expectations formed by members under them and the prospect of the destabilization of the political conception and its basic structure that might result from the frustration of those expectations. Therefore, even protection of an environmental good like the Brazilian rainforest would justify exclusion only through the medium of the political conception of justice.

Similar arguments hold for other kinds of goods, such as national cultures or distributive goods. The reason is, quite simply, that under realistic assumptions any such good would be the source of potential conflicting claims, which ultimately must be determined according to a political conception and its corresponding basic structure. As a further example of the kind often cited by writers who defend immigration restrictions on the basis of national or cultural interests, take devolution of some power over immigrant selection to the Canadian province of Québec, whose policy, among other things, shows a preference for Francophone migrants. Such a policy would be justified, on this view, by the fact that the Canadian political conception of justice recognizes that having a French-language culture is a good to be protected through various means, and that the Québecois have a legitimate expectation of this ongoing protection. Therefore, all else equal, the judgement would be, it is permissible to select Francophone migrants over non-Francophone migrants in order to honour this legitimate expectation.[10] The justifiability of this preference, however, does not rest on the good of French-language culture in Québec independently of the political conception of justice. As an example of a more denatured kind, Michael Blake has recently argued that the imposition of jurisdictional obligations on a state when a migrant immigrates limits the freedom of its members. For that reason, Blake argues, states have a presumptive right to exclude migrants.[11] But the kinds of obligations toward new arrivals that Blake cites, such as to provide protection against crime, are at-large obligations met by already existing institutions. Meeting such obligations generally in no way limits members' freedom or otherwise injures, or even affects, members. The only way, indeed, that freedom can ground the right to exclude is if members have a claim to such freedom under their political conception of justice, holding a legitimate expectation that it will not be limited by virtue of the arrival of immigrants. Therefore, even here any cap must be set according to the stability of the political conception and potential for frustrating members' legitimate expectations.

As the examples suggest, the way that such legitimate expectations might operate to justify exclusion or not may vary considerably from state to state, depending on the nature of its political conception of justice and the goods in play. The arguments that follow in this chapter do not specify any political conception of justice, except that I sometimes assume that any conception will include some principle or principles of distributive justice, institutionalized in the form of social welfare schemes. I make this assumption because I believe that the arguments for restriction that provide the most immediate intuitive appeal are those premised on the need to sustain, and ensure fair access to, the provision of existing social welfare schemes or other aspects of a scheme of domestic distributive justice. In part, this intuitive appeal rests upon the value that egalitarian liberals place upon domestic distributive justice; in part, it rests upon the concern that such institutions would be swamped if borders were opened to allow the global poor free migration. Even Joseph Carens, while advocating open migration, accepts that it may be permissible to impose a waiting period on migrants before they can access the welfare state institutions of a receiving state.[12] Beyond its intuitive appeal, this concern is supported up to a point by the forms of partiality defended in Chapter Three. If a member has legitimate expectations of certain entitlements under an existing scheme of distributive justice, then it would seem, all things considered, unjust to

---

[10] See Miller, 'The Case for Limits', above n 3 at 201. See also the general discussion of Québec in W Kymlicka, *Multicultural Citizenship: A Liberal Theory of Minority Rights* (New York, Oxford University Press, 1995).

[11] See Blake, 'Immigration, Jurisdiction, and Exclusion', above n 3 at 119–20. Blake bases his argument on the claim that there is a presumptive right to be free from others imposing obligations on us without our consent.

[12] Carens, *The Ethics of Immigration*, above n 3 at 281. See also Carens's earlier discussion in JH Carens, 'Immigration and the Welfare State' in Amy Gutmann (ed), *Democracy and the Welfare State* (Princeton, Princeton University Press, 1988) 207.

upset those expectations through the admission of a migrant. Finally, quite apart from all such theoretical support, the fear of such possible effects is likely to be a significant driver of immigration restrictions.

III. The Value of Freedom of Movement

Hannah Arendt says that 'nobody would ever be able to arrive at a place where freedom rules if he could not move without restraint'.[13] Freedom of movement no doubt has some core intrinsic value. It is also instrumentally necessary to all other freedoms, as a result of which historically it is sometimes used synonymously with freedom period.[14] Yet it is also true that our freedom of movement is restricted in all sorts of ways that we do not think unjust.[15] Traffic laws mostly do not offend our sense of justice (though other drivers may), likely because such laws facilitate movement, much as rules of debate facilitate discussion. Property laws are more problematic and clearly can damage important interests, though here too we might think, against the background of a fair society, that they may be justified.[16] A yet more difficult case is restricted access to social entitlements upon relocation. The *Canadian Charter of Rights and Freedoms* allows each province to impose 'reasonable residency requirements as a qualification for the receipt of publicly provided social services' even though such requirements impede internal movement;[17] such restrictions have been considered unconstitutional in the United States.[18] This is, as I said, a difficult case, but many other restrictions on freedom of movement are not. One cannot occupy space taken up by someone else. One cannot run onstage at a concert. One cannot jump onto tube train tracks. One cannot go to the bathroom during takeoff and landing.[19]

---

[13] H Arendt, *On Revolution* (New York, Penguin Books, 1963) 32–33.

[14] Thus when Magna Carta and subsequent charters discuss the right to life, liberty, and property, the middle term refers to 'personal liberty', that is, freedom from personal restraint, what Blackstone called 'the power of locomotion, of changing situation, or moving one's person to whatever place one's inclination may direct, without imprisonment or restraint, unless by due course of law.' (CE Shattuck, 'The True Meaning of the Term "Liberty" in Those Clauses in the Federal and State Constitutions Which Protect "Life, Liberty, and Property"' (1891) 4 *Harvard Law Review* 365, 377.) Enshrinement of this right to personal liberty predates the protection of other liberties most often associated with the idea of freedom—of religion, of speech, and so on (ibid). A modern argument for free movement within a state is found in H Shue, *Basic Rights*, 2nd edn (Princeton, Princeton University Press, 1996) 78–85. Shue excludes international freedom of movement from his discussion: ibid at 79.

[15] Miller, 'The Case for Limits', above n 3.

[16] But see J Waldron, 'Property, Justification, and Need' (1993) 6 *Canadian Journal of Law & Jurisprudence* 185.

[17] *The Constitution Act*, 1982, being Schedule B to the Canada Act 1982 (UK) 1982, c 11, s 6(3).

[18] These cases are discussed in Carens, 'Immigration and the Welfare State', above n 12.

[19] See Miller, 'The Case for Limits', above n 3 at 194: 'These are very familiar observations, but they are worth making simply to highlight how hedged about with qualifications the existing right of free movement in liberal societies actually is.'

Arendt's claim must be qualified to deal with the near-contradictory nature of freedom of movement. Such freedom is vitally important to do anything, but not everything we do is vitally important. It is crucial to live some sort of life, but no one has a claim to be able to live any among the set of all possible lives, come what may. It is easy to see why radical restrictions on freedom of movement, such as imprisonment, require the strong form of justification provided by a criminal trial. It is less easy to see on what grounds more moderate restrictions might be allowed or disallowed.

In the balance of this section, I offer an account of the value of freedom of movement using Martha Nussbaum and Amartya Sen's capabilities approach. I argue that this approach corresponds with our judgements about first-order immigration policy from Chapter Two. I then explore an argument presented by Adam Smith in *Wealth of Nations* for the freedom to move to sell one's labour. I claim that Smith's argument shows that economic migration can also be understood in terms of the capabilities approach. Therefore the value of economic migration is continuous with the value of other forms of migration about which our judgements are more secure.

1. The Capabilities and Our Considered Judgements

Of the considered judgements listed in Chapter Two, four concern first-order policy questions regarding selection, namely that (1) it is wrong to return refugees to states where they face torture or where their life or basic human rights would be threatened; (2) it is wrong to separate, or to keep separate, parents and their young children; and (3) it is wrong for a state to prevent the return of a citizen who cannot naturalize elsewhere. We would also include our first order judgement that (4) it is permissible to restrict the immigration of criminals, or those who present a security threat or public health risk. One way to develop a conception of the value of freedom of migration that unites the first three of these judgements and partly explains the fourth is through a capabilities-based conception of freedom of movement. I set out this conception in this subsection. In the next I extend it to economic migration. In this way, I try to work from firmer judgements to an area where things are less clear.

The human capabilities approach provides a list of potential functionings and measures advantage and disadvantage in terms of those functionings people are actually able to perform. The basic capabilities are plural and interdependent. All of them are necessary in some minimal degree to live a human life, and all rely upon one or more of the others. Martha Nussbaum breaks down our capabilities into a list of ten: life; bodily health; bodily integrity; being able to use the senses, imagination, and thought; emotions, including being able to have attachments to other people; practical reason, including being able to form a conception of the good; affiliation, including having the social bases of self-respect; being able to live with concern for and in relation to animals, plants, and the world of nature; play; and control over one's political and material environment, including rights of political participation and being able to hold property.[20] The list of capabilities seems to provide a plausible way to operationalize the otherwise vague concept of purposiveness more transparently than its alleged rival, Rawls's list of primary goods. The capabilities are, Nussbaum says, 'what people are actually able to do and to be, in a way informed by an intuitive idea of a life that is worthy of the dignity of the human being'.[21] In contrast, Rawls's list is of things people should have.[22]

The list of capabilities reveals how complex human purposiveness is. This complexity can be seen by examining the capability most germane to the concerns of this essay, bodily integrity, which Nussbaum says includes 'being able to move freely from place to place'.[23] This capability depends, of course, upon being alive and healthy to some degree. It depends on being able to think of moving somewhere else and to conceive of this project as good for you, hence requiring thought, imagination, and practical reason. It depends on having the sense that the fact that moving somewhere else would be good for you makes it a worthwhile endeavour, hence having access to the social bases of self-respect that would allow you to see your goals this way. It also depends on having the material means to move, hence having some control of your environment. Finally, moving freely from place to place potentially can be used to improve one's position relative to almost every other capability, perhaps by making work available, perhaps by permitting one to form or deepen affective relationships, and so on.[24] Trivial, unimportant exercises of freedom of movement might add up to make our lives overall significantly better. The list of capabilities, therefore, grounds a conception of the value of freedom of movement in terms of probable marginal changes to one's capability set.[25] The value of a particular move, as opposed to the overall value of the range of free movement one generally enjoys, depends on one's level of capabilities without that particular opportunity to move and the potential change to that level that will result if the opportunity were granted. Conversely, the injury effected by a restriction on movement can be thought of as the deprivation of that probable marginal improvement. While more questions would be need to be answered to

---

[20] M Nussbaum, *Frontiers of Justice: Disability, Nationality, Species Membership* (Cambridge, MA, Belknap Press, 2006) 76–78.

[21] ibid at 70. See also M Nussbaum, *Women and Human Development: The Capabilities Approach* (New York, Cambridge University Press, 2000) 71.

[22] Rawls claims that his list of primary goods—the basic rights and liberties; freedom of movement and free choice of occupation; powers and prerogatives of offices and positions of authority; income and wealth; and the social bases of self-respect—takes into account basic capabilities: J Rawls, E Kelly (ed), *Justice as Fairness: A Restatement* (Cambridge, MA, Belknap Press, 2001) 169. I take Rawls's claim to mean that the primary goods are goods everyone should want given some 'normal' range of human purposiveness. That suggests, however, that the capabilities provide a more direct index of purposiveness. The other potential implications of the capabilities view for Rawls's theory do not, I believe, affect the argument here.

[23] Nussbaum, *Frontiers of Justice*, above n 20 at 76.

[24] ibid at 76–78.

[25] See A Sen, *The Idea of Justice* (Cambridge, MA, Belknap Press, 2009) chapters eleven and fourteen.

work it out (for example, how does one assess the probability of realizing the gains to one's capability set), I will put those aside and refer to this conception as the variable value of freedom of movement or migration.

Defining injury in terms of the reduction of human purposiveness, as represented by the list of capabilities, seems plausible. It allows us to say, for example, that if one were prevented from moving to a place where there was no prospect of an improved capability set, no injury would result at all. This might be the case, for example, if some equally advantageous destination was available. It also allows us to understand better the various restrictions on movement within a state. Traffic laws seem inoffensive to our sense of justice because for the most part they do not diminish the level of our capabilities. In the short term, they may slow us down or force us to take alternate routes; in the long term, they likely make any sort of movement using public thoroughfares possible. Other restrictions may be injurious but justified, and therefore not unjust. Property laws and restrictions on access to social services within a new jurisdiction may fall into this category.

Because this conception of the value of freedom of movement is keyed to probable marginal improvements to one's capabilities set, it further allows us to address an important objection raised by David Miller to claims that there is a human right to migration. Miller argues that what people have is a right to an adequate range of options and that most people have available to them an adequate range of options within their home state. '[A]lthough people certainly have an *interest* in being able to migrate internationally,' he writes, it 'is more like my interest in having an Aston Martin than my interest in having access to *some* means of physical mobility.'[26] There are at least two ways to read this argument. One possible implication is that the marginal improvement to one's capability set from owning an Aston Martin is minor, so the injury is small and easily justified. The second possible implication is that one's interest in having an Aston Martin is so far above what is required by an adequate range of options that it cannot plausibly ground a rights claim. But too much work here is being done by the use of a luxury brand in the example. The gains from owning an Aston Martin could be significant if one did not own a car at all and lived in an area that was not well served by public transport. It might also be significant in non-ideal societies where ownership of luxury goods were seen as a marker of status, thus contributing to one's self-respect. Similarly, whether migration represents an opportunity for a minor or a significant improvement to one's capability set will vary case by case.

This conception of the value of freedom of movement also allows us to respond to Arthur Ripstein's interpretation of Kant's cosmopolitan right, noted in Chapter Three, under which a state enjoys freedom to restrict immigration because decisions to deny admission 'limit only your ability to achieve what you wish, rather

---

[26] Miller, 'The Case for Limits', above n 3 at 195.

than your ability to use what you have to set and pursue your own purposes'.[27] Philip Pettit also makes a suggestion along these lines:

> Nor are people dominated by the States that do not give them a right of entry. Entering another State is not a default option that is taken away from them by the State's boundary, at least not under realistic assumptions about people's baseline alternatives.[28]

This lack of domination, Pettit continues, is because: 'It is a brute fact or historical necessity—an obstacle created by nature—that there is no State-less territory available, and people cannot be dominated by such an obstacle.'[29] These arguments contain the same veiled assertion or assertions, namely that immigration restrictions, at least in ordinary circumstances,[30] are either not injurious because state borders are a natural fact or close to it, or they may be injurious but are not a matter of justice because such injury cannot be traced back to human agency. However, as Rawls says: 'What is just or unjust is how institutions deal with natural limitations and the way they are set up to take advantage of historical possibilities.'[31] Perhaps the division of the world into states, with the inevitable inequalities that follows, is all but a natural fact. Even so, limitations on the ability to migrate to an adjacent country are not like the inability to settle on the ocean floor. If borders result in marginal reductions in the capabilities of non-members, hence injury, the way that the immigration regimes respond to this all-but natural fact requires justification.

Finally, this conception of the value of freedom of movement allows us to explain our first-order judgements regarding immigration. These judgements, we may say, involve reasons to move that are particularly foundational to human life. They are cases where we might be relatively certain that injury, in terms of a pervasive marginal diminishment of a migrant's capability set, can rarely be justified. Children who are not raised by their parents face the prospect of having a lifetime with a stunted capability set; parents committed to raising their children are dealt a particularly decisive injury if they are separated. Here the capabilities most directly implicated seem to be what Nussbaum dubs 'emotion' and 'affiliation'.[32] The rights of refugees not to be returned to a country where they face persecution, and the rights of citizens who cannot naturalize elsewhere to be admitted to or not to be banished from their own country, may be tied to the need to have

---

[27] A Ripstein, *Force and Freedom: Kant's Legal and Political Philosophy* (Cambridge, MA, Harvard University Press, 2009) 296.

[28] P Pettit, 'Law and Liberty' in S Besson and JL Martí (eds), *Legal Republicanism: National and International Perspectives* (New York, Oxford University Press, 2009) 52. Domination is, for Pettit, the antithesis of freedom and a just society is one without domination. So the claim that immigration controls cannot be dominating appears to be an absolutist claim that they cannot be unjust. Note that Ripstein interprets Kant's innate right to freedom as reflecting an idea of non-domination, so it may be that Ripstein and Pettit are making identical claims.

[29] ibid.

[30] For this qualifier, see Ripstein, *Force and Freedom*, above n 27 at 296.

[31] J Rawls, *A Theory of Justice*, revised edn (Cambridge, MA, Belknap Press, 1999) 254.

[32] Nussbaum, *Frontiers of Justice*, above n 20 at 77.

access to a state in which all other capabilities can be secured. Our considered judgements in the case of refugees and young children and their parents are only presumptive. They seemingly may be overridden when migrants are demonstrably criminals, security threats, or dangers to public health, although just when such overrides occur and what their implications are for justice in immigration is a difficult question. Why this does not hold true for returning citizens does not seem to be explained by the capabilities approach. It may be that such exclusion grounds should be applied in these cases as well.

Thus the capabilities approach provides a way to unite our first-order judgements about immigration governance, with one minor shortfall. Migration is of variable value, depending on the initial circumstances of the migrant in his or her home state and the potential circumstances in his or her state of destination. This variable conception of the value of migration does not itself lead us toward judgements regarding the vast majority of cases. In particular, it does not provide us with firm judgements about economic migration and most forms of family migration. I take the point about family migration to be relatively clear. One's family life is clearly an important part of one's capability set. But the value of living with or near a member of one's family would seem to depend on a variety of factors, such as age, the intimacy of the family relationship, and the other family members one already has nearby. It is one thing to say young children presumptively have a liberty to migrate to be with their parents or vice versa. This judgement seems less certain as the relationship becomes more distant and less dependent. I do not believe most of us have a firm judgement that the exclusion of, say, adult siblings or cousins would be unjust. For this important category of migration, we must look for something other than a considered judgement to assess the justifiability of immigration restrictions.

A more acute difficulty arises with respect to economic migration. Nussbaum lists as a capability material control over one's environment, which includes being able to hold property rights on an equal basis with others; having freedom to seek employment on an equal basis with others; and being able to work as a human being.[33] This capability is undefended and includes assumptions of an egalitarian baseline that we cannot adopt here without question-begging. The importance of economic migration once the egalitarian assumption is removed is not as intuitively obvious as those that explain the three considered judgements regarding admission, or even our intuitions about the general importance of family. Indeed, economically motivated migration often seems thought to be morally weightless. In the next subsection, I describe an argument made by Adam Smith that elaborates and justifies the inclusion of material control on the list of capabilities, though not necessarily the egalitarian baseline. More to the point, Smith's argument allows us to conceptualize the value of economic migration.

This argument will unavoidably seem anachronistic. It is couched within a polemic against the Laws of Settlement, early modern restrictions on the mobility

---

[33] ibid at 78.

of common labourers in England. These laws sought to establish who was 'settled' in each English parish, a matter thought vital to the integrity of the Elizabethan Poor Law, which delegated responsibility to local officials for maintenance of the poor. For all the obvious differences, the Laws of Settlement and modern immigration law belong, in a manner relevant to moral evaluation, to a single family of regulations that seek to control the flow of people from one jurisdiction to another; more specifically, at controlling the flow of labour; and more specifically still, perhaps, at controlling the flow of labour in order to preserve a scheme of distributive justice. Smith says that it was 'an evident violation of natural liberty and justice' to remove a man from the place where he chooses to settle in the name of such a scheme. To us it is not evident. In probing why Smith thinks it is, we come to a firmer understanding of the value of freedom of migration for economic reasons.

2. 'An Evident Violation of Natural Liberty and Justice'

The relevant passage from *Wealth of Nations* is as follows:

> To remove a man who has committed no misdemeanour from the parish where he chooses to reside is an evident violation of natural liberty and justice. The common people of England, however, so jealous of their liberty, but like the common people of most other countries never rightly understanding wherein it consists, have now for more than a century together suffered themselves to be exposed to this oppression without a remedy.... There is scarce a poor man in England of forty years of age, I will venture to say, who has not in some part of his life felt himself most cruelly oppressed by this ill-contrived law of settlements.[34]

This is part of Smith's general indictment of any and all restrictions on the 'free circulation of labour from one employment to another'.[35] In the same chapter from *Wealth of Nations*, he criticizes two other limits of this kind, apprenticeships and the exclusive privileges granted to corporations over certain trades. All of this ties into a broader argument in favour of what, in his *Lectures on Jurisprudence*, he calls '*liberi comercii*, a right of trafficking with those who are willing to deal'[36] and which undergirds his advocacy throughout *Wealth of Nations* of the 'obvious and simple system of natural liberty' in which '[e]very man, as long as he does not violate the laws of justice, is left perfectly free to pursue his own interest his own way, and to bring both his industry and capital into competition with those of any other man, or order of men.'[37]

Smith's objections to restrictions on the mobility of labour are therefore connected to his views on 'the right to free commerce'.[38] The value to the individual of free commerce, in turn, has to do with the related values of moral development

---

[34] A Smith, *The Wealth of Nations, Books I–III* (New York, Penguin Books, 1986) 245 [I.x.2].
[35] ibid at 239 [I.x.2].
[36] A Smith, *Lectures on Jurisprudence* (Indianapolis, Liberty Fund, 1982) 8.
[37] A Smith, *The Wealth of Nations, Books IV–V* (New York, Penguin Books, 1999) 273–74 [IV.ix].
[38] Smith, *Lectures on Jurisprudence*, above n 36 at 8.

and independence.[39] Independence is fostered by the freedom to move from place to place to sell one's labour, thereby increasing one's personal stock of wealth and reducing the extent to which one must rely on charity. The moral development argument is that such freedom of movement (and other kinds of freedom) is among the conditions that allow individuals to cultivate prudence, justice, benevolence, and other virtues. It is also among the social bases of self-respect.

Neither moral development nor independence can be had without the other. Independence connotes both the capacity for judgement and the material conditions that allow one to act on one's judgements. A certain degree of independence is necessary to develop one's capacities for judgement; a certain moral maturity is required to be truly independent. At the same time, to be dependent and morally incapacitated is to be in a profound sense unfree.[40] Such unfreedom has consequences that go beyond the individual: forced dependence is subjugation; willing dependence, a form of depravity; both engender social disorder. The debasement that comes with dependence explains why societies with greater numbers of dependents suffer from higher crime. Smith thinks, for example, that servants set free 'are the most helpless set of men imaginable depraved both in mind and body' by idleness, and so turn to 'crime and vices'.[41] We do not have to accept this empirical claim to appreciate the normative point behind it, just as we did not have to accept Kant's relegation of certain groups to the status of passive citizens to draw lessons from his discussion of that status.

Converse to the dynamic through which material dependence begets debasement, Smith sees commercial exchange as a form of intercourse through which our moral capacities are developed.[42] Here the argument returns to the discussion

---

[39] Free commerce also has social effects that conduce to greater liberty: '[C]ommerce and manufactures gradually introduced order and good government, and with them, the liberty and security of individuals [.]' (Smith, *Wealth of Nations, Books I–III*, above n 34 at 508 [III.iv].) See D Winch, *Adam Smith's Politics: An Essay in Historiographic Revision* (New York, Cambridge University Press, 1978) 70: 'The *Wealth of Nations* can be accurately, if not very fully, described as an extended treatise on the reciprocal relationship between commerce and liberty.'

[40] 'Of all the calamities to which the condition of mortality exposes humankind, the loss of reason appears, to those who have the least spark of humanity, by far the most dreadful [.]': A Smith, K Haakonssen (ed), *The Theory of Moral Sentiments* (Cambridge, Cambridge University Press, 2002) 15 [I.i.1.11]. Workers who, because of the division of labour, spend their lives performing one or two simple tasks are reduced to this state of unfreedom. 'The torpor of his mind renders him not only incapable of relishing or bearing a part in any rational conversation, but of conceiving any generous, noble, or tender sentiment, and consequently of forming any just judgement concerning many even of the ordinary duties of private life.' (A Smith, *Wealth of Nations, Books IV–V*, above n 37 at 368–69 [V.i.Art. 2].) See also ibid at 374 [V.i.Art. 2]: 'A man without the proper use of the intellectual faculties of a man, is, if possible, more contemptible than even a coward, and seems to be mutilated and deformed in a still more essential part of the character of human nature.' Rawls thought that the ideal of the social union of social unions, which would be realized in a well-ordered society governed by justice as fairness, would eliminate this concern: Rawls, *Theory of Justice*, above n 31 at 463–64.

[41] Smith, *Lectures on Jurisprudence*, above n 36 at 333.

[42] See eg CJ Berry, 'Adam Smith and the Virtues of Commerce' in JW Chapman and WA Galston (eds), *Nomos XXXIV: Virtue* (New York, New York University Press, 1992) 69; S Fleischacker, *A Third Concept of Liberty: Judgment and Freedom in Kant and Adam Smith* (Princeton, Princeton University Press, 1999); E Rothschild, *Economic Sentiments: Adam Smith, Condorcet, and the Enlightenment* (Cambridge, MA, Harvard University Press, 2001); S Darwall, 'Equal Dignity in Adam Smith' (2004) 1 *Adam Smith Review* 129.

of sympathy set out in Chapter One. There we saw that Smith believes our moral judgements arise socially. All of us are all the time judging one another, anticipating one another's judgements, and adjusting our behaviour and attitudes to meet the judgements of others. In this way our faculty of judgement develops intersubjectively and our moral development is tied to our social context. What is more, the convergence of our judgements through this social interaction helps ensure social harmony. That is especially important when it comes to our judgements of justice, where disagreement would threaten to rend societies apart.

Smith saw commercial exchange as part of the process through which this development takes place. To successfully negotiate an agreement, one must see the world from others' perspective. Such sympathetic exertion allows one to imaginatively determine their wants and needs and, further, gives one the tools for persuading them that what they want and need is what you are selling: 'The offer of a shilling, which to us appears to have so plain and simple a meaning, is in reality offering an argument to persuade one to do so and so for his interest.'[43] This dimension of commerce plays a crucial role in Smith's moral egalitarianism, providing one way that moral rectitude and virtue are made accessible to all or nearly all. Morality would be worth little, and would seem to rest on an unstable foundation, if virtue were available to only a select few. Instead, Smith holds that it is accessible through 'vulgar education' and can be learned through 'ordinary commerce'.[44] The 'simple system of natural liberty' therefore is the system that would maximize the wealth of nations, but it is also that system of government under which men would achieve greatest independence and have the widest range of opportunities for moral development.[45] Smith singled out the Laws of Settlement for criticism because he saw in them a threat to these valuable interests.

First, the poor who could not move were forced into situations of dependence in their original parishes. Going on the parish rolls led, among other things, to loss of the franchise.[46] Second, the Laws of Settlement came to be administered by a series of local officials whose decision making was essentially unconstrained.[47] The discretion bestowed on local officials came on top of a third source of dependency, that is, the dependency of common labourers on parishioners in their new home under some of the approved channels of resettlement, for example by becoming apprentices (Smith thought that apprenticeships generally produced

---

[43] Smith, *Lectures on Jurisprudence*, above n 36 at 352 and 493–94. See the discussion of this point in S Darwall, *The Second-Person Standpoint: Morality, Respect, and Accountability* (Cambridge, MA, Harvard University Press, 2006) 47–48.

[44] Smith, *Theory of Moral Sentiments*, above n 40 at 160 [III.iii.7].

[45] 'Freedom of commerce, in the *Wealth of Nations*, is an emancipation from personal, political, and sometimes physical oppression.': Rothschild, *Economic Sentiments*, above n 42 at 27.

[46] ibid at 63.

[47] For Smith: 'The risk of absolutism becoming despotism increased when discretionary powers were conferred by the executive on subordinate bodies.': Winch, *Adam Smith's Politics*, above n 39 at 95.

'idle and worthless' workmen)[48] or being hired into service and working for a year. Individuals who relocated in accordance with the law would in this way become objectionably dependent on new masters. Those who relocated clandestinely might be even more so. The injustice was sealed by the self-interested manner in which parish overseers and churchwardens enforced the Laws of Settlement, together with its economic irrationality. Restrictions on the flow of labour were irrational because they reduced the overall wealth of society and led to sharp differences in wages, hence greater inequality, between one parish and another.

Smith's argument builds on a conception of the value of freedom of economic migration in terms of independence and moral development. In the next chapter, I will discuss the importance of moral development, relying on Rawls's more schematic division of our moral capacity into two moral powers, the capacity for a sense of justice and the capacity to form, revise, and pursue a conception of the good. More immediately, I think that what Smith means by independence corresponds to purposiveness, as explicated by the capabilities approach. It is an idea that allows us to capture the value of freedom in terms of what we are actu-ally able to do. It is no surprise that being able to move to work holds the promise of improving one's material independence. Smith's argument, however, brings out the full texture of what is at stake. It renders plausible the claim that eco-nomic migration connects with the other capabilities on Nussbaum's list, not just because it promises greater capabilities overall but because it fosters our moral capacities in particular. Anticipating the next chapter, it also renders plausible the connection between economic migration and the development of the two moral powers. In this way it reveals a continuity between economic migration and those forms of migration about whose value we have firm judgements.

Freedom of migration, then, is valuable because it allows for greater indepen-dence: it allows us to have more capabilities. This value underwrites an initial general claim to migrate on behalf of all migrants, including economic migrants. Most migrants today, it may be safely assumed, face the prospect of some marginal increase in their capability set. Otherwise they would not want to migrate. Having a claim, however, is not the same as saying that the claim must be made good. The value of migration is variable and so the actual injury caused by immigration restrictions, and the justifiability of such injuries, will depend on each migrant's initial situation and his or her prospects for betterment. The ultimate justice or injustice of immigration law will depend on weighing these prospects against the anticipated impact of migration on the conditions that allow for maintaining the stability of a state's political conception of justice and the legitimate expectations of members. It remains to be seen if the conception of the variable value of free-dom of migration can lead to more concrete conclusions about which forms of immigration restriction are justified.

---

[48] Smith, *Wealth of Nations, Books I–III*, above n 34 at 226 [I.x.ii]. For discussion of Smith's criticism of apprenticeship, see Rothschild, *Economic Sentiments*, above n 42 at chapter four.

IV. The Global Distributive Justice Alternative

In this section I want to explain how pursuing an account of justice in immigration governance based on a conception of the value of freedom of migration challenges those accounts of justice in immigration that see the value of migration as lying principally in its potential for addressing global distributive injustice. On such accounts, only those migrants whose immigration is dictated by principles of global distributive justice have claims to entry.

A principle of distributive justice, narrowly construed, provides 'moral standards for assessing ongoing methods of distribution of rights to income and wealth that are implicit in any economic system'.[49] Additionally, a principle of distributive justice must apply 'to all existing income and wealth within an ongoing system of production, exchange, and consumption'.[50] A theory of global distributive justice in immigration governance would have to suggest principles for immigration governance that contribute, or deny the need to contribute, to some overall ideal of distributive justice within the global economic system.[51]

A common approach is to see the right to close borders as a right that might be lost or limited if a country does not meet its international distributive justice obligations. The idea at work is that: 'If we cannot move enough money to where the needy people are, then we will have to count on moving as many of the needy people as possible to where the money is.'[52] Perhaps surprisingly, such proposals often appear defensively, in an 'as long as' clause proposed by authors who defend restrictions on immigration yet seek to acknowledge the problem of global economic inequality. Christopher Heath Wellman, for instance, writes:

> I do not deny that political communities must honor their samaritan, restitutive, and egalitarian duties of distributive justice in order to be legitimate, but as long as they do so, they remain entitled to the sphere of political self-determination [which Wellman argues entails the right to exclude].[53]

A more specific version of this view is associated with scholars who are sometimes called liberal nationalists—liberals because they acknowledge the moral equality

---

[49] S Freeman, 'The Law of Peoples, Social Cooperation, Human Rights and Distributive Justice' in *Justice and the Social Contract: Essays on Rawlsian Political Philosophy* (New York, Oxford University Press, 2007) 263. More broadly construed, distributive justice is sometimes used synonymously with social justice.

[50] ibid at 264.

[51] See, eg Cavallero, 'An Immigration-Pressure Model'; Kymlicka, 'Territorial Boundaries'; Macedo, 'The Moral Dilemma of US Immigration Policy'; Ypi, 'Justice in Migration', all above n 3.

[52] R Goodin, 'If People Were Money ...' in Barry and Goodin (eds), *Free Movement*, above n 3 at 8. The idea is also found in Walzer, *Spheres of Justice: A Defence of Pluralism and Equality* (New York, Basic Books, 1983) 47–48.

[53] Wellman, 'Freedom of Association and the Right to Exclude' in Wellman and Cole, *Debating the Ethics of Immigration*, above n 3 at 67. Wellman makes a similar proposal with respect to refugees, that is, that a state may refuse entry to refugees if it has intervened in the refugees' home state to ensure they are adequately protected: 'Refugees' in Wellman and Cole, *Debating the Ethics of Immigration*, above n 3 at 123.

of all persons, but nationalists because they argue for the importance of fostering and preserving liberal forms of nationhood. Their work consists in trying to
reconcile these contrary inclinations. One path to reconciliation is to make the
right to foster national identity through immigration restrictions contingent on
meeting obligations of global distributive justice.

Will Kymlicka provides the most well worked out version of this proposal of
which I am aware. He argues that parties to a global original position, that is, a
global hypothetical social contract, would, first, allow for the creation of national
boundaries and the regulation of immigration as part of a nation-building
strategy;[54] second, choose some form of redistributive tax, requiring wealthier
countries to share their wealth with poorer countries in order to 'ensure that all
people are able to live a decent life in their country of birth';[55] and, third, agree
that: 'If rich countries are unwilling to share their wealth in this way, then they
forfeit the right to restrict admission into their borders.'[56] Kymlicka continues:

> [I]f states do meet their obligations of international justice, then it is permissible
> for them to regulate admissions so as [to] preserve a distinct national community.
> This regulation of mobility is consistent with liberal egalitarianism, I believe since it
> would not involve claiming an unfair share of resources, but would only reserve for
> the nationals of a country what aliens already have in their own country—namely, the
> chance to be free and equal citizens within their own national community.[57]

Kymlicka does not spell out the implications of his account for all aspects of
immigration policy. At times, the approach seems to imply that in cases where
global distributive obligations are fulfilled, then states enjoy broad discretion,
but in cases of non-compliance totally open borders are required. Kymlicka, for
instance, says rich countries that fail to meet their international distributive obligations 'forfeit the right to restrict admission'. Would failure to pay even a small
but non-trivial part of a redistributive tax in a given year mandate open borders?
A more plausible suggestion might link the extent of failure to required openness
by some metric. The larger aim, after all, is to achieve global distributive justice.
So one way to fill out this picture would be to allow countries to decide the extent
to which they meet their obligations by opening their borders or through foreign
aid, rather than being forced to choose one method or the other.

That still leaves many questions. Rather than address them all, I assume that the
liberal nationalist account can be defensibly fleshed out as follows. One principle is
that even when states comply with their other obligations, their immigration policies ought not to undermine the goal of global distributive justice. Additionally,
even a complying state needs some way to deal with others' non-compliance. A
simple proposal would be to subscribe to something like Liam Murphy's collective

---

[54] Kymlicka, 'Territorial Boundaries', above n 3 at 266–67. See also the argument for restricting
immigration in Kymlicka, *Multicultural Citizenship*, above n 10 at 125–26.
[55] Kymlicka, 'Territorial Boundaries', above n 3 at 266–67.
[56] ibid.
[57] ibid.

principle of beneficence, which 'requires agents to promote the well-being of others up to the level of sacrifice that would be optimal under full compliance'.[58] Such a principle eliminates the need to make up for the non-compliance of others. There may, of course, be other obligations, such as an obligation to establish some international institution that could enforce the requirements of the scheme.

That is what a somewhat worked-out liberal nationalist approach to justice in immigration governance might look like when a receiving state meets the demands of global distributive justice. We still need to flesh out the account for cases where a receiving state does not meet those demands. Here a non-complying state should nonetheless be permitted to ensure that immigration does not undermine that which makes it valuable as a state. Also, under the consequent admissions cap, priority of admissions would not only be required not to undermine global distributive justice; it seems admissions ought to somehow promote global distributive justice. That seems to follow reasonably from the fact that admissions policies are now seen as making up for the state's failure to comply with its other obligations of global distributive justice. The basic difference between principles of justice in immigration governance under conditions of compliance and non-compliance, then, is that in the latter case states must employ their immigration policies as tools for achieving global distributive justice instead of merely not undermining this goal. Not unlike the role of background justice in Rawls's theory, contribution to the scheme of global distributive justice on this view gives the state greater scope for its national project.

This is not the only way to reconstruct the liberal nationalist approach, but it is coherent and retains the ideas that make it appealing in the first place. There are two lines of inquiry pertinent to the assessment of this approach. The first asks whether migrant admissions can in fact be used to remedy failures to meet obligations of global distributive justice. Thomas Pogge has argued forcefully that immigration policy cannot be made an effective tool toward achieving global distributive ends.[59] This claim seems plausible.[60] After all, currently, the poorest are not able to finance their own migration.[61] To make migration a tool to help the worst off globally, then, would require subsidizing their migration, which seems an obvious inefficiency. Of course, if Pogge is correct that does not of itself invalidate all possible versions of the liberal nationalist proposal. The requirement

---

[58] L Murphy, *Moral Demands in Nonideal Theory* (New York, Oxford University Press, 2000) 7; see also L Murphy, 'The Demands of Beneficence' (1993) 22 *Philosophy & Public Affairs* 267.

[59] '[T]he number of needy persons in the world—including at least those 1300 million who cannot afford "a minimum, nutritionally adequate diet plus essential non-food requirements"—is simply out of all proportion to the number of needy foreigners which the rich countries admit or could admit.' For every person admitted, 'there will be hundreds, if not thousands, left in desperate need'. T Pogge, 'Migration and Poverty' in Bader (ed), *Citizenship and Exclusion*, above n 3 at 14. See also Miller, 'The Case for Limits', above n 3 at 198–99.

[60] But see HF Chang, 'The Economics of International Labor Migration and the Case for Global Distributive Justice in Liberal Political Theory' (2008) 41 *Cornell International Law Journal* 1, 6–8.

[61] P Collier, *Exodus: How Migration Is Changing Our World* (New York, Oxford University Press, 2013) 154–55.

to open borders may not be aimed at achieving global distributive justice through migration directly, but only indirectly by creating an incentive for wealthy states to meet their redistributive obligations.

A second objection is strictly moral and probably more significant. The argument in Section Three sought to show that migration, even for economic migrants, has wide-open and variable value, which is ignored by an approach that seeks an account of justice in immigration governance through the lens of global distributive justice. Instead, the global distributive justice account reduces the value of migration to its ability to conduce to better global distributive justice. It views migrants as interchangeable in a way that seems disjoint from the moral significance migration might have for migrants themselves. Their ability to access the value *for them* of the migration experience is entirely contingent on whether it will promote global distributive justice. This logic contrasts with, say, that of income taxation, where value is expropriated from otherwise free exercises of subjects' purposiveness. The equivalent domestic regime would be one that allowed people to move between jobs and cities only insofar as that promoted the health of the domestic welfare scheme.

To make this criticism more concrete, take as an example the idea, sometimes mooted, that the goal of either not interfering with or helping promote global distributive justice may justify restrictions on emigration if necessary to fight the brain drain, that is, the loss of valuable professional or other skills in sending states.[62] For example, one quarter of the educated labour force born in Ghana was living in countries belonging to the Organisation for Economic Co-Operation and Development in 1990; the same figure is 60 per cent for Gambia and 80 per cent for Jamaica.[63] Yet limits on the exit of skilled workers would only accord with their rationale if they served to force those workers to work in their chosen profession at home. Perhaps this may seem permissible because what is at stake is often the emigration of the advantaged, for whom freedom of migration may be less valuable in terms of the prospective improvement of their capability set and who are more likely to pursue their chosen profession at home. The same logic, though, would extend to any sector of the economy that happens to be important to a country's distributive welfare. If doctors are important to a receiving state now, construction or road workers might find themselves to be similarly important later on. Global distributive approaches to justice in immigration focusing on the problem of the brain drain therefore support arguments for a conscripted workforce. The answer to concerns about the brain drain is not to subsume the problem of migration under the problem of distributive justice. Rather, it is to work out an account of the right of emigration in light of the variable value of migration for potential emigrants.

Arguments about justice in immigration governance in terms of global distributive justice reduce the value of freedom of migration to a single dimension,

---

[62] See Ypi, 'Justice in Migration', above n 3 at 401ff.
[63] S Commander, M Kangasniemi, and LA Winters, 'The Brain Drain: Curse or Boon?' *IZA Discussion Paper No. 809* (June 2003), available at: http://ftp.iza.org/dp809.pdf.

namely promoting global distributive justice, and are objectionable for that reason. The pursuit of opportunities through migration connects to each migrant's capability set in wide-ranging and morally significant ways that are ignored by such approaches. For these reasons, appeals to concerns about global distributive justice do not provide an adequate basis for theorizing justice in immigration governance. Nor does the fact that a state meets its global distributive obligations provide an adequate defence of immigration restrictions. Such concerns about global justice must be met in a way that adequately account for the value of migration to each migrant.[64]

V. The Indirect Principle

The arguments for the variable value of migration from Section Three provide a way to conceptualize injuries caused by first-order immigration restrictions. These are injuries that result in the denial of a prospective marginal improvement to a capability set through direct interference with freedom of migration. I have identified a set of three first-order considered judgements that suggest it is presumptively unjust to exclude refugees, young children or their parents, or returning citizens who cannot naturalize elsewhere. Above, I also claimed that for the vast majority of economic and family migrants, we do not have any such judgements. Yet for such migrants, migration will not be without value, so their exclusion also needs to be justified. Under the argument so far developed, such a justification would require a showing that: (1) welfare institutions (if these, for example, are part of its political conception of justice) are necessary to the receiving state's political conception of justice; (2) the given forms of first-order immigration restriction are necessary to preserve the stability of welfare institutions and the legitimate expectations that members have formed under the rules of those institutions; and (3) these preservationist goals outweigh migrants' reasons for immigrating. If those claims can be supported, no injustice will have occurred by virtue of a first-order restriction on admission.

To arrive at such a first-order justification, a great deal of normative and empirical information is required. How does one assess the stability of a non-ideal political conception of justice? What legitimate expectations do members have? How does one weigh those against the claims of migrants? What cross-cutting effects might the admission of this or that migrant, or this or that migrant group, have on this stability and these expectations? In the end, a sufficiently impartial judgement of surpassing complexity must be made. We must, Smith says, 'place ourselves completely in [the impartial spectator's] situation' and 'listen with diligent and reverential attention to what he suggests to us'.[65] However, as I noted

---

[64]   M Blake makes a similar point in Blake, 'Immigration, Jurisdiction, and Exclusion', above n 3 at 126.
[65]   Smith, *Theory of Moral Sentiments*, above n 40 at 267 [VI.ii.1.22].

at the end of Chapter One, Smith is sceptical of anyone's ability to take on this perspective when cross-border issues arise. Further, the prescription to consult the impartial spectator does not provide much guidance, by itself, as to when a first-order immigration restriction will or will not be justifiable. The injunction to consult with the impartial spectator to establish the authority of immigration regimes can plausibly be fleshed out institutionally in terms of the Rawlsian account of authority laid out in Section Five of Chapter Five. However, the description of this impartial perspective does not settle what a reasonable conception of just immigration governance might be. For that, another sufficiently impartial perspective for the derivation of such principles is required. This task is taken up in Chapter Seven.

Before attempting to derive principles for first-order immigration governance in this way, more can be said by looking at our second-order judgements. Accordingly, in this section I provide the argument for what I am calling the indirect principle of freedom of migration. As noted, the principle holds that a state may only impose those first-order immigration laws and policies that do not result in second-order oppression. The principle is important since, by virtue of the justificatory overlap between first-order and second-order issues, the presence or absence of second-order oppression provides one indication of when a first-order policy is unreasonably unjust. In this way, it offers a pragmatic way at getting at elusive first-order judgements by attending to the actual or likely unjust effects of an immigration law or policy. The principle also has non-trivial critical force, in light of the number of possible second-order constraints that may be invoked and in light of what I call the countersocial premise, according to which immigration laws and policies that seek to arrive at first-order results contrary to migration pressure are more likely to lead to second-order oppression.

1. The Indirect Principle

The indirect principle seeks to integrate the conception of the variable value of freedom of movement based on marginal improvement to one's capability set and the account of the value of states based on their provision of a stable political conception of justice with the considered judgements from Chapter Two regarding second-order immigration governance. Those second-order judgements are that the following are presumptively unjust: (1) enforcement of immigration policies using excessive or arbitrary force; (2) expulsion of long-term residents without procedural guarantees; (3) imposition of criminal penalties for breaches of immigration law without trial; (4) prolonged detention of migrants who do not pose security or other risks; and (5) private exploitation of migrants by traffickers, smugglers, or employers. A further second-order judgement is that it is just (6) to exclude non-naturalized migrants from voting in national elections, although this judgement is not important to the argument here.

Under the indirect principle, for the vast majority of economic and family migrants a so-called 'right' to migrate is more helpfully thought of as a valuable liberty protected by a series of rights against these forms of second-order oppression. The root idea at work here is one that occasionally surfaces in discussions of freedom or liberty. It is, for instance, at work in Smith's attack against the Laws of Settlement, where his principal arguments focus on the various forms of second-order oppression that arose incidentally to the restrictions on the movement of poor labourers. Both HLA Hart and Wesley Hohfeld aptly illustrate the same idea using a line of cases concerning the right to trade or employ labour. The real issue in such cases, according to Hart, is not whether the liberty 'to earn one's living in one's own way'[66] is to be protected according to some abstract principle, but rather which torts and criminal penalties ought to be available to protect it.[67] And each such question, as Hohfeld says, 'is ultimately a question of justice and policy; and it should be considered on its merits'.[68]

Thus any liberty right can be understood deontically as a permissible activity surrounded by a 'perimeter of protection'[69] made up of other entitlements, which are easiest to conceive of as rights against interference. Accordingly, there are two ways, direct and indirect, to come to an understanding of the extent or limits of any liberty.[70] Direct arguments assert the value of an activity and move outward to specify associated protective rights. Arguments for traditional civil and political rights often will be able to proceed directly, since such rights involve activities whose value can be used to justify a wide range of protections.[71] Indirect arguments, in contrast to direct ones, describe a residuum of free action that cannot be interfered with other than by violating a protective right.[72] Such arguments are less ambitious. They do not rely on, nor do they seek to establish, comprehensive duties not to interfere with an activity based on its value. They ride on the coat-tails of the justifications for ancillary entitlements, which will in some cases be easier to establish because they relate to a person's capabilities in a more basic way.

---

[66] *Quinn v Leathem* (1901) AC 495, 534. The quote is altered. Lord Lindley wrote: 'The plaintiff had the ordinary rights of the British subject. He was at liberty to earn his living in his own way ... This liberty is a right recognized by law; its correlative is the general duty of everyone not to prevent the free exercise of this liberty except so far as his own liberty of action may justify him in so doing.'

[67] HLA Hart, 'Legal Rights' in *Essays on Bentham: Studies in Jurisprudence and Political Theory* (Oxford, Clarendon Press, 1982) 172, fn 53. This point is further discussed in NE Simmonds, 'Rights at the Cutting Edge' in MH Kramer, NE Simmonds and H Steiner, *A Debate Over Rights* (New York, Oxford University Press, 1998) 168–73.

[68] WN Hohfeld, 'Some Fundamental Legal Conceptions as Applied in Judicial Reasoning' (1913) 23 *Yale Law Journal* 16, 36.

[69] See Hart, 'Legal Rights', above n 67 at 170–73 (1982). See also Simmonds, 'Rights at the Cutting Edge', above n 67 at 156–57, 165–73.

[70] For the distinction between direct and indirect arguments, see Kramer, 'Rights Without Trimmings' in Kramer, Simmonds and Steiner, *A Debate over Rights*, above n 67 at 12, fn 3.

[71] Hart says such liberty-rights may be protected by a 'strictly correlative obligation not to interfere by any means with a specific form of activity'. Hart, 'Legal Rights', above n 67 at 172; but see also the same essay at 190–93. Hart's claim may be misleading if it is meant to suggest such rights do not ultimately give way to the kind of analysis that he and Hohfeld apply to less celebrated forms of liberty. It just happens that the most widely-accepted civil and political liberties enjoy sufficient protective entitlements that their guarantee can seem complete.

[72] Kramer, 'Rights Without Trimmings', above n 70 at 12, fn 3

When there are strong reasons to value a particular freedom and those reasons do not vary from person to person, it may still be appropriate to talk in terms of a single, substantive right instead of a constellation of protective rights. This may be the case with, say, freedom of conscience or religion. In the migration context, it may be that in accordance with our considered judgements liberal constitutional democracies ought to constitutionally protect or enshrine rights of asylum or reunification for young children and their parents, just as the right of return for citizens is protected or enshrined in many states and internationally. For the vast majority of migrants, however, there appears to be no strong case for such protection or enshrinement.

Instead we say the following: our first-order considered judgements reflect the judgement that the high value of migration in certain cases will rarely be outweighed by the legitimate expectations of members. They also reflect the belief that the number of such migrants will be relatively small, and so unlikely to undermine the political conception of a receiving state and its basic structure. Our second-order judgements reflect judgements about ways that it is almost always wrong to restrict migration, even in those cases where we do not have a clear first-order judgement. Such a judgement reflects the view that such forms of injury will rarely be justified by the need to safeguard a political conception of justice or by the need to respect members' legitimate expectations. There are reasons to have more confidence in our second-order judgements than our first-order ones. Accordingly, we can rely on our second-order judgements to provide guidance on the permissible outer limits of first-order immigration law and policy.

The argument for the indirect principle of freedom of migration proceeds through two stages. First, an affirmative case for the value of migration is made out. I have argued that the value of migration depends on the prospective increase to one's capability set that will result from migrating. This account establishes an initial claim to migrate for most migrants. Second, there must be a set of arguments for the specific rights of protection, based on our second-order considered judgements, which migrants ought to enjoy even when a receiving state's proposed admissions policy would deny them a right to enter. Such arguments identify forms of injury that ought to be prohibited because they will almost always be irrational or unreasonably partial. Put another way, we must evaluate the extent to which a given second-order injury reduces or limits a migrant's capability set and then ask if such limits are acceptable in light of the probable impact of the migrant's or migrants' immigration on the state. If that injury seems to us to be one that would not be justifiable, then we have identified one limit of immigration law and policy.

The five considered judgements of second-order injustice all seem to identify second-order rights because they zero in on forms of serious injury to migrants that most will recognize as presumptively wrong and that experience demonstrates are likely to result from restrictive forms of immigration governance. Our considered judgement is that it is unlikely that these apparent wrongs can be defended even taking into account the special justificatory considerations that arise in this domain.

2. The Relevance of the Indirect Principle

Under the indirect principle, migration cannot be restricted through second-order oppression, except in exceptional circumstances. Why is this principle important? One reason has to do with the justificatory links between first-order and second-order immigration policy and the way that absolutist governance of immigration potentially trades on those links.

It is sometimes assumed that matters of second-order policy can be divorced from general sovereign discretion over matters of admission and exclusion. Some international instruments, for example, regarding the rights of migrants include what might be called sovereign reserve clauses, setting forth a series of rights to be protected but also including provisions saying that states' discretion over admission remains intact. The International Convention for the Protection of the Rights of All Migrant Workers and Members of Their Families[73] (ICRMW) is a case in point. It sets out a long list of rights for both legal and illegal migrant workers and their families but also includes the following article:

> Nothing in the present Convention shall affect the right of each State Party to establish the criteria governing admission of migrant workers and members of their families. Concerning other matters related to their legal situation and treatment as migrant workers and members of their families, States Parties shall be subject to the limitations set forth in the present Convention.[74]

Articles such as this appear to presume that broad first-order discretion ('the right of each State Party to establish the criteria governing admission') can be preserved notwithstanding restrictions on second-order policy ('other matters related to their legal situation and treatment as migrant workers and members of their families') in the form of rights that migrants present in a state must be afforded. This presumption is questionable, since a state will be unable to admit migrants on the condition that they give up any among the set of protected rights. Such limits, for example, severely limit the range of acceptable guestworker programmes, in turn limiting the number of guestworkers that a country will be willing to admit. Indeed, this connection between first-order and second-order policy is recognized by the strongest absolutist pronouncements. In *Nishimura Ekiu*, for instance, the United States Supreme Court held that a state is free to 'admit [immigrants] only in such cases *and upon such conditions* as it may see fit to prescribe'.[75] On the strongest form of absolutism, the right of a state to implement any first-order policy justifies any means of carrying out such policy.

Further, as I have noted, the immigration regimes of wealthy liberal constitutional democracies often govern as though absolutism were a legitimate moral and legal view. In doing so, their laws and policies often include objectionable

---

[73] International Convention on the Protection of the Rights of All Migrant Workers and Members of Their Families (adopted 18 December 1990, entered into force 1 July 2003) 2220 UNTS 3.

[74] ibid at art 79.

[75] *Nishimura Ekiu v United States*, 142 US 651, 659 (1892) (emphasis added).

second-order elements aimed at achieving first-order aims. Most notable, as discussed in Chapter Four, are the various strategies used to deter asylum seekers from coming to and seeking asylum in a receiving state. Similar strategies are used in other policy areas. Thus, what gives the indirect principle salience is that, in the case of immigration governance, there are historical and structural reasons for thinking receiving states will unduly denigrate migrants' interests and, correspondingly, inflate countervailing interests in favour of immigration restriction, leading them to incorrectly judge that such forms of second-order injury are justified to achieve first-order ends. Our list of second-order judgements reflects particular evils that the historical record shows governments have been willing to visit or have allowed to be visited on migrants in the name of immigration control. Unable to realize desired policy ends at the border, governments have often restricted due process rights to expel migrants, heedless of whether such deportation measures are over inclusive. Unwilling to permanently admit migrants whose labour is needed within the receiving state, governments have a long history of admitting temporary guestworkers or of tacitly tolerating the presence of illegal immigrants as a cheap form of labour—both groups, of course, are more vulnerable to exploitation and abuse. Unable to prevent unwanted immigration, detention and even killing are sometimes relied on by governments to achieve their aims. Therefore, the rights identified by our second-order judgements correspond to wrongs against migrants that governments *actually have committed or allowed to be committed* in the name of achieving desired policy aims.

There are also structural reasons to think such wrongs have not been mere accidents but that the governments of receiving states, left unconstrained, *will continue to commit them* or *continue to allow them to be committed*. As has been emphasized, the immigration regimes of receiving states must, in order to avoid unreasonable injustice, make a series of complex judgements regarding the prospective gains to migrants' capability set; the legitimate expectations of members; and the effect that immigration would have on the stability of the state's political conception of justice. These judgements are both normatively nuanced and require the marshalling of considerable data and the application of difficult economic and social theories. Immigration regimes are liable, therefore, to get these judgements wrong. Besides informational deficits and simple human fallibility, they will fall prey to an undue bias toward the interests of members, a Smithian unreasonable preference. This bias arises because the governments of liberal constitutional democracies are answerable to their own members, large numbers of whom, history suggests, will have propensities toward anti-immigrant sentiment. Moreover, the interests of migrants will seem more remote to the officials of receiving states. As a result, immigration policies will tend to disregard them. That means that serious second-order injury, of the kinds identified by our considered judgements, are likely to be unjust.

And so the argument for the indirect principle is as follows. The judgement required to arrive at a reasonably just first-order immigration policy is extraordinarily nuanced and multi-faceted. What can be said is that no immigration regime may ordinarily, consistent with its claim to authority, violate the basic rights reflected by our second-order considered judgements or create conditions that lead to violations of the basic rights of migrants when implementing a law or policy. Such basic rights include rights to life and security of the person; rights against prolonged and arbitrary detention; rights against criminal liability without trial; rights against enslavement, exploitation, and abuse; and rights of due process when facing expulsion. The case for these rights depends on the significant impact such injuries would have on the capability sets of migrants and the reasonable presumption that such injuries will rarely be justified in light of the set of possible reasons in favour of restriction. It also depends on three further claims. First, the historical record of government action in this area is too poor for us to give governments the benefit of the doubt. Second, this record seems a reflection of the fact that the judgements made by national immigration regimes about whether or not they should respect the liberty of migration in such cases are too liable to error to ground a justification of such basic rights violations in normal circumstances. Further, there are structural reasons for thinking democratic governments will improperly discount the interests of migrants when making such judgements. Therefore an immigration law or policy that leads to one of the five forms of second-order oppression identified will, presumptively, be unreasonably unjust.

3. The Critical Force of the Indirect Principle

Those who believe immigration laws and policies are too restrictive may find the indirect principle unpromising. Clearly, the indirect principle does not challenge sovereign control over immigration as thoroughly as would a general right to free migration. But, as I will argue in the next chapter, there is no convincing case for such a general right. Further, while it may be possible to argue for more rights of migration—more or broader rights, that is, than those corresponding to the three first-order considered judgements that we are working with—even if there is no general right, the effect of such arguments will merely reduce the scope of applicability of the indirect principle. Finally, the indirect principle has more critical force than might at first seem to be the case. In particular, it will support freer immigration governance depending on the kinds of second-order oppression recognized and depending on the validity of what I call the countersocial premise.

First, while I have relied on only five considered judgements of second-order oppression, the potential list of second-order judgements that could be posited is much longer. To see this, one need only consider the potential applicability of general human rights protections in the domain of immigration governance. The United Nations Human Rights Committee has written that 'the general rule is that each one of the rights of the [International Covenant on Civil and Political Rights] must be guaranteed without discrimination between citizens and aliens'.[76] Here, the right to equality before the law without discrimination and the right to the

[76] UNCHR, 'General Comment No. 15: The Position of Aliens under the Covenant' (11 April 1986) UN Doc HRI/GEN/1/Rev1 (1986) at para 2.

enjoyment of one's own culture, religion, or language appear to have the greatest expansionary potential under the indirect principle.[77] The possible limits expand still further once economic and social rights are taken into account. Strikingly, for instance, the Universal Declaration of Human Rights and the International Covenant on Economic, Social and Cultural Rights both include a right to work and other employment rights that are not, on their face, limited to either citizens or even legal migrants.[78] Other common rights that may be applicable include rights to social security,[79] to public health services,[80] and to education.[81] As more rights are accepted as basic rights enjoyed by migrants, the critical force of the indirect principle grows. Each such right removes a set of possible conditions that might have been imposed upon entry, one way in which first-order policies might have been enforced, or one consequence that receiving states can allow to result from such policies.

Beyond the number of rights, the critical force of the principle will depend on the preferences and actions of migrants themselves. This is by virtue of what I call the countersocial premise. In Chapter Two, I noted that the immigration regimes of wealthy constitutional liberal democracies are trying to achieve with their laws and policies outcomes generally opposed to actual migration pressures. That is, their overall inegalitarian laws and policies tend to favour the admission of the better off, whereas the greatest migration pressures come from less advantaged, though not the least advantaged, migrants. The countersocial premise states that this opposition is more likely to lead to second-order oppression than would immigration laws and policies that generally track migration pressure.

The countersocial premise is supported by the common sense supposition that when migrants see themselves as having strong reasons to immigrate into another state, at a certain point they are likely to think those reasons outweigh the foreseeable disadvantages of migrating through injurious channels. In response, immigration regimes wedded to their first-order designs will put in place even more injurious enforcement policies to create further disincentives. Therefore policies that do not track the preferences of migrants will tend to lead to more and harsher second-order injuries. The countersocial premise further rests upon the claim, already discussed, that immigration regimes, however carefully planned, are simply likely to get the complex judgement demanded of them, about the impact of immigration on the state's political conception of justice and the legitimate expectations of members, not only wrong but unreasonably wrong. As a result,

---

[77] International Covenant on Civil and Political Rights (adopted 16 December 1966, entered into force 22 April 1954) 999 UNTS 171, arts 26 and 27.

[78] Universal Declaration of Human Rights (adopted 10 December 1948), UNGA Res 217 A(III), art 23; International Covenant on Economic, Social and Cultural Rights (adopted 16 December 1966, entered into force 3 January 1976) 993 UNTS 3, art 6(1).

[79] Universal Declaration of Human Rights, above n 78 at arts 22 and 25; International Covenant on Economic, Social and Cultural Rights, above n 78 at art 9.

[80] Universal Declaration of Human Rights, above n 78 at art 25(1); International Covenant on Economic, Social and Cultural Rights, above n 78 at art 12.

[81] Universal Declaration of Human Rights, above n 78 at art 26; International Covenant on Economic, Social and Cultural Rights, above n 78 at arts 6(2), 13–15.

there is reason to believe that immigration regimes, or the officials within them, will systematically overestimate the justification for imposing second-order injury upon unwanted migrants. If all this is true, what is implied is that the indirect principle will impose what might be called deontic pressure on immigration regimes to allow in more disadvantaged migrants, hence toward more egalitarian policies. One result of this dynamic is to give migrants a form of standing that in practice is generally denied them—we might call it 'deontic standing'—as immigration regimes adapt their policies to avoid second-order oppression.

VI. Moving on

I have argued that a cap on immigration into a state can only be justified by the Kantian imperative to sustain an authoritative political conception of justice and the need to respect members' legitimate expectations formed within such a conception. The resulting judgements that must be made to arrive at just first-order immigration policies are complex. For the vast majority of migrants, it will be difficult to say when first-order policies cross the line into injustice because of the range of factors that come into play: the variable value of freedom of migration; the empirical impact of migration on states; the nature of that state's political conception of justice and the conditions necessary to support it; and the difficult question of what counts as a legitimate expectation and how far these should be respected. In the face of this uncertainty about first-order policy, the argument for the indirect principle relies instead on the claim that certain forms of second-order injury will rarely be justifiable and that by avoiding these forms of injury a state can approximate the requirements of a just first-order policy.

The indirect principle has non-trivial critical force, but it does not allow for the straightforward assessment of inegalitarian policies. This may be problematic in two cases in particular. First, a geographically isolated state may be able, under the indirect principle, to impose a far more inegalitarian immigration policy than another not so isolated because geographic barriers provide a far more effective deterrent than any second-order policy ever could.[82] For example, the indirect principle may permit an inegalitarian policy for Iceland but not the United States. The second kind of case involves improved technologies of surveillance and humane enforcement. Improved technologies may enable states to impose increasingly inegalitarian polices in keeping with the principle. Such considerations suggest that, while the indirect principle is significant, it should not be our sole means of evaluating the justice or injustice of first-order policies. Accordingly, in the next chapter I seek to develop a principle that allows for first-order evaluation, using a modified Rawlsian original position.

---

[82] I owe this point to Audrey Macklin.

7

Priority of Admission for the Worst-off Migrants

I. Introduction

WE ARE TRYING to develop reasonable principles for just immigration governance. While the indirect principle set out in the previous chapter has non-trivial critical potential, it does not, as its name implies, directly add to an understanding of when we ought to judge first-order laws and policies unjust. In this chapter, I develop an argument for a principle of priority to guide in the selection of migrants for indefinite, or permanent, admission beneath a cap based on the imperative of stability and the related requirement to protect the legitimate expectations of members. This principle allows for the evaluation of first-order inegalitarianism.

Whereas the indirect principle took inspiration from Kant, I now depart from his cosmopolitan right. Kant says that, 'Cosmopolitan Right shall be limited to Conditions of Universal Hospitality', where

> *hospitality* means the right of a stranger not to be treated with hostility when he arrives on someone else's territory. He can indeed be turned away, if this can be done without causing his death, but he must not be treated with hostility, so long as he behaves in a peaceable manner in the place he happens to be in.[1]

If Kant's principle of cosmopolitan right suggests, as it seems to, that there are no constraints on what I call first-order immigration policies, I believe it is a mistaken view of rightful immigration governance. To develop a better alternative, in this chapter I undertake the rather fusty philosophical enterprise of adapting John Rawls's hypothetical social contract device, the original position, to construct principles of first-order selection for indefinite admission. Others have carried out a similar exercise. In Chapter Six, I discussed how Will Kymlicka deploys a global original position to incorporate immigration governance into a principle of global distributive justice.[2] More well-known than Kymlicka's account is

---

[1] I Kant, 'Perpetual Peace: A Philosophical Sketch' in H Reiss (ed), *Kant: Political Writings* (Cambridge, Cambridge University Press, 1970) 105–106.

[2] W Kymlicka, 'Territorial Boundaries: A Liberal Egalitarian Perspective' in D Miller and SH Hashmi (eds), *Boundaries and Justice* (Princeton, Princeton University Press, 2001) 259.

Joseph Carens's use of a global original position for individuals to conclude that a right of migration would be protected as a basic liberty having so-called lexical, or absolute, priority: '[O]ne would insist that the right to migrate be included in the system of basic liberties for the same reasons that one would insist that the right to religious freedom be included: it might prove essential to one's plan of life.'[3] The power of Carens's argument flows from the fact that immigration may indeed prove essential to a migrant's plan of life. Indeed, as will emerge, I agree with Carens that freedom of migration is a liberty that the parties to an appropriately modified original position would choose to protect. He goes wrong, however, in moving too quickly to assume that this right would be given sweeping breadth and absolute priority.

The aim of this chapter, then, is to elaborate with greater care the argument for freedom of migration from a modified original position. As this aim suggests, the argument proceeds for the first time in ideal theory, at least (as I will explain) partly. One reason for this shift to ideal theory is to take advantage of the simplifying assumptions associated with the original position. In addition, in this way we may develop ideal principles that will allow us to evaluate the immigration regimes of wealthy liberal constitutional democracies and, perhaps, provide guidance for their reform.[4] After some preliminary remarks in Section Two about the tension between contextualism and universalism about justice in Rawls's theory, I explain in Sections Three to Five how to adapt the original position to the problem of immigration governance. Sections Six and Seven present the substantive arguments that some central range of migration would be protected as a basic liberty because of its importance to the two moral powers, namely the powers to develop and act on a sense of justice and a conception of the good. I also argue, however, that freedom of migration would not enjoy lexical priority, as do the basic liberties in Rawls's domestic theory of justice. Nonetheless, the case for protecting migration non-lexically yields an account of the importance of migration to the moral powers. In Section Eight, I argue that sensitivity to the relationship between migration and the moral powers yields a prioritarian principle of first-order indefinite admissions. Under this principle, a state should admit as many of the worst-off migrants as possible below the threshold at which the legitimate expectations of existing members would be frustrated and the stability of the political conception of justice compromised. Section Nine then assesses the evaluative power of the prioritarian principle by returning one last time to our first-order judgements and to the problem of inegalitarianism.

---

[3] J Carens, 'Aliens and Citizens: The Case for Open Borders' (1987) 49 *The Review of Politics* 251 at 258.

[4] For discussion, see AJ Simmons, 'Ideal and Nonideal Theory' (2010) 38 *Philosophy & Public Affairs* 5–37, esp 34.

II. Contextualism and Universalism

I begin by explaining what I take to be the nature of Rawls's contextualism regarding social justice. Rawls's presumption in his theory of a closed society entered only at birth and exited only through death accompanies another restriction, confining its principles to the basic structure of a well-ordered society.[5] This second restriction presents us with a series of puzzles about what happens to justice outside the confines of the basic structure. At least three distinct debates have arisen in the literature over whether a theory of justice thus restricted can deal appropriately with issues of gender and the family;[6] over how such a theory addresses personal conduct;[7] and over global and international justice.[8] All three debates flow from the difficulty of sorting out whether and how contexts other than a state's basic structure, but in which seemingly morally significant human interactions take place, can or ought to be regulated by principles of justice. The problem of justice in immigration governance dovetails with this set of puzzles. Migrants are outside the group of persons born into any given basic structure, but they seek inclusion in that group. What does justice say about them?

One way of framing puzzles of this kind is as a question about whether Rawls is committed to a universalist account of social justice, in the sense that he seeks to develop universal principles that may nevertheless apply differently in different contexts, or to a contextualist account, in which distinct first principles exist for each context.[9] On a universalist account of justice the principles of justice spread out over all possible social worlds and vary only in application. So, for example, the difference principle—the principle that social and economic inequalities are to be to the greatest benefit of the least-advantaged members of society—might still apply to individual conduct, but the demands made by that principle on an individual would differ from the demands made on the institutions of the basic structure.[10] On a contextualist account, the principles of justice themselves change from context to context. One would say that individual conduct is not governed by the difference principle but only, say, by a natural duty of mutual aid.[11]

---

[5] J Rawls, *Political Liberalism*, expanded edn (New York, Columbia University Press, 1996) 258; see also J Rawls, E Kelly (ed), *Justice as Fairness: A Restatement* (Cambridge, MA, Belknap Press, 2001) 4.

[6] SM Okin, *Justice, Gender, and the Family* (New York, Basic Books, 1989).

[7] GA Cohen, 'Where the Action Is: On the Site of Distributive Justice' (1997) 26 *Philosophy & Public Affairs* 3; L Murphy, 'Institutions and the Demands of Justice' (1998) 27 *Philosophy & Public Affairs* 251.

[8] See, eg C Beitz, *Political Theory and International Relations* (Princeton, Princeton University Press, 1979); TW Pogge, *Realizing Rawls* (Ithaca, Cornell University Press, 1989).

[9] Here I rely on the distinction between contextualist and universalist accounts of justice in D Miller, 'Two Ways to Think about Justice' in *Justice for Earthlings: Essays in Political Philosophy* (New York, Cambridge University Press, 2013) 40.

[10] See Cohen, 'Where the Action Is' and Murphy, 'Institutions and the Demands of Justice', above n 7.

[11] J Rawls, *A Theory of Justice*, revised edn (Cambridge, MA, Belknap Press, 1999) 297–98.

Rawls in fact makes amply clear that he considers that different principles of justice take hold in different contexts. He seems to be, therefore, a contextualist when it comes to justice. For example, in 'The Law of Peoples' (the published lecture that preceded the book), he writes:

> In justice as fairness the principles of justice for the basic structure of society are not suitable as fully general principles: They do not apply to all subjects, not to churches and universities, or to the basic structures of all societies, or to the law of peoples.[12]

If Rawls is a contextualist about justice, that sets up a superficial tension with another of his firmly held views. According to Rawls, all persons, or the great majority of persons, are owed justice.[13] That is because the great majority of persons are endowed with the sense of justice, which has been so important to earlier argument. This moral capacity provides standing to make demands of justice on one another. As Rawls writes, 'Those who can give justice are owed justice.'[14]

This discussion brings us to Rawls's conception of moral personhood. The nerve of this conception in its mature form is the idea that all persons have two moral powers, a capacity for a sense of justice and a capacity for a conception of the good. The former is 'the capacity to understand, to apply, and to act from the public conception of justice which characterizes the fair terms of social cooperation'. The latter is 'the capacity to form, to revise, and rationally to pursue a conception of one's rational advantage or good'.[15] Rawls mentions three possible elements that conceptions of the good may have: the final ends of the individual; their attachments and loyalties to other individuals or groups; and their religious, philosophical, or moral view of their relation to the world.[16] We would think of the second moral power as the capacity to form, revise, and pursue these different aspects of one's life. In *A Theory of Justice*, Rawls explicitly says the capacity for a sense of justice is a minimal requirement satisfied by the great majority of humankind;[17] I can conceive of no reason for thinking that the second moral power ought not to be thought of in similarly broad terms. We might say that it is due to the second moral power that we face the prospect of unjustified injuries that give rise to conflicts of justice. It is due to the first moral power that we are distinctively sensitive to the prospect of dignitarian insult that haunts such conflicts and also that we have various associated duties as a result, such as the duty to avoid injuring others unjustifiably. It is through his theory of moral personhood, then, that Rawls seems committed to the view that justice and its obligations are universal in reach.

---

[12] J Rawls, 'The Law of Peoples' in S Freeman (ed), *Collected Papers* (Cambridge, MA, Harvard University Press, 1999) 532. See also, eg Rawls, *Theory of Justice*, above n 11 at 119; Rawls, *Political Liberalism*, above n 5 at 272, n 9.

[13] Rawls, *Theory of Justice*, above n 11 at 443.

[14] ibid at 446. See also J Rawls, 'The Sense of Justice' in *Collected Papers*, above n 12 at 96.

[15] Rawls, *Political Liberalism*, above n 5 at 19.

[16] ibid.

[17] Rawls, *Theory of Justice*, above n 11 at 442–43.

That seems to eliminate one way of thinking about Rawls's contextualism. It cannot be that he thinks obligations of justice are not owed beyond the confines of the basic structure. While the two principles established under justice as fairness are special in that they are confined to the basic structure of a closed, well-ordered society, justice itself is not a special relationship. If one encounters others who possess the two moral powers, there is the possibility of obligations of justice toward them. We must try to figure out what these are. If we do not, we are open to potential charges of injustice. Moreover, now returning to Kant, in special cases 'devoid of justice' we are subject to the injunction to 'proceed ... into a rightful condition,'[18] failing which we are guilty of 'wrong in the highest degree'.[19] In sum, whenever we find ourselves in a dispute with another person possessed of the two moral powers, we must strive to find principles of justice to regulate that dispute and, if we are not under one already, place ourselves under a common authority to resolve disagreements over those principles.

We can now understand the various puzzles arising from the closed-state presumption and basic-structure restriction as pointing toward an obligation to reach authoritative settlement of principles of justice for each context that might be characterized by the circumstances of justice, that is, circumstances where there is a potential for injury that cannot be resolved by resort to a common conception of the good. There is also a further quandary, over how to relate the different contextual principles to one another. This second quandary is particularly meaningful in the domain of immigration. Immigration regimes are 'transcontextual' contexts, mediating the conceptions of justice of the state of origin and the state of destination. Further, such regimes also mediate between these conceptions of justice and a conception of global or international justice. If we accept Rawls's contextual approach to justice, we might think of our problem as one that concerns what happens to justice at the intersections of these various conceptions.

III. A Contextualist Universalist Method

Rawls is both contextualist and universalist. His contextualism raises methodological questions about, first, how to appropriately define each context and, second, how to formulate principles for each context so defined. His universalism leads to a duty to figure out the principles of justice that govern various contexts in which the possibility of mutual injury arises. This duty also leads to a question about how the principles of justice in different contexts relate to one another. Finally, there are difficult questions about how to address potential conflicts

---

[18] I Kant, MJ Gregor (trans and ed), *The Metaphysics of Morals* (Cambridge, Cambridge University Press, 1996) 86 [6:307].
[19] ibid at 86 [6:307–308].

among the different principles developed for different contexts. In this section, I offer a Rawlsian approach that resolves these issues.

Rawls can be understood to have offered two primary methods for the derivation of principles of justice, namely wide reflective equilibrium and the constructivist original position. The basics of wide reflective equilibrium have already been explained. It is a method whereby we work back and forth between our considered judgements and a set of explicative principles. The process of wide reflective equilibrium stops when mutual adjustments are no longer necessary to achieve consistency among these judgements and principles. As described, though, wide reflective equilibrium is susceptible to a 'charge of emptiness'.[20] There is nothing it excludes, even other methods of justification. That leads to the question of how we can ever hope to actually develop a set of principles with sufficient structure to merit the designation of being a theory. One role of the original position is to provide such structure.[21]

The idea behind the original position is to model a fair procedure (hence 'justice as fairness') through which parties negotiating a social contract can arrive at an agreement on principles of justice for a well-ordered society. In the domestic original position, each member of society is represented by a party to the social contract. The parties are mutually disinterested and rational. By choosing among a set of alternatives, they seek to establish principles that further the life plans of the members they represent, but they do not know those plans nor do they know various other personal contingencies such as race, class, associative ties, and (in *Political Liberalism*) their comprehensive religious or philosophical beliefs and commitments. In this way no party has an unfair advantage and all parties have reason to agree to principles of justice acceptable to the least advantaged members. That is because, for all they know, the least advantaged might be the members they represent.

The original position relies on wide reflective equilibrium at two points: first, in devising the conceptions of persons, society, and procedural justice that serve as inputs to the construction of the social contract procedure; and second, as a backstop, in checking the results of the procedure against our firmly held convictions. If, once such an exercise were carried out, the principles arrived at through the original position failed, for instance, to protect certain key liberties we may wish to revise the procedure. If all or most of our considered judgements are accounted for, then we can be reasonably confident in our theory for the time being and seek to apply it to more controversial cases. In this way the original position produces a candidate conception of justice that can now be the subject of ongoing debate, in our case debate concerning immigration governance, through public reason.

The general problem in this chapter is how to make use of wide reflective equilibrium and the original position to sort out Rawls's contextualism on the one

---

[20] TM Scanlon, 'Rawls on Justification' in S Freeman (ed), *The Cambridge Companion to Rawls* (New York, Cambridge University Press, 2003) 150–51.
[21] Rawls, *Political Liberalism*, above n 5 at 26.

hand and his commitment to the view that we owe justice to all moral persons on the other. Our specific problem is how to use these methods to develop a principle or principles of justice for governing indefinite admissions.

Rawls discusses the general problem in *Political Liberalism* and in 'The Law of Peoples', in both cases under a section headed, 'How a Social Contract Doctrine is Universal in its Reach'. He suggests proceeding stepwise through each context, beginning with the basic structure of a domestic society and then working

> forwards to principles for the claims of future generations, outward to principles for the law of peoples, and inward to principles for special social questions.... In due course, all the main principles are on hand, including those needed for the various political duties and obligations of individuals and associations.[22]

So we proceed iteratively until we have populated the social realm with principles of justice covering every salient problem of justice—every circumstance in which we may injure one another.

On this iterative approach, it seems the only limit to the number of different conceptions of justice, each potentially with its own distinct set of principles, is our capacity to subdivide the world into social contexts or, what may be the same thing, situations characterized by the circumstances of justice. Another seeming limit is the ability to design and defend a constructivist procedure for each context, as Rawls himself did when addressing justice for the basic structure of a well-ordered society, justice between generations, and international justice. It is unlikely that the original position can be modified to suit every context or even that some other constructivist alternative will always be available, in which case, we must resort to wide reflective equilibrium or some method outside of Rawls's own.

One problem, then, is the design of a suitable original position for each context. A second problem arises once we have divided the world into contexts and developed principles for them. For example, what is to occur if there is a conflict between our duties to provide distributive justice within a state and our duties to provide some form of international aid? What do we say about such potential conflicts or other issues pertaining to the relationship between the sets of contextual principles developed? Rawls offers two suggestions:

> Constructivism assumes ... that there are other forms of unity than that defined by completely general first principles forming a consistent scheme. *Unity may also be given by an appropriate sequence of cases and by supposing that the parties in an original position (as I have called it) are to proceed through the sequence with the understanding that the principles for the subject of each later agreement are to be subordinate to those of subjects of earlier agreements, or else coordinated with and adjusted to them by certain priority rules.* I shall try out a particular sequence and point out its merits as we proceed. There is in advance no guarantee that it is the most appropriate sequence and much trial and error may be needed.[23]

[22] Rawls, 'Law of Peoples', above n 12 at 532. See also Rawls, *Political Liberalism*, above n 5 at 261.
[23] Rawls, 'Law of Peoples', above n 12 at 533 (emphasis added). This is a more general statement of a view also found in Rawls, *Political Liberalism*, above n 5 at 261–62.

Rawls here proposes two ways of proceeding through different constructions of principles of justice for various contexts.

In each case we proceed from context C_1 to C_2 to C_3 and so on, carrying out an original position procedure for each, that is, OP_1, OP_2, OP_3, and so on. The first method proposed applies a rule of paramountcy ('*the principles for the subject of each later agreement are to be subordinate to those of subjects of earlier agreements*'). In case of conflict between the principles developed by OP_1 and OP_2, those of OP_1 govern. The second approach imagines that certain priority rules as between the two original positions are arrived at, allowing us to 'coordinate and adjust' the two sets of contextual principles ('*[T]he principles for the subject of each later agreement are to be … coordinated with and adjusted … by certain priority rules*' with '*those of subjects of earlier agreements*'). I take the second method, which seems to describe a form of wide reflective equilibrium between the results of such constructions, to be the broader and hence more appropriate starting point. There seems no initial reason to assign paramountcy to one or another context: in all contexts, justice is about the need to avoid unjustified injury. Any rule of paramountcy, as well as any proposed priority rule and any ordering of the sequence of original positions, would themselves have to be defended within wide reflective equilibrium.

We use wide reflective equilibrium, then, to square the results of each context's original position with one another until we have eliminated or narrowed, to the extent possible, all such conflicts. Another way of putting this is to say we consider the principles of each original position, relative to the principles of other original positions, as considered judgements to be used in testing those other principles. In some cases, it may be possible to design yet another original position to play this mediating function. At a certain point, despite the 'versatility'[24] of the method, the supply of plausible original positions dries up and we must grope toward a solution using wide reflective equilibrium.

The method I propose to use to address first-order inegalitarianism in immigration governance is the second approach from the above passage. For each new problem, we develop an appropriate original position and see which principles of justice are generated thereby. We then see if these principles can be reconciled with those of earlier original positions. We do not assume the paramountcy of either set. We do, however, seek to assign priorities among different types of claims, if appropriate, within the reconciled set of principles. We must also seek to reconcile these principles with any other considered judgements and with relevant sociological facts at our disposal. That means that in developing principles of justice for immigration governance, we heed the first-order considered judgements concerning young children and their parents, refugees, citizens who cannot naturalize elsewhere, and the permissible exclusion of criminals, and those who present public health and security risks, as well as the second-order judgements taken into account by the indirect principle. In addition, we consider

---

[24] J Rawls, *The Law of Peoples* (Cambridge, MA, Harvard University Press, 1999) 40.

as provisionally fixed the judgement that immigration can be capped in order to adequately safeguard the stability of a political conception of justice and to protect members' legitimate expectations. Finally, we must be sure that a given approach to justice in immigration governance does not conflict with any considered judgements and principles of justice regarding domestic and global justice that we may have at hand. Conflicts between any of these provisional judgements and any principle or principles derived must be resolved through mutual adjustments via reflective equilibrium.

IV. A Constructivist Approach to Immigration

A Rawlsian constructivist procedure adapted for the problem of justice in immigration governance must specify and defend model conceptions of the person, of society, and of the original position appropriate to the context of immigration governance. Relative to these, it must specify the institutions that are its subject and their role. Once these elements are in place, it must seek to develop a principle or principles for the just governance of immigration.

The aim, then, is to adapt the original position to a specific aspect of the basic structure of wealthy liberal constitutional democracies, namely immigration regimes, which would not have been dealt with in developing principles for a closed society. This adaptation necessarily requires enlarging the group of persons represented behind the veil of ignorance. It is then hoped that the principles yielded by the modified original position can provide a sufficiently impartial perspective from which the conflicts that characterize immigration can be resolved. In this way, it is hoped that any principle or principles produced might serve as the foundation for the application of the Rawlsian ideal of reciprocity in immigration governance.

Over the next two sections, I want to defend the following three claims: first, that an original position designed to select principles for justice in immigration governance would veil from the parties knowledge of whether they are migrants or members; second, that the immigration policy of a liberal country ought to have in view the maintenance of the public conception of justice[25] of a well-ordered domestic society and just relations with the world outside its borders; third, that migrants seeking admission to a constitutional democracy, while not accorded political equality with members, should nevertheless be conceived of as free and equal moral persons. I will spend most time defending the most contentious claim, regarding the way that migrants are to be conceived as free and equal. This claim is most contentious because it may seem to presuppose that the

---

[25] Note that I now use 'public conception of justice' to signal that the argument from this point proceeds in ideal theory, assuming that we are searching for principles of just immigration governance for a well-ordered society.

interests of members and non-members ought to be given equal weight. It returns us, that is, to the question of partiality addressed in Chapter Three.

The aim is to tailor the original position as narrowly as possible to the subject, namely the immigration regimes of wealthy liberal constitutional democracies. Further, the goal is to provide for an ideal principle or principles, so we begin by holding provisionally fixed the Rawlsian liberal ideal of a well-ordered society as the receiving state. Rawls defines a well-ordered society as a society in which members accept, as compatible with their sense of justice, and know that all other members accept in the same way, a reasonable political conception of justice that regulates all major social and political institutions, that is, the basic structure.[26] We further assume that this conception is liberal, constitutional, and democratic insofar as it provides a list of basic rights, assigns priority to some of these over other types of claims, and includes measures for ensuring members of the well-ordered society have adequate means to make use of their freedoms.[27] To be effectively regulated by such a conception, we assume that the members of the society are jointly juridically integrated and cooperate with one another fairly within the framework that it provides. And we assume that it is wealthy enough to be attractive to a significant number of migrants from at least one other state. A new original position is now embarked upon, in which the members of this well-ordered society are represented, along with the population of potential migrants who want to enter it. Because we are at this point exclusively concerned with first-order policies for selecting migrants for indefinite admissions, migrants in the modified original position will be non-members outside a state who wish to enter it indefinitely.

Immigration and its governance confront a well-ordered society with its place in the world. What sort of world is it appropriate to have in mind in designing the modified original position? As was noted in the Introduction, Rawls provided only brief and scattered remarks about immigration governance in *The Law of Peoples* because he considered that, once other problems of international justice had been addressed, immigration would no longer be a serious problem.[28] This seems unsatisfactory in part because the governance of immigration is a problem that faces us here and now. I will therefore proceed as though the well-ordered receiving society is situated in a non-ideal world like ours, assuming that Rawls is correct that our non-ideal world circumstances are what makes the problem of justice in immigration governance pressing. There is a risk to taking this approach. It may be that the principles developed will undermine the prospects of reaching an international or global justice ideal, for example, by undermining

---

[26] Rawls, *Justice as Fairness*, above n 5 at 8–9; Rawls, *Political Liberalism*, above n 5 at 35; Rawls, *Theory of Justice*, above n 11 at 397–405.

[27] Rawls, *Political Liberalism*, above n 5 at 156–57; see also J Rawls, 'The Idea of Public Reason Revisited' in *Collected Papers*, above n 12 at 581–82; Rawls, *Law of Peoples*, above n 24 at 14.

[28] Rawls, *Law of Peoples*, above n 24 at 9.

or further undermining the stability of sending states. We cannot know if the principle or principles developed will have such an effect unless we also have on hand the results of an international or global original position, and also, perhaps, a modified original position to deal with emigration. Such alternative original positions would address the perspectives of non-members who are not migrants. Embarking on all these different original positions, however, would be far too heroic an undertaking than is possible at this stage.

Finally, an original position aimed at the problem of immigration governance would veil the place of birth or, what is the same thing here, whether the parties represent members or non-members of the receiving well-ordered society. The leading idea behind the various ignorances in the original position is the idea of fairness.[29] What is or is not fair depends on the nature of the disagreements or potential disagreements that must be resolved. For governing principles to find acceptance, they must not reflect any one individual or group's unfair advantage in the context of that particular conflict. Thus in the case of justice in immigration governance we look first to the nature of the conflicts at issue. These do not have to do with laying claim to the shared output of social cooperation, as Rawls characterized it in the domestic setting, but to gaining access to the cooperative arrangements that produce such outputs. It follows that parties should not know whether they already have such access. This knowledge would give them an unfair bargaining advantage in the original position. It further means that parties should be deprived of knowledge of other aspects of individuals' social position that would lead them to advocate for principles of admission that favoured one group over another, either members or migrants or a subgroup of members or migrants. These are the kinds of knowledge already restricted by Rawls's original position.[30]

V. Free and Equal Migrants

I do not think the modified original position as set out so far presents much difficulty. But the requirement of conceiving of the persons represented by the parties to the modified original position as free and equal persons runs into important objections that merit discussion. The idea of equal moral personhood here is the

---

[29] Questions of fairness arise 'when free persons, who have no authority over one another, are engaging in a joint activity and among themselves settling or acknowledging the rules which define it and which determine the respective shares in its benefits and burdens. A practice will strike the parties as fair if none feels that, by participating in it, they or any of the others are taken advantage of, or forced to give in to claims which they do not regard as legitimate.': J Rawls, 'Justice as Fairness' in *Collected Papers*, above n 12 at 59.

[30] In veiling the place of birth, we make the veil of ignorance 'thicker rather than thinner', just as Rawls veiled knowledge of a represented citizens' generation or the stage of civilization of their society in seeking to develop principles for justice between generations: Rawls, *Political Liberalism*, above n 5 at 273; Rawls, *Theory of Justice*, above n 11 at 254–55.

Rawlsian conception mentioned above, namely that all persons possess the capacity to understand, to apply, and to act from principles of justice and the capacity to form, revise, and pursue a conception of the good. They are free because they see themselves as 'self-originating sources of claims' and are capable of taking responsibility for and revising their ends.[31] They are equal in that they are represented as having these powers and capacities in equal measure. One objection to conceiving of migrants as free and equal persons has to do with the possibility of divergent conceptions of moral personhood within different political, national, ethnic, or other sorts of communities. A second objection is that it is impossible to square the idea that migrants are to be thought of as moral equals with the forms of justified political inequality defended in Chapter Three.

With respect to the first objection, the specific issue confronting the immigration regimes of well-ordered societies is how to treat migrants who come from states where other conceptions of the person prevail. One likely source of divergence has to do with the revisability of an individual's conception of the good. Liberal societies, let us assume, celebrate individualism and self-creation. Non-liberal societies may have more limited conceptions of the range of options available to a person over the course of their life, with limits based on such things as gender, communal identity, or other characteristics. In this sense, potential immigrants to a well-ordered society may see themselves or others as less free. Another likely source of divergence has to do with inequality: in a non-liberal state, the claims that an individual may make against their government and other members of their non-liberal society may depend on their position within that society. In this sense, potential migrants who have come to moral maturity within such a society may not consider humankind a community of equal persons. If we attempted to model these variations in the conception of the person, however, it would be impossible to try to develop a conception of just immigration governance through a modified original position, since the original position requires equality at some level among the parties.[32]

One response to the concern about representing migrants who may not view themselves as free and equal in keeping with Rawls's conception of moral personhood is to say that this conception is simply true of all, or nearly all, humans. That is, the response is simply to deny that any but a small number of individuals might be said not to have the two moral powers. This response seems coherent and, despite Rawls's own disavowal of claims of truth, wholly adequate. To the extent that prospective migrants might hold different conceptions of their own or others' personhood, they are simply wrong.

---

[31] See the discussion of freedom in J Rawls, 'Kantian Constructivism in Moral Theory' in *Collected Papers*, above n 12 at 330–32. Rawls further discusses these ideas of freedom in J Rawls, 'Justice as Fairness: Political Not Metaphysical' in *Collected Papers*, above n 12 at 404–408.

[32] 'Only equal parties can be symmetrically situated in an original position': Rawls, *Law of Peoples*, above n 24 at 70.

To those who disagree, a further reply is as follows. It is one thing to concede that non-liberal states and their members may conceive of moral personhood differently. It is another to say the members of a well-ordered liberal society should honour those different conceptions when deciding what justice requires in immigration governance. The point is not to deny that it would be possible for other states or their members to hold different conceptions of the person. It is that a well-ordered society should not base its principles of immigration governance on foreign conceptions. Say an immigrant comes from a state where people do not admit to the power to revise their conception of the good or perhaps where they admit of the power, but hold that some beliefs and tenets are non-negotiable, so that there are limits to the revisability. Should we, in an attempt at avoiding conceptual imperialism, think of our obligations of justice toward such a migrant in a manner consistent with his or her home state's conceptions of the person, constructing a way of thinking about justice in immigration based on this home conception?

There are many reasons to think that we should not. First, it may be that the migrant does not share the same conception of the person as other members of his or her home state. One way to characterize refugee migration, for example, is as the flight of individuals who conceive of their own freedom and equality differently than their governments or fellow members, a disagreement that may be grounded in a difference in conceptions of moral personhood. Second, at the limit the suggestion would require a well-ordered society to organize its immigration regimes in accordance with as many different conceptions of justice in immigration governance as there are conceptions of the person among sending countries, which seems unworkable both in practice and from an evaluative perspective. Third, some migrants will indeed become members, at which point all liberal democrats would agree that the receiving state's government has to treat them as free and equal moral members, in every respect, just as it does birthright members. It seems absurd to conceive of the moral powers, in their innate not developed form, of migrants differently before and after immigration. Coming at the same point in a different way, the modified original position relies on a conception of the person as free and equal persons because it cannot be said that migrants are free and equal *members*. But, further, they rely on this conception because to become juridically integrated in a liberal state, migrants eventually have to come to see themselves as free and equal members. To do this, they must first see themselves as free and equal persons.

The second objection listed at the beginning of this section flows from the thought, often advanced by opponents of cosmopolitanism, that compatriots are permitted or required to show partiality toward one another, similar to the partiality commonly thought justifiably to apply among family members. The idea is roughly that we have stronger or more numerous moral responsibilities to fellow members than we do to the world at large. In light of permissible or required partiality among compatriots, the objection continues, it is not appropriate to conceive of members and migrants as free and equal moral persons. This objection is misconceived. The point of the arguments in Chapters Three and Five is that in developing immigration laws and policies we must recognize migrants as free and equal in the minimal sense of acknowledging that they cannot be subject, without appropriate justification, to damage to their purposiveness. As was argued, such recognition supports a demand that immigration regimes strive to be non-oppressive in order to be rightful. Justified political inequality is the form of partiality implicit in the conception of the well-ordered receiving society that parties to this modified original position adopt, since it is part of the necessary conditions for maintaining and fostering the stability of such a society. On its face, there does not seem to be any reason to accept that this form of partiality is inconsistent with recognizing moral equality in immigration governance.

However, in one sense, the objection is a salutary warning, and the answer to it comes too soon. The point of the entire inquiry into just immigration governance is to see if it is possible to reconcile political inequality and moral equality.

VI. A Basic Liberty

Principles of social justice specify how institutions should distribute rights and duties, benefits and harms, to eliminate oppression. The conjecture of any original position is that symmetrically-situated rational parties in a fair choice situation will adopt principles that achieve such a result. In Rawls's *A Theory of Justice*, the parties to the original position proceed by choosing among alternative principles drawn from the traditions of moral and political philosophy. It would be artificial to seek to present such alternatives where the subject is the immigration regime of a well-ordered state, since the historical tradition of moral and political philosophy has not, in general, engaged with matters of immigration, other than Kant's brief discussion of cosmopolitan right and Sidgwick's stark binary between an absolute right to close borders and an absolute right to migrate freely.[33] The strategy here will therefore be to simply imagine the parties asking a sequence of questions: first, would migration be protected as a basic liberty; if so, would that liberty have lexical priority; if not, what sort of principles govern its regulation. These questions are to be asked against the background assumption that the receiving state is a well-ordered society effectively governed according to a reasonable public conception of justice. In this section, I address the first question: whether migration would be protected as a basic liberty.

Rawls nowhere details all the basic liberties nor describes specifically how they are to work together in a single scheme.[34] He satisfies himself with a broadly-

---

[33] H Sidgwick, *The Elements of Politics* (New York, Cosimo Inc, 2005) 295.

[34] Rawls's most extensive discussion of a liberty addresses freedom of speech: Rawls, *Political Liberalism*, above n 5 at 340–56. Otherwise, he deals at greatest length with the political liberties generally, freedom of conscience, and the rule of law. Rawls, *Theory of Justice*, above n 11 at §§33, 36–37, and 38.

worded list, which other than on one occasion does not expressly include freedom of movement. That should not detain us since Rawls's various formulations of the list of basic liberties are either expressly non-exhaustive, as in *Theory*,[35] or so general as to be effectively non-exhaustive, as in *Political Liberalism*[36] or *Justice as Fairness*. In this last work, his list is as follows:

> [F]reedom of thought and liberty of conscience; political liberties (for example, the right to vote and to participate in politics) and freedom of association, as well as the rights and liberties specified by the liberty and integrity (physical and psychological) of the person; and finally, the rights and liberties covered by the rule of law.[37]

The issue at this stage in the development of our account of justice in immigration governance is whether freedom of movement can be read into such a list.

Rawls proposes an analytical method for answering the question of whether a liberty ought to be considered basic.[38] According to this method, the parties ask, 'which liberties are essential social conditions for the adequate development and full exercise of the powers of moral personality over a complete life'.[39] Recall once again that moral personality comprises two moral powers, the capacity to have a sense of justice and the capacity to form and pursue a conception of the good.[40] Conceptions of the good may comprise, among other things, the final ends of the individual; their attachments and loyalties to other individuals or groups; and their religious, philosophical, or moral view of their relation to the world.[41] These may be thought of as the set of commitments that may come to structure an individual's purposiveness. Recall also that within the modified original position migrants are considered to have these two powers.

Note also the reason for focusing on the moral powers. In Chapter Six, I argued that Smith considered moral development and independence to be mutually supporting. The argument for the indirect principle in Chapter Six focused, however, on independence or purposiveness, which was explicated through the capabilities approach. That allowed us to develop an account of the variable value of freedom of movement, which we saw was consistent with our first-order considered judgements. But while the capabilities approach includes certain of what we might

---

[35] Rawls, *Theory of Justice*, above n 11 at 53

[36] Rawls, *Political Liberalism*, above n 5 at 291.

[37] Rawls, *Justice as Fairness*, above n 5 at 44.

[38] He also proposes a historical method, whereby we look to historical examples by surveying the list of liberties that have been 'normally protected' in democratic constitutions that 'have worked well': Rawls, *Political Liberalism*, above n 5 at 292–93; Rawls, *Justice as Fairness*, above n 5 at 45. In this way, the parties to the original position can be presented with candidate liberties to consider.

[39] Rawls, *Political Liberalism*, above n 5 at 293.

[40] ibid at 332–33. Rawls's exposition of this idea runs via the idea that there are two 'fundamental cases', corresponding to the two powers: 'The first of these cases is connected with the capacity for a sense of justice and concerns the application of the principles of justice to the basic structure of society and its social practices.... The second fundamental case is connected with the capacity for a conception of the good and concerns the application of the principles of deliberative reason in guiding our conduct over a complete life.' (ibid at 332.) Use of this terminology seems to me unnecessary to an argument already overladen with Rawlsian jargon.

[41] ibid at 310.

consider to be the traditional liberal basic liberties in its list, it does not explain why we would single out those liberties for special protection or provide a basis, so far as I can tell, for giving a special place to certain kinds of capabilities over others and, perhaps more importantly, over other kinds of interests.[42] This seems to be a problem when asking about when and how freedom of movement, which has wide-ranging instrumental value, deserves protection as a right. What we need is a way to structure our reasoning about this freedom by allowing us to discriminate among its potential instrumentalities. A focus on moral development, conceptualized in terms of the two moral powers, allows us to do so. It is these powers that are most centrally concerned with what it means to be a person living in a moral world.

On Rawls's account, to show that the parties to the modified original position would select a given liberty for protection, it must be shown that the candidate liberty would be significant to the development and exercise of either moral power. Alternatively, it must be shown that the liberty indirectly supports other basic liberties more directly implicated with the two powers. Rawls's only mention of freedom of movement as a basic liberty takes up this alternative possibility. He says freedom of movement is a basic liberty because it plays a role 'supporting' other basic liberties:

> The equal political liberties and freedom of thought are to secure the free and informed application of the principles of justice, by means of the full and effective exercise of citizens' sense of justice, to the basic structure of society.... Liberty of conscience and freedom of association are to secure the full and informed and effective application of citizens' powers of deliberative reason to their forming, revising, and rationally pursuing a conception of the good over a complete life. The remaining (and supporting) basic liberties—*the liberty and integrity of the person (violated, for example, by slavery and serfdom, and by the denial of freedom of movement and occupation)* and the rights and liberties covered by the rule of law—can be connected to the two fundamental cases by noting that they are necessary if the preceding basic liberties are to be properly guaranteed.[43]

This implies that the 'central range of application'[44] of freedom of movement is simply the range necessary to support the exercise of the other basic liberties. But this is not the only mention that Rawls makes of freedom of movement within his theory. He more often mentions this freedom not as a basic liberty but as an aspect of fair equality of opportunity, under which those who have the same level of talent and ability are to have the same chance of success at achieving social positions or public offices regardless of class of origin.[45] Finally, although this is not said, the protection of freedom of movement seems to belong to the 'general

---

[42] See A Sen, *The Idea of Justice* (Cambridge, MA, Belknap Press, 2009) 299: 'There is no claim here that the capability perspective can take over the work that other parts of Rawlsian theory demand, particularly the special status of liberty and the demands of procedural fairness.'

[43] Rawls, *Political Liberalism*, above n 5 at 334–35 (emphasis added).

[44] Rawls, *Justice as Fairness*, above n 5 at 111.

[45] ibid 58; Rawls, *Political Liberalism*, above n 5 at 181.

presumption against imposing legal and other restrictions on conduct without a sufficient reason'.[46] This principle does not provide for anything like a right but, importantly, it includes a requirement of justification contrary to the absolutist ethos.

Rawls is not being inconsistent. These three different forms of protection for freedom of movement reflect its complex relationship to the moral powers.

First note that some basic range of freedom of movement seems an inescapable aspect of physical and psychological integrity. In this respect it seems necessary for its own sake and not insofar as it supports other liberties. To see this, all you need to do is imagine the initial horror of, say, waking up paralyzed or the torture of solitary confinement. In the last-quoted passage above, Rawls seems to suggest that the integrity of the person plays only an instrumental role in relation to the other liberties, a position which seems to overlook a core of intrinsic value. Having said this, the range of freedom of movement whose guarantee is needed to protect this core is likely not very extensive. It almost certainly does not require freedom of migration.[47]

But freedom of movement also plays an ongoing role in the general development of our moral powers, other than through the exercise of the other basic liberties. This is a Smithian point about the quotidian disciplining effect of sympathetic intercourse with those we encounter, corresponding to what Rawls calls the highest-order interest that we all have in securing social conditions under which the development of our moral powers, and in particular our 'original allegiance and continued devotion' to our ends, take place under conditions that are free.[48] There is a real sense in which a series of exercises of freedom of movement, trivial in themselves, may significantly foster our moral maturity by providing ever more opportunities for sympathetic intercourse with others.

Here we get a sense of the range of the connection between freedom of movement and the development of our two moral powers. Minimally, some core range of freedom of movement must be protected for its own sake. Maximally, greater freedom of movement will lead to more and more opportunities for moral maturity, suggesting both why there is a general presumption against restrictions to this freedom and what sorts of reasons would be needed to justify restriction.

Why would we not seek to protect freedom of movement *as a basic liberty* maximally instead of merely to the extent necessary to protect the other basic liberties, as Rawls suggests? Past a certain point, having maximal freedom of movement would interfere with the liberties of others. In particular, it would interfere with the right to own real property and the exercise of other basic rights, such as rights to the practice of one's religion or the right of freedom of association.

---

[46] Rawls, *Justice as Fairness*, above n 5 at 44; Rawls, *Political Liberalism*, above n 5 at 292.

[47] Here I partly agree with David Miller: D Miller, 'Immigration: The Case for Limits' in AI Cohen and CH Wellman (eds), *Contemporary Debates in Applied Ethics* (Oxford, Blackwell, 2005) 194–95.

[48] J Rawls, 'Fairness to Goodness' in *Collected Papers*, above n 12 at 283.

In general, the other liberties require some degree of control of the environment in which their exercise takes place, including the right to prevent or limit others from entering certain spaces: to bar employers from union halls, tourists from churches, or strangers from the home. Indeed, the need to restrict the movement of others becomes clearer when we move down a notch to the more modest and obvious fact that individuals need some degree of control of their material environment to pursue reasonable life projects. Such control implies limitations on others' freedom of movement. It seems any attempt to protect freedom of movement maximally would make it impossible to develop an adequate scheme for resolving conflicts among the basic liberties. It would also interfere unacceptably with each person's ability to pursue their own conception of the good. On the other hand, since the other basic liberties are themselves protected based on their significance to the two moral powers, it is a reasonable surmise that by protecting freedom of movement so far as necessary to support the other basic liberties, these powers will receive adequate protection.

There is nothing in this argument to distinguish migration from freedom of movement generally. As a result, it follows that the parties to the modified original position would choose to protect freedom of migration as a basic liberty for the same reason that it would be protected within a well-ordered society, namely to instrumentally protect the exercise of other basic liberties that are crucial to the exercise and development of the two moral powers. Neither is there anything in the argument denying that, within a well-ordered society, there may be additional reasons for guaranteeing freedom of movement. These reasons may include rational ends like the promotion of solidarity or economic growth. Freedom of movement may play a crucial role in supporting certain range-limited principles, including the equal exercise of political liberties among the members of a state and protection of equality of opportunity among members.[49] More generally, within a well-ordered society there is a general reason to provide all members with the same amount of freedom, to aim at an ideal, that is, of equal freedom for all.[50] But, and this is the last point of this section, we also see that both within the well-ordered society and in the modified original position, a way of structuring our thinking about freedom of movement has emerged. Restrictions on freedom of migration, as with all freedom of movement, are protected by the general presumption against restriction without sufficient reason. Notwithstanding the perhaps additional reasons for protecting freedom of movement within a well-ordered society, the reasons for restricting immigration must in the first instance address the importance of movement to the two moral powers to count as sufficient.

---

[49] For discussion of some of these other reasons, see A Hosein, 'Immigration and Freedom of Movement' (2013) 6 *Ethics & Global Politics* 25.

[50] See P Pettit, *On the People's Terms: A Republican Theory and Model of Democracy* (New York, Cambridge University Press, 2012) 92ff.

VII. A Non-lexical Liberty

It follows from (1) the fact that freedom of movement would be protected as a basic liberty in the modified original position, and from (2) the inclusion of both migrants and members in the modified original position, that (3) freedom of movement across borders, or freedom of migration, would also be protected as a basic liberty. Such protection would extend to exercises of liberty necessary to support the exercise of the other liberties. This conclusion is both less radical and more important than it may seem. It is less radical because it does not follow that freedom of migration has absolute priority over range-limited principles guaranteeing distributive justice in the receiving society or the legitimate expectations that members have built up under those principles; such absolute priority would be required to support anything resembling an open borders view. It is important, however, because it provides us with a way to prioritize the selection of migrants for admission by being duly attentive to the potential importance of migration to a migrant's moral powers. These points will be made over the next two sections, beginning with the refutation of lexical priority here.

Rawls claims that, within his domestic conception of justice as fairness, the basic liberties would have lexical priority over claims of distributive justice. If freedom of migration is 'basic' in the same way as in Rawls's theory, migrants might enjoy a freedom to move across borders that also could not be subordinated to distributive justice in the receiving state.[51] On the other hand, Rawls holds that a basic liberty can be restricted for the sake of another basic liberty, in the name of creating an adequate scheme of liberties. Extending this to the modified original position, it seems that the scheme of basic liberties in the well-ordered society and members' legitimate expectations in their basic liberties, including the political liberties, might be protected notwithstanding the basic liberty of migration, or at least that the freedom of migration should be included in an adequate scheme that includes the domestic basic liberties. The resulting picture would be that immigration could be restricted only for the sake of the basic liberties inside the well-ordered society, while allowing that the principles and institutions of distributive justice would be subject to disruption.

I do not think this principle of lexical priority for freedom of migration would be adopted. Such a conclusion is confirmed, as I will now explain, by examining the three arguments presented by Rawls for the lexical priority of liberty, none of which carry over to the basic liberty of freedom of migration.

Rawls's first argument for the lexical priority of the basic liberties is that the parties to the original position would affirm such priority to assure an equal distribution of the social bases of self-respect, which he counts as the most important

---

[51] Rawls, *Theory of Justice*, above n 11 at 214; Rawls, *Political Liberalism*, above n 5 at 334ff.

of human goods.[52] I have explained in Chapter Three the way in which members' self-respect is at stake within their own state's conception of justice. That conception plays a role in the constitution of their sense of justice, and the sense of justice determines their sense of their own standing to make claims against other members and against society's major social institutions in general. Because our self-respect is jointly implicated in this way, it may be injured when members are treated unequally, such as by being relegated to unequal status or by not being provided with certain benefits in equal measure without a sufficient reason for departing from a baseline of equality.

Rawls argues that in a well-ordered society governed by justice as fairness, self-respect is assured not by one's relative position in terms of, say, wealth but in part by granting the same rights under a scheme of equal liberties. This way of apportioning self-respect allows everyone to have 'equal and secure status when they meet to conduct the common affairs of the wider society', that is, using his later idea, when they engage in public reason.[53] The lexical priority of the basic liberties is guaranteed, therefore, because equality of those liberties takes the place of economic and social status as a guarantor of members' self-respect. The members of a state are not allowed to trade off liberty for greater wealth, because that would lead to an unequal distribution of the social bases of self-respect in the important realm of public reason.

Migrants' self-respect is not at stake in the same way. Migrants may undergo a process of juridical integration, as I developed that idea in Chapter Three, through which their sense of justice will come to substantively fit and orient itself toward a well-ordered society's public conception of justice. Once juridical integration has occurred, the migrant will have committed himself or herself to continue to cooperate with other members no matter what their joint decisions about justice turn out to be, so long as these are not unreasonably unjust. Prior to juridical integration, however, no such commitment has been made. Exactly how the transition from non-commitment to commitment is to be negotiated is a subtle question, dealt with in practice by the structuring of immigration regimes as status regimes. Until such commitment occurs, however, migrants' self-respect will not depend in the same way as members' on their treatment within that conception. This is why a migrant would not have a claim to, for example, redistribution under strong egalitarian terms. Migrants' self-respect will be tied instead, at the outset, to their enjoyment of rights according to the political conception of justice in their home state. This claim holds, I should note, even for refugees. Refugees may in effect be migrants who can no longer remain juridically integrated in their home state

---

[52] Rawls, *Political Liberalism*, above n 5 at 318–20; Rawls, *Theory of Justice*, above n 11 at §82. Helpful exposition of this argument, as it was originally made, is found in H Shue, 'Liberty and Self-Respect' (1975) 85 *Ethics* 195.

[53] Rawls, *Theory of Justice*, above n 11 at 477. Self-respect is also guaranteed by the fair value of the political liberties and the difference principle: Rawls, *Political Liberalism*, above n 5 at 319.

without accepting their own domination. That may make their claim for entry an urgent one. Nonetheless, the fact remains that they are not juridically integrated with their receiving state, suggesting that something less than lexical priority for freedom of migration is called for even in their case.

Rawls's second argument for lexical priority is that the parties would be unwilling to gamble away the conception of the good of those they represent, whatever it may turn out to be, or their ability to deepen or revise their commitment to that conception under conditions of freedom.[54] Carens's claim—that 'one would insist that the right to migrate be included in the system of basic liberties for the same reasons that one would insist that the right to religious freedom be included: it might prove essential to one's plan of life'[55]—is a version of this argument. In addition to not knowing if they represent migrants or members, the parties to the original position would not know the specific content of their constituents' conceptions of the good, what actions might need to be taken to act on or pursue any such conceptions, nor what circumstances might lead them to wish to alter their conceptions. They would know, however, that freedom of movement will be required to form or pursue all final ends, attachments, or religious, philosophical, and moral commitments to a greater or lesser extent. Therefore they would seek to protect the freedom to migrate lexically.

David Miller's argument, discussed in the previous chapter, that people only have a right to an adequate range of options responds to this kind of claim. According to Miller:

> What a person can legitimately demand access to is an adequate range of options to choose between—a reasonable choice of occupation, religion, cultural activities, marriage partners, and so on…. So although people certainly have an interest in being able to migrate internationally, they do not have a basic interest of the kind that would be required to ground a human right. It is more like my interest in having an Aston Martin than my interest in having access to *some* means of physical mobility.[56]

Miller's argument, however, would not be accepted in a modified original position. From behind the veil of ignorance, parties seek to protect themselves against the worst contingencies. Accordingly, they would not take the chance that they might come from a state where, for instance, practice of a certain religion was outlawed because that could be the very religion of the person they represent. The argument once again points, though, to the variability of the value of migration, and of freedom of movement more broadly. This variability poses a difficulty for the claim of lexical priority made by Carens. Thus note that Miller's argument seems far more plausible with respect to 'choice of occupation' than it does with respect to 'religion' or 'marriage partners' because we think, in general, that being able to choose any religion or any marriage partner is crucial to whether we see

---

[54] See Rawls, *Political Liberalism*, above n 5 at 310ff; Rawls, *Theory of Justice*, above n 11 at §33.
[55] Carens, 'Aliens and Citizens', above n 3 at 258.
[56] Miller, 'The Case for Limits', above n 47 at 196.

our lives as good. These latter intuitions are, in fact, reflected in the widespread recognition of a right to immigrate to join one's spouse[57] or the breadth of protection offered against religious persecution in the 1951 Convention Relating to the Status of Refugees, which does not suggest that the right to practice religion is restricted to only a reasonable range of options.[58] For some migrants, then, it may be that migration is essential for exercises of purposiveness that are centrally related to their moral powers. Those cases, though, can probably be accommodated without granting lexical priority to freedom of migration for all. Freedom of migration is not, in this respect, like freedom of conscience, of vital importance to any sort of human life. It will be vitally important to some migrants but not others. Parties to the original position would be satisfied if they could guarantee movement for those cases for which migration is crucial.

The last argument offered by Rawls for the priority of the basic liberties is one that operates in a very different way. Rawls argues that the priority of liberty helps secure for persons represented in the original position the value of a 'social union of social unions' in which a person's conception of the good, whatever it is, may be 'enlarged and sustained'.[59] The underlying idea behind this argument is that a well-ordered society governed by just institutions 'is the preeminent form of human flourishing'[60] because it allows each members' purposiveness to be exercised cooperatively with others. Such cooperation may take place in the first instance within smaller social unions, such as families, friendships, and those associations of persons who join together to play games or to pursue business, knowledge, understanding, or artistic achievement. The well-ordered society, however, provides a social union of all these smaller social unions, within which

---

[57] *Immigration and Refugee Protection Regulations*, SOR/2002-227, s 117(1)(a).

[58] See UNHCR, 'Guidelines on International Protection No. 6: Religion-Based Refugee Claims under Article 1A(2) of the 1951 Convention and/or the 1967 Protocol relating to the Status of Refugees' (Geneva 2004).

[59] Rawls, *Political Liberalism*, above n 5 at 323; the complete argument is presented in *Political Liberalism* at 320–24. Note that an exegetical puzzle arises here. In 'Reply to Habermas' (in *Political Liberalism*, above n 5 at 372), Rawls says that in *Political Liberalism* he set out to 'rebuild' the argument for the stability of justice as fairness in the third part of *A Theory of Justice*. That argument, he says, had been based 'on the conception of a social union of social unions and its companion idea of stability, which depends on the congruence of the right and the good' (ibid 388, fn 21). This may suggest that Rawls in *Political Liberalism* no longer wishes to rely on the idea of a social union of social unions to support his account of stability (as is pointed out by Paul Weithman: P Weithman, *Why Political Liberalism? On John Rawls's Political Turn* (New York, Oxford University Press, 2010) 293–96). Why, then, would Rawls continue to rely on this idea in his argument for the priority of the basic liberties? In *Political Liberalism* at 207, fn 39, Rawls says of the argument for the lexical priority of the basic liberties based on the ideal of a social union of social unions: 'I am not entirely satisfied with that argument but I think it not without some force.' Weithman contends that Rawls, in his last writings, sought to replace the ideal of a social union of social unions with a similar but weaker ideal of democratic governance, under which members value the successful carrying out of just institutions but not the common aim of cooperating together to realize their own and others' nature: Weithman, *Why Political Liberalism?* at 296. Perhaps, if Weithman is right, Rawls thought this weaker ideal was still sufficient to ground the kind of argument for the priority of liberty that he made relying on the ideal of a social union of social unions.

[60] Rawls, *Theory of Justice*, above n 11 at 463.

all members can count the flourishing of one another as also in some sense their own.[61] Since each of us has manifold possible lives but can only live one, in this way we may achieve 'the same totality of capacities latent in each' of us in just union with others.[62] It is not an exaggeration to say that the social union of social unions, for Rawls, represents the highest possible realization of the two moral powers: 'Only in a social union is the individual complete.'[63] Rawls claims that the priority of the equal basic liberties, together with the second principle, best secure, the attitude of mutual regard and the appreciation of reciprocity necessary to realize this immensely valuable shared good.

In assessing the place of this argument in the consideration of justice in immigration governance, we should remember once again that we are assuming an ideal, well-ordered society within a non-ideal world. The assumption for our purposes is that the receiving society provides for this preeminent form of human flourishing to a degree not realized among sending states. While global economic inequalities occupy much of the literature, from the perspective of the well-ordered society we should be concerned primarily with the unequal realization of this form of human flourishing. This takes us back to an idea presented for the first time in Chapter One but raised again at various stages of this essay. The justification of immigration governance is part of the overall justification of the various, often very considerable, inequalities between members and non-members of states. Following Scanlon's three-level strategy for justifying inequality, any justification of the advantages that accrue to the members of a state based on the fact of membership alone cannot be wholly self-supporting. Further justification is required at a second-level by showing that there is no unfairness in the way that one may become a member. This second-level justification must in turn be supported by a third-level of justification that shows that the fair process at the second-level is not undermined by unfair access to qualifying characteristics allowing some but not others to succeed.

Justice in immigration governance is part of the second level of justification for global inequality. Membership in a state is determined primarily by birthright, which is justified by the assumption that if one is born in or to members of a state, one's sense of justice will mature within it, one will become juridically integrated with it, and one will develop legitimate expectations based on its political conception of justice. However, the vast majority of humans are possessed of the two moral powers, and so I have assumed here that the vast majority of humans would be able to become juridically integrated as members into a well-ordered society. In light of this potential for juridical integration, from the perspective of the ideal well-ordered society, the problem of justice in immigration governance is the problem of justifying who should be given the opportunity to integrate into the social union of social unions alongside those members who have been born

---

[61] ibid at 462.
[62] Rawls, *Political Liberalism*, above n 5 at 321.
[63] Rawls, *Theory of Justice*, above n 11 at 460, fn 4.

to and come to moral maturity within the society, thus becoming free and equal members entitled to share in such a great good with their new fellow members. The third level of justification would require an account of international or global justice, to ensure that the conditions supporting potential juridical integration are fairly distributed worldwide. But this problem, as I have noted several times, is bracketed here.

It should be clear from seeing the problem of justice in immigration governance this way that the argument made by Rawls for the lexical priority of the basic liberties based on the idea of a social union of social unions cannot also support lexical priority for freedom of migration. Rawls's argument based on the social union of social unions supports lexical priority within a well-ordered society because it helps secure, for all members, the conditions under which this great good may be achieved. The parties would not extend lexical priority to freedom of migration, however, because prior to juridical integration, migrants are simply not among the members who can partake in the social union.

The conclusion from this long discussion that freedom of migration would not be given lexical protection is confirmed when one stands back from Rawls's three arguments and focuses simply on the need to ensure and foster the stability of a well-ordered society. The well-orderedness of a society does not depend on its basic liberties alone but also on its distributive principles. The disruption of legitimate expectations based on those principles would be perceived as an injustice and would tend toward instability. Indeed, at the limit lexical priority for freedom of migration suggests that any principles of distributive justice adopted within a well-ordered society would in effect be adopted only contingently, based on the hope that they would not be undermined by immigration. Such contingency is at odds with the important role principles of distributive justice would play in guaranteeing adequate means to make use of one's freedoms within a well-ordered society. Distributive principles avert large inequalities of wealth, income, and other goods, as well as of the capabilities needed to make use of those goods. If such large inequalities arose, our ability to act on and develop our moral powers would also become, eventually, unequal past the point consistent with well-orderedness. Thus a principle of lexical priority for freedom of migration would be inconsistent with the reason that would motivate migration: to gain access to a well-ordered society where the basic liberties could be exercised adequately in a way consistent with one's self-respect. It follows that since lexical priority would not be given to this freedom within the modified original position, an open borders principle would not be accepted by the parties.

VIII. Prioritizing the Worst off

From the perspective of Rawlsian ideal theory, the question of justice in the indefinite admissions policies of a well-ordered society is the question of the just distribution of the opportunity to become juridically integrated into a social union of social unions. By becoming so integrated, the migrant would enlarge his or her capacity to develop and exercise his or her two moral powers. Such enlargement would be most important for those migrants deprived of one or more basic liberties in his or her state of origin. For such migrants, then, we would say migration is protected as a basic liberty, because migration instrumentally supports the exercise of one or more other basic liberties. Migration, like all movement, also has general value supporting the development and exercise of the moral powers. Moreover, the two moral powers have priority, in the assessment of human interests related to purposiveness, over the other capabilities, since they are more centrally concerned with what it means to be human. In the provision of reasons to justify immigration restrictions, immigration regimes must give priority to considerations relating to the moral powers over considerations relating to the capabilities generally.

It seems then that we should prioritize for indefinite admission those migrants who enjoy fewest basic liberties in their state of origin. For greater specificity, we might say that we should prioritize for admission those migrants who are deprived of more liberties of greater importance to the moral powers. It is these migrants whose moral powers are most compromised: who live in a condition of greatest remove from their potential human flourishing. Of course, the question of which liberties are more important than others is a difficult one, and I will not go into it other than to say that however a ranking of the relative importance of the liberties is arrived at, it should be amenable to reasonable justification to reasonable migrants conceived of as free and equal persons. With such a ranking in place, the well-ordered society should admit first those migrants deprived of a greater number of more significant liberties, then those migrants deprived of fewer and less important basic liberties, and so on. If the supply of migrants facing deprivations of their basic liberties does not exhaust the number that can be admitted below the cap set in accordance with the imperative of stability and the need to respect members' legitimate expectations, remaining migrants should be prioritized for admission based on the potential importance of migration to their two moral powers.

This all seems unhappily vague. However, we can say more. In Rawls's domestic conception of justice, the priority of the equal basic liberties is not defended in isolation, but in tandem with principles of socio-economic distribution. These are, first, the principle of fair equality of opportunity, which ensures that all members have a fair chance to attain public offices and social positions; second, the difference principle, which requires that social and economic inequalities be to the greatest benefit of the least-advantaged members of society; and third, the provision of a social minimum that meets the essential needs of its members and, further, that prevents the most disadvantaged from either becoming resentful to the point of violent action or withdrawn and distant from political society. These principles are important because of a distinction Rawls makes between liberty and its worth: '[L]iberty is represented by the complete system of the liberties of equal citizenship, while the worth of liberty to persons and groups depends upon their capacity to advance their ends within the framework the system defines.'[64] The first principle of justice as fairness guarantees the equal liberties as such, not their equal worth. Rawls acknowledges that those with greater wealth, power, or authority will be able to make more of their liberties, that is, take advantage of them to greater effect in the development and exercise of the two moral powers.[65] We might add, in amendment, that the worth of a liberty to us depends more generally on our entire capability set.

Here Rawls seems to allow inequalities of wealth and power to determine the fullness with which individuals can develop their moral personhood. It is hard at first to see how this kind of inequality is consonant with the ideal of reciprocity central to his theory. As Norman Daniels has noted, there is a real sense in which if I lack the means to act on or enjoy the benefits of a given liberty, than I do not enjoy that liberty.[66] Rawls answers this objection by requiring that the equal worth of the political liberties, such as the right to vote and run for office, be guaranteed for all.[67] He rejects, however, a broad guarantee of the equal worth of the other basic liberties. Such a guarantee, he claims, would be irrational if it sought to guarantee equal wealth and income to all; superfluous, given the difference principle and the social minimum, if it aimed to insure a certain base level of income and wealth; and potentially divisive if it sought to guarantee equal worth of the basic liberties measured against each individual's conception of his or her own good, since some members would then have a right to far more wealth than others.[68] For these other liberties, differences of value are addressed only through the difference principle and the social minimum: 'Taking the two principles together, the basic structure is to be arranged to maximize the worth to the least advantaged of the complete scheme of equal liberty shared by all.'[69]

Now, it is an open question whether socio-economic principles or some principle of equal political liberty ought to apply within a conception of international or global justice. I have not sought to answer that question and have assumed an ideal society in a non-ideal world. That is, we are considering the problem of justice in immigration governance for a well-ordered society in a world of states falling somewhere along the spectrum between well-orderedness and collapse, in which either there are no obligations of global distributive justice or in which there are such obligations, but they are largely unmet. There is no global provision of a social minimum, no adherence to a global difference principle, no fair global equality of opportunity, and no global protection of equal political liberty. In such a world, our world, there seems to be no basis for not taking into account the

---

[64] ibid at 179.
[65] ibid.
[66] N Daniels, 'Equal Liberty and the Unequal Worth of Liberty' in N Daniels (ed), *Reading Rawls: Critical Studies on Rawls's 'A Theory of Justice'* (Oxford, Blackwell, 1975).
[67] Rawls, *Justice as Fairness*, above n 5 at 149.
[68] ibid at 151.
[69] Rawls, *Theory of Justice*, above n 11 at 179.

value of freedom of movement in regulating immigration. Otherwise Daniels's objection could not be met in this context.

The selection of migrants for indefinite admission, then, must be guided not only by the number and importance of deprivations of the basic liberties faced in their home state, but also by the worth of their remaining liberties to them assessed by looking at their capabilities set. Finally, once more, if a well-ordered state can admit more migrants once it has already admitted all those facing deprivations of one or more basic liberties, it should do so on the basis of a judgement of the potential importance of migration to their two moral powers in light of their overall capability set. Under this conception, priority of admission would be granted first to the migrants falling under one of two categories—those deprived of all liberties and those deprived of a minimal, sufficient level of capabilities. For all other migrants, difficult judgements must be made.

IX. Principles for the Just Governance of Immigration

A well-ordered society, then, would prioritize the indefinite admission of the worst-off migrants, where 'worst-off' connotes a judgement that takes into account the deprivation of their liberty and their level of capabilities in their state of origin. Selection on this basis would take place beneath a cap set in accordance with the need to maintain and foster the stability of the well-ordered society's public conception of justice and to respect its members' legitimate expectations. Any resulting policy would also have to avoid second-order oppression, in accordance with the indirect principle. Finally, within the limits set by these principles, states are permitted to govern immigration through the creation of a regime of status, including temporary statuses, provided also, again in keeping with the indirect principle, that these do not result in oppression. However, should a migrant become juridically integrated within a state, a matter that is neither wholly in the migrant's control nor the state's, then naturalization is required. If an immigration regime strives to comply with these principles, then it can be said that immigration regimes are not unreasonably unjust. Such a regime would have authority with respect to migrants.

Do these principles help make sense of our considered judgements? I think that they do. In the last chapter, I argued that the capabilities approach is consistent with our first-order judgements that it is presumptively unjust to exclude refugees, citizens who cannot naturalize elsewhere, and young children or their parents. These considered judgements were confirmed because they all involved cases where denying migration would result in a diminishment of all or nearly all the capabilities. The account in this chapter seems also to suggest that such migrants have a basic liberty to be admitted. The uniting consideration is that, for such migrants, the exercise of the moral powers is comprehensively compromised by the form of deprivation faced should they be excluded, in addition to the general, pervasive diminishment of their capability set. For instance, to qualify as a refugee, one must face a well-founded fear of persecution. But persecution con-notes not just any risk of a violation of human rights. A qualifier is always added. The denial of human rights must be 'serious',[70] 'sustained or systemic',[71] or 'so oppressive or likely to be repeated or maintained that the person threatened can-not be expected to tolerate it'.[72] What do these qualifiers seek to capture? On the account provided here, they seek to capture the sense that the violation of human rights faced by a refugee claimant is such that either the violation itself, or the fear of it, would comprehensively undermine their ability to exercise their two moral powers within their state of origin. Hence the basic liberty of migration is protected for refugees. The same could be said of a returning citizen who cannot naturalize in another state or a young child separated from his or her parents. In both cases, the basic liberty of migration is protected in that it is instrumentally necessary to a core aspect of freedom of association.[73] However well off such migrants might be in terms of income and wealth, depriving them, in the one case, of any state into which they might be juridically integrated without oppression or, in the other, of the good of being raised by the adults that one would normally expect to be best motivated to raise them in a loving and caring manner, would comprehensively undermine the development or exercise of their moral powers and their ability to act on any other basic liberties they might have. Putting together the argument from the moral powers here and the capabilities-based account from Chapter Six, we may say that these first-order judgements are supported by considerations of both the Smithian values of independence and moral capacity.

Therefore there is a convergence with our first-order judgements. There is also, it should be noted, a convergence between the account of prioritization and the indirect principle. That principle, I suggested in Chapter Six, will push the immigration laws and policies of wealthy liberal constitutional democracies toward less inegalitarian policies because, according to the countersocial premise, immigration policies that are responsive to migration pressures will give rise to less second-order oppression. The seeming convergence of these two principles should give us some measure of confidence in both. In this same regard, these principles also seem to allay a concern about global distributive justice raised in Chapter Six, namely that a prioritarian principle that tends toward the admis-sion of the worst off is unlikely to aggravate global inequality by encouraging the emigration of more advantaged migrants. This result has been reached, however, not by subsuming the problem of justice in immigration governance within the problem of global distributive justice. Rather, it has been reached by taking seri-ously the value of migration.

---

[70] UNHCR, Handbook on Procedures and Criteria for Determining Refugee Status under the 1951 Convention and the 1967 Protocol relating to the Status of Refugees (Geneva 1979, re-edited 1992) para 51.
[71] JC Hathaway, *The Law of Refugee Status* (Toronto, Butterworths, 1991) 108.
[72] *MIMA v Ibrahim* [2000] HCA 55 at para 65 (per McHugh J, dissenting).
[73] Here I agree in part with M Lister, 'Immigration, Association, and the Family' (2010) 29 *Law and Philosophy* 717, 723.

This convergence, and the prioritarian principle in particular, seems to provide a means of evaluating inegalitarianism in immigration law and policy. Laws and policies that favour the indefinite admission of the advantaged and exclude or impose greater restrictions on the less advantaged on their face seem to offend the prioritarian principle. Note, however, that this conclusion cannot be stated with confidence. It will always be open to argue on behalf of a regime that by design it admits more of the advantaged so that it can admit more of the disadvantaged. The admission of a group that is thought likely to juridically integrate successfully, and without compromising the stability of the receiving state's political conception of justice, might supply the political and other capital needed to support the admission of more of the less advantaged. If a regime began from the least advantaged and worked its way up, the number of migrants admitted might in the end be quite small. Whether actual inegalitarian policies can be justified in these terms is not something I have examined. The progress that has been made in this essay, then, has not led to the condemnation or endorsement of inegalitarianism. It has instead illuminated the kinds of reasons that must be offered in its defence and in establishing, against absolutism, the duty to offer such a defence.

Note finally how this account leads us to revise the considered judgement that states should have broad control over immigration. This considered judgement, on the principled account, reflects the imperative of ensuring and fostering the stability of receiving state's political conception of justice. States control immigration because the balance of reasons, absent alternative candidates, seems to favour such control by them. However, on the principled account their discretion is not an unfettered form of licence. Rather, what states have is a right to exercise their own judgement, from a suitably impartial perspective, about how to maintain their own political conception of justice, as well as the legitimate expectations that members might have in goods protected or fostered by this political conception, in light of the claims to admission made by migrants. If the political conception of a state is threatened with instability and collapse, then, at the limit, a state would have the right to restrict all immigration. (Of course, such a society is unlikely to be a destination of choice.) Absolutist discretion over immigration governance has been replaced by a structured judgement, and many of the kinds of reasons that would have to be given to justify such a drastic policy, or any policy, on an impartial basis have been brought out. Importantly, these reasons are ones that both reasonable migrants and reasonable members of the receiving state can accept. Reasonable migrants will be able to accept them because such judgements, suitably made, are duly attentive to their most important interests. The excluded migrant will know others were admitted before him or her because they had a more urgent need. The admitted migrant will not have to worry that his or her immigration was unfair to other migrants or that it will be perceived as illegitimate by members. Finally, reasonable members will accept such a policy because they will know that the stability and, one hopes, the progress of their state toward a well-ordered ideal is being sustained and supported by relations between themselves and the world outside that are marked by reciprocity.

Conclusion

I HAVE SOUGHT in this essay to demonstrate the implausibility of absolutism, the label I use for a view that denies the constraining power of justice over immigration governance. The argument has taken the form, first, of a denial that social justice is a special relationship; second, a denial that immigration regimes can have authority without striving to be just; and third, the denial that justice makes no demands in immigration governance. In place of absolutism, I have taken steps toward a principled alternative consistent with the ideal of reciprocity, under which we attempt to realize a form of immigration governance based on a symmetrical reasonableness between the members of and migrants to a state. With this ideal of reciprocity as guide, I have proposed the following principles for just immigration governance:

(1) Immigration laws and policies of liberal constitutional democracies must admit migrants up to a threshold determined by two considerations: (a) first, the point where the stability of a state's political conception of justice would be undermined, such that stability is conceived as the tendency of the major social institutions of a state to remain within or progress toward a reasonable political conception of justice; (b) second, the need to respect the legitimate expectations of its members. Other authors have claimed other bases for capping immigration. I have argued, however, that these other considerations all reduce to the need to preserve the stability of the political conception of justice and the need to respect members' legitimate expectations.

(2) Under the cap set in accordance with this first principle, immigration laws and policies of liberal constitutional democracies must give priority of indefinite, or permanent, admission to the worst off, where 'worst off' is determined according to some function of the number of restrictions to a migrant's basic liberties in his or her state of origin, the importance of those liberties, and the capabilities that the migrant has to take advantage of those basic liberties he or she enjoys. These first two principles appear generally to support our judgements that, all else equal, states should admit refugees, young children or their parents who would otherwise be separated, and non-member citizens who cannot naturalize elsewhere. These categories of migrants enjoy a basic liberty to migrate. All such migrants face what might be thought of as a comprehensive threat to their basic liberties, and their numbers are likely small enough that their admission would not compromise either the stability of a receiving liberal constitutional democracy or the legitimate expectations of its members. Beyond these categories, however, difficult judgements must be made based on the prioritarian principle.

Further, (3) any cap and principles of selection must avoid second-order oppression of migrants; this is the indirect principle. The indirect principle may seem underwhelming, but it is an important corrective to actual practice as well as a guide to permissible first-order policy with respect to the vast majority of economic and family migrants. It also has considerable critical potential. First, it may be successfully argued that the list of considered judgements of second-order oppression that I have worked with should be expanded. Second, what I have called the countersocial premise suggests that the indirect principle may give migrants something like a form of standing. The requirement of avoiding second-order oppression, that is, will nudge states toward policies that will more closely correspond to the desired purposes of migrants.

(4) Within these limits, states may govern immigration through the imposition of differential status, where the rights and duties attached to any status may aim (so long as this can be done without oppression) at either juridical integration, for those migrants admitted indefinitely, or not, for those migrants admitted on a temporary basis. Once migrants are juridically integrated into a receiving constitutional liberal democracy, the various forms of required partiality toward members must be extended to them. Therefore, upon juridical integration, migrants must be granted membership, which in practice likely means allowing them to naturalize to the status of formal citizenship. Here, states have no discretion.

Beyond the general concern to refute absolutism, a more immediate motivation in seeking these principles has been to develop, if possible, tools useful for the critique of the inegalitarian laws and policies pursued by the immigration regimes of wealthy constitutional liberal democracies. Inegalitarianism was found troubling because it seems to lead to a disturbing correlation between disadvantage and vulnerability to injury during the process of migration. However, whatever principles were developed would also have to recognize the challenge faced by states when confronting immigration. At the limit, this can be a challenge to the very achievement of being a state whose major social institutions successfully embody a political conception of justice. The principles proposed seem to hold the promise of adequately addressing the dual concern with the vulnerability of migrants on the one hand and the stability of states on the other. If these principles were applied perspicuously by immigration regimes, I believe that members of states would be reconciled to the consequent loss of some sovereign control over immigration, so jealously guarded since the end of the nineteenth century. Similarly migrants would accept the need to restrict immigration in order to ensure the stability of the state and to reasonably protect its members' legitimate expectations. Applied by immigration regimes assiduously and in good faith, the hope is that these principles would minimize the vulnerability of migrants to oppression and the risk to the destabilization of states. If this can be done, migration can, without anxiety, become part of the ongoing project of building up and reproducing stable and just states.

Having said all that, I do not wish to claim more than my arguments can establish. The above principles propose considerations that must feature in the justification of immigration laws and policies. They do not—far from it—address all the questions a fully worked out theory of justice in immigration governance would need to address, not to mention the fine-grained questions that immigration policymakers and lawyers must answer. Nor can I say, and I doubt anyone can, whether these principles would lead to more open or more restrictive immigration policies in any particular state. The humility that is advisable for immigration lawyers and policymakers should equally be adopted by those seeking to explore the political morality of this form of governance.

Such humility is needed in particular because the arguments do not fully explore three key conceptual building blocks: the ideas of stability, legitimate expectations, and juridical integration. First, it will not be obvious at what point immigration might endanger the stability of the political conception of justice of a well-ordered receiving society. There is of course a great deal of empirical work on the effects of immigration. More philosophical work, however, needs to be done on the question of stability. By 'stable', I have not meant that the basic structure embodying the political conception of justice should not change, which seems undesirable. Nor have I meant that the political conception of justice of a state will itself not change over time. Rather, stability must mean that as the institutions and rules associated with major social institutions change over time, they will do so through a process of reasonable evolution. Thus I take it that a stable political conception of justice is not one that is faithful to a single conception of justice, but to a family of reasonable conceptions that may transform over time, the succeeding conceptions connected to one another perhaps like one of Ronald Dworkin's chain novels[1] or perhaps like the threads in Derek Parfit's account of personal identity.[2] For this progression to be stable, each new set of principles of a political conception of justice must seem reasonable from the perspective of those juridically integrated into it. Perhaps also, it must be that any such evolution must be toward an ideal public conception of justice whose stability will be of a more enduring kind. Whatever the eventual picture, this idea of stability implies that the account here is concerned not with whether immigration brings change or not, but with the *pace* of change.[3] The important nuance that stable does not mean stagnant adds considerable complexity to the question of when immigration can be capped.

Second, the idea of legitimate expectations, which I claimed is central to the question of when an exclusion can be justified, is little discussed in the academic philosophical literature. As Henry Sidgwick remarked, the reconciliation between legitimate expectations, which are likely grounded in some non-ideal conception of justice, and tendencies to seek reform toward some ideal 'is the chief problem of political Justice'.[4] Immigration governance, my argument suggests, returns us

---

[1] R Dworkin, *Law's Empire* (Cambridge, MA, Belknap Press, 1986) 228.

[2] D Parfit, *Reasons and Persons* (Oxford, Clarendon Press, 1984).

[3] S Fine, 'The Ethics of Immigration: Self-Determination and the Right to Exclude' (2013) 8 *Philosophy Compass* 254, 261.

[4] H Sidgwick, *The Methods of Ethics*, 7th edn (Indianapolis, Hackett Publishing Co, 1981) 273.

to this chief problem. More work needs to be done to identify where an expectation should be considered legitimate. Further, work needs to be done on the strength of different kinds of expectations when held up as a claim against fellow members or migrants. When there is a conflict between legitimate expectations and a contrary well-founded claim that threatens to frustrate those expectations, it is more plausible to aim for some form of accommodation between the two. How such accommodation is to be reached is unclear. Such questions are hard, perhaps even frightening, because they force us to confront the way our moral relationships with one another may change over time. It is unnerving to think that the moral world in which one lives may not be there in twenty or thirty years.

Finally, the idea of juridical integration has been central to the preceding argument. Juridical integration is the process whereby a person's sense of justice comes to fit and to be oriented toward the political conception of a state. The juridical relationship among the members of a state, I have argued, is all important. Indeed, the connection between juridical integration and self-respect is the basis for two of the most important claims made, namely, that migrants who become juridically integrated must be allowed some form of membership and that the freedom of migration does not enjoy absolute priority over other social interests. But although everyone has a capacity for a sense of justice, and although I have said that all could in principle become juridically integrated, this assumption ought to be the subject of further inquiry. A person's sense of justice, it would be reasonable to presume, may have finite elasticity. Moreover, the conditions that would harden a person's sense of justice into a form incompatible with the prospect of juridical integration within a wealthy liberal constitutional democracy may be most likely to exist in the kinds of outlaw and burdened states from which disadvantaged migrants would be most likely to come. A full account of juridical integration would have to confront this possibility and its implications for the application of the prioritarian principle, the indirect principle, and more specifically for our judgements about which migrants it is permissible to exclude. Here is where an account of global or international justice seems most likely to connect to the problem of justice in immigration governance. One of the projects of global or international justice might be to ensure that all persons are able within a reasonable period of time, and with minimum psychological trauma, to juridically integrate into all states, and to eliminate the conditions nullifying this possibility. It may be in this sense that Rawls was correct to conclude that in a realistic global utopia, immigration would be 'eliminated as a serious problem'.[5] The problem would not be eliminated by the unrealistic assumption that people would no longer wish to move from state to state in such a world. It would be eliminated because most migrants would indeed have the capacity for juridical integration into most states.

---

[5] J Rawls, *The Law of Peoples, with 'The Idea of Public Reason Revisited'* (Cambridge, MA, Harvard University Press, 1999) 9.

These conceptual gaps suggest that the refutation of absolutism is not complete. Absolutism, I believe, is an attitude toward the governance of immigration that is motivated in some cases by fear and uncertainty, in other cases by scepticism and pessimism. It can only be fully answered by providing a thorough framework for the justification of immigration laws and policies. The conceptual gaps just discussed correspond to empirical gaps in our knowledge. In particular, we do not know, for example, how robust the political conceptions of our non-ideal states are. Any account of stability must be complemented by an account of instability. And it is not obvious that we should be concerned with only instability for the right reasons. If immigration would destabilize a society's political conception of justice because of intolerance and ignorance, that seems as much of an evil as destabilization created by more reasonable attitudes. The potential for instability is compounded by the fact that there are many more ways to be unjust than just.

If our political conceptions of justice are fragile, as they might be, then maybe highly restrictive policies will be necessary. At that point, the considered judgements, that the injurious exclusion of refugees, young children or their parents, or non-member citizens who cannot naturalize elsewhere are presumptively unjust, might give way. Indeed, even some of what may seem reflexively to be second-order injustices might be justified. That, it seems to me, would be a dire result, one that can only be associated with the worst times. How can we avoid it? The answer has been implicit in much of the foregoing: The attitude of reasonableness and impartiality, of openness to the concerns and views of others, and a willingness to make decisions based on proper forms of inductive logic and reasoning. It is just possible that Adam Smith is right. If we diligently, perhaps even reverentially, strive for such an attitude, it may be that the voice of the impartial spectator will not deceive us.[6] Adopting such an attitude need not be naive. It may be less naive than an absolutist pessimism that gives up on reasonableness at the border.

---

[6] A Smith, K Haakonssen (ed), *The Theory of Moral Sentiments* (Cambridge, Cambridge University Press, 2002) 267 [VI.ii.1.22].

BIBLIOGRAPHY

Abizadeh, A, 'Democratic Theory and Border Coercion: No Right to Unilaterally Control Your Own Borders' (2008) 36 *Political Theory* 37

—— 'Liberal and Egalitarian Arguments for Closed Borders: Some Preliminary Critical Reflections' (2006) 4 *Ethique/cs & Economique/cs* 1

—— and Gilabert, P, 'Is There a Genuine Tension between Cosmopolitan Egalitarianism and Special Responsibilities?' (2008) 138 *Philosophical Studies* 348

Ackerman, BA, *Social Justice and the Liberal State* (New Haven, Yale University Press, 1980)

Aleinikoff, TA, 'Aliens, Due Process, and "Community Ties": A Response to Martin' (1983) 44 *University of Pittsburgh Law Review* 237

Anderson, E, 'What is the Point of Equality?' (1999) 109 *Ethics* 287

Anderson, MJ, 'A License to Abuse: The Impact of Conditional Status on Female Immigrants' (1983) 102 *Yale Law Journal* 1401

Applbaum, AI, 'Legitimacy without the Duty to Obey' (2010) 38 *Philosophy & Public Affairs* 215

—— 'Democratic Legitimacy and Official Discretion' (1992) 21 *Philosophy & Public Affairs* 240

Arendt, H, *On Revolution* (New York, Penguin Books, 1963)

Bader, V, 'The Ethics of Immigration' (2005) 12 *Constellations* 331

—— *Citizenship and Exclusion* (New York, St Martin's Press, 1997)

—— 'Fairly Open Borders' in Bader, V (ed), *Citizenship and Exclusion* (New York, St Martin's Press, 1997)

Barry, B, 'John Rawls and the Search for Stability' (1995) 105 *Ethics* 874

—— 'Intimations of Justice' (1984) 84 *Columbia Law Review* 806

—— and Goodin, RE (eds), *Free Movement: Ethical Issues in the Transnational Migration of People and of Money* (University Park, Pennsylvania State University Press, 1992)

Beitz, C, *Political Theory and International Relations* (Princeton, Princeton University Press, 1979)

Bell, D, *Beyond Liberal Democracy: Political Thinking for an East Asian Context* (Princeton, Princeton University Press, 2009)

Benhabib, S, *The Rights of Others: Aliens, Residents, and Citizens* (Cambridge, Cambridge University Press, 2004)

Berry, CJ, 'Adam Smith and the Virtues of Commerce' in Chapman, JW and Galston, WA (eds), *Nomos XXXIV: Virtue* (New York, New York University Press, 1992) 69

Bhabha, J, 'The "Mere Fortuity of Birth"? Children, Mothers, Borders, and the Meaning of Citizenship' in Benhabib, S and Resnik, J (eds), *Migrations and Mobilities: Citizenship, Borders, and Gender* (New York, New York University Press, 2009) 187

Blake, M, 'Immigration, Jurisdiction, and Exclusion' (2013) 41 *Philosophy & Public Affairs* 103

—— 'Immigration, Association, and Antidiscrimination' (2012) 122 *Ethics* 748

—— 'Immigration and Political Equality' (2008) 45 *San Diego Law Review* 963

—— 'Immigration' in Wellman, CH and Frey, RG (eds), *The Blackwell Companion to Applied Ethics* (Oxford, Blackwell, 2003) 224–37

—— 'Discretionary Immigration' (2002) 30 *Philosophical Topics* 273

Brighouse, H and Swift, A, 'Legitimate Parental Partiality' (2009) 37 *Philosophy & Public Affairs* 43

Brock, G, *Global Justice: A Cosmopolitan Account* (New York, Oxford University Press, 2009)

Brown, PG and Shue, H (eds), *Boundaries: National Autonomy and Its Limits* (Totowa, Rowman & Littlefield, 1981)

Camayd-Freixas, E, 'Interpreting the Largest ICE Raid in US History: A Personal Account' *The New York Times* (13 June 2008)

Carens, J, *The Ethics of Immigration* (New York, Oxford University Press, 2013)

—— 'Who Should Get In? The Ethics of Immigration Admissions' (2003) 17 *Ethics & International Affairs* 95

—— 'Realistic and Idealistic Approaches to the Ethics of Migration' (1996) 30 *International Migration Review* 156

—— 'Immigration and the Welfare State' in Gutmann, A (ed), *Democracy and the Welfare State* (Princeton, Princeton University Press, 1988) 207–30

—— 'Aliens and Citizens: The Case for Open Borders' (1987) 49 *The Review of Politics* 251

Carter, DM, *States of Grace: Senegalese in Italy and the New European Immigration* (Minneapolis, University of Minnesota Press, 1997)

Castles, S, 'The Factors that Make and Unmake Migration Policies' (2004) 38 *International Migration Review* 852

—— and Miller, MJ, *The Age of Migration: International Population Movements in the Modern World*, 4th edn (New York, Guilford Press, 2009)

Cavallero, E, 'An Immigration-Pressure Model of Global Distributive Justice' (2006) 5 *Politics, Philosophy & Economics* 97

Chang, HF, 'The Economics of International Labor Migration and the Case for Global Distributive Justice in Liberal Political Theory' (2008) 41 *Cornell International Law Journal* 1

Christiano, T, 'Authority' in Zalta, EN (ed), *The Stanford Encyclopedia of Philosophy* (Spring 2013 edn)

—— 'The Authority of Democracy' (2004) 13 *Journal of Political Philosophy* 266

Cohen, GA, 'Where the Action Is: On the Site of Distributive Justice' (1997) 26 *Philosophy & Public Affairs* 3

Cole, D, *Enemy Aliens: Double Standards and Constitutional Freedoms in the War on Terrorism* (New York, New Press, 2003)

—— 'In Aid of Removal: Due Process Limits on Immigration Detention' (2002) 51 *Emory Law Journal* 1003

Cole, P, *Philosophies of Exclusion: Liberal Political Theory and Immigration* (Edinburgh, Edinburgh University Press, 2000)

Cole, RP, and Chin, GJ, 'Emerging from the Margins of Historical Consciousness: Chinese Immigrants and the History of American Law' (1999) 17 *Law and History Review* 325

Collier, P, *Exodus: How Migration Is Changing Our World* (New York, Oxford University Press, 2013)

Commander, S, Kangasniemi, M and Winters, LA, 'The Brain Drain: Curse or Boon?', *IZA Discussion Paper No. 809* (June 2003)

Cornelius, WA, and Rosenblum, MR, 'Immigration and Politics' (2005) 99 *Annual Review of Political Science* 99

Cox, AB and Posner, EA, 'The Second-Order Structure of Immigration Law' (2007) 59 *Stanford Law Review* 809

—— and Rodríguez, CM, 'The President and Immigration Law' (2010) 119 *Yale Law Journal* 458

Daniels, N, *Justice and Justification: Reflective Equilibrium in Theory and Practice* (Cambridge, Cambridge University Press, 1996)

—— 'Equal Liberty and the Unequal Worth of Liberty' in Daniels, N (ed), *Reading Rawls: Critical Studies on Rawls's 'A Theory of Justice'* (Oxford, Blackwell, 1975) 253–81

Darwall, S, 'Authority and Second-Personal Reasons for Acting' in *Morality, Authority, & Law: Essays in Second-Personal Ethics I* (Oxford, Oxford University Press, 2013)

—— *The Second-Person Standpoint: Morality, Respect, and Accountability* (Cambridge, MA, Harvard University Press, 2006)

—— 'Equal Dignity in Adam Smith' (2004) 1 *Adam Smith Review* 129

—— 'Sympathetic Liberalism: Recent Work on Adam Smith' (1999) 28 *Philosophy & Public Affairs* 139

De Genova, NP, 'Migrant "Illegality" and Deportability in Everyday Life' (2002) 31 *Annual Review of Anthropology* 419

Dent, JA, 'No Right of Appeal: Bill C-11, Criminality, and the Human Rights of Permanent Residents Facing Deportation' (2002) 27 *Queen's Law Journal* 749

Dummett, M, *On Immigration and Refugees* (New York, Routledge, 2001)

Dunn, J, *The History of Political Theory and Other Essays* (Cambridge, Cambridge University Press, 1996)

Dworkin, R, *Law's Empire* (Cambridge, MA, Belknap Press, 1986)

Fine, S, 'The Ethics of Immigration: Self-Determination and the Right to Exclude' (2013) 8 *Philosophy Compass* 254

—— 'Freedom of Association is Not the Answer' (2010) 120 *Ethics* 338

Finnis, J, *Natural Law and Natural Rights* (Oxford, Clarendon Press, 1980)

Flatham, R, *Political Obligation* (New York, Atheneum, 1972)

Fleischacker, S, *A Short History of Distributive Justice* (Cambridge, MA, Harvard University Press, 2005)

—— *On Adam Smith's Wealth of Nations: A Philosophical Companion* (Princeton, Princeton University Press, 2004)

—— *A Third Concept of Liberty: Judgment and Freedom in Kant and Adam Smith* (Princeton, Princeton University Press, 1999)

Flikschuh, K, 'Reason, Right, and Revolution: Kant and Locke' (2008) 36 *Philosophy & Public Affairs* 375

'Forced Labor' (7 September 2010) *The New York Times* (Opinion)

Freeman, S, *Justice and the Social Contract: Essays on Rawlsian Political Philosophy* (New York, Oxford University Press, 2007)

—— *Rawls* (London, Routledge, 2007)

Galloway, D, *Immigration Law* (Concord, Irwin Law, 1997)

Gardner, J, 'The Virtue of Justice and the Character of Law' (2000) 53 *Current Legal Problems* 1

Gaus, G, *The Order of Public Reason* (New York, Cambridge University Press, 2011)

Gibney, MJ, *The Ethics and Politics of Asylum: Liberal Democracy and the Politics of Asylum* (New York, Cambridge University Press, 2004)

Goodin, R, 'If People Were Money ...' in Barry, B and Goodin, RE (eds), *Free Movement: Ethical Issues in the Transnational Migration of People and of Money* (University Park, Pennsylvania State University Press, 1992)

Goodwin-Gill, GS and McAdam, J, *The Refugee in International Law*, 3rd edn (New York, Oxford University Press, 2007)

—— *International Law and the Movement of Persons between States* (Oxford, Clarendon Press, 1978)

Haakonssen, K, *The Science of a Legislator: The Natural Jurisprudence of David Hume and Adam Smith* (New York, Cambridge University Press, 1981)

Hahamovitch, C, 'Creating Perfect Immigrants: Guestworkers of the World in Historical Perspective' (2003) 44 *Labor History* 69

Hardimon, MO, 'Role Obligations' (1994) 91 *The Journal of Philosophy* 333

Hart, HLA, *The Concept of Law*, 2nd edn (Oxford, Clarendon Press, 1994)

—— 'Legal Rights' in *Essays on Bentham: Studies in Jurisprudence and Political Theory* (Oxford, Clarendon Press, 1982)

—— 'Are There Any Natural Rights?' (1955) 64 *Philosophical Review* 175

Hathaway, JC, *The Rights of Refugees under International Law* (Cambridge, Cambridge University Press, 2005)

—— *The Law of Refugee Status* (Toronto, Butterworths, 1991)

—— 'The Evolution of Refugee Status in International Law: 1920–1950' (1984) 33 *International & Comparative Law Quarterly* 348

—— and Neve, RA, 'Fundamental Justice and the Deflection of Refugees from Canada' (1996) 34 *Osgoode Hall Law Journal* 103

Heeren, G, 'Pulling Teeth: The State of Mandatory Immigration Detention' (2010) 45 *Harvard Civil Rights-Civil Liberties Law Review* 601

Helton, AC, 'Asylum and Refugee Protection in Thailand' (1989) 1 *International Journal of Refugee Law* 20

Heyman, MG, 'Judicial Review of Discretionary Decisionmaking' (1994) 31 *San Diego Law Review* 861

Higgins, R, 'The Right in International Law of an Individual to Enter, Stay in and Leave a Country' (1973) 49 *International Affairs* 341

Higham, J, *Strangers in the Land: Patterns of American Nativism* (New York, Atheneum, 1981)

Hobbes, T, Ruck, R (ed), *Leviathan* (Cambridge, Cambridge University Press, 1996)

Hohfeld, WN, 'Some Fundamental Legal Conceptions as Applied in Judicial Reasoning' (1913) 23 *Yale Law Journal* 16

Horton, J, *Political Obligation* (Houndmills, Basingstoke, Hampshire, Macmillan, 1992)

Hosein, A, 'Immigration and Freedom of Movement' (2013) 6 *Ethics & Global Politics* 25

Hume, D, Warner, SD and Livingston, DW (eds), *Political Writings* (Indianapolis, Hackett Publishing Co, 1994)

Joppke, C, 'Why Liberal States Accept Unwanted Immigration' (1998) 50 *World Politics* 266

Julius, AJ, 'Nagel's Atlas' (2006) 34 *Philosophy & Public Affairs* 176

—— 'Basic Structure and the Value of Equality' (2003) 31 *Philosophy & Public Affairs* 321

Kanstroom, D, 'The Better Part of Valor: The REAL ID Act, Discretion, and the "Rule" of Immigration Law' (2006/7) 51 *New York Law School Law Review* 161

—— 'Deportation, Social Control, and Punishment: Some Thoughts on Why Hard Laws Make Bad Cases' (2000) 113 *Harvard Law Review* 1890

—— 'Surrounding the Hole in the Doughnut: Discretion and Deference in US Immigration Law' (1997) 71 *Tulane Law Review* 703

Kant, I, Gregor, MJ (trans and ed), *The Metaphysics of Morals* (Cambridge, Cambridge University Press, 1996)

—— Reiss, H (ed), *Political Writings* (Cambridge, Cambridge University Press, 1970)

Kersting, W, 'Politics, Freedom, and Order: Kant's Political Philosophy' in Guyer, P (ed), *The Cambridge Companion to Kant* (New York, Cambridge University Press, 1992) 342

Klein-Solomon, M, 'GATS Mode 4 and the Mobility of Labour' in Cholewinski, R, Perruchoud, R, and MacDonald, E (eds), *International Migration Law: Developing Paradigms and Key Challenges* (The Hague, TMC Asser Press, 2007)

Klosko, G, *The Principle of Fairness and Political Obligation*, 2nd edn (Lanham, MD, Rowman & Littlefield, 2004)

Kraut, R, *Socrates and the State* (Princeton, Princeton University Press, 1984)

Kukathas, C, 'The Case for Open Immigration' in Cohen, AI and Wellman, CH (eds), *Contemporary Debates in Applied Ethics* (Oxford, Blackwell, 2005) 207–20

—— 'Immigration' in LaFollette, H (ed), *The Oxford Handbook of Practical Ethics* (New York, Oxford University Press, 2003) 567

—— 'Territorial Boundaries: A Liberal Egalitarian Perspective' in Miller, D and Hashmi, SH (eds), *Boundaries and Justice* (Princeton, Princeton University Press, 2001) 259

Kymlicka, W, *Multicultural Citizenship: A Liberal Theory of Minority Rights* (New York, Oxford University Press, 1995)

Lister, M, 'Who Are Refugees?' (2013) 62 *Law and Philosophy* 345

—— 'Immigration, Association, and the Family' (2010) 29 *Law and Philosophy* 717

Locke, J and Laslett, P (ed), *Two Treatises of Government* (Cambridge, Cambridge University Press, 1960)

Lomasky, LE, 'Liberalism Beyond Borders' (2004) 24 *Social Philosophy and Policy* 206

McAdam, J, *Complementary Protection in International Refugee Law* (Oxford, Oxford University Press, 2007)

Macedo, S, 'The Moral Dilemma of US Immigration Policy: Open Borders Versus Social Justice?' in Swain, C (ed), *Debating Immigration* (Cambridge, Cambridge University Press, 2007)

MacIntyre, A, *After Virtue, A Study in Moral Theory*, 2nd edn (Notre Dame, University of Notre Dame Press, 1984)

Macklin, A, 'Freeing Migration from the State: Michael Trebilcock on Migration Policy' (2010) 60 *University of Toronto Law Journal* 315

Martin, DA, 'Introduction: The New Asylum Seekers' in Martin, DA (ed), *The New Asylum Seekers: Refugee Law in the 1980s* (Dordrecht, Martinus Nijhoff, 1988)

Martin, PL and Teitelbaum, MS, 'The Mirage of Mexican Guest Workers' (2001) 80 *Foreign Affairs* 117

Martinez, S, *Peripheral Migrants: Haitians and Dominican Republic Sugar Plantations* (Knoxville, University of Tennessee Press, 1995)

Massey, DS et al, *Worlds in Motion: Understanding International Migration at the End of the Millennium* (New York, Oxford University Press, 1998)

Meilaender, PC, *Toward A Theory of Immigration* (New York, Palgrave, 2001)

Meissner, D and Kerwin, D, *DHS and Immigration: Taking Stock and Correcting Course* (Washington, Migration Policy Institute, February 2009)

Menz, G, *The Political Economy of Managed Migration: Nonstate Actors, Europeanization, and the Politics of Designing Migration Policies* (New York, Oxford University Press, 2009)

Mill, JS, *Utilitarianism* (New York, Oxford University Press, 1998)

Miller, D, 'Justice and Boundaries' in Miller, D, *Justice for Earthlings: Essays in Political Philosophy* (New York, Cambridge University Press, 2013) 142–64

—— 'Two Ways to Think about Justice' in Miller, D, *Justice for Earthlings: Essays in Political Philosophy* (New York, Cambridge University Press, 2013) 40–69

—— 'Why Immigration Controls Are Not Coercive: A Reply to Arash Abizadeh' (2010) 38 *Political Theory* 111

—— 'Democracy's Domain' (2009) 37 *Philosophy & Public Affairs* 201

—— 'Immigration, Nations, and Citizenship' (2008) 16 *Journal of Political Philosophy* 371

—— 'Introduction' in Walzer, M, *Thinking Politically: Essays in Political Theory* (New Haven, Yale University Press, 2007) vii–xxi

—— 'Immigration: The Case for Limits' in Cohen, AI and Wellman, CH (eds), *Contemporary Debates in Applied Ethics* (Oxford, Blackwell, 2005) 193–206

—— 'The Ethical Significance of Nationality' (1998) 98 *Ethics* 647

—— *On Nationality* (Oxford, Clarendon Press, 1995)

Motomura, H, 'Immigration Law after a Century of Plenary Power: Phantom Constitutional Norms and Statutory Interpretation' (1990) 100 *Yale Law Journal* 545

Mouffe, C, 'Carl Schmitt and the Paradox of Liberal Democracy' in *The Democratic Paradox* (New York, Verso, 2005)

—— *The Democratic Paradox* (New York, Verso, 2000)

Murphy, JG, *Kant: The Philosophy of Right* (London, Macmillan, 1970)

Murphy, L, *Moral Demands in Nonideal Theory* (New York, Oxford University Press, 2000)

—— 'Institutions and the Demands of Justice' (1998) 27 *Philosophy & Public Affairs* 251

—— 'The Demands of Beneficence' (1993) 22 *Philosophy & Public Affairs* 267

Nagel, T, 'The Problem of Global Justice' (2005) 33 *Philosophy & Public Affairs* 113

—— 'Personal Rights and Public Space' in Nagel, T, *Concealment and Exposure & Other Essays* (New York, Oxford University Press, 2002) 31–52

—— *Equality and Partiality* (New York, Oxford University Press, 1991)

—— *The View From Nowhere* (New York, Oxford University Press, 1986)

—— *Mortal Questions* (Cambridge, Cambridge University Press, 1979)

Neuman, G, 'Discretionary Deportation' (2006) 20 *Georgetown Immigration Law Journal* 611

Ngai, M, *Impossible Subjects: Illegal Aliens and the Making of Modern America* (Princeton, Princeton University Press, 2005)

Nozick, R, *Anarchy, State, and Utopia* (New York, Basic Books, 1974)

Nussbaum, M, *Frontiers of Justice: Disability, Nationality, Species Membership* (Cambridge, MA, Belknap Press, 2006)

—— *Women and Human Development: The Capabilities Approach* (New York, Cambridge University Press, 2000)

—— and Sen, A (eds), *The Quality of Life* (Oxford, Clarendon Press, 1993)

Okin, SM, *Justice, Gender, and the Family* (New York, Basic Books, 1989)

O'Neill, M, 'What Should Egalitarians Believe?' (2008) 36 *Philosophy & Public Affairs* 119

Parfit, D, *Reasons and Persons* (Oxford, Clarendon Press, 1984)

Pettit, P, *On the People's Terms: A Republican Theory and Model of Democracy* (New York, Cambridge University Press, 2012)

—— 'Law and Liberty' in Besson, S and Martí, JL (eds), *Legal Republicanism: National and International Perspectives* (New York, Oxford University Press, 2009) 39–59

—— 'Capability and Freedom: A Defence of Sen' (2001) 17 *Economics & Philosophy* 1

Pevnick, R, *Immigration and the Constraints of Justice: Between Open Borders and Absolute Sovereignty* (Cambridge, Cambridge University Press, 2011)

—— 'Social Trust and the Ethics of Immigration Policy' (2009) 17 *Journal of Political Philosophy* 146

Plato, Jowett, B (trans), *Five Great Dialogues* (New York, Walter J Black, 1942)

Plender, R, *International Migration Law*, 2nd edn (Leiden, Sijthoff, 1988)

Pogge, T, 'Migration and Poverty' in Bader, V (ed), *Citizenship and Exclusion* (New York, St Martin's Press, 1997)

—— *Realizing Rawls* (Ithaca, Cornell University Press, 1989)

Rawls, J, *Lectures on the History of Political Philosophy* (Cambridge, MA, Belknap Press, 2007)

—— *A Theory of Justice*, revised edn (Cambridge, MA, Belknap Press, 1999)

—— *The Law of Peoples, with 'The Idea of Public Reason Revisited'* (Cambridge, MA, Harvard University Press, 1999)

—— *Political Liberalism*, expanded edn (New York, Columbia University Press, 1996)

Rawls, J, Freeman, S (ed), *Collected Papers* (Cambridge, MA, Harvard University Press, 1999)

Rawls, J, Kelly, E (ed), *Justice as Fairness: A Restatement* (Cambridge, MA, Belknap Press, 2001)

Raz, J, *The Authority of Law: Essays on Law and Morality*, 2nd edn (New York, Oxford University Press, 2009)

—— *Practical Reasons and Norms* (Oxford, Oxford University Press, 2002)

—— *Ethics in the Public Domain: Essays in the Morality of Law and Politics* (Oxford, Clarendon Press, 1994)

—— *The Morality of Freedom* (Oxford, Clarendon Press, 1986)

Reichert, JS, 'A Town Divided: Economic Stratification and Social Relations in a Mexican Migrant Community' (1982) 29 *Social Problems* 411

Ripstein, A, *Force and Freedom: Kant's Legal and Political Philosophy* (Cambridge, MA, Harvard University Press, 2009)

Risse, M, *On Global Justice* (Princeton, Princeton University Press, 2012)

—— 'On the Morality of Immigration' (2008) 22 *Ethics & International Affairs* 25

Rodríguez, CM, 'Guest Workers and Integration: Toward A Theory of What Immigrants and Americans Owe One Another' (2007) *University of Chicago Legal Forum* 219

Rothschild, E, *Economic Sentiments: Adam Smith, Condorcet, and the Enlightenment* (Cambridge, MA, Harvard University Press, 2001)

Ruhs, M and Chang, H-J, 'The Ethics of Labor Immigration Policy' (2004) 58 *International Organization* 69

Salyer, L, *Laws Harsh as Tigers: Chinese Immigrants and the Shaping of Modern Immigration Law* (Chapel Hill, University of North Carolina Press, 1995)

Sangiovanni, A, 'Global Justice, Reciprocity, and the State' (2007) 35 *Philosophy & Public Affairs* 3

Sassen, S, *Guests and Aliens* (New York, New Press, 1999)

—— *Globalization and Its Discontents: Essays on the New Mobility of People and Money* (New York, New Press, 1998)

Scanlon, TM, 'Equality of Opportunity', 3rd lecture in *When Does Equality Matter? Uehiro Lectures in Practical Ethics* (December 2013)

—— 'Contractualism and Utilitarianism' in Scanlon, TM, *The Difficulty of Tolerance: Essays in Political Philosophy* (Cambridge, Cambridge University Press, 2003) 124–50

—— 'Due Process' in Scanlon, TM, *The Difficulty of Tolerance: Essays in Political Philosophy* (Cambridge, Cambridge University Press, 2003) 44

—— 'Rawls on Justification' in Freeman, S (ed), *The Cambridge Companion to Rawls* (New York, Cambridge University Press, 2003) 139–67

—— 'The Diversity of Objections to Inequality' in Scanlon, TM, *The Difficulty of Tolerance: Essays in Political Philosophy* (Cambridge, Cambridge University Press, 2003) 202–18

Schapiro, T, 'What is a Child?' (1999) 109 *Ethics* 715

Scheffler, S, 'Immigration and the Significance of Culture' (2007) 35 *Philosophy & Public Affairs* 93

—— 'The Conflict Between Justice and Responsibility' in Scheffler, S, *Boundaries and Allegiances: Problems of Justice and Responsibility in Liberal Thought* (New York, Oxford University Press, 2001) 82–96

Scheuerman, WE, *Carl Schmitt: The End of Law* (Lanham, MD, Rowman & Littlefield, 1999)

Schmitt, C, 'Der Begriff des Politischen' (1927) 58 *Archiv für Sozialwissenschaft* 4 in Scheuerman, WE, *Carl Schmitt: The End of Law* (Lanham, MD, Rowman & Littlefield, 1999

—— Kennedy, E (trans), *The Crisis of Parliamentary Democracy* (Cambridge, MA, MIT Press, 1985)

—— Schwab, G (trans), *Political Theology: Four Chapters on the Concept of Sovereignty* (Cambridge, MA, MIT Press, 1985)

—— Schwab, G (trans), *The Concept of the Political*, expanded edn (Chicago, University of Chicago Press, 1976)

Schotel, B, *On the Right of Exclusion: Law, Ethics and Immigration Policy* (Abingdon, Routledge, 2012)

Schuck, PH, 'The Transformation of Immigration Law' in *Citizens, Strangers, and In-Betweens* (Boulder, Westview Press, 1998)

Seglow, J, 'The Ethics of Immigration' (2005) 3 *Political Studies* 317

Sen, A, *The Idea of Justice* (Cambridge, MA, Belknap Press, 2009)

Schwartz, WF (ed), *Justice in Immigration* (New York, Cambridge University Press, 1995)

Semple, K, 'For Some Immigrants, Voting Is a Criminal Act' (15 October 2010) *The New York Times*

Shapiro, I, 'On Non-Domination' (2012) 62 *University of Toronto Law Journal* 293

Shattuck, CE, 'The True Meaning of the Term "Liberty" in Those Clauses in the Federal and State Constitutions Which Protect "Life, Liberty, and Property"' (1891) 4 *Harvard Law Review* 365

Sheppard, C, 'Women as Wives: Immigration Law and Domestic Violence' (2000) 26 *Queen's Law Journal* 1

Shue, H, *Basic Rights*, 2nd edn (Princeton, Princeton University Press, 1996)

—— 'Liberty and Self-Respect' (1975) 85 *Ethics* 195

Sidgwick, H, *The Elements of Politics* (New York, Cosimo Inc, 2005)

—— *The Methods of Ethics*, 7th edn (Indianapolis, Hackett Publishing Co, 1981)

Simmons, AJ, 'Ideal and Nonideal Theory' (2010) 38 *Philosophy & Public Affairs* 5–37

—— 'Natural Duties and the Duty to Obey the Law' in Simmons, AJ and Wellman, CH, *Is There a Duty to Obey the Law?* (New York, Cambridge University Press, 2005) 121–88

—— 'Justification and Legitimacy' in Simmons, AJ, *Justification and Legitimacy: Essays on Rights and Obligations* (New York, Cambridge University Press, 2001) 122–57

—— 'The Principle of Fair Play' in Simmons, AJ, *Justification and Legitimacy: Essays on Rights and Obligations* (New York, Cambridge University Press, 2001) 1–26

—— *Moral Principles and Political Obligations* (Princeton, Princeton University Press, 1979)

Simmonds, NE, 'Rights at the Cutting Edge' in Kramer, MH, Simmonds, NE and Steiner, H, *A Debate Over Rights* (New York, Oxford University Press, 1998)

Smith, A, *The Wealth of Nations: Books I–III* (New York, Penguin Books, 1986)

—— *The Wealth of Nations: Books IV–V* (New York, Penguin Books, 1999)

—— Haakonssen, K (ed), *The Theory of Moral Sentiments* (Cambridge, Cambridge University Press, 2002)

—— Meek, RL, Raphael, DD, and Stein, PG (eds), *Lectures on Jurisprudence* (Indianapolis, Liberty Fund, 1982)

Sohn, LB and Buergenthal, T, *The Movement of Persons Across Borders: Studies in Transnational Legal Policy (No 23)* (Washington, DC, American Society of International Law, 1992)

Soper, P, *The Ethics of Deference: Learning from the Law's Morals* (Cambridge, Cambridge University Press, 2002)

Sztucki, J, 'Who Is a Refugee? The Convention Definition: Universal or Obsolete?' in Nicholson, F and Twomey, P (eds), *Refugee Rights and Realities: Evolving International Concepts and Regimes* (New York, Cambridge University Press, 1999) 55

Tienda, M, 'Demography and the Social Contract' (2002) 39 *Demography* 587

Waldron, J, *Dignity, Rank, and Rights* (New York, Oxford University Press, 2012)

—— 'The Primacy of Justice' (2003) 9 *Legal Theory* 269

—— 'What is Cosmopolitan?' (2000) 8 *Journal of Political Philosophy* 227

—— *Law and Disagreement* (Oxford, Oxford University Press, 1999)

—— 'Kant's Legal Positivism' (1995) 109 *Harvard Law Review* 1535

—— 'Property, Justification and Need' (1993) 6 *Canadian Journal of Law & Jurisprudence* 185

—— 'Special Ties and Natural Duties' (1993) 22 *Philosophy & Public Affairs* 3

Walton, K, 'The Particularities of Legitimacy: John Simmons on Political Obligation' (2010) 26 *Ratio Juris* 1

Walzer, M, 'What Does It Mean to Be an "American"?' (2004) 71 *Social Research* 633

—— *Thick and Thin: Moral Argument at Home and Abroad* (Notre Dame, University of Notre Dame Press, 1994)

—— *Interpretation and Social Criticism* (Cambridge, MA, Harvard University Press, 1987)

—— *Spheres of Justice: A Defense of Pluralism and Equality* (New York, Basic Books, 1983)

—— 'Philosophy and Democracy' (1981) 9 *Political Theory* 379

—— *Obligations: Essays on Obedience, War, and Citizenship* (Cambridge, MA, Harvard University Press, 1970)

Weinrib, J, 'Kant on Citizenship and Universal Independence' (2008) 33 *Australian Journal of Legal Philosophy* 1

Weithman, P, *Why Political Liberalism? On John Rawls's Political Turn* (New York, Oxford University Press, 2010)

Wellman, CH, 'Immigration' in Zalta, EN (ed), *The Stanford Encyclopedia of Philosophy* (Spring 2014)

—— and Cole, P, *Debating the Ethics of Immigration: Is There a Right to Exclude?* (New York, Oxford University Press, 2012)

Winch, D, *Adam Smith's Politics: An Essay in Historiographic Revision* (New York, Cambridge University Press, 1978)

Young, IM, *Justice and the Politics of Difference* (Princeton, Princeton University Press, 1990)

Ypi, L, 'Justice in Migration: A Closed Borders Utopia?' (2008) 16 *Journal of Political Philosophy* 391

INDEX

Abizadeh, Arash
  democratic governance, 144
Absolutism
  anti-liberalism, 95
  asylum-seekers, 94
  authority
    absolutist authority, 45–47
    authority without justice, 8–9, 93
    immigration law, 114
    lack of authority, 114
  brutality, 97, 105, 113
  communitarian absolutism
    see **Communitarian absolutism**
  designation of migrants, 94–95
  detention, 93
  discretionary doctrine, 45–47, 57, 93
    see also **Discretionary doctrine**
  expulsion, 93
  immigration governance, 3–5, 7, 92–93, 98,
    149–50, 176, 214
    see also **Immigration governance**
  implausibility, 15, 40, 210–11, 214
  inegalitarian admissions, 93–94
  injustice, 40
    see also **Injustice**
  justice, 31, 61, 97–99, 102, 113
    see also **Justice**
  lack of principle, 96–97
  legitimacy, 93, 96
  liberal absolutist accounts, 95–96
  liberal pessimism, 107–111
    see also **Liberal pessimism**
  minimal moral conditions, 96
  moral obligations, 97–98, 102
  obligations of virtue, 97
  oppression in immigration, 94
  pessimism, 214
  political morality, 93, 96
  preventing heterogeneity, 94
  principled account required, 8
  procedure, 93
  refugees, 94
  restrictive immigration policies, 96
  right of exclusion, 62
  social justice, 7, 9, 15, 96–97
    see also **Social justice**
  universality of justice, 20–23
    see also **Universality of justice**

Admission policies
  admission conditions, 44–45
  admission rights, 48
  advantaged migrants, 2, 38, 49, 54–55, 179, 208
  affirmative criteria, 48
  asylum seekers, 177
  cap-setting, 152–56, 188, 205, 207, 210–11
  economic migrants, 49
  fear of prosecution, 48, 50
  freedom of migration, 9–10, 172
    see also **Freedom of migration**
  global distributive justice, 170
  grounds of inadmissibility, 48
  guest workers, 176
  human rights, 48
  indefinite admission, 4, 204–5, 207, 209–10
  inegalitarianism, 7–8, 10, 39, 93–94
    see also **Inegalitarianism**
  injury caused, 49
  injustice, 10
  juridical integration, 209
  policy goals, 48
  priority of admissions, 2, 10, 181–83,
    187–88, 199
    see also **Priority of admissions for
      worst-off migrants**
  quotas, 48
  rationale for admission, 88
  refugees, 48, 50
  right of admission, 1
  well-ordered society, 205
Arbitrary force
  indirect principle, 173
  injustice in immigration, 40
Arendt, Hannah
  freedom of movement, 158–59
Arrest
  powers of arrest, 39
Asylum seekers
  admission, 177
  detention, 55
  discouraging inflows, 94
  motivation, 48
  residence and naturalization, 54–55
  right of asylum, 54, 175, 177
Authority
  absence of authority, 83
  authoritative governance, 82–83

behaviour of officials, 20
defiance, 20
democracy, 20
democratic theories, 117
due process, 20
government/subjects relationship, 20
human rights protection, 20
illegal immigration, 35
immigration law, 114–26, 141
    see also **Authority of immigration law**
immigration regimes, 34–37
immigration restrictions, 35, 37
individual's obligations, 20
justice and authority, 20
    see also **Justice**
legal authority, 19–20, 35–37
legitimacy, 17–18
legitimate power, 19, 36–37
legitimate regimes, 114–15
liminality, 35
moral justification, 17
non-ideal theory relative to justice,
    18–19
normative theory, 17–18
obedience, 20, 37
political obligation, 17–18
political authority, 17, 19–20, 35–37
political participation, 36–37
procedural/institutional mechanisms, 20
rule of law, 20
social justice, 17–19
submission, 20
theory of legitimacy, 17–18
Authority of immigration law
absolutist position, 114
accountability, 116
acquired obligation, 115, 117
consent, 115, 117–21
    see also **Consent**
democratic theories, 117
differential status, 117, 211
duty of civility, 116, 136, 138–40,
    143, 145
fairness, 115, 122–26
    see also **Fairness**
illegal immigrants, 114
indeterminacies, 115–16
institutional conditions, 116
institutional reflective equilibrium, 116
just governance, 115–16
    see also **Just governance**
legal obligations, 115
legal regimes, 114–15
natural duty of justice, 116, 126–31, 133–34,
    140, 145–46
    see also **Natural duty of justice**
political obligations, 115–16
striving to be just, 114–16, 126, 140–41, 146

Barry, Brian
social domination, 100
Basic liberty
capabilities approach, 195–96
conceptions of the good, 195
essential social conditions, 195
freedom of migration, 198–99, 201
    see also **Freedom of migration**
freedom of movement, 196–97, 199
    see also **Freedom of movement**
legitimate expectations, 199
lexical priority, 194, 199–201
modified original position, 195–96, 198–99
moral personality, 195
moral powers, 195–96, 198
protection of migration, 194
special protection, 196
well-ordered society, 194, 198
Blake, Michael
exclusion of migrants, 157

Canada
Canadian Charter of Rights and Freedoms, 158
discretionary doctrine, 46
family migrants, 53
immigration policy, 156–57
multiculturalism, 11
political conception of justice, 156
Québec, 11, 156–57
social services, 158
Cap-setting
immigration governance, 152–56, 188, 205,
    207, 210–11
Carens, Joseph
access to welfare benefits, 157
migration right, 182, 201
original position, 182
Children
best interests of the child, 46
separation from parents, 40, 53–54, 159,
    162–63, 172, 175, 188, 214
status, 90
Citizenship
acquired citizenship, 48
dual citizenship, 43
equal citizenship, 107, 206
return to country of citizenship, 41, 159, 162,
    172–75, 188, 208, 214
status, 86–87, 211
Communitarian absolutism
see also **Absolutism**
complex equality, 100–6
    see also **Complex equality**
distribution of valued goods, 100, 104
domination, 100–1, 104
spheres of justice, 100
thin morality, 100–6
    see also **Thin morality**

Complex equality
communal self-understanding, 103–4
conception of justice, 21–22, 102–4
distributive justice, 102
domination
brutality, 105
distribution of goods, 104
exclusion of refugees, 105
freedom from domination, 100–1
immigration policies, 104–6
injustice, 105
minimizing domination, 105
immigration law, 104
immigration restrictions, 103–4
justification, 105
kinship principle, 102
local understandings, 100
membership, 22, 77, 99, 102
mutual aid, 102
non-coercive inclusion, 101–4
particularist approach, 100, 102
principled governance, 106
rule against conversion, 101–4
shared understandings, 101–6
structural requirements, 100–2, 104
thin morality, 100–6
Consent
acquired political obligation, 115,
117, 121
authority of immigration law, 115
see also **Authority of immigration law**
coercive governance, 118
compliance with immigration law, 119
continued residence, 118
duress, 119
illegal immigration, 120–21, 123
indeterminate nature, 121
interpersonal obligations, 117
involuntary consent, 119
legal obligation, 118
natural freedom, 118
political participation, 118
tacit consent, 118–20, 123
unjust regimes, 117–18, 121
validating wrongful actions, 118
voluntariness, 119
Constructivist approach to immigration
basic structure of society, 189–91
constructivist original position, 186–88
free and equal migrants, 189–90
see also **Free and equal migrants**
global justice, 190–91
juridical integration, 190
original position, 189–91
partiality, 190
political equality, 189
principles of justice, 189
well-ordered society, 189–91

Contextualism
see also **Contextualist universalist method**
basic structure of society, 2, 5–6, 183, 185, 187
principles of justice, 183–85
social justice, 183
well-ordered society, 183, 185, 187
Contextualist universalist method
conflict of duties, 187
constructivist original position, 186–88
principles of justice, 185–89
priority rules, 188
see also **Priority of admission for worst-off
migrants**
reflective equilibrium, 186, 188–89
Contractualism
inegalitarian immigration policies, 111
status distinctions, 111
theory of justice, 110–11
theory of legitimacy, 110–11
Criminals
deportation, 48
exclusion of criminals, 42, 48, 159,
162, 188

Daniels, Norman
enjoyment of liberty, 206–7
Deportation
criminals, 48
demands on social entitlements, 48
discretionary doctrine, 44, 46
guest-workers, 52
illegal immigrants, 55, 80
migrants, 80
security threats, 48
Detention
absolutism, 93
see also **Absolutism**
arbitrary detention, 178
asylum seekers, 55
indefinite detention, 45–46
powers of detention, 39, 48
prolonged detention, 41, 43, 173
suspected terrorists, 41, 43
Deviation from justice
see **Reasonable deviation from justice**
Discretionary doctrine
absolutist theory, 45–47, 57, 93
see also **Absolutism**
admission conditions, 44–45
best interests of the child, 46
Canadian case decisions, 46
current status, 45
deportation, 44, 46
detention, 45–46
discretionary control, 150
domestic immigration law, 44
due process, 46
expulsions, 45–46

human rights protection, 47
immigration power, 44–45
international legal doctrine, 44, 46–47
principled interpretation, 46–47, 57
public policy, 44
reinterpretation, 57
substantive immigration policies, 46
US case decisions, 44–46
Distributive justice
global distributive justice, 151, 168–72
see also **Global distributive justice**
immigration governance, 1, 16, 21, 30, 32, 63, 102, 157, 168–69
non-lexical liberty, 199
Due process
authority, 20
lack of due process, 41
right to due process, 46, 177–78
Dworkin, Ronald
chain novels, 212
natural duty of justice, 129–30

Economic migrants
admission, 49
effects/impact, 50
exclusion, 172
freedom of movement, 159, 163
see also **Freedom of movement**
guest-worker programmes, 49, 51–52
indirect principle, 173
inegalitarianism, 39
labour certification, 51
labour supply, 51
motivation, 48, 163
property rights, 158, 163
protectionism, 51
state intervention, 51
status, 87
value, 163, 171
Egalitarian justice
distributive amelioration, 107
egalitarian justification, 107–9
equal citizenship, 107
equality of opportunity, 107
immigration governance, 109
impartial egalitarian motive, 110
juridical integration, 107
see also **Juridical integration**
legitimacy criteria, 108, 110
non-discrimination, 107
pre-political human rights, 108, 112
principles of democracy, 107
self-oppression, 107, 109
self-respect, 107
universalizability, 108–9
Exclusion
criminals, 42, 48, 159, 162, 188
economic migrants, 172

exclusion from voting, 173
family migrants, 172
freedom of migration, 9–10
see also **Freedom of migration**
immigration law, 39, 48
inegalitarianism, 7–8, 10, 39
see also **Inegalitarianism**
injustice, 10
migrants, 142, 155–57, 209
right of exclusion, 1, 62
refugees, 105, 172, 188, 214
Expulsion
absolutism, 93
see also **Absolutism**
discretionary doctrine, 45–46
see also **Discretionary doctrine**
long-term residents, 173
mass expulsions, 41
migrants, 121
powers of expulsion, 39

Fairness
acquired political obligation, 115, 117
authority of immigration law, 115
see also **Authority of immigration law**
benefit of public goods, 122–25
discretionary public goods, 122–24
distribution of goods, 122, 124, 126
immigration regimes, 123
justice condition, 124–25
legal obligations, 122, 126
migrants, 123, 125, 206
presumptive benefits, 122–26
principle of fairness, 122–26
Family migrants
advantaged migrants, 54
Canada, 53
consanguinity, 48
educational opportunities, 52
exclusion, 172
family reunion rights, 40, 53–54, 159, 162–63, 172, 175, 214
indirect principle, 173
inegalitarianism, 39, 53–54
labour market access, 52
motivation, 48
sponsorship, 48, 53
status, 87
United States of America, 11, 53
First-order areas of governance
admission and exclusion, 39, 48, 51, 153, 155, 172, 175, 181–82
aims, 177
capabilities approach, 207
convergence, 208–9
deportation, 49
detention, 49
discretion, 176

enforcement of policies, 39
first-order injury, 49
first-order policies, 39, 48, 112–13, 150, 154,
    159, 162, 176–77, 179–82, 190
freedom of migration, 153
freedom of movement, 195
immigration governance, 93, 163, 172–73,
    188, 207
independence, 208
inegalitarianism, 49, 51, 56, 151,
    181–82, 188
justice, 39
justification, 172
moral capacity, 208
oppressive measures, 113
Free and equal migrants
conception of the good, 192–93
equal moral personhood, 191
inequality, 192
juridical integration, 193
modified original position, 191–93
moral equality, 194
moral personhood, 192–93
moral powers, 192–93
non-liberal states, 192–93
partiality, 193–94
political inequality, 194
principles of justice, 192
refugees, 193
self-originating sources of claims, 192
well-ordered societies, 192–93
Freedom of migration
see also **Freedom of movement**
absolute priority, 199
admission/exclusion restrictions, 9–10, 172
asylum rights, 175, 177
basic liberty, 198–99, 201
    see also **Basic liberty**
citizens' right of return, 41, 159, 162, 173–75,
    188, 208, 214
direct interference, 172
global distributive justice, 168
    see also **Global distributive justice**
human rights protection, 161
immigration restrictions, 161–62, 172, 198
impartial judgement, 172
indirect principle
    see **Indirect principle**
legitimate expectations, 172
    see also **Legitimate expectations**
lexical priority, 204
migration right, 161, 173–74
modified original position, 182
non-lexical liberty, 199
protection, 199
relative importance, 202
religious persecution, 202
social interests, 213

unification of children/parents, 40, 53–54,
    159, 162–63, 172, 175
value, 150, 155, 159, 167–68, 171, 180
Freedom of movement
see also **Freedom of migration**
basic liberty, 196–97, 199
    see also **Basic liberty**
capabilities approach, 159–63, 167, 172
economic migrants, 159, 163
    see also **Economic migrants**
equality of opportunity, 198
independence, 165, 167
intrinsic value, 158, 161–62
Laws of Settlement, 26, 163–64, 166, 174
migration
    see **Migrants; Migration**
moral development, 165, 197
moral powers, 197–98
non-lexical liberty
    see **Non-lexical liberty**
political liberties, 198
protection, 196–99
purposiveness, 167
    see also **Purposiveness**
range, 197
relative importance, 158–59
restrictions, 158–59, 161–62, 164, 167, 198
social entitlements, 158
sympathetic intercourse, 197
value, 195

Global distributive justice
admission policies, 170
application, 168
closure of borders, 168
constructivist approach to immigration,
    190–91
    see also **Constructivist approach to
        immigration**
emigration restrictions, 171
equal political liberty, 206
freedom of migration, 168
    see also **Freedom of migration**
immigration governance, 168–72, 204, 208
liberal nationalist approach, 168–70
moral standards, 168
national projects, 170
promotion, 171–72
redistributive obligations, 171
social minimum, 206
value of migration, 168
Guest-worker programmes
admission policy, 176
creation, 51
deportation, 52
economic migrants, 49
exploitation, 117
forced labour, 52

remittances, 52
status, 88–89
workers' rights, 52

Ha-Joon Chang
consequentialist nationalism, 93
Hall, William Edward
non-naturalized migrants, 120
Hart, H L A
political obligations, 122, 124
Hobbes, Thomas
consent theory, 121
Human rights
admission policies, 48
arbitrary detention, 178
criminal liability without trial, 178
due process right, 46, 177–78
education rights, 179
enjoyment of culture, religion,
    or language, 179
enslavement, 178
equality before the law, 178
exploitation, 178
freedom of movement, 159–60, 162, 167
    see also **Freedom of movement**
human rights protection, 20, 47, 110, 174–78
humanitarian intervention, 32
injustice, 40, 159, 177
just governance, 208
    see also **Just governance**
life and security of the person, 178
migration right, 161
public health right, 179
refugees, 54
social security rights, 179

Illegal migration
deportation, 55, 80
enforcement measures, 55–56
identification issues, 55
illegal entry, 120, 125–26
illegal migrants
    absence of rights, 49
    authority, 35, 114
    clandestine entrants, 120
    consent, 120–21, 123
    disadvantaged migrants, 55
    immigration law, 114
    skilled migrants, 55
    United States of America, 11
policy-making, 55
status difference, 56
Immigration control
administrative tribunals, 50
exclusive control, 83
identification systems, 50
immigration governance, 209, 211
quotas, 48

state power, 1
visas, 50
Immigration governance
absolutism, 3–5, 7, 92–93, 149–50, 176,
    209, 214
    see also **Absolutism**
alarmism, 2
authority, 20, 35–37, 82–83
    see also **Authority**
cap-setting, 152–56, 188, 205, 207, 210–11
constraints, 8
cosmopolitan ideal, 149–50
demands of justice, 9
democratic states, 10–11
destabilizing effects, 1–2
discretionary doctrine
    see **Discretionary doctrine**
distributive justice, 1, 16, 21, 30, 32, 63, 102
duty of obedience, 133
economic inequalities, 203
effects of immigration/emigration, 33
egalitarian justice, 109
    see also **Egalitarian justice**
enforcement, 152–55
equality before the law, 178
exclusion of migrants, 142, 155–57, 209
first-order areas, 93, 163, 172–73, 188, 207
    see also **First-order areas of governance**
freedom of migration, 9–10
    see also **Freedom of migration**
full equality, 154
general will, 142
global distributive justice, 168–72, 204,
    208, 213
governance through law, 9, 98
human rights protection, 178–79
    see also **Human rights**
immigration policy, 142
immigration restrictions, 5, 156, 158,
    176–77
incorporation, 152–53
indirect principle, 173
    see **Indirect principle**
inegalitarianism, 7–8, 10, 38–39, 151
    see also **Inegalitarianism**
inequality, 69, 194
    see also **Inequality**
injury caused, 7, 25, 27–28, 31, 51, 56, 150
    see also **Injury**
international instruments, 11
juridical integration, 142, 149, 203–4
    see also **Juridical integration**
just regimes, 61–62, 68, 86, 149, 207–8, 210
    see also **Just governance**
justice
    see **Justice**
justification, 37–38, 69, 142, 203–4
legal doctrine, 2–3

legitimacy, 8, 110–11
legitimate expectations, 156–58, 175, 177,
    180–82, 189, 199, 203
    see also **Legitimate expectations**
liberal democracies, 2, 10–11
migration governance distinguished, 152
migration regimes, 11
moral equality, 194
moral powers, 203
morality, 154
national ideal, 3, 5, 149
non-oppression, 91
normative framework, 152, 154
original position, 182
partiality, 154–55, 157, 214
    see also **Partiality**
policy framework, 152, 154
political conception of justice, 142–43
political inequality, 7–8, 142, 149, 189, 194
political morality, 2, 82, 151
principled account, 8, 91–93, 96, 106, 113,
    150, 209
properly public purpose, 2
public right, 8
purpose, 152
reasonableness, 210, 214
reciprocity, 141, 143, 189, 209–10
regulation of private relations, 152–55
rightful condition, 149
rightful governance
    see **Rightful governance of immigration**
second-order areas, 39, 48, 51, 56
    see also **Second-order areas of governance**
selection of migrants, 152–53, 155
social welfare, 157
stability of society, 6–7
stable/wealthy states, 10–11
state discretion, 3
Immigration law
acquired citizenship, 48
admission and exclusion provisions, 39,
    48–50
asylum seekers, 48
authority, 114–26, 136, 138–41, 143, 145
    see also **Authority of immigration law**
compliance, 119
deportation, 48
discretionary doctrine, 7–8
    see also **Discretionary doctrine**
economic migrants, 48
family migrants, 48
inegalitarianism, 7–8, 10, 209
    see also **Inegalitarianism**
justification, 212
refugees, 48
Immigration regimes
absence of authority, 83
authoritative governance, 82–83

conceptions of justice, 185
deviation from justice, 134–37
    see also **Reasonable deviation from justice**
duty of obedience, 133
enforcement issues, 84–85
entry into a rightful condition, 84–85
exclusive control of immigration, 83
fairness, 123
historical wrongs, 85
indeterminacy, 84
juridical integration, 81–82
    see also **Juridical integration**
just regimes, 61–62, 68, 86, 149
legality, 126
legitimacy, 110
legitimate expectations, 82
    see also **Legitimate expectations**
liminal nature, 86, 117
maintaining a rightful condition, 81–82,
    84, 88
natural duty of justice, 126
    see also **Natural duty of justice**
political conception of justice, 82, 86, 88,
    90, 92
political obligation, 126
postulate of public right, 126
    see also **Postulate of public right**
rightful governance
    see **Rightful governance of immigration**
rightful non-oppression, 86
sense of justice, 86, 88
status
    see **Immigration status**
trans-contextual contexts, 185
unjust regimes, 117–18, 121, 133–37
Immigration status
assignment of status, 87
children, 90
citizenship, 86–87, 211
democratic legal systems, 86
differential status, 87–89, 91, 211
discretion, 91–92
economic migrants, 87
explanations, 90
exploitation, 88
family migrants, 87
guest workers, 88, 88–89
juridical control, 92
juridical integration, 90–91
justifiable status, 89–91
migrants, 87–88
naturalization, 91
non-oppression, 91–92
permanent status, 87, 91
political conception of justice, 90
refugees, 87
status regimes, 117
students, 88

temporary status, 87–88, 91, 207
tourists, 88
unequal status, 35–36, 88–90
Indirect principle
admission criteria, 176
ancillary entitlements, 174
arbitrary force, 173
avoiding oppression, 173
capabilities approach, 195–96
convergence with prioritization, 208–9
deontic standing, 180
economic migrants, 173
egalitarian policies, 180
excessive force, 173
exclusion from voting, 173
exploitation of migrants, 173
expulsion of long-term residents, 173
family migrants, 173
immigration governance, 173
immigration laws/policies, 173
importance, 173
imposing criminal penalties, 173
independence, 195
juridical integration, 213
liberty of migration, 178
migrants' protective rights, 174–78
    see also **Human rights**
migration restrictions, 176–77
migration right, 173–74
non-trivial critical force, 173, 180–81
oppression, 176, 207, 211
perimeter of protection, 174
prolonged detention, 173
purposiveness, 195
    see also **Purposiveness**
relevance, 176–78
rights against interference, 174
substantive rights, 175
violation of protective rights, 174
Inegalitarianism
admission and exclusion policies, 7–8, 10, 39,
    93–94
advantaged migrants, 49–50
deportation, 112
disadvantaged migrants, 49, 211
discretionary doctrine
    see **Discretionary doctrine**
economic migrants, 39, 51–52
    see also **Economic migrants**
egalitarian policies, 56
enforcement issues, 112
exclusion policies, 112
family migrants, 39, 53–54
    see also **Family migrants**
first-order policies, 112–13, 181–82, 188
global inequality, 57
illegal migration, 39, 55–56
    see also **Illegal immigration**

immigration governance, 2, 38–39, 151, 209
    see also **Immigration governance**
inegalitarian policies, 57, 112–13
injury caused, 50–51
injustice in immigration, 40–41
    see also **Injustice**
legitimacy, 111
oppression, 112–13
public benefit schemes, 56
second-order policies, 112–13
social welfare programmes, 56
vulnerability, 211
Inequality
difference principle, 205
distribution of opportunities, 32
economic inequality, 203
fairness in selection process, 32
free and equal migrants, 192
    see also **Free and equal migrants**
global inequality, 208
justification, 31–32, 61, 69
members of states, 32, 37
political (in)equality, 7–8, 62–63, 142, 149,
    189, 194
superior positions, 31
unequal status, 35–36, 88–90
worst-off migrants, 206
    see also **Priority of admission for worst-off
    migrants**
Injury
damage to purposiveness, 26–27
dignity of injured party, 28
disadvantage and vulnerability, 211
injury caused, 7, 25, 27–28, 31, 37, 49–51,
    56, 150
judgements about justice, 25, 27–28
justification for injury, 7, 28, 31, 77
reasons for action, 27
responsibility for injury, 16
undue partiality, 27
unjust injury, 27
unjustified injury, 7, 25, 28–29, 37, 137
Injustice
absolutism, 40
    see also **Absolutism**
acceptance, 134
banishment, 41, 159, 162
burdens, 134
controversial exclusionary areas
    dual citizenship, 43
    guest-worker programmes, 43
    historic wrongs, 43
    public health risks, 43, 159, 162
    security threats, 43, 159, 162
    terrorist suspects, 43
    victims of climate change, 43
destabilizing potential, 30
detention, 41, 43

domination, 105
excessive force, 40
human rights threatened, 40, 159
immigration governance, 40–41
impartial justification, 28
inegalitarianism, 40–41
injury caused, 25, 27–28, 49–51
judgements about (in)justice, 20, 25–28,
  40–41
justifiable exclusionary actions
  exclusion from voting, 42
  exclusion of criminals, 42, 159, 162
  exclusion of spouses, 43
  exclusion on racial grounds, 42–43
  prohibition on emigration, 42–43
lack of due process, 41
likelihood of torture, 40, 43, 159
mass expulsions, 41
motives, 25, 27
object of resentment, 25
oppression, 37, 40–41
penalties without trial, 41
personal injustice, 17, 22
real and positive hurt, 26
reflective equilibrium, 40
refugees, 40, 159, 162–63, 172
resentment, 28
return to country of citizenship, 41, 159, 162,
  172–75, 188, 208, 214
revenge, 28
separating parents/children, 40, 53–54, 159,
  162–63, 172, 175
social injustice, 16–17, 22, 37, 129
unjustified injury, 7, 25, 28–29, 37
unreasonable injustice, 177
victimization, 41

Juridical integration
admission policy, 209
constructivist approach to immigration, 190
  see also **Constructivist approach to
    immigration**
egalitarian justice, 107
  see also **Egalitarian justice**
entry into rightful condition, 71
free and equal migrants, 193
  see also **Free and equal migrants**
global justice, 213
immigration governance, 142, 149,
  203–4
immigration regimes, 81–82, 142, 149
immigration status, 90–91
importance, 213
indirect principle, 213
  see also **Indirect principle**
joint juridical integration, 74
just governance, 207, 211–13
  see also **Just governance**

legitimate expectations, 76
  see also **Legitimate expectations**
meaning, 71
migrants, 200, 205, 207, 211, 213
moral standing of states, 71–73
  see also **Moral standing of states**
political conception of justice, 74
prioritarian principle, 213
proximity requirement, 72
refugees, 200–1
self-respect, 213
sense of justice, 71, 74, 213
stability of the state, 72–73
subjection to state authority, 71–72
Just governance
capabilities approach, 207
differential status, 211
human rights protection, 208
indefinite admissions, 4, 204–5, 207,
  209–10
juridical integration, 207, 211–13
legitimate expectations, 207, 210, 212–13
political conception of justice, 207, 210,
  212, 214
stability of the state, 211–12
Justice
absolutism, 31, 40
  see also **Absolutism**
background justice, 170
claims for justice, 34, 72
classical understanding, 7
commutative justice, 30
conception of justice, 7, 29–30, 34, 64–65, 73,
  102–4, 185, 200, 207
condition devoid of justice, 79, 83
conflicts of interest, 31
conflicts of justice, 32–33
constraining influence, 3, 210
cosmopolitan conceptions, 109
demands of justice, 9
determination of justice, 75
deviation from justice, 134–37, 141, 144
  see also **Reasonable deviation from justice**
disagreements about justice, 79, 137, 139
distinctive features, 32–33
distributive justice, 1, 16, 21, 30, 32, 63, 102,
  151, 157, 168–72, 199
  see also **Distributive justice**; **Global
    distributive justice**
economic inequality, 31
egalitarian justice, 107–8, 110, 112
  see also **Egalitarian justice**
elimination of oppression, 16
equal respect, 29
excessive force, 30
expansion of justice, 30
fairness, 186, 199–200
humanitarian intervention, 32

immigration governance, 21–22, 206, 208, 210, 212
  see also **Immigration governance**
impartiality, 37–38
indeterminacy, 8
inequalities, 31–32
injury caused, 16, 28–29, 31
  see also **Injury**
injustice
  see **Injustice**
international justice, 1, 5–6, 9
judgements of justice, 21–22, 40–41
justice as constraint, 15
limited scope, 21–22
migrants, 32–33
national prejudice, 37
natural duty of justice, 9, 116, 126–31, 134–35, 140, 143, 145–46
  see also **Natural duty of justice**
natural partiality, 37
nature of justice, 67
non-ideal theory relative to good, 18–19
obligations of justice, 3–4, 6, 8, 142–43
personal justice, 16, 30
political boundaries, 21–22
political conception of justice, 6–9, 22, 61, 69–76, 79, 82, 86, 88, 90, 92, 142–44, 149, 155–57, 175, 177, 180, 182
political inequality, 7–8, 69
primacy of justice, 29, 61
principles of justice, 3–4, 6–7, 29, 65, 84, 183–89, 192
provisional nature, 84
purposiveness, 15
  see also **Purposiveness**
reasonable conception of justice, 9, 149
reasonable deviation from justice, 134–40
  see also **Reasonable deviation from justice**
reflective equilibrium, 40
  see also **Reflective equilibrium**
resentment, 28
revenge, 28
rules of justice, 69
sense of justice, 6, 28–30, 32, 65, 70–72, 74, 76, 79, 81, 86, 88, 129, 136, 167, 184, 200, 213
shared understandings, 21–22
social justice, 7, 9, 15–16, 30, 107, 183
  see also **Social justice**
special relationship, 21, 30–31
spheres of justice, 100
stable relations of justice, 85
state powers, 33
striving for justice, 114–16, 126–27, 140–41, 145–46
unequal access, 31
universality of justice
  see **Universality of justice**
unknown variables, 34

value of justice, 107
viability of justice, 2
victimization, 17

Kant, Immanuel
categorical imperative, 108
citizenship, 86–87, 89, 165
common conception of good, 78
cosmopolitan right, 78–79, 150, 161, 181, 194
duty of obedience, 127, 134
entry into rightful condition, 62, 64–66, 68–69, 78, 84–85, 127, 134, 185
  see also **Rightful condition**
historic wrongs, 85, 127
hypothetical state of nature, 62
idea of reason, 69
innate right to freedom, 78
justice
  conception of justice, 64–65
  indeterminacy of justice, 8
  nature of justice, 67
  political conception of justice, 8, 180
justification of the state, 62, 65, 68–70, 73, 121, 127, 132–33
legitimacy of the state, 126
normative authority, 126
political philosophy, 8
postulate of public right, 62–63, 78, 92, 126, 146
  see also **Postulate of public right**
principles of justice, 3
property rights, 64
public right, 8
right of resort, 78
role of proximity, 66–68, 72
universal principle of right, 63–64
Klosko, George
fairness principle, 122–24
Kymlicka, Will
distributive justice, 169, 181

Legitimacy
criterion for legitimacy, 110
human rights protection, 110
immigration governance, 8, 110–11
legitimate world order, 111
moral justification, 17
relationship to authority, 17–18
theory of legitimacy, 110
Legitimate expectations
admission restrictions, 172
basic liberty, 199
  see also **Basic liberty**
conception of justice, 207, 212
frustration, 76–77
honouring entitlements, 75
immigration restrictions, 77, 156–58, 175, 177, 180–82, 189, 199, 203

juridical integration, 76
just governance, 207, 210, 212, 213
   see also **Just governance**
migration, 172
non-lexical liberty, 199
partiality, 75–77
   see also **Partiality**
political conception of justice,
   75–77
priority of admission, 181–82
protection, 77, 82
range-limited principles, 75
sense of justice, 76
Liberal pessimism
egalitarian justice, 107–10, 112
   see also **Egalitarian justice**
pessimism about legitimacy
   global morality, 111
   human rights violations, 110
   immigration governance,
     110–11
   immigration regimes, 110
   inegalitarian immigration policies, 111
   legitimate world order, 111
   theory of legitimacy, 110
Locke, John
consent theory, 118, 120
determinate natural laws, 66
executive power, 66
principles of justice, 66

MacIntyre, Alasdair
attitudes of justice, 21
Migrants
see also Migration
ability to litigate, 36
admission policy, 209
admission rationale, 88
advantaged migrants, 2, 38, 49–50, 54–55,
   179, 208
basic liberties, 205, 207–8, 210
clandestine entrants, 120
conflicts of interest, 31–33
consent theory, 117–21
deportation, 80
disadvantaged migrants, 39, 49, 55, 119,
   180, 213
diversity, 36
due process rights, 177
economic migrants
   see **Economic migrants**
equal standing, 34
ethical relationship with the state, 120
exclusion, 142, 155–57, 209
exploitation, 173
expulsion, 121
fairness principle, 123, 125, 206
   see also **Fairness**

family migrants
   see **Family migrants**
free and equal migrants, 191–94
   see also **Free and equal migrants**
freedom of migration
   see **Freedom of migration**
guest workers
   see **Guest workers**
heterogeneous nature, 36, 116
ICRMW provisions, 176
illegal migrants, 11, 35, 39, 49, 55–56, 114,
   120–21, 123, 125–26
   see also **Illegal migration**
immigration governance
   see **Immigration governance**
impact of migrants, 33–34
indefinite admission, 4, 204–5, 207, 209–10
indeterminacy, 80
inegalitarianism, 38–39
   see also **Inegalitarianism**
interaction with states, 78–79
international instruments, 176
juridical integration, 79, 81–82, 200, 205, 207,
   211, 213
limitation of rights, 121
meaning, 10
migrant-member conflicts, 32–33
migration flows, 1–2, 49–50
moral powers, 199, 202, 205, 207
naturalization, 91
negative duty, 120
non-lexical liberty, 199
obligations of justice, 8
overstaying a visa, 120
political participation, 36–37, 82, 91, 117, 124
political obligations, 113, 133
political reception, 34
protective rights, 174–78
proximity of migrants, 32–33
purposiveness, 31, 50, 79–81, 194, 202
   see also **Purposiveness**
refugees
   see **Refugees**
relocation, 79
removal, 33
right of return, 41, 159, 162, 173–75, 188, 208
self-determination, 82–83
self-oppression, 107, 109
self-respect, 91, 200
sense of justice, 6, 32, 200
special vulnerability, 1–3, 211
state powers, 33
status
   passive citizens, 87
   permanent status, 87, 91
   political status, 87
   temporary status, 87–88, 91
   unequal status, 35–36, 88–90

tacit consent, 120, 123
transience, 36, 116, 142
unjust regimes, 117–18, 121, 133–37
victimization, 41
worst-off migrants, 182, 205–8
    see also **Priority of admission for worst-off migrants**
xenophobia, 81
Migration
administrative tribunals, 50
basic liberty, 205
economic migrants
    see **Economic migrants**
family migrants
    see **Family migrants**
freedom of migration
    see **Freedom of migration**
freedom of movement distinguished, 198
    see also **Freedom of movement**
identification systems, 50
global distributive justice, 151, 168–72
human rights protection, 161
illegal migration, 11, 35, 39, 49, 55–56, 114, 120–21, 123, 125–26
    see also **Illegal migration**
immigration restrictions, 161–62, 164, 167
juridical nature
    condition devoid of justice, 79, 83
    disagreements about justice, 79
    juridical integration, 79, 81–82, 107
    lack of shared membership, 79
    maintaining a rightful condition, 81–82
    political conception of justice, 79
    pursuit of opportunities, 80
    redirecting purposiveness, 79–80
    sense of justice, 79, 81
freedom of migration, 9–10
    see also **Freedom of migration**
legitimate expectations, 172
    see also **Legitimate expectations**
migration control, 50, 209, 211
migration flows, 1–2, 49–50
migration right, 161, 173–74
moral powers, 182
opportunity structures, 50
partiality, 175
    see also **Partiality**
presumptive wrongs, 175
priority of admission, 181–83, 187–88
    see also **Priority of admission for worst-off migrants**
protection, 194
right of return, 41, 159, 162, 173–75, 188, 208, 214
value of migration, 163, 150, 155, 159, 163, 167–68, 171–72, 175, 208
visa systems, 50
welfare institutions, 172

Miller, David
migration right, 161, 201
restrictive immigration policies, 96
reunification of spouses, 43
Moral personhood
equal moral personhood, 2, 191
free and equal migrants, 191–93
    see also **Free and equal migrants**
Moral standing of states
basic structure of the state, 69–70, 72–73
claims of justice, 72
coercive power, 73
extant states, 78
general will, 78
juridical integration, 71–73
    see also **Juridical integration**
justification of the state, 69
natural allegiance, 70, 73
orientation to a state, 71
political conception of justice, 69–73
proximity requirement, 72
sense of justice, 70–72
stability of states, 72–73
Murphy, Jeffrie
determinacy of justice, 68
Murphy, Liam
principle of beneficence, 170

Nagel, Thomas
absolutist views, 9, 107, 146
contractualism, 111–12
cosmopolitan conceptions of justice, 109
egalitarian justice, 107–8, 110, 112
enforcement issues, 112
global morality, 111
immigration governance, 96, 98, 108–9, 112
legitimacy, 110–11
obligations of justice, 142
political morality, 108
test of universalizability, 108–10, 113
value of justice, 107
Natural duty of justice
action-guiding, 132–33
application requirement, 130–32
background justice, 129
duty of obedience, 127–28, 133
immigration governance, 9, 126
no limitations of range, 129–30
political obligations, 126–31, 133–34, 139, 145
postulate of public right, 126
    see also **Postulate of public right**
public reason, 127–28
reasonable deviation from justice, 134–35
    see also **Reasonable deviation from justice**
reasonableness requirement, 143, 145
rightful condition, 132–33
rule by law, 127
sense of justice, 129

social injustice, 129
special relationships, 131
striving for justice, 126–27, 140, 145–46
sufficient guidance, 130
voluntary obligations, 131
Non-lexical liberty
admission of migrants, 199
distributive justice, 199
freedom of migration, 199
see also **Freedom of migration**
legitimate expectations, 199
see also Legitimate expectations
lexical priority, 199–200, 204
protection of liberties, 199
Nozick, Robert
fairness principle, 122, 130
Nussbaum, Martha
freedom of movement, 159–60, 162, 167
social justice, 27

Parents
separation from children, 40, 53–54, 159,
    162–63, 172, 175, 188, 214
Parfitt, Derek
personal identity, 212
Partiality
common sense morality, 73, 76
constructivist approach to immigration, 190
see also **Constructivist approach to**
    immigration
determination of justice, 75
equal respect, 74
exclusionary force, 76
free and equal migrants, 193–94
see also **Free and equal migrants**
immigration restrictions, 75, 154–55, 157,
    175, 214
impartiality, 24–25, 37–38, 86, 214
joint juridical integration, 74
justification, 73, 75–76
legitimate expectations, 75–77
see also **Legitimate expectations**
natural partiality, 24, 37
partiality among compatriots, 73
permitted partiality, 73–74
political conception of justice, 73–76
political inequality, 69, 189, 194
political participation, 74
proximate individuals, 75
range-limited principles, 75
reasonable forms, 73
self-respect, 74–76
self-worth, 74
undue partiality, 27
Persecution
fear of persecution, 48, 50, 54, 94, 208
Pettit, Philip
immigration control, 162

Pevnick, Ryan
guest worker programmes, 88–89, 118–19, 121
Pogge, Thomas
immigration policy, 170–71
Postulate of public right
central authority, 65
conception of justice, 64–65
conception of the good, 65
cosmopolitan right, 78–79
distributive justice, 63
entry into a rightful condition, 62, 64–66, 68
equal freedom, 63–65
immigration regimes, 126
innate right to freedom, 63–64
justification of states, 62, 65, 68–69
meaning, 63
natural duty of justice, 126
see also **Natural duty of justice**
nature of justice, 67, 84
property rights, 64
rightful governance, 93
rightful non-oppression, 86
role of proximity, 66–68
sociable bonds, 66–67
stable relations of justice, 85
united general will, 63
universal principle of right, 63–64
Priority of admission for worst-off migrants
absolute priority, 182
basic liberty
see **Basic liberty**
constructivist approach to immigration,
    189–91
see also **Constructivist approach to**
    immigration
contextualism, 183
contextualist universalist method, 185–89
see also **Contextualist universalist method**
first-order immigration policies, 181–82
first-order inegalitarianism, 181–82, 188
free and equal migrants, 191–94
see also **Free and equal migrants**
just governance, 207–8
see also **Just governance**
legitimate expectations, 181–82
non-lexical liberty, 194–204
see also **Non-lexical liberty**
permanent admission, 181, 187
prioritarian admissions principle,
    2, 10
priority rules, 188
worst-off immigrants
admission policy, 182
basic liberties, 205, 207–8
cap-setting, 205
difference principle, 205
equality of opportunity, 205
fairness, 206

inequality, 206, 208
political liberties, 206
Private relations
regulation, 39, 152–55
Public health risks
immigration governance, 188
injustice in immigration, 43, 159, 162
Purposiveness
capabilities, 27, 195–96
conception of one's own good, 26
damage to purposiveness, 26–27
indirect principle, 195
see also **Indirect principle**
migrants, 31, 50, 79–81, 194
moral powers, 26–27
redirecting purposiveness, 79–80

Rawls, John
application of rules, 138–39
basic liberty, 194–95, 199, 203
see also **Basic liberty**
basic structure of society, 2, 5–6, 183,
185–87, 190
burdens of judgement, 64
causes of immigration, 5
citizenship, 87
closed society presumption, 2, 5–6, 21, 107,
110, 141, 183, 185
conception of the good, 65, 167, 184
considered judgements, 7, 20–21, 40–43
consistency of laws/policies, 138
constructivism, 10, 189
contextualism, 183–86
deliberative democracy, 140
difference principle, 129
duty of civility, 116, 136, 138–40
duty of obedience, 128
elimination of immigration, 213
equal liberty, 129, 200
equality of opportunity, 129, 196
fair play principle, 122
fairness, 6, 21, 69, 122, 124, 128–29, 186,
199–200, 206
see also **Fairness**
freedom of movement, 196
see also **Freedom of movement**
immigration governance, 190
inequality, 206
just distribution, 205
just legal order, 138
justice
background justice, 170
conception of justice, 29–30, 73–74, 129, 205
international justice, 5–6
justice requirement, 124–25
natural duty of justice, 9, 116, 127–30,
133, 135
political conception of justice, 6–7

principles of justice, 3–4, 6, 29, 138, 183–87
reasonable deviation from justice,
134–35, 137
sense of justice, 6, 29–30, 65, 70, 136,
167, 184
social (in)justice, 22, 107, 129, 183
theory of justice, 21, 102, 107, 182, 183
legitimacy principle, 127, 134, 136
lexical priority of liberty, 199–202
liberal legitimacy, 9
liberty, 205
limiting immigration, 5
method of justification, 3–4, 20, 22
moral powers, 184–85, 192, 197, 203
original position, 10, 138, 180–81, 186, 189,
191, 194, 199
political obligations, 116, 128–30, 137
public reason, 4, 6, 9, 22–23, 116, 127–28,
134–36, 139–41
publicity, 140
reasonableness, 135–36, 141
reciprocity, 141, 189, 203
reflective equilibrium, 20, 23, 138–39, 141,
186, 188
self-respect, 74, 200
social conditions, 197
social contract device, 10, 22, 138, 181
social union, 203
socio-economic distribution, 205
stability of society, 6, 73
sufficiency conditions, 146
universalism, 183–85
well-ordered society, 156, 183, 185–87, 190,
194, 204
Raz, Joseph
authority, 19, 35
duress invalidating consent, 119
legal obligations, 114
legal regimes, 114
self-representation, 35
Reasonable deviation from justice
accountability requirement, 140
authoritative equilibrium, 140
conflicts of interest, 137
disagreement about justice, 137, 139
duty of civility, 136, 138–40
indeterminacy, 137
injustice
accepting injustice, 134
burdens of injustice, 134
institutional conditions, 138, 140, 146
institutional requirements, 134
limits of institutional design, 137
moral attitudes, 134
natural duty of justice, 134–35
see also **Natural duty of justice**
permanent minorities, 134
political obligations, 137

public reason, 134–37, 139–40
publicity requirement, 140
reasonableness, 135–38, 141, 144
reciprocity, 137, 141
relevant circumstances, 137–38
sense of justice, 136
terms of cooperation, 137
unjustifiable injury, 137
Reasonableness
  absolutist pessimism, 214
  acquired obligations, 142–43
  democratic decision-making, 144
  deviation from justice, 135–38, 141, 144
    see also **Reasonable deviation from justice**
  duty of civility, 136, 138–40, 145
  immigration governance, 141–43, 149, 214
  indeterminacy of justice, 144
  institutional conditions, 138, 146
  natural duty of justice, 143, 143, 145
    see also **Natural duty of justice**
  political conception of justice, 142–44
  public reason, 134–37, 139–40
  reciprocity, 141, 143
  reflective equilibrium, 138–39, 141, 144–45
  social cooperation, 141
  symmetrical reasonableness, 210
Reflective equilibrium
  absolutist objection, 20–21, 23
  contextualist universalist method
    see also **Contextualist universalist method**
  injustice, 40
  institutional reflective equilibrium, 116
  reasonableness, 138–39, 141, 144–45
Refugees
  absolutist policy, 94
    see also **Absolutism**
  admission, 48, 50
  asylum, 54
  consent theory, 119
  definition, 54–55
  exclusion, 105, 214
  fear of persecution, 48, 50, 54, 94, 208
  free and equal migrants, 193
    see also **Free and equal migrants**
  international refugee law, 54
  juridical integration, 200–1
  motivation, 48
  overriding legal rules, 115
  protection
    human rights protection, 54
    non-refoulement, 54
    procedural means, 55
    scope of protection, 55
  return of refugees, 40, 159, 162–63, 172, 188
  status, 87
Rightful condition
  entry into rightful condition, 62, 64–66,
    68–69, 71, 78, 84–85, 134, 149, 185

maintaining a rightful condition, 81–82, 84, 88
natural duty of justice, 132–33
Rightful governance of immigration
  absolutism, 61–62
    see also **Absolutism**
  acquired rights, 78
  authoritative control, 61
  demand for respect, 61–62
  demonstrating reasonable preference, 78
  discretionary control, 61, 91–92
    see also **Discretionary doctrine**
  enforcement mechanisms, 61
  entry into rightful condition, 78
  general will, 78
  innate right to freedom, 78
  jurisdiction, 61
  just regimes, 61–62, 68
  justification of inequality, 61–63, 69
  justification of injury, 77
  moral discretion, 61
  moral equality, 68
  moral standing of states, 68–69, 78
    see also **Moral standing of states**
  national competence, 61
  non-oppression, 91
  partiality, 69
    see also **Partiality**
  political conception of justice, 61
  political inequality, 69
  political morality, 61
  postulate of public right, 62–68
    see also **Postulate of public right**
  primacy of justice, 61
  right of a guest, 78
  right of resort, 78
  social institutions, 61, 64
  state authority, 77–78
Ripstein, Arthur
  immigration restrictions, 161
  right to freedom, 78–79
Rousseau, Jean Jacques
  consent theory, 118
Ruhs, Martin
  consequentialist nationalism, 93
Rule of law
  authority, 20
  rules of justice, 69

Sassen, Saskia
  migration strategies, 50
Scanlon, T M
  contractualism, 108, 110–11
  equality of opportunity, 31
  justifying inequalities, 203
Scheffler, Samuel
  effects of immigration/emigration, 33
Schmitt, Carl
  immigration governance, 94–95, 97

Schotel, Bas
immigration governance, 98
Second-order areas of governance
constraints, 150, 173
enforcement of policies, 39
exercise of power, 75
expulsion powers, 39
immigration governance, 153–54, 173, 175, 188
implementation, 39
incorporation issues, 153–54
indeterminacy, 80
injury, 39, 49, 51, 56, 175, 177, 179–80
justice, 39, 175
law and policy, 39–40, 48–49, 55, 112, 153, 176–77, 180
oppressive measures, 112–13, 121, 150–51, 173–74, 178–80, 207–8
regulation of private relations, 39
resident immigrants, 39
violations of basic rights, 178
Security risks
deportation, 48
immigration governance, 188
injustice in immigration, 43, 159, 162
Sen, Amartya
freedom of movement, 159
social justice, 27
Sidgwick, Henry
absolute right, 3, 194
cosmopolitan ideal, 5
immigration governance, 149–50
legitimate expectations, 212
Simmons, A J
consent theory, 118
justice condition, 124–25
legal obligations, 124
political obligations, 131–32
postulate of public right, 66–67
refusal of benefits, 125
sociable bonds, 66–67
Smith, Adam
divergences in judgements, 64
economic migration, 167
equal respect, 27
free commerce, 164–66
freedom of movement, 159, 163–65, 174
impartiality, 24–25, 37–38, 172–73, 214
independence, 27, 165, 167, 195
justice
commutative justice, 30
corruption of judgement, 24–25
injury through oppression, 30
injustice, 23, 25–28, 37
judgements of justice, 15–16, 23, 28
judgement of others, 23–25
principles of justice, 3, 7, 68
rules of justice, 25, 28
self-deception, 24–25

self-evidence, 26
sense of justice, 28, 70
social justice, 30
Laws of Settlement, 26
mechanism of sympathy, 23–24
moral maturity, 27, 164–66, 195
natural partiality, 24
freedom of migration, 9
sympathetic intercourse, 197
Social justice
absolutism, 7, 9, 15, 96–97
see also **Absolutism**
authority, 17–19
see also **Authority**
conception of the good, 15
contextualism, 183
distribution of rights, 16
elimination of oppression, 15
immigration governance, 7, 30
see also **Immigration governance**
questions of membership, 22
reform, 17
social injustice, 16–17
Sympathy
judgement of others, 23–24
social harmony, 24
sympathetic approval, 23
sympathetic identification, 23, 72
sympathetic resentment, 28

Terrorists
security risks, 43, 159, 162
Thin morality
complex equality, 100–4
see also **Complex equality**
immigration policy, 106
inevitable parochialism, 106
limits, 104
minimalism, 106
shared understandings, 106
Torture
likelihood of torture, 40, 43, 159

United States of America
discretionary doctrine, 44–46
family migrants, 11, 53
illegal immigration, 11
Universalism
contextualist universalist method, 185–89
see also **Contextualist universalist method**
difference principle, 183
principles of justice, 183
Universality of justice
absolutist objection
communal shared understandings, 21–22
considered judgements, 20–21
judgements of justice, 21–22
political boundaries, 21–22

public reason, 22–23
reflective equilibrium, 20–21, 23
judgements about justice
injury, 25, 27–28
injustice, 25–28
motives, 25–26
object of resentment, 25–26
purposiveness, 26–27
rules of justice, 25, 28
three-way sympathetic intercourse, 25

Waldron, Jeremy
circumstances of politics, 19
natural duties, 132
principles of justice, 132
Walzer, Michael
absolutist views, 9, 146
basic principle of justice, 101

complex equality, 100, 102, 105
see also **Complex equality**
conception of justice, 104
discriminatory policies, 99
distributive justice, 102
domestic justice, 99
domination within spheres, 100, 104
guest worker programmes, 88, 99, 103
health care, 100
illegal migration, 120–21
immigration governance, 88, 95–96, 98–99,
  102, 104, 106
membership, 77
theory of justice, 21–22
thin morality, 100–3, 105–6
Wellman, Christopher Heath
distributive justice, 168
exclusion of migrants, 96

www.ingramcontent.com/pod-product-compliance
Lightning Source LLC
Chambersburg PA
CBHW061152220326
41599CB00025B/4457